The End of Politics in America

The End of Politics in America

Experience and Possibilities

Michael Leiserson
University of California, Berkeley

Little, Brown and Company   *Boston*

LIBRARY OF CONGRESS CATALOG CARD NO. 72-11455
FIRST PRINTING
Published simultaneously in Canada
by Little, Brown & Company (Canada) Limited

PRINTED IN THE UNITED STATES OF AMERICA

To Channing Grigsby

An educated man knows how complicated things are;
An intelligent man knows how simple things must be.

Preface

This book represents an optimistic critical analysis of the quality of politics and public life in the United States. The play on the word "end" in the title expresses my belief that the truth about our national situation today can be revealed only by fundamental criticism (politics is finished) *and* by analysis of the possibilities of fundamental change (politics is the way out). But the book is not a polemic. I have dropped the pretense of textbookish objectivity, but not the teacher's awkward commitment to present truth while permitting diverse conclusions. And I have not hidden my biases; in Part I, I introduce and summarize the book, explaining the judgments about politics, learning, and America on which the book rests.

I have tried to select and organize materials so as to make the book accessible and useful to students in introductory courses on American government and politics, or on social problems or contemporary political issues. The book can be used either as a text or as a source of additional readings to supplement a text. But one possible confusion should be clarified here. So-called radical texts and readers, and people concerned about the plight of the United States today, usually focus on the extraordinary. We usually assume that life for *most* Americans is okay: whether we sympathize with the "frontlash" or the "backlash," our implicit premise is that "the silent majority" is well-off and satisfied except insofar as the less-well-off bothers the majority. In this view—which seems to me quite widespread—serious problems exist only for Americans who are colored, foreign-born, poor, or draftable. The rest of us have problems merely because of the reactions of these groups to their oppression. This view is found almost as often in leftist and minority-group statements as in more establishmentarian and rightist opinions. (The black nationalist who says that all whites are the enemy and the white conservative who says that the racial problem is black violence and extremism are basically agreed in their analysis, differing only, for example, in their loyalties.) But my argument in this book directly opposes the idea that for the vast majority of Americans there is little or nothing the matter, if only the dissidents and deprived would quiet down. In other words, I strongly disagree with the hope (or fear) that groups and classes who presently object to the way they are treated by the society could be made satisfied without changing the way of life of virtually everyone in our nation. The source of our troubles, in my view, is neither "racism," "big business," or "imperialism," on one hand, nor "troublemakers," "striped-pants aristocrats," or "communists," on the other. The problems of the oppressed minorities are part of the sickness infecting the world of the oppressive majority. And that sickness will continue even if "big business" is nationalized or if all the "troublemakers" and "agitators" are bought off or jailed.

The studies in this book, therefore, deal more than might be expected with the ordinary, with how normality looks in our country. For example, the injustices meted out to black and poor people in our country in most courtrooms may reveal no more about American justice than the irrationality of the normal, reasonable trial of a successful white man described in selection 11 by Larner. The exclusion of most people of color from the American dream may reveal no more than does the fact that the dream also excludes white grandparents. My point is not that atrocities are not committed in and in the name of the United States; they are, and they are atrocious—whether in Vietnam, Harlem, the Cumberland region of Appalachia, or wherever. Rather, my position is "Look at what things are like when we behave normally!" and "It begins to make sense that we commit atrocities when *this* is what we call normality."

To repeat, this book's focus on ordinary, not-very-spectacular events and situations is *not* because I think everyone in the United States suffers equally. To consider the oppression of the white suburban middle class (which does exist) as qualitatively similar to the exploitation and domination that are the lot of most working-class and nonwhite people in this society would be fatuous, even if well-meant. But equality does enter the picture when we consider the question of action. Poor and discriminated-against people face neither an easier nor a harder task than do comfortable white people in resolving the real problems. My intent in this book is to make those basic problems clear, and to suggest ways of starting to struggle with them.

Michael Leiserson

Acknowledgments

Thanks are due to the authors and copyright holders of the selections reprinted here for their permissions to edit and use their materials as I have.

This book would have been impossible for me to conceive before I came to talk and work with people in Berkeley over the past five years. I am especially indebted to Hanna Pitkin for discussions on the nature of politics and political knowledge; to Ed Roberts and Susan Gumpert for first challenging me to take seriously the sorts of ideas represented here in Parts IV and V; to Lonnie Hicks, Mark Morris, Brian Murphy, and Jack Wikse who worked out with me a course that suggested what has become the present Part VI; and to David Schumann, Jeff Lustig, and particularly Jack Schaar for discussions that helped me to handle Part II. I first tried out some of the ideas behind this book in an introductory course on American politics in the winter quarter of 1971, and I used preliminary versions of this book in noncredit courses sponsored by the Associated Students of the University of California at Berkeley and by the Educational Liberation Front in 1971 and 1972; I was encouraged and assisted by students in those courses. Dona Boatright located several of the articles reprinted here, and assisted in various ways when I began working on the book. Norman Jacobson and Bob Peyton influenced my understanding of teaching in ways that have left a mark on this book, and Lonnie Hicks and Bob Waterman have spent many hours showing and explaining to me what it means to teach politics well. I will be content if this book proves as helpful to them as they have been to it.

The suggestion to do the book came from Alfred Browne of Little, Brown and Company. The present book is better than the original prospectus thanks in part to the comments made by several reviewers. Bob Waterman read an earlier version of the book and helped me improve it.

M. L.

Contents

I

Introduction: The Meaning of "The End of Politics in America"

Imagine a doctor talking with a patient after a thorough checkup. The patient is a middle-aged man, successful in worldly ways, who insists that there's nothing seriously wrong with him. But he has several mysterious ailments that appear and disappear without apparent cause or warning. For example, although the patient is a former athlete, sometimes he loses all his strength and can barely lift his briefcase. He has sporadic stomach pains, occasional headaches, and once in a while frightening dizzy spells. Perhaps because of these discomforts, the patient has become increasingly moody and temperamental, and occasionally gets into a fight with one or another of his neighbors. Recently, repairing the garage door in an irritated frame of mind, he hit his thumb with the hammer and got so angry that he threw the hammer at his dog. Last year he changed jobs, hoping things would improve, but it didn't seem to make any difference. Now he has come to see if the doctor can prescribe some medicines, or perhaps some sort of rest cure.

The doctor is at a loss for words: the checkup has shown that the patient does not have any familiar disease. In some way that medical science cannot explain precisely, however, the doctor is quite sure that the patient's basic constitution and his way of living are the source of his discomforts. And because the source of these aches and pains is deep-rooted, it will be difficult to produce any real change. The easy prescription would be to suggest a pain-killer, tranquilizers, and a vacation. But the doctor has tried such "remedies" before. People return from vacations, after all, and pains that are not treated at the source often become stronger and more resistant to drugs. On the other hand, the doctor's experience has shown that people do not take kindly to being told that they will have to live in fundamentally different ways in order to cure themselves. Confronted with such advice, patients become alarmed or angry, and go off to find another physician who will give them less frightening and demanding prescriptions. And this reaction is not just a matter of fear. The doctor knows that most people really do not understand how a person's basic constitution and the quality of his whole life might be the cause of specific ailments such as headaches or a bad temper. This patient is no different. He wants simple, straightforward cures for what he sees as, and hopes are, unrelated and not fundamental or constitutional problems—"my stomach problem, my dizzy spells, my temper." And since experts are specialists (internists, surgeons, psychiatrists, etc.), it is always possible to find several doctors who are willing to deal with the patient's problems as separate and distinct and in that sense superficial. (Indeed, these experts could hardly treat the patient in any other way; they feel incompetent to deal with the whole man, and so they have come to believe that the whole man cannot be treated at all.)

Now imagine a "doctor of national health" talking with Uncle Sam about the condition of his body—our body politic, as it were. Uncle Sam is complaining about his problems; he has unemployment pains, poverty pockets, discrimination tensions, pollution headaches, general unrest, twinges of crime, and a semipermanent condition of war. He wants to know the cures for each one. And just like the patient, he doesn't want to hear that his problems won't go away without some radical changes in his constitution and his way of life.

Uncle Sam's health is, of course, the health of the United States. This book is a sort of diagnosis of the health of our body politic. The diagnosis is rather harsh. Our problems are not superficial and unrelated; our nation is seriously ill. Overseas wars, domination based on sex, race, or class, ecological destruction and other social irrationalities, and the absence of genuine self-government are not "problems" to be "solved" by experts, but are parts of the underlying sickness of our body politic. Moreover, when we do finally attempt to solve a social problem such as racial discrimination, we only make the underlying sickness worse, because our remedies for these evils are like mere patent medicines being applied to the symptoms of a disease. Just as additional doses of patent medicines for reducing a fever may ignore the real sickness or even actually aggravate it, further use of our conventional institutions and practices seems only to perpetuate our national sickness or even to make it worse. Instead, we will have to start living differently as a nation, to make changes affecting our basic constitution, and to develop healthy antibodies to fight the disease in our system.

Our body politic, of course, is not really an organism like a human body. Such a phrase as "our national sickness" is a metaphor, a way of pointing at a truth without describing it precisely. And like all metaphors, the notion that our nation is a body that can be healthy or sick can be misleading. So since I am using the metaphor, it is only fair to warn against some possible confusion that it might produce.

First of all, an important similarity exists between a nation and a body, a similarity that is evident in the word *constitution.* We speak of a person's constitution in such words as "He has a sound (sickly, robust, delicate, etc.) constitution." We also speak of a nation's constitution, referring not to the supreme law (e.g., the American Constitution) but describing *the system of fundamental principles and institutions according to which the nation is really governed.* Just as a person's constitution or basic makeup is intimately connected with character, disposition, and temperament, so a nation's constitution shapes its disposition—the qualities and tendencies inherent in and characteristic of the nation as a whole. (Our national constitution and our written Constitution are related, but are not at all the same.)

Much of the time we make no mistake when we speak of a nation's constitution. For example, it is no more metaphorical or misleading to say that our nation has a constitutional tendency toward expansion and war than it is to say that a person is constitutionally hyperactive and aggressive. But there is one crucial difference between the constitution of a person and that of a nation, a difference in the way each constitution *governs.* To see this difference we need to look at a constitution that is easier to see but governs in somewhat the same way as a national constitution. Take, for example, the constitution of a family. Speaking very loosely, it is not unreasonable to say that any family has a government, and that the family's government lays down laws and policies. For example, one of a family's laws might be that children should be not too noisy at the dinner table, and one policy might call for harmonious conversation during dinner. In one sense of the word "govern," such laws and policies govern the children, just as the draft and income-tax laws and the government's economic policy govern citizens, since it is difficult and painful to disobey them. But these laws and policies, and in fact the family's government itself, are governed in a deeper sense by some principles and institutions that underlie the family's very existence. The family's government and all its laws rest in part upon the institution of parenthood and upon the principle that at certain times the parents' wishes should and do outweigh the children's.* This institution and this principle make up part of what we would mean if we spoke of a family's constitution. A family is governed by its constitution in the sense that everything that normally goes on in the family is consistent with its constitutional institutions and principles (such as parenthood). Or, in other words, the constitutional institutions and principles are fundamental to the life of the family, since the family's government and laws—to say nothing of its economics, its morality, its sexual practices, and so on—derive from its constitution.

To put it in one sentence, a family's (or a nation's) constitution governs in the sense that the significant happenings are consistent with and based upon or guided by the constitutional principles and institutions. Does this notion of governing sound somewhat soft or permissive? It might, because the word "govern" usually includes the notion that things *must* be a certain way. A person's body is governed by the biological laws that govern any organism. (You simply cannot disobey them.) A government governs its people by laws that are always backed up by the threat of force. (Disobey this law and you go to jail. Refuse to go to jail and the police will come to take you. Refuse to go and you will be overpowered and taken by force.) But a nation's constitution is neither necessarily obeyed, as are the laws of biological science, nor is it enforced by the threat of irresistible legal force, as are a government's laws and policies. A nation's constitution governs, if you will, unnecessarily and resistibly—that is, by a power that is neither the force of gravity nor simply the force of a policeman's gun, a judge's gavel, and a jail-cell lock. The power of a constitution is rooted in human emotion and human relationships—in fear, superstition, dependence, love, and habit —although this power does also underlie and receive expression in the

*This example shows how I'm using the words "institution" and "principle." An institution is not simply a huge, permanent organization like the Methodist Church or the Supreme Court. It is fundamentally a stable pattern of human relationships that people believe should be as they are—such as, for example, a church or a court. Just as the Methodist Church and the Supreme Court are specific examples of the institutions of church and court, usually "capital-letter" institutions are specific cases of basic (or "lower-case") social institutions. Also, a principle is not simply an ideal like the Golden Rule. It is an actual standard that people really try to live by, such as obeying the law. (Obviously, principles and institutions are closely related—so closely, in fact, that it isn't possible to talk about one without the other.)

government's use of force. Such a power may *sound* soft when compared to power that arises from the force of nature or of coercion, but it is precisely this power, and not simply the force of nature or of coercion, that leads us to follow our constitution. So it is the constitution and its peculiar power, and not the necessary force of nature nor the irresistible force of coercion, that are ultimately responsible for our national illness.

This difference between the power of a constitution and the force of nature or of coercion is a matter of life and death. If our national constitutional illness resulted from natural forces or irresistible coercion, then we as a nation would be as good as dead. When a person has a constitutional illness, then barring some miracle he or she is doomed to suffer that illness until death. But if a nation has some constitutional defect, it is possible and no miracle for the people to act and modify the constitution, thereby curing the constitutional sickness. Of course, the people might not act. Then a constitutionally sick nation (unlike a person) might stagger on indefinitely in its diseased condition, perhaps patched up from time to time by reforms that allay discontent without touching the basic illness that produces the discontent. Or there might even be some sort of revolution or civil war, as happened to the United States in the 1860's, perhaps leading to basic constitutional change or even to the creation of two or more nations out of the old one. (Even this, notice, is hardly the same thing as the literal death of a person.) A nation's constitutional illness, then, is open-ended, its possible outcome indefinite, in contrast to a person's constitutional disease. And it is in this openness, this indefiniteness, that creative action can take place.

In other words, to say that a constitution's power is "unnecessary and resistible" is to say that our constitution and its effects are man-made. The symptoms of our constitutional illness (including, for example, the decay of the cities and of local government, the growing power of the military, our inability to deal with institutional racism, and the continuing exploitation of much of the working population) may feel inevitable and unbeatable. But these trends represent the intended and unintended results of countless individual and collective decisions by men and women. And, since no human decision necessarily must be what it is, this means that things could be different. Therefore, to understand our constitution and its effects—to understand our national illness and its causes and possible remedies—we need to look not at some natural or scientific laws, not for some necessary and irresistible force, but at what we are, what we do, how we act.

The word that describes what we are, what we do, how we act as a nation is *politics*. Politics, you might say, is the constitution in action. So, to rephrase the previous paragraph, in order to understand our national illness and its causes and possible remedies we need to look at our politics.

If politics represents the constitution in action, then it must also be true that a significant change in the way we do politics would mean a change in the constitution. The creative action made possible by the "unnecessary and resistible" nature of a constitution's power will be creative political action. Once this fact is recognized, the double meaning of the word "end" in the title of this book should become clear. As long as we as a nation continue to engage in politics as usual, we will merely maintain and re-produce our constitution—and therefore maintain and reproduce the basic source of our national illness. In this sense, politics is at an end, a dead end. But if we as a nation change what we are, what we do, how we act—if, in other words, we engage in creative political action—then we will at the same time be changing our constitution, and thus contributing to the solu-tion of our national illness. In this sense, then, the end or goal of politics is to contribute to our national health, by making fundamental changes in our constitution.

Now you have the general position taken in this book. Before describing the contents more concretely, I want to deal with an objection to what I have said here that may have occurred to you. One possible reaction to my position might be that it is too pessimistic or ideological, or perhaps even anti-American. But is a doctor who diagnoses a serious illness necessarily a pessimist, an ideologue, or "anti" the person who has the illness? Obvi-ously, what matters here is: what are the facts? If the United States suffers from a constitutional illness—and this book shows that we are—then there is no point in attacking the people who call attention to that fact. It is absurd to argue, even though some otherwise intelligent people do argue, that "the racial problem," for example, is primarily a matter of the anger or violence of black people, rather than the fact of racial oppression. Obviously, as long as racial oppression exists, *that* is the problem, not the anger or extremism of militant blacks. Likewise, as long as our constitutional illness exists, *that* is the source of gloom rather than any critic's pessimism or ideology.

THE ARGUMENT OF THIS BOOK

The preceding pages have been rather abstract. Now I will describe more concretely what this book says about the United States and our futures.

Recall the analogy between our body politic and an individual person. If we were to describe an individual's makeup or constitution, we might talk about the person's physical and psychological development, major activi-ties, quality of character, values, habits, and life style, or about the person's hopes and visions and possibilities of achieving them. The following five parts of this book will deal with facets of our national constitution that are analogous to all these aspects of an individual's constitution. Part II is a review of the original context of our politics, a description of our early political principles and institutions and their interaction and historical evolu-tion up to the present. In Part III the focus is on the governmental policies that result from our politics, and on the structure of power and interests that shapes those policies. In Part IV the quality of our political public life is described. Part V concerns the less visible but no less significant politics of everyday life: some of the ways in which ordinary Americans are encour-aged or required to perpetuate our constitution rather than to change it. And Part VI deals with actions and movements designed to change the American constitution by doing politics differently than as described in Parts II through V. The following paragraphs describe the contents of these parts in more detail.

Part II, "The Dried-Up Tradition," views our politics from an historical perspective. One selection describes the core of our traditional national character, American individualism. Two essays show how certain traits in the American character elicited certain key features of the Constitution of 1787, and how conversely some of the features of our Constitution have shaped our national character as well as our way of doing politics. Then a lengthy article analyzes the evolution of our national character and basic institutions from their condition in the largely white Protestant, rural, small-scale America before the Civil War to their condition in the industrial, urban, multiethnic, centralized America of today. A final essay describes how our institutions and our national character combined to produce a kind of politics—a national way of acting collectively—that, whatever its merits two hundred years ago, clearly cannot cope with the issues of survival and sanity that prevail today.

Part III, "The Basic Structure of Power, Interest, and Policy," concerns politics as we usually think of it. The argument is simple. The section on "Our National Priorities" shows that our basic national goals are economic (corporation) prosperity and international power, explains why these are our goals, and points out how some other goals are ruled out by these priorities. Thus, for example, attempts to deal with problems of the cities are limited or virtually strangled by the "requirement" that we spend over half of our public (tax) income on war and preparation for war, and by the "requirement" that we not violate the property rights of influential corporations. The section on "The Politics of Accommodation" describes how certain interests, such as those of organized farmers and workers, get satisfied within the context of our basic national commitments. Finally, the concluding selection shows that these national priorities do not result from democratic decision-making—that is, it is not true that the people have been presented with a genuine alternative to these priorities and have still chosen these.

Part IV, "The Shape of American Public Life," describes the quality of American politics in terms of Americans' own personal experiences. It shows the sorts of experiences we have all had with "justice," "community," and "leadership" in our society. By "justice" I mean the principles that underlie the fundamental relationships among the people and institutions of our society, particularly the principles that justify the ways considered reasonable for resolving or preventing conflicts in our nation. By "community" I mean the feelings and relationships that are present when members of our society call themselves "we." By "leadership" I mean the special qualities of—the values expressed by, what there is to emulate in—the people who exercise authority in our society. Of course, a description of our experiences with justice, community, and leadership in our society tells not only about our experience but also, implicitly, about our expectations. So Part IV is a description of what we expect to see as American justice, community, and leadership—and in that sense a description of what American politics is. The description shows that our "justice" rests on fundamentally bureaucratic principles. Our "community" consists of private, possessive, exclusive, and conformist feelings and relationships. Our "leadership" teaches us to behave like the "marks" at a carnival, citizens of a land occupied by a foreign power, children with their fingers in the cookie jar.*

Part V, "The Boundaries of Life in the United States," deals with the theme of social control or what has been called "the reproduction of everyday life," emphasizing especially the frustration and meaninglessness of many of the ordinary lives that our national way of life presently "requires." The section on "The Dominant Ideology" describes the present plight of American individualism, showing how our individualistic values and ways of thinking both shape and are reshaped by the way our corporate, technological society works. (At the same time, any reader should find many of his or her own "personal" habits and feelings described here.) The section "Invisible Control Mechanisms" then describes some important social practices and institutions that work to make us dependent on the present system, unable to see or achieve any alternative to the status quo.

Part VI, "Freedom and Political Action," raises the obvious question of whether and how it is possible to live as one might really want to—to build upon or transcend the background of Part II, to struggle against the power and interests so as to achieve different policies from those of Part III, to enjoy a better quality of justice, community, and leadership than those of Part IV, and to resist and overcome the limits of Part V. At first glance, of course, one might say that to live as one really wants would *not* involve any

---

*It is important to recognize that (*a*) we each do have some *personal* experience with the quality of our national public life, and (*b*) these sorts of political experiences (with justice, community, leadership) do matter to us as individuals as well as to the sorts of political outcome we achieve. Regarding (*a*), we each have some personal experience with the ways that are considered reasonable in our society to resolve or prevent conflicts. We each have some personal experience with the sorts of situations and feelings that go along with being a part of some "we." And we each have some personal experience with the qualities (even a manipulated "image" has its own particular quality) of the people who exercise authority in our society. And, regarding (*b*), it is precisely these experiences that make the difference between, say, fearing that there's little point to life except a fast buck, a quick thrill, mere duty, or escape, on one hand, and knowing that life makes sense, that one's own life can be worthwhile, on the other. Why should these political experiences be so important? Very briefly, they are important because of who we are and because of what politics is. "No man is an island": we rely upon the resonance that we ourselves set off in our fellows; we retreat if our principles and values receive no confirmation in the world. And politics is precisely the realm where men and women act or fail to act (collectively) to make their values and principles actual in the world. In short, *it is the politics of our society* (including our experience with American justice, community, and leadership, as well as the broad policies that are shaped in part by those things) *that shapes and limits the values and hopes that we as individuals can live by.* To describe our political experiences, then, is to describe (though of course not completely) the meaning of our lives at the same time as describing (again, not completely) the kind of world we live in and help to perpetuate and change.

of these things! But the intent in Part IV, V, and VI together is to show how living freely must involve some sort of struggle against the system described in the previous parts of the book; this argument is made explicitly in the introduction to Part VI. The selections in Part VI then attempt to provide the basis for—and to pose some of the major questions that will be asked in—any serious discussion of the human and political possibilities of our day, all in the process of describing some well-known contemporary political groups and movements.

In other words, Parts III, IV, and V—dealing with the basic structure of power, interest, and policy, the quality of our public life, and the boundaries of life in this country—describe the main features of our constitutional politics today. These three facets of our politics are equally significant, but different, sides of a single reality, namely, our constitution. They are, in a sense, the *what,* the *how,* and the *who* of our contemporary politics. One way to define politics is as *the interactions among people who are attempting to achieve or prevent certain possibilities for their community.* Then the basic structure of power-interest-policy = what? = the possibilities that *are* regularly achieved by our national community. The quality of our public life = how? = the *nature* of the interactions among Americans as they attempt to achieve or prevent certain possibilities for their community. The boundaries of life in this country = who? = the *kinds* of people that we are.

But what about the *why* of our politics? Why are our political "what," "how," and "who" as they are? That is, why do we regularly achieve the outcomes or policies that the Part III analysis of the basic structure of power, interest, and policy describes? Why do we customarily interact in the way that the Part IV analysis of the quality of our public life describes? Why are we the kinds of people—why do we think and behave in the way—that the Part V analysis of the boundaries of life in this country describes?

It is tempting to answer these questions by finding one or a very few "basic causes" that are supposed to determine everything else about our politics and our national life. "Power," "technology," "the economy," and "the social structure" are some of the factors that we often hear about as "the basic cause" of almost everything from the Vietnam War to the rising divorce rate. But, although these notions are helpful, I think that the attempt to find a few "basic causes" is misguided. Rather, I think, once you know the who, what, and how of a story, then there is no more to say, no "why?" question that hasn't been answered, except for historical questions. (One might have said that "why?" concerns the reasons that people have for doing what they do the way they do it, but I've already included people's motivations and reasons in my definition of "who" as the kinds of people that we are.) In my view, to ask "why?" about our political "what," "how," and "who"—about, that is, our basic structure of power-interest-policy, the quality of our public life, and the boundaries on life in this country—is to ask why these things came to be as they are. In other words, "why?" is historical in that its answer locates our present constitutional politics in an historical process or narrative, not in some fixed cause-effect mechanism.

This is the significance of the description in Part II of "The Dried-Up Tradition." To describe our national traditions is simply to describe our national constitution as it has existed and changed over time. All three facets of our contemporary constitutional politics are also visible in the historical narrative. But here the focus is on their interaction and evolution, rather than on their description. To talk about our traditions, then, is not merely to provide "historical background" but to describe the evolution of our constitution, to speculate about its deep-rootedness and permanence, and to wonder about the potential for constitutional change in our society today.

Recall once again the earlier analogy between our body politic and an individual person. Parts III, IV, and V—the what, how, and who of our constitutional politics—are related to each other in much the same way that an individual person's major activities, qualities of character, and values and life style are related. One of the three is not *the* cause of the others, but each influences the others. To understand an individual, then, involves describing that person's major activities, qualities of character, and values and ways of thinking. If, after that description, someone asks you "But why?," there really isn't much left to say, except to turn to the individual's personal history and try to describe the process by which his or her activities, character, and values came to be as they are today. And that historical description would involve showing how activities, character, and values mutually influence each other, gradually evolving over time.

It is this sort of historical description that is attempted in Part II in order to answer "why?" the contemporary pictures in Parts III, IV, and V are as they are. For example, the basic structure of power-interest-policy in the past can be seen as bringing out certain qualities in our public life, and as imposing certain restrictions or boundaries on the lives that Americans customarily led as private individuals. And, on the other hand, just as an individual's character often seems to dictate future values and priorities, so the quality of our public life—especially the quality of justice, community, and leadership we accepted—can be seen to have encouraged the growth of a certain sort of basic structure of power-interest-policy, with its consequent priorities for the nation. Likewise, the kinds of limitations and restrictions that Americans learned to accept on their lives were not merely the result of certain national priorities, but were themselves an important part of the basic institutional structures that generated those priorities. Similarly, the quality of our national public life and the quality of our private lives obviously influenced each other.

(These interrelations between our political what, how, and who are *not* spelled out explicitly in Parts III, IV, and V. So it is important to keep in mind that the connections do exist, and to figure out how they work.)

In short, then, Part II deals with change in the past, whereas Parts III, IV, and V describe the present as though it were not changing. Part VI then opens up the possibility of change in the future. Just as Part II, where the changes over time in all facets of our constitution are described, had to include consideration of "what," "how," and "who" simultaneously, so Part VI, where the possible ways we might change our constitution are discussed, has to deal at once with the possibilities to be achieved, the nature of the interactions among people, and the kinds of people who will act, if constitutional change is to occur. If Part II answers "why?" and Parts III, IV, and V answer "what?," "how?," and "who?," then Part VI raises the question, "whither?"

"THE THINGS WE DO, AS A NATION ..."

It will be clear by now that the ideas in this book are unconventional. Not only have I claimed that an accurate description of American politics must at the same time be a critical evaluation, but also I have equated the word "politics" with phrases such as "our constitution in action" and "the things we do as a nation." And such talk is not only irritatingly vague, it's downright nonsense, when you think about how people usually use the word "politics." The dictionary on my desk has eight definitions of "political" and five definitions of "politics," and *all* those definitions involve the idea that politics is a matter of *government*. This dictionary accepts the conventional view—which is shared by newspapers, television news, civics textbooks, and so on —that politics is essentially the operations and effects of government. But I have not talked about government much at all. Obviously there is a basic difference between my notion of politics and the conventional notion. Do I have the right to use the word "politics" so differently? Does it make any sense?

For example, I've spoken rather vaguely about the way we are, as a nation —what we do, how we act. But people usually imagine that what is done in the United States results from *government* policy, and from the actions of other enormously powerful organizations such as business corporations. The usual view seems to be that it is the government and major business corporations who decide what will be done in, and in the name of, our nation. But again, I think this view is mistaken. The things we do as a nation are not decided by, nor are they the result of, government and corporation policy alone. Rather, the things we do as a nation are a part of national policy in a broader sense. But to speak of "national policy in a broader sense" can be misleading. The word "policy" suggests some specific, definite goal or set of goals. So, for a policy in that sense to exist, there must be some authoritative spokesman (such as the official spokesman for the president) or some authoritative statement (such as a law) that says just what goals we as the nation are committed to achieving. But clearly there is no authoritative spokesman or final statement that says just what our broad national policy is at any specific point in time (though of course government policy and laws are a part of that broader national policy). Nevertheless, I will continue to speak of our "broad national policy," while recognizing that this "policy" is of necessity not to be discovered simply by reading presidential statements and acts of Congress. Our "broad national policy," rather, is the basic direction that our nation is in fact moving toward, the fundamental commitments that shape our future.

To illustrate, consider for example the racial situation in this country. What is happening overall in racial relations is not decided by nor the result of government and corporation policy alone. It seems obvious that the actions of millions of private individuals, plus the decisions of labor unions, television and movie producers, universities, churches, and school boards, plus the demands and confrontations of nongovernmental political groups from the American Independent Party to the Urban League to the Black Panther Party all contribute to the overall evolution of racial relations. It's obvious, too, that there is nowhere you can go to find out in clear and definite terms just what the nature of the overall racial situation is today, the way you can get copies of the civil-rights acts or of presidential press-conference statements. There can be no final and definitive statement about the *present* direction that the racial situation is really moving toward, because whether it is true that "we are heading toward two separate and unequal societies, one white and one black," for example (as the National Commission report puts it), depends on what happens in the *future*.

Two very specific differences exist between "broad national policy" and "government policy." Government policy is *made;* a relatively small number of people consciously choose to commit "the U.S." to achieve certain goals. And government policy can be *enforced;* the police and the courts stand ready to punish anyone who attempts to obstruct the methods the government chooses to achieve its policy goals. But national policy in a broader sense—the basic directions in which our nation is moving—is not made nor is it enforceable in the way that government policy is made and can be enforced. I do not mean that choice and force play no part in the evolution of our broad national policy. After all, government policy which is chosen and enforced is a key element of our broad national policy. All I am insisting on is that our broad national policy *as a whole* is not chosen and cannot be enforced. There is no one and no thing that decides and requires the overall, basic pattern in what we will do tomorrow regarding the racial situation, for example. Nevertheless, obviously, what will happen tomorrow in the United States regarding the racial situation is hardly a matter of pure chance or accident. Rather, what we will do as a nation tomorrow about the racial situation will have to depend on the way we really are, as a nation, today and tomorrow—the fundamental commitments we truly follow, the basic directions in which our nation is in fact moving. And "what we are as a nation," the fundamental commitments we truly follow, are simply vague ways of talking about our national constitution. So what will happen tomorrow about the racial situation must depend not simply on government but on the nature of our constitution, and on the ways we put that constitution in action or change that constitution by action—depend, in other words, on our politics and not simply on the government.

These observations should help explain how a book such as this one, which describes very little about the machinery of government or about how specific policies of government come into being, can still be about our politics. The constitution does not, by itself, explain specific concrete events —does not explain, for example, (1) why the labor-union members of the Nixon administration's Pay Board resigned in 1972, or (2) why Shirley Chisholm was not elected president in 1972, or (3) why the AFL-CIO backed pro-Vietnam War candidates rather than Eugene McCarthy for the 1968 Democratic presidential nomination, or (4) why and how the Environmental Protection Agency was set up in Washington to fight pollution. Rather, the constitution, and politics as I am using the term, explains tendencies and *types* of events—explains, for example, (1) why our government's policies regularly benefit large corporate interests more than the interests of working people, (2) why women and black people do not exercise significant national power in our country, (3) why there was no strong open opposition to the Vietnam War from the major organizations in the country until after the government announced its intention to withdraw, (4) why "ecology" is a much more popular issue than is exploitation of people in their jobs, and so on.

THE NATURE OF POLITICS

It is still true, nevertheless, that I am using the word "politics" in a strange way. Ordinarily politics has to do with the activities that go on in the halls of Congress, during election campaigns, when pressure groups lobby city hall, when the President visits China, and so on. This is natural; the television news and the newspapers report certain sorts of things to us as "political news," so naturally we come to think that those sorts of things make up the heart of politics. But such thinking is confused. Politics represents a kind of *activity,* as do farming, worship, drawing, building, athletics, teaching, and conversation. And like those other activities, *politics is properly understood (defined) in terms of its meaning for, and its effects on, the people who engage in it.* Just as it is an obvious mistake to equate the essence of religious faith with any one established church's dogma and rituals, it is an error to define politics in terms of governmental institutions and the conventional and ritualized practices of one country.*

But it is difficult, and not terribly helpful, to formulate precise definitions for basic human activities such as politics—and the same goes for art, love, or religion. (What have you understood about religion when you have merely memorized a definition or a proof that God does or does not exist?) It is much

---

*Take this example. What's wrong with understanding (defining) love in terms of the institution of marriage, thus: "Love is the activity concerned with creating, maintaining, and improving a marriage"? What's wrong is that *that definition* of love, *if you really do believe it and act on it, will make you confused and unable to think and act as you should be able to* about love or marriage. Just imagine: Jill: "Jack, I don't think you love me anymore." Jack: "Sure I do, Jill. Just yesterday I emptied out the garbage, and that's part of maintaining our marriage, which (according to the definition) shows I love you." Jill: "It does??!!" Since marriage is an institution, in some ways like government, the obvious point that love and marriage should not be too closely identified in our thinking (if we don't want to get confused about each one) suggests that, likewise, we should not try to understand what politics is simply by referring to governmental institutions and ritualized practices.

more significant, I think, to understand the ways in which a fundamental activity such as politics is similar to but different from other activities such as religion, warfare, management, friendship, or education. But this is not the place for that sort of discussion. Provisionally, as I suggested earlier, *politics can be thought of as the interactions among people who are attempting to achieve or prevent certain possibilities for their community.* But the *best* way to get a sense of the possible meaning of politics for people who (might) engage in it is to think about the *reasons* people might have for taking political action or even for thinking seriously about politics.

The usual reason for studying politics is "to be a well-informed citizen." But a well-informed citizen is someone who has the knowledge and know-how that are relevant to choices and actions *he or she is able to make.* A well-informed car driver is someone who has the knowledge and know-how relevant to driving a car, not someone who knows, for example, how to become an effective president of General Motors or how to improve the assembly lines in Detroit factories. Likewise, a citizen—the reader of this book—needs to have knowledge and know-how that are relevant to the actual political situations he or she lives in and wants to deal with, not information about, for example, how to become elected president or how to improve the workings of Congress.

More simply put, what we know about politics ought to be of use to us as (potentially) free men and women. The famous Russian scientist and revolutionary, Prince Peter Kropotkin, put it quite well:

> *Think about the kind of world you want to live and work in. What do you need to know to build that world? Demand that your teachers teach you that.*

Who would bother to learn about car engines if her life had little to do with cars, or if there were no chance of car engines breaking down, or if there were no chance of being able to work on them or of being able to do anything about them? Now for "car engines" substitute "politics and government." Who would bother to learn how politics and government work if her life had little to do with (what she understands as) politics and government, or if there were no chance of (what she understands as) politics and government needing repairs, or if there were no chance of being able to work on them or of being able to do anything about them?

I put the phrase "what she understand as" into the last questions because people are more confused about what politics and government are than about what car engines are. Depending on what you understand or define as politics and government, they may indeed be irrelevant and not worth knowing about. (Surely this is true of much of the "news" we are supposed to absorb from daily television programs and newspapers!) But how you understand or define politics and government may or may not be correct. Now I want to show that a correct definition reveals that for most people politics *is* quite relevant to how they live their lives.

Look back at those words of Kropotkin. Is the world you live in now the kind of world you want to live and work in? What in this world belongs in the world you want to live in, and what does not belong there? How can you build the kind of world you want to live and work in, salvaging what is good in this world and changing the rest to make it better? Isn't *this* what you really need to know? ("This," incidentally, *is* political.)

Don't worry about answering those questions right away. When most people hear a question like "Is the world you live in now the kind of world you want to live and work in?," they have complicated reactions. We need to admit these reactions, to look at them and try to sort them out, before even attempting to answer the question. Most people react to that question with a mixture of feelings such as:

I don't like people to ask me that question. It makes me feel uncomfortable.

No, of course the world isn't perfect. But it never will be. You've just got to accept that.

The problem isn't with the world, it's with me! If only I could be the sort of person I should be. I can't take on the world's problems until I can handle my own, and respect myself.

It doesn't make any difference anyway.

I'm well aware that my world isn't the world I want to live in for the rest of my life. But in a little while, after I finish school [move to another city, grow up, get promoted, have a baby, buy a house, raise the children, retire, etc.], things will be different.

There are some things about this world that really ought to be changed. But I don't know what to do about them, and I certainly don't have the ability to make any changes.

These are all perfectly reasonable reactions to that question about whether you like the world you live in. I listed them not because they are silly or wrong but because while they are reasonable and perhaps correct they are also very revealing, and I want to talk about what they reveal. In order to discuss these reactions, it will be helpful to have a label for each one, so I'll call them (in order) the reactions of anxiety, fatalism, passiveness, meaninglessness, unconnectedness, and powerlessness. When I say that these reactions are reasonable and perhaps correct, I mean that it is "natural" for a person in our society to feel anxious, fatalistic, passive, meaningless, unconnected, and powerless when confronted with such a question.

By saying that these reactions are "revealing," I mean, first, that they result largely from the kind of society we live in, from what we are as a nation—from our constitution. Second, these reactions help to perpetuate the kind of world we live in; that is, they are part and parcel of our politics. Third, these reactions prevent us from seeing and believing in (and so, naturally, prevent us from achieving) many of the possibilities that are in fact under our noses—different and better kinds of politics that would involve less anxious, meaningless, passive, unconnected lives for us all.

To see how a feeling such as anxiety results from life in our society, we must be able to see the connection between *personal* troubles and *social* facts. Of course, it's easy to see how some social facts are connected with personal troubles—unemployment obviously means that some people have no jobs, and racial discrimination obviously means that individuals of one race are treated very badly. Indeed, almost every social fact implies certain personal experiences. Try thinking about it. When you hear or read that our society is becoming more urbanized, that the cities are decaying, that inflation is too high, that technology runs our lives, or that there is a problem of law and order, what personal troubles do you know some people are experiencing?

Take this concrete example. You often hear that our society is increasingly centralized and bureaucratic. This social fact implies that more and more people in our society are having more and more of certain kinds of personal experience. What kinds of experience does one have, living in a bureaucratic society? A bureaucracy is best described in terms of the metaphor of a machine. To oversimplify, you might say that the personal experience of living in a bureaucratic society is the experience you would have if you tried to become a cog in a machine! A bureaucracy is the coordination and control of people by means of: centralized, hierarchical order-giving; specializing the tasks of any one person; preventing any person from owning what he or she works with; and regulating every person's job by written rules. So the personal experience of living in a bureaucratic society must include: continually being told what to do by one's superior; working on tasks that are specialized and cut off from the larger context that would make them interesting or meaningful; lacking control over what one works with and works on (the tools are not one's own, and the product is taken away); and continually being required to behave in ways that make no sense in terms of who one is, but make sense only in terms of the job one performs. Now, stop and think about how those four kinds of experience feel, what their impact is on a person. I think it's clear that experiences like these naturally lead people to feel powerless, passive, unconnected, meaningless, and fatalistic—and so, naturally, very anxious. The fact that our society is increasingly bureaucratic, then, is an important reason why more and more people in our society have these kinds of troubled feelings.

What should we say then? That powerlessness is a personal trouble experienced by many people in our society? Or that powerlessness is a major social issue confronting our country? Obviously, the choice between these two is a *political* choice, because the choice you make has implications for the future of our national community. It is political because the choice you make has implications for the ways in which Americans will interact with each other in attempting to achieve certain possibilities for their community. Do we send people complaining of powerlessness to the psychiatrist? Or do people who experience powerlessness join together and act collectively to overcome that condition? Or both? Or, is there something else?

The stuff of politics properly understood is the continual debate and struggle over the connection between personal troubles and collective or constitutional facts and issues. A generation ago, in the Great Depression of the 1930's, the major political choice facing Americans was whether to regard the condition of joblessness as a personal trouble of some workers, or as a social fact that should be dealt with by a certain sort of collective action. As a nation we chose to see joblessness as unemployment, a social fact that deserved to be remedied by government action. In the 1960's the major political choice facing Americans was whether to regard the condition of legal racial discrimination as a personal trouble of some whites and blacks, or as a social fact that should be dealt with by political action. As a nation we chose to see legal racial discrimination as illegal (that is, to redefine the boundaries of legality), making racial discrimination a crime punishable in the courts. As you might guess, my own judgment is that these issues were indeed political, but that our constitutional illness infected both the way we perceived these issues and the steps we took to resolve the issues, leaving us still with racial discrimination and with more, equally serious, political choices. These choices, for example, between bureaucratic organization and its "personal" troubles and a more democratic form of social organization, are the political agenda—the public life agenda—of the coming years.

  To sum up, as C. Wright Mills taught, politics occurs in the intersection between personal troubles and social (constitutional) issues. The results of political choices and political action are to perpetuate or change social (constitutional) facts, and in the process to perpetuate or change (or perhaps even eliminate) personal troubles. But equally important, the process of political action itself is a new kind of social fact for us. It, too, can produce new (for us) kinds of personal experience, and these new experiences might change or eliminate some personal troubles. In fact, for some personal troubles, such as the experience of living in a meaningless and oppressive society, or the experience of being powerless, it may well be that the *only* new social fact that could significantly change and resolve those troubles would be political (collective, public) action itself! This may sound both odd and extreme, since we Americans usually think of politics as at best something that we suffer as a necessary evil. I won't try now to argue against this traditional (indeed, constitutional) prejudice against politics. The selections in Part VI make that argument well enough, anyway. But it is worth mentioning that many of the greatest thinkers and actors in history have thought (and lived by the thought) that self-fulfillment can occur only in the context of political commitment and collective action.

II

The Dried-Up Tradition

A nation's traditions matter, to the present, just as a person's character relates to her present choices. But we Americans have always been at once fascinated by our history and indifferent to our traditions. We are more interested in "making" history than in understanding or transcending our traditions. It is traditional in the United States not to take tradition seriously —unless, as we would say, tradition is all you've got left (and when we say that, we are not envious!). Nevertheless, the purpose of the selections in this part is to show that we do have traditions, to describe some of those traditions, and to illustrate how those traditions matter to us today.

Referring to the discussion in Part I about our national constitution, you might say that our national traditions are nothing more than our national constitution as it has existed and evolved over time. But if tradition and the constitution represent two different ways of talking about the same things, why not talk about only one or the other? The answer is that looking at our constitution historically, in terms of traditions, makes it possible to see the facts of change and continuity, of lost possibilities and new roads taken, of beginnings and growth and struggle, that we miss when we talk only about our constitution in the present. To talk about our traditions, in other words, is to talk about *why* we have the national constitution we have today, as well as to describe some of the ingredients of our constitution as it exists today. It is also, at the same time, to speculate about the deep-rootedness and permanence of our constitution, and to wonder about the potentiality of constitutional change in our society today.

One word of caution: For anyone to describe our national traditions is in a sense as presumptuous and as difficult as it would be to describe the character of a person one has never met personally. In fact, the two are more alike than "in a sense" suggests. When Slater says, for example, in the selection, "A National Character," that individualism is traditional with us, and describes individualism, he is in fact describing the character of individual Americans. That includes the character of each reader of this book. Certainly it is presumptuous and difficult, *unless* the writer makes completely clear the intention of the description. If I were to describe an individual's character, naturally you would expect that my intention would be to describe what is most important about that particular individual, what "makes her tick," and what distinguishes her from other people. But even though a description of national traditions does involve a description of individuals' characters, the intention here is not to describe what is most important about each and every particular individual, and certainly not to show what distinguishes those individuals from each other. The intention is not those things, since they would get in the way of giving a description of what makes the whole nation tick, what makes all of us as a nation be as we are. If any of the basic characteristics described in the following selections were to change, many individual Americans might feel themselves only a little different, but the society as a whole (which is what these selections are trying to describe) would become a very different place to live in. So even though it *is* important to relate the following selections to one's own personal experience, it is also important to keep in mind that these selections cannot be a completely accurate description of all of any individual's experiences and feelings and beliefs and goals. Therefore, to find in these selections things that are not true of oneself would be easy—but trivial. The point is to see things that *are* true. Only if there is *nothing* significant about yourself in the descriptions in these selections should you conclude that they are not talking about you.

Another difficulty with trying to talk about our national traditions arises from the fact that there has always been a lot of diversity and conflict in our society. To say, for example, that private property or individualism is a basic tradition in our country might sound as though I'm saying that there was never *any* challenge to private property, or that *no* one has ever tried to live communally. Or it might sound as though I'm saying that all people *spontaneously,* without being influenced by the structure of power and interests and policy, *wanted* private property to be part of our constitution, or *wanted* to be lonely. *If* I were saying such things, I'd be wrong. But I'm not. The attitudes and behaviors described in "In the Beginning . . ." *are* traditional, but they did not occur spontaneously, were not arrived at without any struggle and conflict, and are not without opposition today.

In other words, when the following selections make generalizations about what "an American" is like, or talk about "the American experience," they do not mean that all citizens of this land are just the same. What they do mean is that, in spite of the very great differences among people, groups, and classes in our nation, we do share some things. Our traditions, our "national character," exist in the present in those things—experiences, feelings, beliefs, habits, predispositions to action—that we do all share.

A good example of the difficulties posed by talking about our traditions is a question that should not be avoided in any consideration of United States history: Is democracy part of our basic traditions? It is not a simple yes-or-no type of question, and needs closer attention than it usually gets. At the levels of principles and of institutions, democracy is and is not traditional with us. And about this fact, as with the bottle that is both half-empty and half-full, you can be disappointed or optimistic.

We generally agree that democracy is "government of the people, by the people, and for the people." We generally agree that we want democracy. And we generally agree that certain of our key institutions, most centrally the whole system of elections, are democratic. And then FCC Commissioner Nicholas Johnson tells us that ours is "a government of the people, but by the corporations, and for the rich!" Is Johnson a cynic, are we naive, or what? The problem is that there is an uncertainty embedded right in the middle of our belief in democracy and right in the middle of our key democratic institution, elections. The uncertainty is over just *who,* in a democracy, does the governing.

Ordinarily this uncertainty is hidden by talking in terms of "direct democracy" versus "indirect democracy" or "representative democracy." The standard line goes something like: "A direct democracy is a system in which every citizen participates directly in making policy, but obviously this is impossible when the number of citizens gets very large so only some of the citizens can participate directly in policy-making; but this will still be democratic if all the citizens choose through elections a group of representatives who will do the direct participating." This looks so obvious and reasonable that, if you don't watch closely, it's hard to see the non sequitur. But what have "every citizen participates directly in making policy" and "all the citizens choose through elections a group of representatives" got to do with each other? Is it so obvious and reasonable to say that "direct marriage" and "representative marriage" are equally marriage, only in one you participate yourself and in the other you choose a person who participates for you?!

A marriage, of course, *is* only a two-person thing, and a political community does have a problem of size. Nevertheless, the basic point remains valid. A government can be said to be *democratic* only to *the extent that the people do exercise control over the government's actions.* Elections certainly are a necessary part of a large democracy, but the mere fact that an election occurs hardly guarantees that a government responds to the will of the people. A host of connected and vital questions remain, including who can run for office, who can really vote, how frequently elections occur, can an elected official be recalled from office by the constituents, can an incumbent be reelected or must there be rotation in office, and, of course, what do the laws permit an elected official to do?

The historical fact is, as Hofstadter shows in his selection on "The Founding Fathers," that our Constitution was written by men who not only saw the significant differences between more democratic and less democratic forms of government, but who worked hard to make sure that our government would be *less* democratic than it might have been. (The constitution of 1787 was, for example, less democratic than several of the state constitutions in existence at the time.) That's why some of the heroes of the Revolution, like Sam Adams, Patrick Henry, and "Lighthorse Harry" Lee, opposed the Constitution when it was first written. That's also why, in the popular voting on whether to accept the Constitution, in spite of the near-unanimous backing of the press for the new document, the outcome was so close that historians still cannot say for certain whether a majority was in favor of ratification or not. (Probably, the *opposition* had a tiny majority!) But of course—and as an indication of our Founding Fathers' lack of commitment to democracy—the overall popular vote was not decisive anyway. All that was needed was the approval of a majority of the delegates in the state conventions of only nine of the thirteen states.

Three fundamental aspects of our Constitution reveal how far removed it was and is from the practice of democracy. *First,* popular control over the members of the national government is weakened by the length of terms of office (especially the six years for senators), by the absence of any provision enabling the people to recall an incumbent from office during his term if he does something they oppose, and particularly by the failure to limit the number of successive terms to which an incumbent may be reelected. (It is well known that the most powerful people in Congress come from "safe" districts where they face no competition and so are reelected many times. These districts are mostly very untypical of the country as a whole. To prevent incumbents from staying in office for long would eliminate those long-term legislators, making Congress far more accessible to the nation as a whole.) Also, popular control over the members of the government is weakened by the fact that the most democratic branch, the House of Representatives, is weaker in significant ways than the Senate and the presidency. And also, all the three million civilian officials and the 3.5 million military personnel below the president in the executive bureaucracies, and the members of the federal court system including the Supreme Court, are not elected at all.

Second, popular control over the national government as a whole is critically weakened by provisions in the Constitution that have the effect of making the government legally *omnipotent:*

1.   The Constitution is supposedly a supreme law that regulates and limits the actions that the national government can take (a government of law, not of men), but only the national government itself has the power to say just what the supreme law means.

2.   The Constitution gives the national government definite superiority over any other government in the nation, thereby making it practically impossible to counterbalance the national government by some other government (as South Carolina discovered as early as the "nullification" struggle in the 1830's).

3.   The Constitution gives the national government the power to tax, and to use its funds to pay its own bureaucracy and maintain a standing army —which, in light of points 1 and 2, means that the national government will always have a preponderance of nonlegal *force,* as well as legal power.

All three of these features of the Constitution were strongly attacked in 1787 as both undemocratic and not at all required by the financial and commercial difficulties that had caused the widespread dissatisfaction with the earlier Articles of Confederation and produced the Constitutional Convention in the first place. And all three have had the most profound influence on our development as a nation away from the kind of democracy we enjoyed immediately after the Revolution.

This judgment may need a little explaining, since it flies in the face of the apparent fact that today the national government is the most progressive and responsive major power center in the nation. The national government freed the slaves; the national government pushed the welfare system; the national government has pushed state and local governments to be less racist; the national government has consistently been the place where general public and consumer interests get the most favorable hearing, while the state governments are "the playground of the special interests"; and so on. Where the position of the opposition to the national Constitution in 1787 was that "the rich will have enough advantages against the poor without [these] political advantages," today many people would be more inclined to say that without the national government the poor would be even worse off than they are now.

The dispute here is partly over the facts and partly over the meaning of words. Is a democracy a country that takes care of the interests of the poor or a country where the poor take care of their own interests? I will return to this conceptual issue in a moment. As for the facts, consider these two generalizations. First, as explained in the introduction to Part III, the government has interests of its own, and elections do not determine government policy. Lincoln did not free the slaves because of a democratic commandment from the people; he freed the slaves because of the interest of the government in winning the war or, as he said, "of the Union." Second, in every one of the examples listed at the beginning of the preceding paragraph, showing that the national government is progressive and democratic, the fact is that the national government was directly responsible for first establishing the situation that, many years later, it helped to reform in partial ways. The national government actively opposed welfare and labor unions for years and years, aiding the giant corporations to establish their dominance over the economy, before it finally permitted labor unions and a welfare system that even today is paltry compared with the ones in most other advanced industrial nations. The national government actively participated in the establishment of white supremacy and legal segregation. The post-1896 system of racism was not at all a simple continuation of patterns and attitudes continued from the days of slavery. The slave society had been broken by the Civil War, and the new kind of racism that was established could have been neither started nor maintained without the help of the national government. And so on.

But the consequences of the undemocratic nature of the Constitution as listed earlier in points 1–3 can be illustrated better, perhaps, by facts whose cause is not so hard to see. For example, these three aspects of the Constitution ensured that our Bill of Rights freedoms would be diluted, and that power in the nation would be centralized and continually expanding. The liberties in the Bill of Rights were guaranteed in *absolute* terms ("Congress shall make no law . . . abridging the freedom of speech, or of the press; or the right of the people peaceably to assemble. . . ."; "The right of the people to be secure . . . against unreasonable searches and seizures, shall not be violated. . . ."; and so on), but Congress and the Supreme Court have always been able to interpret those phrases in *relative* terms ("but of course in this sort of situation . . ., and in this one . . ., and this one . . ., obviously something must be done or else we'll have anarchy or subversion or . . ."), because there is no one to challenge the government's own interpretation of the limits imposed on it by the Constitution. For the same reason, it has always been impossible—legally, or with force short of civil war—to prevent the national government from extending its power into new areas of our lives, or from doing whatever it wanted to do under the banner of "emergency," "national security," or "the general walfare." Also, our national government has never been a genuinely federal government. In the nation as a whole power has always been more centralized (in order to capture or influence that pinnacle of ultimate power, the national government) than decentralized. The solid South, as I said before, existed not because of federalism or "states' rights," but because of decisions taken at the *central* government level, backed up by the power of the South in *national* politics. The government has always had more money and force at its disposal than any state government. The troops and marshals requiring compliance with desegregation in Little Rock and the University of Mississippi were nothing compared to the armed troops sent by the president over the strenuous objections of the Illinois governor in 1894 to crush the most successful railroad strike up to that time.

The fact that the Constitution required national power to be centralized and ever-expanding is related to the *third* major undemocratic aspect of the Constitution, namely, that it imposed a kind of structure upon our national politics that must be described as legalistic and bureaucratic. As John Schaar points out in "Our Constitutional Psyche and Its Politics," our national political unity is basically a commitment to rules and procedures. Our public space is so criss-crossed with those rules and procedures that they come to shape not only the form but even the substance of what we can do, politically, as a nation. That is, much of the reason for our legalism and bureaucratic organization stems directly from the sort of Constitution that was laid on us at the founding. If these effects were a rather long time in becoming visible (though I think the outlines began to show fairly quickly, and were quite apparent in the rise of national bureaucratized political parties in the 1830's), the reason for the delay is not that the Constitution was not the key influence, but that the nation was small enough in the early days to function without needing the Constitution so much. A baby might grow up in a straitjacket for some years before finding his movements severely restricted.*

To paraphrase the political scientist E. E. Schattschneider, if in a democracy the people are really the sovereign, then in the United States the sovereign can speak only when spoken to, and then has a vocabulary limited to only two words, "yes" and "no." Moreover, the sovereign's governors

---

*It is customary for critics of our contemporary problems to find the major cause of our national bureaucratization in the industrialization that followed the Civil War. But this view is inadequate for two reasons. First, the national government encouraged and even partially subsidized the growth of the national corporations that later came to dominate the society. And second, if we had not had a strong central government, but rather had required that business corporations adjust themselves to a variety of state or regional governments, is it likely that powerful nationwide corporations would have emerged in the form and with the power that they did? Surely that development would have depended much more than our own industrial growth did on the political choices made by the people in the states and regions, just as the governments and diverse peoples of the nations of Europe have had a decisive influence on the failure of European corporations to operate on a truly Europe-wide basis—at least until after World War II.

are discouraged by the Constitution from speaking openly to him, and are encouraged to do his thinking for him, paying much more attention to each other than to the sovereign they supposedly serve. And this feebleness of the sovereign people in our nation corresponds to a certain feebleness in our commitment to democracy. We can never quite make up our minds whether we are really as concerned that government be *by* the people as, merely, *for* the people. (This is the confusion over what the notion of democracy really means that I mentioned a moment ago.) Generally, our traditional attitude has been that as long as things are pretty much okay—as long as my rights are being protected and my interests satisfied—then it does not matter much whether the government that is behind things is democratic ("by the people") or not. But, on the other hand, we do believe in government by the people, and when things start going badly then our deep belief that we have the right to govern ourselves asserts itself—and sometimes causes our political institutions to look more democratic than by themselves they really are.

In other words, we are often confused into taking the *responsiveness* of our government as an indication of its *democratic* nature, forgetting that *any* government will have to be responsive in *some* ways to *some* of its people's serious aspirations and frustrations. Responsiveness, like elections, is only a necessary (not a sufficient) condition of democracy. The fact that a government responds does not in itself show that it is truly "by the people"—nor, even, truly "for the people." A clever dictator like Bismarck, or a wise and paternalistic ruling class like England's in the nineteenth century, would naturally be responsive in some way to the population, giving "bread and circuses" and concessions of special kinds, precisely in order to preserve their *un*democratic rule!

This discussion of democracy in America has ignored the question of just who "the people" are. The point of the brief selection by Slater is that Americans have traditionally been antidemocratic in a profound sense— antidemocratic in that, since democracy necessarily and always involves politics, our antipolitical attitudes have prevented us from getting seriously involved in the business of governing ourselves. The individualist that Slater describes may never have existed in such pure form, but there is surely no doubt that the desire in all of us to get away from each other, to escape the "confines" of society and to look out for "number one," has had as one result the abdication of our original potential as self-governors, and the handing-over of that role to professionals who will do the "dirty" business of politics for us.

Still, even though it is true that some of the deepest features of our characters have worked against democracy, it is also true that the institutions our Founding Fathers saddled us with have not made it any easier for us to achieve and maintain a genuine democracy. The selections by Hofstadter and by Schaar reveal quite clearly the truth of the profound insight that men's and women's characters and actions are shaped by their basic political institutions. When Hofstadter begins with the observation that our government is based on the philosophy of Hobbes and the religion of Calvin, he is saying (in the typically indirect way of the academic) that this government is based on *fear*—that the Founding Fathers' fear of ordinary people led them to create institutions which would work only if people behaved as if they were worthy of being feared, and that over time people developed the habit of behaving in a fearful way, so that it became true in fact that one has to fear other people in order to know how to operate in American society. Similarly, Schaar shows that the "everyman" postulated by the Founding Fathers, as part of the theoretical justification for our Constitution, has actually been brought into existence by the operations of the political institutions created by the Constitution. And Schaar shows some of the political consequences of our being molded by the Constitution. For example, people today deny the possibility of treating each other differently in politics than in other areas of social life, and this denial makes it "natural" for people to behave in ordinary (selfish, fearful) ways in public, and to be "naturally" indifferent to the public good and private-centered. In other words, Schaar suggests that our Constitution has made it virtually impossible for us to govern ourselves, because it has taught us to want to behave in ways that are antithetical to the requirements of genuine self-government. This is not to say, of course, that we *must* accept the conditioning imposed by our institutions, only that it is very hard for us to escape or transcend our institutionally imposed antipolitical tendencies.*

No discussion of democracy in America or of our basic national traditions, even one as hasty as this, can be left without some mention of the profound changes that occurred in our society between the Civil War and World War I. In 1860, to an extent that we postwar Americans can hardly conceive, the United States consisted essentially of farms and small towns inhabited by Anglo-Saxon Protestants. The countryside dominated, very few organizations had nationwide operations (aside from the national government), and most people could be on their own almost as much as they chose to be. But by 1920 everything had changed. Millions of non-WASP immigrants and former slaves, huge cities, factory industry, enormous nationwide organizations, and the close of the frontier were now some of the basic facts of daily life. In less than one lifetime the society "modernized." And, hardly less than happens in the "modernizing" nations of today, we went through a profound crisis during our "modernization," and had to make some very basic choices about the way we as a nation would continue to exist.

The selection by William Appleman Williams describes some of the changes that occurred during this period. Here I want to stress that we, as a nation, *chose* to handle our crisis of "modernization" by means of the sort

---

*To stress the fact that our Constitution is not particularly democratic, either in intention or in effect, is not to say that there were no people two hundred years ago who wanted our nation to be a democracy. Such people did exist, in large numbers, but they were defeated by the men we have been taught to call the "Founding Fathers." It is a great mistake when people today, who desire basic change in our politics and society, ignore our own history as a source of inspiration and examples.

of undemocratic, centralized, and bureaucratic organization that was fore-shadowed in our Constitution. It may have been a measure of our national commitment to electoral democracy, as Robert Wiebe says, that the frustra-tions and bitterness of two decades of intense social and economic conflict played themselves out in the election of the Republican McKinley as presi-dent in 1896. But it was an indication of the quality of the "democracy" we were committed to that the direct result of that election was our imperialis-tic "splendid little war" (to quote the secretary of state at the time) with Spain over Cuba and the Philippines, the establishment of white supremacy in the South, and the destruction of Populism and of all serious political opposition to the growing power of the huge industrial and financial corpo-rations.

Centralized control of the economy (and indirectly of the society), huge cities, and the problems of "mass society" are generally taken to be "inevita-ble" by-products of a process of industrialization. But I insist that these developments were not absolutely necessary in this country, and came about as the result of choices and human action and inaction. Contrast what we as a nation did in the 1890's with what we did in the crisis that was produced after 1765 by the clash between our own desires and Britain's colonial policies. At that time the "inevitable" outcome was for the colonies to remain colonies. But the colonists came together as a people, chose to resist the inevitable, and worked successfully, politically as well as militarily, to reshape the world they lived in. They saw their problem as not merely economic, and not just military, but as political—involving the future consti-tution of their body politic—and they acted on that perception. In the last two decades of the nineteenth century, by contrast, although there was a good deal of resistance, as a nation we gave in to "the inevitable." Less dramatically, there was not enough popular determination to break out of the constraints imposed by our constitutional traditions and by the already overwhelming power of the corporations and of the national government, and so the outcome of what struggle there was had to eventually fit in with and thereby reinforce those traditions and that structure of power.

It was a time not unlike our own. Many people at that time believed that there was a real possibility that basic social and political change might occur. And most people were seriously dissatisfied with the conditions of their lives, many to the point of seeing the society as beyond mere reform. But few people took the notion of making some constitutional changes seriously. Instead of acting on the insight, as the colonists had against colonialism itself a hundred years earlier, that constitutional institutions and the Constitution were part of the problems facing them, discontented peo-ple either rallied to *defend* those institutions or tried to make *use* of them to solve their problems! The Populists, for example, although they certainly did make radical demands and did try to develop new kinds of institutions, chose to make their major political struggle into an attempt to gain control over the national government via the presidential elections, and they chose to do this *within* one of the two major existing parties! People in all parts of the country who still had hopes for "making it big" saw that the way to the top for an individual looked a bit easier when aided by contacts within the established parties. Comfortable, educated reformers in the cities became frightened of what might happen if basic structural changes were permitted, and so drew back from the Populists to throw in their lot with more "responsible" voices. Factory workers who were disorganized and downtrodden had a hard time seeing any connections between the predominantly rural-oriented program of the Populists and their own desperate needs. Immigrant groups were either too disestablished to be able to do much in politics, or were established enough that their own group interests appeared to lie in the direction of protecting gains already made and paving the way for more by staying on the good side of those with power. Farmers in the Midwest and East were generally not so badly off as the southern and western Populists, and so could not bring themselves to break with tradition and the major parties. And very critically, of course, there was virtually no split among the powerful businessmen, financiers, and politicians, and therefore very little established or experienced leadership for the Populists to work with in attempting to reach these other oppressed groups in the population.

In short, *given* that these other groups had not yet reached the point of seeing the crisis as so severe as to make their continued pursuit of private or exclusive group interests irrelevant or ignoble, and *given* that in spite of their lack of ties with those groups the Populists still chose to wage their struggle through traditional institutions, not surprisingly, the people who controlled and benefited most from those traditional institutions won the struggle. But this hardly makes the outcome unavoidable; neither "given" *had* to be true. The question for today is whether simular sorts of "givens" can be overcome.

The final selection in this part, by Grant McConnell, describes more specifically how these "givens" have contributed to our traditional style of politics, and then shows how "the new politics" attempts to overcome that tradition. The reason for including this selection here is not to argue that the "new politics" of the late 1960's is *the* answer to all our problems. McConnell's article is especially valuable for his description and explanation of the way we usually behave as a nation. In the process of showing how the "new politics" differs from our traditional politics, he suggests the kinds of profound changes in our national way of life that a different kind of politics will probably require.

"In the Beginning..."

1   The Founding Fathers

Richard Hofstadter

Long ago Horace White observed that the Constitution of the United States "is based upon the philosophy of Hobbes and the religion of Calvin. It assumes that the natural state of mankind is a state of war, and that the carnal mind is at enmity with God." Of course, the Constitution was founded more upon experience than any such abstract theory; but it was also an event in the intellectual history of Western civilization. The men who drew up the Constitution in Philadelphia during the summer of 1787 had a vivid Calvinistic sense of human evil and damnation and believed with Hobbes that men are selfish and contentious. They were men of affairs, merchants, lawyers, planter-businessmen, speculators, investors. Having seen human nature on display in the marketplace, the courtroom, the legislative chamber, and in every secret path and alleyway where wealth and power are courted, they felt they knew it in all its frailty. To them a human being was an atom of self-interest. They did not believe in man, but they did believe in the power of a good political constitution to control him.

This may be an abstract notion to ascribe to practical men, but it follows the language that the Fathers themselves used. General Knox, for example, wrote in disgust to Washington after the Shays Rebellion that Americans were, after all, "men—actual men

possessing all the turbulent passions belonging to that animal." Throughout the secret discussions at the Constitutional Convention it was clear that this distrust of man was first and foremost a distrust of the common man and democratic rule. As the Revolution took away the restraining hand of the British government, old colonial grievances of farmers, debtors, and squatters against merchants, investors, and large landholders had flared up anew; the lower orders took advantage of new democratic constitutions in several states, and the possessing classes were frightened. The members of the Constitutional Convention were concerned to create a government that could not only regulate commerce and pay its debts but also prevent currency inflation and stay laws, and check such uprisings as the Shays Rebellion.

Cribbing and confining the popular spirit that had been at large since 1776 were essential to the purposes of the new Constitution. Edmund Randolph, saying to the Convention that the evils from which the country suffered originated in "the turbulence and follies of democracy," and that the great danger lay in "the democratic parts of our constitutions"; Elbridge Gerry, speaking of democracy as "the worst of all political evils"; Roger Sherman, hoping that "the people . . . have as little to do as may be about the government"; William Livingston, saying that "the people have ever been and ever will be unfit to retain the exercise of power in their own hands"; George Washington, the presiding officer, urging the delegates not to produce a document of which they themselves could not approve simply in order to "please the people"; Hamilton, charging that the "turbulent and changing" masses "seldom judge or determine right" and advising a permanent governmental body to "check the imprudence of democracy"; the wealthy young planter Charles Pickney, proposing that no one be president who was not worth at least one hundred thousand dollars—all these were quite representative of the spirit in which the problems of government were treated.

Democratic ideas are most likely to take root among discontented and oppressed classes, rising middle classes, or perhaps some sections of an old, alienated, and partially disinherited aristocracy, but they do not appeal to a privileged class that is still amplifying its privileges. With a half-dozen exceptions at the most, the men of the Philadelphia Convention were sons of men who had considerable position and wealth, and as a group they had advanced well beyond their fathers. Only one of them, William Few of Georgia, could be said in any sense to represent the yeoman farmer class which constituted the overwhelming majority of the free population. In the late eighteenth century "the better kind of people" found themselves set off from the mass by a hundred visible, tangible, and audible distinctions of dress, speech, manners, and education. There was a continuous lineage of upper-class contempt, from pre-Revolutionary Tories like Peggy Hutchinson, the governor's daughter, who wrote one day: "The dirty mob was all about me as I drove into town," to a Federalist like Hamilton, who candidly disdained the people. Mass unrest was often received in the spirit of young Gouverneur Morris: "The mob begin to think and reason. Poor reptiles! ... They bask in the sun, and ere noon they will bite, depend upon it. The gentry begin to fear this." Nowhere in America or Europe— not even among the great liberated thinkers of the Enlightenment—did democratic ideas appear respectable to the cultivated classes.

Whether the Fathers looked to the cynically illuminated intellectuals of contemporary Europe or to their own Christian heritage of the idea of original sin, they found quick confirmation of the notion that man is an unregenerate rebel who has to be controlled.

And yet there was another side to the picture. The Fathers were intellectual heirs of seventeenth-century English republicanism with its opposition to arbitrary rule and faith in popular sovereignty. If they feared the advance of democracy, they also had misgivings about turning to the extreme right. Having recently experienced a bitter revolutionary struggle with an external power beyond their control, they were in no mood to follow Hobbes to his conclusion that any kind of government must be accepted in order to avert the anarchy and terror of a state of nature. They were uneasily aware that both military dictatorship and a return to monarchy were being seriously discussed in some quarters—the former chiefly among unpaid and discontented army officers, the latter in rich and fashionable northern circles. John Jay, familiar with sentiment among New York's mercantile aristocracy, wrote to Washington, June 27, 1786, that he feared that "the better kind of people (by which I mean the people who are orderly and industrious, who are content with their situations, and not uneasy in their circumstances) will be led, by the insecurity of property, the loss of confidence in their rulers, and the want of public faith and rectitude, to consider the charms of liberty as imaginary and delusive." Such men, he thought, might be prepared for "almost any change that may promise them quiet and security." Washington, who had already repudiated a suggestion that he become a military dictator, agreed remarking that "we are apt to run from one extreme to the other."

Unwilling to turn their backs upon republicanism, the Fathers also wished to avoid violating the prejudices of the people. "Notwithstanding the oppression and injustice experienced among us from democracy," said George Mason, "the genius of the people is in favor of it, and the genius of the people must be consulted." Mason admitted "that we had been too democratic," but feared that "we should incautiously run into the opposite extreme." James Madison, who has quite rightfully been called the philosopher of the Constitution, told the delegates: "It seems indispensable that the mass of citizens should not be without a voice in making the laws which they are to obey, and in choosing the magistrates who are to administer them." James Wilson, the outstanding jurist of the age, later appointed to the Supreme Court by Washington, said again and again that the ultimate power of government must of necessity reside in the people. This the Fathers commonly accepted, for if government did not proceed from the people, from what other source could it legitimately come? To adopt any other premise not only would be inconsistent with everything they had said against British rule in the past but would open the gates to an extreme concentration of power in the future. Hamilton saw the sharp distinction in the Convention when he said that "the members most tenacious of republicanism were as loud as any in declaiming the vices of democracy." There was no better expression of the dilemma of a man who has no faith in the people but insists that government be based upon them than that of Jeremy Belknap, a New England clergyman, who wrote to a friend: "Let it stand as a principle that government originates from the people; but let the people be taught . . . that they are not able to govern themselves."

If the masses were turbulent and unregenerate, and yet if government must be founded upon their suffrage and consent, what could a Constitution-maker do? One thing that the Fathers did not propose to do, because they thought it impossible, was to change the nature of man to conform with a more ideal system. They were inordinately confident that they knew what man always had been and what he always would be. The eighteenth-century mind had great faith in universals. Its method, as Carl Becker has said, was "to go up and down the field of history looking for man in general, the universal man, stripped of the accidents of time

and place." Madison declared that the causes of political differences and of the formation of factions were "sown in the nature of man" and could never be eradicated. "It is universally acknowledged," David Hume had written, "that there is a great uniformity among the actions of men, in all nations and ages, and that human nature remains still the same, in its principles and operations. The same motives always produce the same actions. The same events always follow from the same causes."

Since man was an unchangeable creature of self-interest, it would not do to leave anything to his capacity for restraint. It was too much to expect that vice could be checked by virtue; the Fathers relied instead upon checking vice with vice. Madison once objected during the Convention that Gouverneur Morris was "forever inculcating the utter political depravity of men and the necessity of opposing one vice and interest to another vice and interest." And yet Madison himself in the Federalist number 51 later set forth an excellent statement of the same thesis:*

Ambition must be made to counteract ambition. . . . It may be a reflection on human nature that such devices should be necessary to control the abuses of government. But what is government itself, but the greatest of all reflections on human nature? If men were angels, no government would be necessary. . . . In framing a government which is to be administered by men over men, the great difficulty lies in this: you must first enable the government to control the governed; and in the next place oblige it to control itself.

Political economists of the laissez-faire school were saying that private vices could be public benefits, that an economically

---

*Cf. the words of Hamilton to the New York ratifying convention: "Men will pursue their interests. It is as easy to change human nature as to oppose the strong current of selfish passions. A wise legislator will gently divert the channel, and direct it, if possible, to the public good."

beneficent result would be providentially or "naturally" achieved if self-interest were left free from state interference and allowed to pursue its ends. But the Fathers were not so optimistic about politics. If, in a state that lacked constitutional balance, one class or one interest gained control, they believed, it would surely plunder all other interests. The Fathers, of course, were especially fearful that the poor would plunder the rich, but most of them would probably have admitted that the rich, unrestrained, would also plunder the poor. Even Gouverneur Morris, who stood as close to the extreme aristocratic position as candor and intelligence would allow, told the Convention: "Wealth tends to corrupt the mind and to nourish its love of power, and to stimulate it to oppression. History proves this to be the spirit of the opulent."

What the Fathers wanted was known as "balanced government," an idea at least as old as Aristotle and Polybius. This ancient conception had won new sanction in the eighteenth century, which was dominated intellectually by the scientific work of Newton, and in which mechanical metaphors sprang as naturally to men's minds as did biological metaphors in the Darwinian atmosphere of the late nineteenth century. Men had found a rational order in the universe and they hoped that it could be transferred to politics, or, as John Adams put it, that governments could be "erected on the simple principles of nature." Madison spoke in the most precise Newtonian language when he said that such a "natural" government must be so constructed "that its several constituent parts may, by their mutual relations, be the means of keeping each other in their proper places." A properly designed state, the Fathers believed, would check interest with interest, class with class, faction with faction, and one branch of government with another in a harmonious system of mutual frustration.

In practical form, therefore, the quest of the Fathers reduced primarily to a search for constitutional devices that would force various interests to check and control one an-

other. . . . [These "devices" are our familiar "checks and balances."] . . .

It is ironical that the Constitution, which Americans venerate so deeply, is based upon a political theory that at one crucial point stands in direct antithesis to the main stream of American democratic faith. Modern American folklore assumes that democracy and liberty are all but identical, and when democratic writers take the trouble to make the distinction, they usually assume that democracy is necessary to liberty. But the Founding Fathers thought that the liberty with which they were most concerned was menaced by democracy. In their minds liberty was linked not to democracy but to property.

What did the Fathers mean by liberty? What did Jay mean when he spoke of "the charms of liberty"? Or Madison when he declared that to destroy liberty in order to destroy factions would be a remedy worse than the disease? Certainly the men who met at Philadelphia were not interested in extending liberty to those classes in America, the Negro slaves and the indentured servants who were most in need of it, for slavery was recognized in the organic structure of the Constitution and indentured servitude was no concern of the Convention. Nor was the regard of the delegates for civil liberties any too tender. It was the opponents of the Constitution who were most active in demanding such vital liberties as freedom of religion, freedom of speech and press, jury trial, due process, and protection from "unreasonable searches and seizures." These guarantees had to be incorporated in the first ten amendments because the Convention neglected to put them in the original document. Turning to economic issues, it was not freedom of trade in the modern sense that the Fathers were striving for. Although they did not believe in impeding trade unnecessarily, they felt that failure to regulate it was one of the central weaknesses of the Articles of Confederation, and they stood closer to the mercantilists than to Adam Smith. Again, liberty to them did not mean free access to the nation's unappropriated wealth. At least fourteen of them were land speculators. They did not believe in the right of the squatter to occupy unused land, but rather in the right of the absentee owner or speculator to preempt it.

The liberties that the constitutionalists hoped to gain were chiefly negative. They wanted freedom from fiscal uncertainty and irregularities in the currency, from trade wars among the states, from economic discrimination by more powerful foreign governments, from attacks on the creditor class or on property, from popular insurrection. They aimed to create a government that would act as an honest broker among a variety of propertied interests, giving them all protection from their common enemies and preventing any one of them from becoming too powerful. . . .

. . . the Fathers' image of themselves as moderate republicans standing between political extremes was quite accurate. They were impelled by class motives more than pietistic writers like to admit, but they were also controlled, as Professor Beard himself has recently emphasized, by a statesmanlike sense of moderation and a scrupulously republican philosophy. Any attempt, however, to tear their ideas out of the eighteenth-century context is sure to make them seem starkly reactionary. Consider, for example, the favorite maxim of John Jay: "The people who own the country ought to govern it." To the Fathers this was simply a swift axiomatic statement of the stake-in-society theory of political rights, a moderate conservative position under eighteenth-century conditions of property distribution in America. Under modern property relations this maxim demands a drastic restriction of the base of political power. A large portion of the modern middle class—and it is the strength of this class upon which balanced government depends—is propertyless; and the urban proletariat, which the Fathers so greatly feared, is almost one-half the population. Further, the separation of ownership from control that

has come with the corporation deprives Jay's maxim of twentieth-century meaning even for many propertied people. The six hundred thousand stockholders of the American Telephone & Telegraph Company not only do not acquire political power by virtue of their stock ownership, but they do not even acquire economic power: they cannot control their own company.

From a humanistic standpoint there is a serious dilemma in the philosophy of the Fathers, which derives from their conception of man. They thought man was a creature of rapacious self-interest, and yet they wanted him to be free—free, in essence, to contend, to engage in an umpired strife, to use property to get property. They accepted the mercantile image of life as an eternal battleground, and assumed the Hobbesian war of each against all; they did not propose to put an end to this war, but merely to stabilize it and make it less murderous. They had no hope and they offered none for any ultimate organic change in the way men conduct themselves. The result was that while they thought self-interest the most dangerous and unbrookable quality of man, they necessarily underwrote it in trying to control it. They succeeded in both respects: under the competitive capitalism of the nineteenth century, America continued to be an arena for various grasping and contending interests, and the federal government continued to provide a stable and acceptable medium within which they could contend; further, it usually showed the wholesome bias on behalf of property which the Fathers expected. But no man who is as well abreast of modern science believes any longer in unchanging human nature. Modern humanistic thinkers who seek for a means by which society may transcend eternal conflict and rigid adherence to property rights as its integrating principles can expect no answer in the philosophy of balanced government as it was set down by the Constitution-makers of 1787.

2   The Pursuit of Loneliness

Philip E. Slater

Once upon a time there was a man who sought escape from the prattle of his neighbors and went to live alone in a hut he had found in the forest. At first he was content, but a bitter winter led him to cut down the trees around his hut for firewood. The next summer he was hot and uncomfortable because his hut had no shade, and he complained bitterly of the harshness of the elements.

He made a little garden and kept some chickens, but rabbits were attracted by the food in the garden and ate much of it. The man went into the forest and trapped a fox, which he tamed and taught to catch rabbits. But the fox ate up the man's chickens as well. The man shot the fox and cursed the perfidy of the creatures of the wild.

The man always threw his refuse on the floor of his hut and soon it swarmed with vermin. He then built an ingenious system of hooks and pulleys so that everything in the hut could be suspended from the ceiling. But the strain was too much for the flimsy hut

and it soon collapsed. The man grumbled about the inferior construction of the hut and built himself a new one.

One day he boasted to a relative in his old village about the peaceful beauty and plentiful game surrounding his forest home. The relative was impressed and reported back to his neighbors, who began to use the area for picnics and hunting excursions. The man was upset by this and cursed the intrusiveness of mankind. He began posting signs, setting traps, and shooting at those who came near his dwelling. In revenge groups of boys would come at night from time to time to frighten him and steal things. The man took to sleeping every night in a chair by the window with a loaded shotgun across his knees. One night he turned in his sleep and shot off his foot. The villagers were chastened and saddened by this misfortune and thereafter stayed away from his part of the forest. The man become lonely and cursed the unfriendliness and indifference of his former neighbors. And in all this the man saw no agency except what lay outside himself, for which reason, and because of his ingenuity, the villagers called him the American.

3 Our Constitutional Everyman and His Politics

John H. Schaar

The great liberal and constitutional theorists of the modern era (Locke, Kant, Madison, Bentham) all rested their political theories on conceptions of human nature. Their commentators never tire of pointing out that all of these conceptions are grossly oversimplified. Such criticism, however, is beside the point: it misses their intention.

These writers did not try to develop an exhaustive psychology. Rather, they devised a political psychology. They abstracted from the infinite diversity of human actuality the one trait or factor that mattered most in the building of a political order along constitutionalist lines. When a political order is deliberately contrived, when the builder deliberately sets out to build a structure that will hold political forces in certain predetermined shapes, then it is important that he have uniform and standard materials to work with. The need for a uniform building material is inherent in the very idea of building a constitutional edifice. The constitutional architect requires men of a standard size and shape, just as the "real" architect requires building materials of specified and uniform properties. In sum, the first reason for the assumption of human equality and uniformity made by these writers is simply that such an assumption is inherent in the constitutionalist way or style of thinking about politics.

If the first reason is inherent in the style of constitutionalist thought, the second is central to its basic substantive intention. All of these writers shared the view that the chief purpose of the constitutional edifice was to provide a secure framework within which men might pursue their private ends. The ba-

Reprinted from "Some Ways of Thinking about Equality," *The Journal of Politics,* 26 (November 1964), by permission.

sic distinction in constitutionalist thought is the distinction between public and private, and the main purpose of the public institutions is the protection of private rights (typically conceived as property and liberty). Now, the most distinctive proposition of the constitutionalists is the idea, which all of them expressed with one or another degree of clarity and comprehensiveness, that the most efficient way to preserve variety and difference—individuality—in the private sphere is by treating men uniformly—equally—in the public sphere. In a phrase, these theorists postulated public equality in order to preserve private inequalities. This is the point of their "oversimplified" conceptions of human nature, which are all really conceptions of human equality.

This is why criticisms of their theories of human nature on empirical grounds are largely beside the point. These writers were constructing a psychology for political purposes, not scientific ones. It is obvious that their conceptions of human nature owe little to observation. The man of whom they write is a creature of the theoretical reason, not a flesh-and-blood resident of the world. This theoretical everyman is conceived as having but one or, at most, a few attributes which are relevant to the construction of a political order. He is a generalized and diminished man, reduced to fear (Hobbes) or will (Kant) or interest (Madison) or the passion for distinction (John Adams) or pleasure-pain (Bentham). He is an elementary stimulus-response mechanism, a quantum of energy which is set into motion under specifiable conditions and directed toward specifiable ends. All that matters about him for political purposes is his external behavior, which is regular, predictable, and subject to the general laws of political motion. These laws are as precise and comprehensive in the political realm as the general laws of motion are in the physical realm.

Provided with these uniform materials, the political architect can build states of great size and admirable symmetry. He need hardly bother with real men at all. Real men —the complex, variable, disorderly creatures who move about in the world—are not needed in the political order erected by the constitutionalists. Conversely, these real men do not need the political order except as a shelter within which they may safely pursue their important (private) interests. Put differently, every one of the great constitutional theorists tried to invent a self-regulating mechanism, a system which would run by its own laws and require the least possible amount of deliberate human care and guidance. Machinery would replace character and fortune as the governing principle of states. James Madison's "new science of politics" was new in the exact sense that it showed political architects how to design institutions which would work in certain ways and produce certain results regardless of the qualities and intentions of the men who occupied them.

Everything about men except the one thing which the theorist held as the basic component of the stimulus-response mechanism is ignored in the construction of the polity and excluded from the meaning of citizenship. This state of being ignored is exactly what the constitutionalists meant by freedom. Freedom rests on being left alone by the public authority, and consists in the unhampered pursuit of one's private interests. As Hobbes put it, liberty exists where the laws are silent. And when the laws speak, they say the same thing to everyone. Constitutionalist theory first asserts that, for political purposes, all men shall be regarded as equal in certain respects. It then says that when the state deals with these equal men it shall deal with them equally. Hence, the state specifies that all men shall, within a prescribed area, behave in the same way. It then defines or constitutes this area in which behavior must

be uniform as the public realm: the public realm *is* the area of uniform and equal behavior. This space is kept as small as possible, so that the private space can be as large as possible. Liberty, which expresses men's inequalities and diversities, resides within the zone of privacy. The fundamental convention, then, is that all men shall be treated as equals in the public realm, in order that they will be able to express their inequalities in the private realm. By assigning the principle of equality to one territory and the principle of inequality to another, the constitutionalists thought that both could be preserved without conflict. It is an ingenious idea, and one with many ramifications.

The radical separation of public and private has some important consequences for the theory of moral personality—the conception of the good man, and the understanding of how natural man develops into moral man. The most important of these consequences is the idea that no man's real worth shall be judged in the public forum and by public criteria. The inner self is entirely private, invisible to the public gaze, shielded from public judgment. This means that the public realm is without authority either to validate or to invalidate a man. Conversely, no man can achieve validation in the public realm. The concept of equal citizenship requires that each man be treated in public *as if* he were as good—or as bad—as any other man, and it forbids a public judgment as to whether he *really* is. That judgment may be made only in the private sphere.

The constitutionalists' everyman has often been criticized on esthetic and moral grounds. Such criticism misses the point as much as the empirical criticism does. Everyman was never meant to be an attractive figure, but only a useful one, and in that he succeeds.

First of all, the construct of public equality serves as a mask behind which one's inner self can hide from the probing, judging eyes of anonymous others. In the huge and heterogeneous polities of today that is a very important protection, for the fact is that each of us must today live much of his life among virtual strangers, and no man can safely endure or morally accept judgments of his worth made by strangers. No man can turn himself over for moral judgment to others who do not share his hopes and fears, his code of righteousness, his loves and hates. In the constitutional polity, with its postulate of equality, each of us in effect is under a contract of strictly limited public liability. This is probably the only technique which can protect any meaningful liberty and personal integrity in the giant states of today. Despite the Biblical injunction to the contrary, one cannot love the public as himself. The very division between familiars and strangers makes it necessary in the huge political societies of today to find a means to ensure familiars that they will not be compelled to treat strangers as though they were intimates, and, at the same time, to guarantee the strangers that they will not suffer by reason of being outside the pale. When an aggregation of men exceeds the (very small) number that can be included within the circle of familiars, it seems both necessary and reasonable that the ties that bind them should be affectively neutral, and that they should benefit no man at the expense of others.

Secondly, the postulate of equality has the utility of sparing us the risk and trouble of actually looking at the crowds of anonymous others among whom we must live. The postulate requires (and therefore permits) us to treat everyone alike. Hence, we have a ready justification for callous behavior when efficiency or necessity requires us to deal with large numbers of people or when we are in charge of apportioning a scarce resource. It is not necessary to examine and judge individual claims: all fall under an equal rule; so first come, first served. The rule of equality, in case after case, relieves us of the obligation of really *looking* at the actual person before us and treating him in the one way uniquely appropriate to his own individuality. We need not attend to and make a judgment on *that* person, and we need not accept the responsibility for acting on our judgment. We need only apply the rule. This too is a real utility, for it reduces the personal risk of living in a complex world, and it lets us save our energy for the task of building a private estate in a busy and complex world. So useful is this rule of equality, and so wide its application in our society, that about the only time one can count on being treated as an individual is when he is sick.

The construct, then, has very real utilities. But it also has some consequences which we may not be so eager to accept. I shall point only to a few of the more obvious ones.

First of all, the sharp distinction between public and private, and the subordination of the former to the latter, narrows the stage of public action. When the public space is so circumscribed, the perils of contingent action are surely reduced—and this was a major aim of the constitutionalists—but so too are the possibilities. Citizenship is not a moral adventure or an educational experience. It is merely a legally defined bundle of rights and powers which the individual may use to defend and advance his interests. The public stage is not regarded as a place where men gather to seek self-understanding and self-enlargement by presenting themselves to others in an open dialogue of thought and action. The citizen is expected to disclose but a fraction of himself to the public gaze, and that will be the same fraction which others expose. The citizen even performs his most obviously public act, the act of voting, in the privacy of the voting booth; and that institution perfectly symbolizes the idea that the citizen need account to no one for his choices. We expect and regard it as entirely legitimate that he will seek to translate his private will into public policy through whatever political instruments are available to him, and we assume that he has a right to keep his political opinions and conclusions to himself. Politics quickly comes to be thought of as a distinctly second-order and instrumental activity and occupation, subordinate to the primary concerns of the private life. John Adams showed a firm grasp of the point when he wrote that he had to give himself to politics in order that his son might pursue the useful sciences, such as engineering, and in order that his son might devote himself to the graceful arts, such as music and literature. This movement from the necessary through the useful to the pleasurable is simultaneously a movement from the public toward the private, and it accurately expresses what happens to the conception of politics in the equalitarian and constitutionalist regime.

A second troublesome consequence of this way of thinking about politics appears when we reflect on the obvious fact that what is "political" is in large part what men think is political. The "political" is not a category or object of nature, like the stars or the sun, which, no matter how our ways of thinking about them change, are not themselves changed by our ways of thinking about them. We may think of the sun as a god, or as the home of a god, or as a huge mass of very hot particles of matter, and none of those conceptions alters in any way what the sun is. The political, on the other hand, is what men think it is, and it changes as their ways of thinking about it change. Hence, when the political realm is defined as the constitutionalists defined it, it tends in fact to become this way: the conception realizes itself.

The most important concrete consequence of this way of thinking about politics is that men come to regard the public arena as a place where ordinary men will appear as naturally and act as capably as extraordinary men. The public realm is not seen as the place where great men most naturally gather and where great actions most naturally take place. Rather, the political arena, being itself a place of second-rate action, is the place where second-rate men gather to pursue their second-rate ends. This process unfolded in all its major phases during the first century of our independent political life. Thus, at the time of the founding, the public stage held a virtual monopoly of men of the highest excellence. Then, during the time of Jackson, the doctrine was officially proclaimed that excellence was not needed even in the highest places of state. That doctrine achieved its practical fulfillment in the "hard cider" election of 1840. And finally, during post-Civil War America the field of grand action and large enterprise manifestly became the realm of the economic, not of the political.

Finally, the narrowing of the political stage and the downgrading of the political vocation means that many of those (always relatively few) men whose natures demand political expression are condemned to frustration for want of a noble and spacious place in which to act. And many other men, who find joy in watching political action, are deprived of a commodious theater and noble plays to attend. When the political stage is narrowed at the rear by the rule of bureaucracy (which is the very model of the regime which acts by the rule of equality) and shortened at the front by the noisy and unedifying private performances of factions, hopeful political actors and spectators are left with little that is worth doing or seeing. Henry Adams would have spared himself much lugubrious whining and regret had he accepted his ancestor's forecast of the progress of the constitutional machine. The earlier Adams had labored precisely to build a machine which would not need future Adamses to tend it, but Henry never quite understood this, and felt abandoned in the cold of private life while his nature yearned for the warmth of public life.

So, there are gains and losses here, a price paid for every advantage obtained.

The intent of the constitutionalists was generous, even noble. They worked to build a political order which would acknowledge that common men had as much claim to dignity and importance in their lives as uncommon men had in theirs. They accomplished this by sharply distinguishing the public and the private, and by insisting that all men be treated in public as if they were equals.

On the other hand, the everyman of the constitutionalists is not a generous or noble, not even an interesting figure. The man hypothesized (and even created) by Locke or Madison, say, cannot matter much to us. We cannot love him, and we cannot hate him either. Surely we cannot see him as a friend.* Such men will to live together out of a recognition of mutual convenience, and on the understanding that they won't have to live together very closely. Each must respect the privacy of others.

None of the great constitutional theorists argued that his everyman was admirable and ought to be accepted for himself. They argued, rather, that equality of public treatment would secure private diversity and inequaltiy. Formal public equality sets the framework within which a multiplicity of private differences and inequalities can flourish. Constitutionalism accepts the formal unity—a unity of rules and procedures—on the public level in order to protect a diversity of substantive unities—unities of sentiment, value, and interest—in the private sphere. The rules of the road tell us how we must drive, but they do not tell us where we must go. The basic assumption of the whole system is very clear: no partial community may impose its substantive vision of the good life on the whole community. On the level of the whole, our unity is formal, not substantive.

The whole point of the postulate of equality in constitutional theory, then, is that it provides the basis for a public order and unity. Now, it is of course true that real men, not hypothetically equal men, act in that public order. However, two qualifications are set on this action; and these qualifications are so important that they greatly shape the tone and content of action in the public realm.

*One can understand much of the spirit and intention of modern constitutionalist theory if he remembers that it has neither need nor place for friendship in the polity, whereas in Aristotle's time, "those who frame the constitutions of states set more store by this feeling than by justice itself." *Ethics*, Book 8. In the modern view, friendship has no place in public life because it corrupts the rule of law. The political machines of an earlier America were hated by the liberal reformers precisely for this reason. As Tim Campbell, the boss of one of those machines, said, "What's the Constitution among friends?"

In the first place, the laws and institutions of the constitutional system encourage some kinds of actions and discourage others. Specifically, they encourage actions which are in conformity with the nature of the hypothesized everyman, and they discourage actions which divert greatly from that norm. In other words, the laws and institutions produce an expectation that certain actions will take place in public and that others will not. I am suggesting that if you institutionalize a conception of man as the pursuer of interest, for example, that in itself tends to produce the kind of behavior it predicts: the hypothesis creates the facts that confirm itself. The workings of this process in American politics are very plain. With us, all political action is assumed to be action in pursuit of interest: that is what politics is; anything else is virtually illegitimate.

In the second place, although action in the public realm is action undertaken by real men, the rules of the game require us to treat those actions *as if* they were the actions not of real men, but of the hypothetical man posited by the laws and institutions. We look at action in the public realm through a special lens which filters out much of what is really going on and admits only selected aspects of the whole. Everything that we see and do in the public realm is constrained by deliberate rules. We agree to see only certain things, and to call those things the whole. We agree not to "pierce the veil," not to probe beneath the surface of rule and convention to the realities within. To see how thoroughgoing this distinction is between public and private, consider again the radical difference we have established between criminal and moral guilt. In the perfectly realized constitutional state, all relations between men would be governed by rules, not by feelings. Above all, every manifestation of public authority would be impartial, general, and anonymous, for the constitutionalist regards personal judgment and authority as dangerous in practice and as illegitimate in principle. The ideal is "a government of laws, not of men."

The Going Gets Tougher

4   From the Nineteenth to the Twentieth Century:
      "Syndicalism" Replaces Individualism

William Appleman Williams

THE AGE OF LAISSEZ NOUS FAIRE

*It is said to be the age of the 1st person
singular.*
Ralph Waldo Emerson, 1827

*I care for nothing about clamors, sir, mark me!
I do precisely what I think just
and right.*
Andrew Jackson, 1828

*In the book from which this selection is taken, Williams describes American
history as a progression from the Age of Mercantilism (1740–1828) through
the Age of Laissez Nous Faire (1819–1896) into the Age of Corporation Capitalism (1882–   ). He describes each of these Ages—which might be renamed, more simply, the Ages of the Founding Fathers, of Individualism, and
of Big Business—by analyzing the Weltanschauung, or world view, that most
people at the time shared, to see how the people of the Age understood and
tried to deal with their common problems. This selection omits the Age of
Mercantilism, and begins with the Age of Laissez Faire, whose spirit is expressed by the two quotations from Emerson and Jackson.—Ed.*

Dynamic, liberating, and creative, the soaring spirit and animal vigor of the Age of
Laissez Nous Faire transformed America
from an established newcomer in the society

of nations into the world's leading industrial
country in less than three generations. Yet its
twin dogmas of expansion and competition
exacted a high price for success. Civil war,
grave social disorders, and the progressive
disillusionment and alienation of a sizable
segment of society were the scars and open
wounds it bequeathed to its heirs. The open

field for fair play became first a military battleground and finally the restricted arena dominated by the giant corporation.

For a time, however, the majority of Americans were probably blessed with more liberty than any men in the modern age have known. In a spectacle that was at once terrifying and ennobling, they came unbelievably close to shaping themselves and their world in their own image. . . .

As generally presented and accepted, the *Weltanschauung* of laissez faire was based on what was presumed to be a simple if not obvious truth. Individualized free competition in an open and fair society would produce specific happiness and the general welfare. But the assumption of free competition was actually predicated upon three other unspoken premises: that domestic society was sufficiently balanced and unfettered to ensure that such conflict remained creative, that the marketplace continued to expand, and that other nations accepted and acted on the key axioms. All other things being equal, ran the argument, competition would generate progress.

Yet as Madison, Monroe, and other mercantilists often pointed out, these essential other things never were equal. Various individuals and groups were always insisting that they needed assistance, either to enter the game as an equal or to remain competitors. Often they did need it. Even under the most favorable circumstances, the very process of competition led to the destruction, failure, or bare survival of the less successful. While it promised a diversity of life, therefore, the dynamic of the system carried it toward a situation in which a few triumphant elements dominated the political and social economy. Hence the system always required a considerable amount of tinkering in order to keep it in working condition. . . .

THE WELTANSCHAUUNG OF LAISSEZ FAIRE ENGENDERS A CIVIL WAR

Long after it has ceased to be an effective weapon of personal recrimination or political strategy, Americans remain haunted by the Civil War. One is sometimes tempted to conclude that never have so many said so much about the same thing that is redundant or irrelevant. Underlying that persistent involvement is the realization that the war undercuts the popular mythology that America is unique. Only a nation that avoided such a conflict could make a serious claim to being fundamentally different. In accordance with the logic and psychology of myth, therefore, it has become necessary to turn the war itself into something so different, strange, and mystic that it could have happened only to the chosen people.

Whatever the appeals and sublimations of that approach, it seems more pertinent to history as a way of learning to examine the Civil War through the convergence of the three moralities of laissez faire that began in the late 1830's and reached an early climax in the Free Soil movement. As they merged in a consolidated system, the religious, political, and economic ethics were also distilled into a few key symbols. These handholds of thought, discourse, and judgment became the most potent and yet inclusive words of the age: *expansion, antislavery, freedom.* As indicated by their use as early as Jackson's time, as well as by their more formal denotations and connotations, they implied that the integrated value system of laissez faire was almost wholly negative. Freedom was defined as release from restriction. Expansion and antislavery were but the two sides of the coin that bought such liberty. But while the defining of evil is a vital function, it is no more than half the responsibility of any philosophy. Lacking a creative vision of community, laissez faire was weak in an essential respect: it provided no basis upon which to deal with evil in a nonviolent way. Its solutions were persistently aggressive and acquisitive.

For these reasons, the northern critics of the Compromise of 1850 were more influential than the southern extremists whose first fuse sputtered out at the Nashville Convention. While many of these northerners were ostensibly anti-expansionists, their position was in reality far more complex. They favored overseas economic expansion and defined the rest of foreign policy largely in terms of the trans-Mississippi west. Most westerners and eastern would-be capitalists shared the latter part of this outlook, and on the issue all of them were vigorous expansionists. Since that region was in fact America's colonial (i.e., underdeveloped) empire, their view was realistic.

But it was also extremely provocative because it defined the issue in very severe terms: would expansion into the trans-Mississippi west be undertaken within the framework of the Constitution, or would that basic law be rewritten in accordance with the abstract principles of laissez faire? The compromises under which the Constitution was adopted, the clauses of that document pertaining to representation in the Congress (which counted three-fifths of each slave) and the rights of states, and the pattern of legislation, and the decisions of the Supreme Court all pointed to a choice between two ways of handling the western territories. Either they would be opened to slaveholders as well as nonslaveholders, or the region would be divided into slave and nonslave areas. Southerners were willing to accept either of these solutions. So were a good many northerners.

But the advocates of antislavery laissez faire insisted that no one who did not accept their version of the axioms of laissez faire should be permitted to share the territorial empire. And as far as they were concerned, slavery was a violation of those principles. For them, at any rate, the arrival of the Age of Laissez Nous Faire meant that the Constitution had to be interpreted—that is, rewritten —in the light of this outlook. Since the divergence of opinion ultimately defined *the* question, the basic cause of the Civil War was the *Weltanschauung* of laissez faire. Unwilling to compete within the framework and under the terms of the Constitution, northern antislavery advocates of laissez faire finally undertook to change the rules in the middle of the game—and in the middle of the conti-

nent—by denying the south further access to the expanding marketplace.

In the meantime, from 1851 to 1861, the nation and its politicians fruitlessly sought a way to reconcile laissez faire with the Constitution. But since all their proposals hinged on expansion, they never broke free of the impasse. Seward had the keenest insight into this determining factor. "I cannot exclude the conviction," he concluded as early as 1846, "that the popular passion for territorial aggrandizement is irresistible." Small wonder, therefore, that he later called the struggle between north and south an "irrepressible conflict." Nor is it surprising that most leaders of the decade offered little more than Polk's strategy of balancing the gains between competing expansionist elements. Any more positive approach was almost discredited. One congressman with a sense of history expressed the attitude with great perceptiveness: any efforts to coordinate and balance the country's development "should be expunged as a disgrace to the country and to the nineteenth century." President Franklin Pierce vented the same spirit in his inaugural assertion that he would "not be controlled by any timid forebodings of evil from expansion." President James Buchanan put it even more bluntly. "Expansion is in the future the policy of our country, and only cowards fear and oppose it."

Thus the issue became dangerously oversimplified: expansion for whom? Throughout the 1850's, moreover, the debate took place against a backdrop prepared by America's first female primitive artist in words and ideas. *Uncle Tom's Cabin,* Harriet Beecher Stowe's landscape of slavery, was published in March 1852. Though the form had not really been established (Erastus Beadle launched it in 1860), it might fairly be called the first dime novel. It was a crude, jerky, inaccurate, and violent morality play based on the manipulation of a few type-cast characters in one black-and-white situation.

By populating the south exclusively with evil slaveholders and Negroes, Stowe stereotyped the south as evil. There was nothing of the anxiety and hesitance of the area, let alone its initial propensity to accept the Compromise of 1850. The moral was provided by her misleading picture of the Negro as a man who could in "one generation of education and liberty" take his place in society as a fully matured and developed individual. An application of the principles of laissez faire would enable everyone to live happily ever after. Many southerners thought Stowe no more than a typical emancipated female—"part quack and part cut-throat"—and initially discounted the importance of the book. But the polemic became a guidebook to an enemy—the south—that had already been defined by the value system of laissez faire as it emerged in the program of the Free Soilers and the generalized antislavery spirit. Perhaps nothing defines the essence of laissez faire quite as well as the parallels between the Jacksonian campaign against the bank and the antislavery agitation. Both were negative. Both defined the enemy in secular moral terms. Both were closely tied to economic objectives. Both lacked any positive program for dealing with the problem. And both were undertaken in the name of expansion and freedom. . . .

A BALANCE SHEET
FOR LAISSEZ NOUS FAIRE

Given the dilemmas and contradictions inherent in their outlook, and granted their failure to complete the revolution implicit in the antislavery campaign, the leaders of the Age of Laissez Nous Faire fulfilled their *Weltanschauung* to a remarkable degree. For by 1897, when they formally surrendered power to the spokesmen of a new conception of the world, they had begun to recover from their third major depression, were underselling England and Germany in the world steel market, and had provided major testaments to the importance and the dignity of the individual human being. And despite the dangers in the romantic exaggerations of Emerson and Thoreau, that emphasis on individual men and women could be dismissed

as merely an agrarian myth only at the price of accepting a substitute conceived of statistical data and born of computing machines.

As suggested by the conflict between private and social property in the Age of Mercantilism, the word and concept *fulfillment* have two different meanings that are usually combined in using the term. The denotation bespeaks the culmination of a given logic or pattern of development. But the connotation adds a favorable judgment. It is particularly important to keep these two aspects separate in evaluating the Age of Laissez Nous Faire. For while its advocates stressed individual liberty, opportunity, and achievement, some of their actions which represented a fulfillment of the axioms and logic of the system did not, even by their own standards, warrant the favorable connotation of the term.

This was apparent, for example, in the way that Andrew Jackson's attitude and policy toward the Indians culminated during and after the Civil War. That bitter and violent antagonism produced one general western war which cost $223,891,264, and did not end until 1882. As one of the commanders who defeated the natives, General Philip F. Sheridan left a harsh judgment of the enterprise. "In other words," he reported to the secretary of war in 1878, "we took away their country and their means of support, broke up their mode of living, their habits of life, introduced disease and decay among them. . . . It was for this and against this," he added, "that they made war." Chief Joseph of the Nez Percé tribe, after having narrowly failed in 1877 to escape across the Canadian border, provided a moving epitaph for all Indians. "I want to have time to look for my children and see how many of them I can find. . . . My heart is sick and sad."

President Chester A. Arthur candidly acknowledged in 1881, "the appalling fact" that even then the problem remained unsolved. Mercantilists viewed the Indians as men with an organized society, and had hoped to resolve the conflict by giving them land as a tribal unit and then encouraging and helping them to shift over to a fixed agricultural economy in which they would work out their own compromises between the two cultures. Laissez-faire leaders pursued a fundamentally different policy. Dramatized in 1871 by the formal decision to destroy tribal society and culture, their approach was to force the Indian to accept the institution of private property and ultimately enter the marketplace as an individual entrepreneur. Congress acted on that axiom in 1887, after Indian resistance had collapsed, and opened up an era of more subtle but hardly less effective economic warfare.

Though it produced a different *policy,* the same classic concern with the marketplace manifested itself in connection with the immigrant. Maintaining their own great fecundity (population increased 25 per cent between 1860 and 1890), and confronted with the economic and social problems of a prolonged depression, Americans began to restrict the foreigner's entry into competition. "The nation has reached a point in its growth," observed a citizen in a letter to the editor of *The New York Tribune* in 1881, "where its policy should be to preserve its heritage for coming generations, not to donate it to all the strangers we can induce to come among us."

Religion continued to play a part in such antagonism, but the immigrant's role in the economic and social marketplace became the focus of attack. Native labor opposed the competition and at the same time agreed with upper-class spokesmen on the immigrant's inferiority. Both groups resolved the non sequitur by invoking the central laissez-faire argument about the danger of class conflict. Since they accepted the promises of laissez faire, neither the higher orders nor the workers wanted such social war and feared that the immigrant might precipitate it. That specter of devolution into social violence became one of the strongest themes of the era and strongly influenced the first restrictive legislation of 1882 and the organization of the American Protective Association in 1887.

Both the treatment of the Negro *and the Negro's response* also developed within the *Weltanschauung* of laissez faire. Since 90 per cent of the Negro population remained in the south until the era of World War I, and because the northern antislavery coalition had never been vigorously pro-Negro (and had collapsed), the Negro confronted and grappled with his fate as a freedman within that region. He also did so primarily as an agrarian. As they reestablished their authority, white southerners did not immediately exclude the Negro legally from political action. The black man was lynched, threatened, bullied, and cajoled, and tricked, foxed, and hoodwinked; but he was also voted at the appropriate times and places as a pawn in the white man's game.

Negro reaction was appropriate to the environment: Negroes accepted the self-interest philosophy and its definition of success and began to build a parallel society. Negro newspapers declared, for example, that high income was "real success," and the class of 1886 at Tuskegee Institute chose the slogan "There Is Room at the Top" as their motto. The Negro community rather quickly stratified itself in replicas of the wealthy white entrepreneur and his aspiring competitors. At the bottom were the miserable and maltreated convict laborers leased out to such gigantic white firms as the Tennessee Coal, Iron and Railroad Company for even less than their keep, which was literally infinitesimal. At the top were Negro professional men and capitalists whose incomes were far greater than those of many whites in any section. Within a short time, the latter group developed a vested interest in segregation that was only very slowly overcome.

Yet the Negro was potentially dangerous to white leaders because he could vote. This reservoir of power and trouble was tapped in the late 1880's as the agrarian *interest* and to some extent the lower *classes* (fearing a lowering if nothing else) began to collaborate across the color line. Keeping well within the perimeter of laissez-faire politics in which interest was the benchmark of decision, the Negro saw that he held a potentially winning hand as a minority capable of delivering a bloc vote to the highest-bidding white faction. Neither the whites nor the Negro offered any strong corporate or commonwealth sentiment or program. It was classic laissez-faire interest and class politics, and the result was the fulfillment of that logic. Southern whites, whipped up by such demagogues as Baptist minister Thomas Dixon of North Carolina, or candidly lectured on their interests by upper-class spokesmen like Carter Glass of Virginia, collaborated in a drive that *legally* segregated and disfranchised the Negro. Southerners searched their souls and found their interests.

The dominant group of Negro leaders did likewise. Accepting their minority position, they argued that it was neceesary to rise to a competitive position within the system in order to extend their rights and opportunities. Coming from Booker T. Washington, who enjoyed entrée into the society of Standard Oil executives, railroad magnates, and Andrew Carnegie, the strategy was persuasive. Washington avowed his loyalty to laissez faire, took his stand in the south as a southerner, and accepted social inequality for the foreseeable future. Blocked by the power of the whites and told by their own spokesman that "white leadership is preferable," most Negroes followed the advice to start climbing up a separate and identical but longer competitive ladder of laissez faire. Only much later did other Negro leaders effectively challenge Washington's influence.

In the meantime, Washington's position was made almost impregnable through the generosity of northern white philanthropists who liked his ideology (which included a code of labor quietism and even strikebreaking). Offered within the broad framework of a humanitarian and extremely hardheaded desire to prevent social upheavals by directing and controlling reform, their help established such educational centers as Howard University and Tuskegee. Judged within its own assumptions, the gravest weakness of such philanthropy was that it was a poor and ineffective second-best for the wholly legitimate (if for the time revolutionary) laissez-faire principle of giving the freed Negro a property stake in the system. For granted the premises and the logic of laissez faire, the periodic redistribution of property is the most internally consistent approach to sustaining that political economy. Though unquestionably noble, philanthropy is a feeble and wasteful substitute. . . .

The undeniable achievement of the laissez-faire entrepreneur, from Carnegie to the Wyoming dry-goods merchant, is that he sustained the momentum of economic development through a long-wave depression (and an era of steadily falling prices) that lasted from 1873 to 1898. Up to 1893, at any rate, per capita income, real wages, and gross national product all continued to increase. That tremendous surge of industrial strength changed the face, the food, and the ideas of America and provoked serious re-evaluations of diplomacy in European and Asian capitals. It also extracted a terrible cost in death and physical injury, in psychic and emotional wounds, and a process of moral leaching that carried away a great amount of American idealism. Judged against the facts that the nation was completely free from any danger of foreign attack, and further graced with fantastic natural wealth and skills, the relative and absolute cost of those economic gains can only be described as exorbitant. Had America been truly unique, it would have pared the social and personal costs of free enterprise to a fraction of their actual total. . . .

A contributor to the *Atlantic Monthly* in 1882 wrote that America's "happy immunity from those social diseases which are the danger and the humiliation of Europe is passing away." And no doubt thinking of such outbreaks of violence as the Haymarket Massacre of 1886 in Chicago and other urban riots, a local Kentucky politician fretted that "the times are strangely out of joint. . . . The rich grow richer, the poor become poorer;

the nation trembles." The same either-or theme is at the heart of Henry George's powerful analysis of the paradox of *Progress and Poverty,* which became a best seller in the 1880's. Desperately concerned over the decline of democracy, and aware of the "widespread feeling of unrest and brooding revolution," George concluded that the tendency to barbarism "is an increasing one." Ignatius Donnelly, a leader of the agrarians, emphasized the same danger of "terrible social convulsions." So did Henry Demarest Lloyd, a newspaper writer who became a reform (and ultimately a radical) publicist. But conservatives like Presidents Harrison and Grover Cleveland commented on the same possibility, as did Senator George F. Edmunds of Vermont, Federal Judge Gresham, and William T. Harris, who was national commissioner of education and an influential writer.

REFORMERS ATTEMPT TO SUSTAIN THE SYSTEM

This broad consensus affords an insight into the upsurge of social and political agitation that climaxed the Age of Laissez Nous Faire. However haltingly, and despite great mutual suspicions and bitter conflicts of interest, the conservative and the liberal defenders of laissez faire cooperated in a belated and unsuccessful effort to save that system. Other conservatives, along with their enemies the radicals, agitated each in his own way for a new system. In the crisis, of course, all conservatives and liberals stood fast against the radicals, but the differences within the coalition against the left provide the fundamental explanation of the political ferment of the era.

As one whose idea of taking the unearned increment of land values had its roots in physiocratic doctrine, George made no sweeping attack on private property. "We declare the true purpose of government," he explained in 1886, "to be the maintenance of that sacred right of property which gives to everyone opportunity to employ his labor

and security that he shall enjoy its fruits." He argued in classic laissez-faire logic that the decline in property holding would create a mass of men "who feel no direct interest in the control of government." That would facilitate the rise of demagogues who would destroy political democracy. George was offering a way of maintaining the circulation of property to avoid such devolution. It appealed to a number of middle-class property owners as well as laborers, and for a time undercut the strength of the currency inflation movement. While George was not a radical in the sense of attacking the system itself, his program to purify and thereby preserve it was both extensive and rigorous. It is very misleading and rather supercilious to call such men (including the Populists) either backward or reactionary. They were vigorous reformers acting on the first principles of laissez faire.

The fulfillment of the laissez-faire labor movement came with the subsequent organization of the American Federation of Labor and the Knights of Labor. In opening its membership to all but a tiny minority of so-called workers (bankers, layers, doctors, and men of the liquor trade were excluded), to the unskilled as well as the skilled, and to Negroes along with the whites, the Knights offered moral leadership of a high order. Accepting the principles of laissez faire, leaders like Grand Master Workman Terence V. Powderly recognized the reality of class conflict and labored to end it. His opposition to the wage system was not an attack on laissez faire; it was merely a kind of hardheaded idealism about the marketplace.

He argued that an interim improvement in working conditions through various reforms such as an eight-hour day and the arbitration of disputes with capital would prepare the way for the worker to become a property owner in the marketplace through the organization of producer cooperatives. Far from being an adaptation of socialism, the Powderly program was a premature and fuzzy vision of later profit-sharing plans. As the basis of his ultimately successful competition with the Knights, Samuel Gompers offered a more routine laissez-faire objective: accept the system and get as much as possible within it. Concentrating on the skilled elite of the labor force, his early views and programs developed wholly within the assumptions of individual private property and the marketplace.

Despite certain indications to the contrary, the agrarian protest movement also developed within them. Like many vigorous reformers who operate within a given system, the Populists accentuated certain weaknesses of the existing order. Some of its leaders combined the prejudices and demagoguery of the Jacksonians with others borrowed from aristocratic bigots in the east. Thus foreigners and Jews were attacked for irrelevant reasons. Yet much criticism of the Populists on these counts is grossly exaggerated and distorted because it derives from the narrow and anemic modern definition of tolerance. Hence it misses or obscures the important point that the target of their anger was the wholly real malfunctioning of the system itself. Jews and immigrants became symbols of that failure; and though the syllogism was mistaken and unfair, it was nevertheless quite a different matter from attacking these groups as such.

Farmers caught the full impact of the declining *rate* of economic growth that became apparent in the late 1880's. They observed the ground rules of laissez faire, applied the new technology, used the new machinery, specialized in regional crops, and produced more—yet their share of the system's income decreased. Freight rates and other industrial prices fell about 67 per cent between 1865 and 1896, but farm prices dropped about 75 per cent. During the same years, moreover, the exportable surplus of wheat jumped 16 per cent. And by 1885, even the federal land commissioner acknowledged "that the public domain was being made the prey of unscrupulous speculation and the worst forms of land monopoly through systematic frauds."

Farmers were bedeviled by the patent racket (as in barbed-wire fencing), losing money on cows as well as on wheat and corn, and reduced to making chattel mortgages at up to 35 per cent interest to secure capital for machinery and land that in some states was doubling in price in less than a decade. With considerable justification, they reacted negatively to supercilious lectures from easterners whose knowledge of dirt came from formal gardens and croquet lawns or from city parks and summer estates. In an analogy with colonialism, the farmer accurately charged that a sizable share of his agricultural production ended up as locally undistributed profits that went east to banks and other absentee landowners. Farm tenancy was rising steadily, as was the consolidation of holdings into large farms. Even those great individualist craftsmen of the age, the cowboys, resorted to strikes in Texas. And their will finally broken by a run of bad weather in the late 1880's, thousands of farmers in Kansas and Nebraska gave up their land.

As that reverse migration of the failures suggests, the Populist movement was in large measure an uprising of *surviving* farmers against existing leadership. However tenuously, they still held on to their land. Cleveland's pious invocations in behalf of "a healthy and free competition" struck them as arrogant nonsense, and they equated the Republicans with Carnegie. Beginning with a revival of the Southern Farmers Alliance (it had originated in Texas in 1875 as a protest against absentee capital in ranching), the agitation spread rapidly into the north and west. Employing the ideas and invoking the names of Jefferson and Taylor, Jackson and Benton, the farmers developed a program that consolidated the general antagonism against railroads and other giant entrepreneurs.

Conservatives as well as reformers began to act. After extended hearings around the country in 1886–1887, a Senate committee reported "that upon no public question are the people so nearly unanimous as upon the proposition that Congress should undertake in some way the regulation of interstate commerce." The Interstate Commerce Act of 1887 was the result. Avowedly a serious compromise effort to adjust and stabilize the framework of the marketplace within the assumptions of laissez faire, it attempted to remove existing abuses and prevent future inequities in the railroad system.

During the next three years, moreover, four agrarian states were admitted to the union, more funds were provided for agricultural science and education, and a cabinet post was added for agriculture. Rapidly gaining strength and confidence, the farmers began, as in their St. Louis meeting of 1889, to work out an alliance with the Grange, the Greenbackers, and some elements of labor. Before their full program was settled, but as their power was becoming apparent in the enactment of laws against trusts and monopoly in southern and western states, men like Senator George F. Edmunds of Vermont and George F. Hoar of Massachusetts, who feared grave social disorders if the system were not put back in balance, joined with reformers to write and pass the misnamed Sherman Anti-Trust Act of 1890. Whatever its weaknesses (it did not offer definitions of trust or monopoly, for example), and however it was emasculated and abused in later years, the law was one of the major symbols of the fulfillment of the Age of Laissez Nous Faire. It represented the essential principle of that *Weltanschauung*—competition throughout a national marketplace.

Populists also demanded broad educational assistance, for the south as well as for other sections, and free trade to expand their exports and strengthen competition in the home market for manufactures. They also proposed a commodity credit plan that would regulate marketing throughout a given crop-year and facilitate the sale of surpluses while giving the farmer short-term loans. And in their most dramatic, and generally misunderstood, proposal, they called for the nationalization of the commercial arteries of the marketplace. Far from becoming agrarian socialist, the Populists were in this plan to nationalize the railroad, telegraph, and telephone systems merely carrying the logic of laissez faire to its classic fulfillment. Given the absolutely essential role of an open and equitable marketplace in the theory and practice of laissez faire, they concluded that the only way to guarantee the cornerstone of the system was by taking it out of the hands of *any* entrepreneur. "It is simply a battle for liberty," explained Populist presidential candidate James B. Weaver of Iowa in 1892. "Having secured the power we will work out the details." While some of the reformers ultimately became true radicals, the movement itself was radical only in the sense that it reasserted and attempted to act on the basic axioms of the existing order.

The party's decision to endorse William Jennings Bryan of Nebraska for president in 1896 underscored its fundamental attachment to laissez faire and the existing political system. So did their argument that the unlimited coinage of silver at 16 to 1 would create more economic opportunity; this was the same kind of inflationary logic that antislavery radicals like Thad Stevens had used in the 1860's. Citing Jackson and Benton as reliable guides, Bryan reiterated the axioms of laissez faire and infused them with the righteous emotional ardor of the early Jacksonians. "We say to you," he thundered in his famous Cross of Gold Speech, "that you have made the definition of a businessman too limited in its application." By Bryan's criteria, almost everyone was a businessman. "The man who is employed for wages . . . the attorney in a country town . . . the merchant at the crossroads . . . the farmer . . . the miners . . . are as much business men [as others]. We come to speak for this broader class of business men."

Bryan and the Populists were attempting to restore and sustain the system of laissez faire in the same way that Jackson had made clear he would maintain the framework of the system. Jackson had attacked South Carolina planters and New England speculators; Bryan assaulted eastern industrialists and New York financiers. But having defeated the mercantilists by splitting the shield of social property with the sword of private property, the true believers of laissez faire found themselves naked on the battlefield. Their attempt to use liberty and private property to attack private property and liberty was doomed from the outset. Such proposals as the nationalization of the communications network appalled the privates in their own ranks. Only a new and at least in part more social basis of criticism could make any headway against the power of laissez faire.

THE PERSISTENT DILEMMAS OF EXPANDING THE MARKETPLACE

This became apparent as the advocates of a reformed laissez faire confronted the dilemmas of their system in foreign policy and philosophy. Since the continuing expansion of the marketplace was the *sine qua non* of laissez faire, President Rutherford Hayes explained in 1877, the "long commercial depression ... directed attention to the subject" in a concerted manner. For that matter, some entrepreneurs had already been talking to Grant's Secretary of State Hamilton Fish about foreign policy as a way "to relieve business distress." Some companies had begun to expand into Canada in 1870, and by 1887 their total was 48. Others were increasing their holdings, or entering the market in China or, like the Singer Sewing Machine Company, moving into Great Britain and other European nations.

Politicians responded quickly. Persistently reminded of the importance of expansion and the necessity of government assistance by such men as Charles Dalton of the textile industry and H. K. Slayton, a dry-goods merchant, Senator John T. Morgan spoke for a growing consensus of congressmen as early as 1882. "Our home market is not equal to the demands of our producing and manufacturing classes and to the capital which is seeking employment. ... We must enlarge the field of our traffic," he concluded in a typical either-or warning, "or stop the business of manufacturing just where it is." Numerous congressmen offered similar analyses and spoke increasingly of China as "our India," and of the nations to the south as "twenty American Indies, if only we shall do our duty toward grasping their trade." This explicit analogy with Britain's empire is one

of the most revealing aspects of the mature foreign policy of laissez faire. ...

As in many ways the symbol of the best that laissez faire could produce, William James offered leadership in the anti-imperialist movement, made fundamental contributions to the theory of individualist psychology, and offered an appropriate statement of the laissez-faire outlook in his pragmatic philosophy. Along with his friend, William Graham Sumner, James pushed the axioms of his age as far as they would go. On the one hand, his basic assumption that the world is chaos, and that the mind serves only to guide the will, led him to attack science and to assert the anti-intellectual claim that contemplation was unhealthy. By that standard he proclaimed that "truth is what happens to an idea." Hence the "cash values of ideas" was their final determinant. And his appropriately "tough-minded" man, who could survive and flourish in such a cosmos, exhibited many traits of the driving entrepreneur, or what later social psychologists have called the authoritarian personality. As James implied in some of his own comments, this side of his pragmatism offered a way to get rich and reform the world in one's own image. "We seem set free," he proclaimed, "to use our theoretical as well as our practical faculties ... to get the world into a better shape, and all with a good conscience."

On the other hand, James realized that what he called the "bitch goddess SUCCESS" did not always let the truth happen to the best ideas. Hence he had to admit that error, or evil, did exist. Drawing upon the transcendentalist version of the Romantic Movement's assertion that the individual could separate truth from evil through one of what James called the varieties of religious experience, he was then able to offer the individual a way out of the dilemma. Yet in society at large, and particularly in foreign affairs, James understood that violence or war was the usual way that truth happened to an idea. His answer—find a moral equivalent for war —was a magnificent and moving plea against imperial expansion and its consequences. But it also revealed the central weakness of laissez faire; for war was a social phenomenon, and James was attempting to resolve it on an individual basis. The circle could not be squared.

As one of James's major opponents who saw the danger of the romantic and transcendental conception of the individual, Josiah Royce argued that men had to commit themselves to something bigger than themselves. Such idealism was essential; otherwise the "cash value of ideas" would always win out. Yet he also understood that idealism could be the spur to the most virulent kind of aggression. His solution, which he never thoroughly worked out, was a creative regionalism in which men could work together to build a truly human society. But both James and Royce were spokesmen of a passing era. The men who took charge of the effort to resolve the dilemmas of laissez faire were aware that it had to be done around some idea of a corporate system, yet they were determined to avoid the pit of social property as well as the pendulum of class war. Their proposals, and the momentum of their institutions, created a system based on the political economy of the large corporation and a more active government charged with the task of maintaining some check on the increased power of private property. . . .

THE NATURE AND THE POWER OF THE LARGE CORPORATION

Powerful and productive in the world of things, and capable of sustaining and strengthening the oligarchies that created them, the large corporations (and their leaders) dominated American history from 1896 until past the middle of the twentieth century. In its industrial and financial forms, the corporation transformed the fears of men like Madison and Jefferson, and the expectations of others like Seward, into a reality that crossed every economic, political, and social boundary, affected every branch of government, and permeated every aspect of the individual citizen's life. Ostensibly created to

facilitate the rational and efficient production of goods to meet the needs of men, the corporation (like the sorcerer's apprentice) ultimately began creating in men the demand for goods they had never seen, observed in use, or even known they needed. And in many cases the original judgment had proved correct—they did not need them.

Undertaking a shopping trip in pursuit of an item first seen on the television screen produced by a corporation that very probably also provided the air time for the program, a housewife in the 1950's [or 1970's —Ed.] could easily have put on a dress made of synthetic fibers made by a corporation that exercised a large influence in the corporation that built the car (or bus) that she used for transportation. The insurance company that underwrote her trip may very well have financed the car itself, the garage in which it was parked, and the city streets upon which she drove. The gasoline that powered the car might have been produced by a corporation that could easily have had some share in the supermarket where she shopped. If not, the vegetables she purchased could have been grown on a contract farm owned by the corporation that also made the detergent or soap with which she washed the dishes from which the vegetables were eaten.

Even if he were, superficially, an independent businessman, her husband was still more intimately involved with these same, or similar, corporations. Most of the couple's entertainment was provided by corporations, as was the news they read in their newspapers and magazines, or heard and viewed over the television set that provided the starting point in the entire web of relationships. The political and economic issues in this news were defined largely by the policies and the programs of the corporations and their leaders. As man and wife, their own efforts to organize or participate in other functional groups that attempted to check or balance this power of the corporation were at best productive of little more than occasional minor victories, and more generally of an uninspiring and enervating stalemate that left the large corporation in its position of predominance.

The couple's fears for the future were centered on one of three major issues: upon their inability to break out of the pattern of installment living produced, packaged, and promoted by the advertising and public-relations adjunct of the corporations; upon the possibility that the corporation economy might falter and flatten them along with its dividend payments; or upon the tension in foreign affairs that was very largely the result of the conflict between the expansion of those corporations and the opposition to them manifested by vigorous and militant rivals. With overseas direct investments of 29 billion dollars, sales of overseas agencies of 30 billion dollars (with an average profit of 15 per cent), and direct exports of between 15 and 20 billion dollars, the overseas economic empire of the United States in 1957 amounted to a total stake of twice the gross national product of Canada and was larger than the same total for the United Kingdom.

The problems of that empire provided most of the national headlines in the 1950's [or 1970's—Ed.], just as very similar foreign fears and antagonisms had greeted the new corporation system at the turn of the century. Writing in 1902 of *The Americanization of the World,* William Thomas Stead of England termed it the "greatest political, social, and commercial phenomenon of our times." "In the domestic life," echoed his countryman Fred Mackenzie in *The London Daily Mail,* "we have got to this: The average man rises in the morning from his New England sheets, he shaves with 'Williams' ' soap and a Yankee safety razor, pulls on his Boston boots over his socks from North Carolina, fastens his Connecticut braces, slips his Waltham or Waterbury watch in his pocket, and sits down to breakfast. There he congratulates his wife on the way her Illinois straight-front corset sets off her Massachusetts blouse, and he tackles his breakfast, where he eats bread made from prairie flour (possibly doctored at the special establishments on the lakes) ... and a little Kansas City

bacon. ... The children are given 'Quaker' Oats. ...

"He rushes out. ... [And] at his office, of course, everything is American. He sits on a Nebraskan swivel chair, before a Michigan roll-top desk, writes his letters on a Syracuse typewriter, signing them with a New York fountain pen, and drying them with a blotting-sheet from New England. The letter copies are put away in files manufactured in Grand Rapids. ... At lunch-time he hastily swallows some cold roast beef that comes from the Mid-West cow ... and then soothes his mind with a couple of Virginia cigarettes. To follow his course all day would be wearisome. But when evening comes he ... finishes up with a couple of 'little liver pills' [that were] 'made in America.' "

Germans and Frenchmen revealed similar uneasiness about American expansion, and the high Russian newspaper *Novoye Vremya* expressed its concern by pointing specifically to the example of Great Britain, "Everything," it lamented, proves that Great Britain is now practically dependent upon the United States, and for all international intents and purposes may be considered to be under an American protectorate. ... The United States has but just entered upon the policy of exploiting the protected kingdom." While such estimates were obviously exaggerated as of 1900, the reality moved ever closer to them throughout the twentieth century in the Western Hemisphere, in Europe, and throughout the rest of the world. Very candidly, and with considerable forethought, America pushed its way into the struggle for economic empire between 1895 and 1898. This involvement was dramatized and extended by the war with Spain, and in 1899 and 1900 culminated in the famous Open Door Notes which demanded equal opportunity for America's tremendous economic power, a weapon that the nation's leaders felt confident would produce world economic supremacy without the limitations and dangers of old-fashioned colonialism.

Likewise, even as the nation emerged from the bloody strife and suffering of the depression of the 1890's, the inclusive nature and extensive power of the corporation was clearly revealed at home. Its triumph established a new political economy, a system of organized and controlled interrelationships and influence that was developed and put in operation during the presidential campaign of 1896. Whereas laissez faire had required at least two elections to establish its primacy under Jackson, the leaders of the age of the corporation scored an impressive victory in their first test. Organized and managed by Mark Hanna, one of the new order's more perceptive and effective spokesmen, this victory established the modern pattern of politics as an expensive, extensive, and centrally coordinated, high-pressure effort.

Despite the flamboyance and extremism of the rhetoric on both sides (itself a reminder of the campaign of 1828), and the emotional ardor of his supporters, Bryan never seriously approached victory in the election of 1896. The rise of the large industrial corporation had given the urban manufacturing and commercial centers and their spheres of influence in the surrounding agrarian areas a predominance in the political economy that would never be successfully challenged by a purely and narrowly laissez-faire interest party such as the Democrats were under Bryan. For that matter, many western farmers responded to the Republican argument that overseas markets for surpluses would solve their particular problem while bringing general prosperity. The real issue was not whether the new order would triumph, but who was to control and direct it; that is, how it was to maintain an internal balance, accomplish the necessary domestic and overseas expansion, and in what way meet and master its political, economic, and philosophic competitors at home and abroad.

With considerable exaggeration, the beginnings of the age of the corporation might be dated from the first textile-mill town (complete with minister and teacher supplied on contract by the owner) established in New England early in the nineteenth century. But the foundations of the new system were actually started by the post-Civil War operations of men like James J. Hill in railroads and associated enterprises, the integrated organization of the Cambodia Iron Works near Pittsburgh, and the development of the Rockefeller and Carnegie empires during the 1880's. After the adoption of favorable holding-company legislation by Delaware, Maryland, and New Jersey during the same decade and the concurrent consolidation of the House of Morgan, the rise of the large life-insurance companies and such firms as the American Telephone and Telegraph Company made it clear that the corporation had moved rapidly into a position of predominance, a position that has never been challenged in a fundamental way.

None of the early firms, however large, revealed all the basic features of the corporation either in their specific organization and operations or in their impact upon the society at large. And in the case of Carnegie, of course, the overall characteristics represented a culmination of the laissez-faire entrepreneur. For this very reason, however, he and Rockefeller, along with Hill, offer apt illustrations of how the corporation economy emerged as a function or consequence of laissez-nous-faire competition. But each of these enterprises did develop one or more of the essential aspects of the corporation that enabled it as an institution to create a distinctive new order once it came to control the key elements of the system. While the secondary characteristics and indirect ramifications of the corporation are numerous, even today not wholly known, its central features are clear.

Beyond the obvious fact of size, of authority and power as *one* unit over the rest of the economy, perhaps the main element introduced by the large corporation was a fundamental change in ideas about economic activity itself. Laissez-faire operators and spokesmen thought of the marketplace as a scene of individualized and somewhat random activity. But the spokesmen and directors of the new order, though they accepted the traditional premise of private property and the vital role and necessity of an expanding marketplace, defined economic activity as making up an interrelated *system*. It was not just the sum of innumerable parts operating in an essentially casual and ad-hoc fashion. The political economy had to be extensively planned, controlled, and coordinated through the institution of the large corporation if it was to function in any regular, routine, and profitable fashion.

This view developed in part from the narrow or interest drive of the corporation entrepreneurs to rationalize and control as much of the marketplace as possible—to make it *their* system. But it was soon generalized as the result of observation and reflection on broader issues. They concluded that Adam Smith's Hidden Hand was often so hidden that it failed to provide the guidance which should have prevented individual and general crises. Also, competition proved in practice to be inefficient, redundant, and wasteful. Finally, from being directly associated with both of these considerations, they grew more and more fearful that the end result of laissez faire would be economic breakdown and social revolution. "The panic of last year is nothing," warned Hill in 1894, "compared with the reign of terror that exists in the large centers. Business is at a standstill, and the people are becoming thoroughly aroused." Like the advocates of laissez faire, the corporation leaders feared social upheaval, but they provided a different answer to the question of how to avoid it. In their way, therefore, the proponents of a system based on the large corporation were capitalists who accepted, on the evidence of their own experience as well as their casual and distorted knowledge of his ideas, the analysis made by Karl Marx, and set about to prevent his prophecy of socialism and communism being fulfilled.

These broad ideas provided the background for understanding the nature and the ramifications of the corporation itself. It was and remains a form of organization designed to accumulate large amounts of capital, resources, and labor and apply them to the rational, planned conduct of economic activity through a division of labor and bureaucratic routine. Acting within this framework, corpo-

ration leaders directly and indirectly exerted several major influences on the political economy. They consolidated the main elements and processes of the economic system in a small number of giant firms. By the end of World War II (1947), for example, when the United States produced approximately 50 per cent of all manufactured output in the world, a mere 139 corporations owned 45 per cent of all manufacturing assets in the country. These behemoths further centralized power within their own group and within specific corporations. Such centralization meant that the rights of the participants (directors and managers, as well as stockholders) were limited in a hierarchical fashion so that control over many units might be maintained with a comparatively small investment and a few firms dominate the general consolidation of the political economy.

In striving to achieve their various objectives, corporation leaders produced two kinds of integrated organization. One was horizontal, pulling together a number of operations at the same stage of production or service. Its purpose was to control the market. The other was vertical, several levels of production (from raw materials to distribution) being acquired and coordinated for becoming independent of the market. In later years, particularly after World War I and the Great Crash of 1929, such power was extended even further as giants like the House of Morgan, Procter and Gamble, and insurance companies began to acquire and operate various real-estate (including farm) holdings.

In all its manifold features and enterprises, and in finance as well as in industry, the corporation operated within an oligarchic framework. Individual propertyholders (today stockholders) no longer enjoyed the kind of direct authority they had wielded in the age of laissez faire. And the labor unions neither sought nor received such power in the area of basic investment or operational decisions. This separation of literal ownership from practical control became progressively greater during the twentieth century. As it did so, some observers concluded that corporation leaders were no longer guided by the philosophy and ideology of private property, but had in effect become dehumanized managers who abstractly kept the system going for its own sake. Another argument maintained that the managers had become public servants driven only by a desire to create the good society.

In the narrowest sense, these interpretations overlook two relevant factors. Up to World War I, and even later in specific cases, a bloc of voting stock large enough to sway key decisions was often held by one or two individuals. And in subsequent years the evidence has suggested strongly that however small their personal holdings, the directors and managers who staff the corporation still *think* and *act* as though the firm belonged to them. In an even more fundamental way, they have continued to define the system created and ordered by the corporation as one based on private rather than on social property. A typical sector of the corporation economy—say the automobile industry—would be a different phenomenon if it were organized and operated as a socialized enterprise. Such features as built-in obsolescence, indifference to safety factors, and redundancy of design would be avoided. For that matter, automobile production might be cut back very sharply in favor of a social investment in modern public-transportation systems.

Though it may seem strange in view of the later inefficiency of the corporation system, the drive for efficiency was one of the motives that powered the merger mania of the period between 1889 and 1903. Capitalized at 25 millions, for example, the Illinois Steel Company of Chicago was organized with the claim of having a plant more efficient as well as larger than that of Carnegie. Rockefeller's Standard Oil Company abandoned the ambiguous partnership-trust form it had used after the reorganization of 1882 and became a gigantic holding company with clearly apparent corporate characteristics. And J. Pierpont Morgan successfully corralled the skittish and maverick railroad entrepreneurs

in a consolidated and centralized railroad system in the east. "The purpose of this meeting," he bluntly told them, "is to cause the members of this association to no longer take the law into their own hands ... as has been too much the practice heretofore. This is not elsewhere customary in civilized communities, and no good reason exists why such a practice should continue among railroads."

"Consolidation and combination are the order of the day," judged Walker Hill, president of the American Bankers Association in 1899; and the chief statistician of the Census Bureau verified this estimate in 1900. "A startling transformation" had occurred in the previous decade, he reported, one which "set at naught some the the time-honored maxims of political economy, which must readjust many of our social relations, and which may largely influence and modify the future legislation of Congress and the States." Joined by such men as August Belmont, and such firms as Lee, Higginson of Boston and Kuhn, Loeb of New York, Morgan's crusade for what he called a "community of interest" produced more than 300 consolidations between 1897 and 1903.

Morgan's own formation of the gargantuan United States Steel Company symbolized the entire epoch, but the appearance of the Amalgamated Copper Co., the American Tobacco Co., the Standard Distilling Co., the National Biscuit Co., the International Harvester Co., and the reorganization of the du Pont firm were just as important. And by 1900, the year after 1,028 firms had disappeared, the American Telephone and Telegraph Co. had become a $250 million corporation. Similar expansion and coordination completed the integration of such firms as Macy's, John Wanamaker's, and Woolworth's into the new political economy. Marshall Field and Sons exemplified the pattern with its wholesale purchasing, functional organization of the store, ownership of some supplying factories, and even in its benevolent creation of the Chicago Manual Training School.

THE CRISIS OF THE 1890's
AND THE SPECTER OF CHAOS

Not only did the many business failures of the 1890's create circumstances favorable to such consolidation and centralization, but the crisis convinced most remaining doubters that laissez faire was unable to cope with the tensions and problems of mature industrialism. Beginning with Black Friday, the Panic of 1893 initiated an intense and double-cycle depression that lasted until 1898. Signifying the end of the easy investment opportunities and massive profits that had been provided since 1789 by the dramatic and once-over development of the continental west, and signifying also the completion of the basic steel, transportation, and power segments of the industrial economy, the depression of the 1890's profoundly shocked even the advocates of the new system.

Following upon the Haymarket Riot of 1886, the sequence of a general strike of Negro and white workers in New Orleans and bread riots and other disturbances throughout the south and the north reached a portentous peak of violence in the bloody and prolonged strike against Carnegie's Homestead plant in 1892. While willing to use troops in such emergencies, most capitalists realized that the economic system could not be operated on the basis of private and government soldiers maintaining production. Nor was the trouble limited to the east. Army units were also used during the same summer in the Utah copper strike. Then, coming after the depression had started, and seeming to verify the worst of the nightmares produced by the Homestead affair, the even more violent and extensive strike against the Pullman Company and the railroads in 1894 dramatized beyond any question the need for a new approach.

Though in many ways the culmination of the old nineteenth-century pattern of company towns originated by textile mills, the circumscribed community and society founded and controlled by the Pullman Company was widely regarded before the upheaval as a model of, and for, industrial relations. More perceptive architects of the emerging corporation system such as Mark Hanna, the Ohio entrepreneur and politician, understood its weaknesses, but they did not immediately alter that general impression of the company. "Oh, hell! Model —!," he thundered to a group of industrialists and bankers. "Go and live in Pullman and find out." But most of his associates initially mistrusted him rather than the supposedly ideal solution to labor problems, and they did not begin to modify their opinions until the continuing crisis forced them to admit the need of a broader outlook. Hence their fears were further intensified by what they thought was a revolutionary march on Washington by Coxey's Army. The army was actually a rather pathetic and motley band of unemployed men who wanted relief rather than revolution.

Already prone to interpret such events in either-or terms, however, American leaders responded to the economic depression and its associated social unrest by intesifying their efforts to formulate ideas that would account for the crisis and provide practical solutions. As they developed such explanations and recommendations, they emphasized increasingly the role of foreign policy in solving domestic troubles and consciously initiated a broad program of sophisticated imperialism. For that matter, the triumphant corporation system rode in on the crest of what John Hay, in a revealing if indiscreet moment, called "a splendid little war." Underlying that expansion, and sustaining it on into the twentieth century, was the central idea that overseas economic expansion provided the *sine qua non* of domestic prosperity and social peace. Gradually transforming this initially conscious interpretation of the crisis of the 1890's into a belief or article of faith—an unconscious assumption—Americans by the middle of the twentieth century had established a network of investments, branch factories, bases, and alliances that literally circled the globe. Just as the sun had never set on the British Union Jack in the nineteenth century, neither did the Stars and Stripes know any darkness in the twentieth century.

Also starting in the 1890's, Americans concurrently evolved a set of attitudes and ideas to rationalize and reform the political economy created by the large corporation. But even though they began with the urge to reform themselves, by 1917 they had concluded that such domestic progress depended upon first reforming the rest of the world. And despite periods of enforced preoccupation with domestic failures, this propensity to link improvements at home to conditions overseas remained an axiom with American reformers. Though the full development and convergence of these domestic and foreign programs did not occur immediately, it is nevertheless useful to preview the underlying assumptions and basic features of such new ideas.

For example, it is almost impossible to overemphasize the importance of the very general—yet dynamic and powerful—concept that the country faced a fateful choice between order and chaos. Not only did it guide men in the 1890's; it persisted through World War I, the Great Depression, World War II, and emerged more persuasive than ever in 1943–1944 to guide the entire approach to postwar opportunities and problems. Only the anarchists and a few doctrinaire laissez-faire spokesmen seemed willing to accept the possibility of chaos. Arguing that it was both necessary and possible, most Americans reformulated and reasserted their traditional confidence in their ability to choose and control their fate. This romantic axiom had been a central theme of American history ever since the 1820's, and it carried over into the new age. But given a consensus on the sanctity of private property, and confronted by the increasingly obvious failure of laissez faire, this faith could be verified only by controlling the marketplace. While this tangle of ideas produced enough ideological rope for many a tug-of-war over who was to control the system and by what standard it was to be done,

all such contests found the victors basing their program on overseas expansion.

THE INCEPTION OF AN AMERICAN SYNDICALISM

Within this framework, and originating largely as a reaction within the ministry against the failure of the church to sustain its old relevance and appeal as the source of values and inspiration, the idea of religion as the guide for creating an ordered and balanced system produced a movement known as the Social Gospel. Protestants as well as Catholics were influenced in such thinking by Pope Leo XIII's famous encyclical *Rerum novarum* (1891) on the nature and role of labor in an industrial society. Recommending the renewed study of St. Thomas Aquinas, and stressing the ideals of cooperation and equity between capital and labor, his ideas were particularly relevant to the political economy of the large corporation.

Even though in stressing the role of the Church it offered a different kind of unifying theme, such a fundamentally functional and syndicalist approach reinforced similar analyses provided by sociologists and industrial spokesmen. It also influenced the large number of American labor leaders who were Catholics, for it reinforced their preference for improving labor's position without attacking private property. Yet just as in earlier centuries, the advocates of a Christian solution for the problems of society divided over whether the commonwealth should be based on private or social property. While a minority asserted the stronger logic and the greater equity of Christian Socialism and exerted some influence in the early years of the century, the great majority in the Social Gospel movement favored Christian Capitalism.

Even within the ministry, such Christian Capitalists soon accepted the necessity and wisdom of American expansion and played a crucial role in reinvigorating the missionary movement. Arguing that it was necessary for effecting Christian reforms and for creating the circumstances in which men would turn to Christ, they also supported economic expansion. Reverend Francis E. Clark thought missionaries played a key role in "the widening of our empire." Robert E. Speer, secretary of the Presbyterian Board of Foreign Missions, reported that his church accepted commercial expansion and "welcomes it as an ally." And Henry Van Dyke of Princeton presented an argument that sounded like the expand-or-stagnate thesis of industrial prosperity. "Missionaries are an absolute necessity," he explained, "not only for the conversion of the heathen, but also, and much more, for the preservation of the Church. Christianity is a religion that will not keep."

Another persuasive idea was different in being a secular thought that became a religion, and in initially placing little weight on overseas expansion as such. Clearly arising out of the needs and desires of various interests to strengthen their own position within the corporation political economy, the idea that efficiency was crucially important to prosperity and the socially tolerable functioning of the system soon gained wide acceptance. Though some businessmen had stressed the axiom earlier, the general discussion was launched by engineering and scientific journals in the 1880's. Then it was adapted by Frederick W. Taylor to the needs of management. That in turn opened the way for a theory (and ideology) of rationalizing the political economy under the direction of the corporation that was evolved under the general leadership of Elton Mayo of the Harvard Business School. An initial stress on efficiency thus led to the view that the corporation was the feudal lord of a new corporate society.

Finally, and in a way that provided the foundation for all such thought and discussion, Americans came increasingly to see their society as one composed of groups—farmers, workers, and businessmen—rather than of individuals and sections. Almost unconsciously at first, but with accelerating awareness, they viewed themselves as members of a bloc that was defined by the political economy of the large corporation. Perhaps nothing characterized the new *Weltanschauung* more revealingly. For given such an attitude, the inherent as well as the conscious drift of thought was to a kind of syndicalism based on organizing, balancing, and coordinating different functional groups. In part a typical example of the way interests and experiences influence thought, but also the product of abstract analysis and interpretation, that kind of corporation syndicalism became by 1918 the basic conception of society entertained by Americans. That outlook provides the underlying explanation of the persistent conflicts between the units, and of the continued difficulty of developing any broad truly inclusive program for balancing and directing the system. In one sense, the corporation was merely one of the functional units. But it exerted more power and influence than the others, and its approach to organizing and balancing the political economy remained an interest-conscious conception even though it did become progressively more sophisticated.

One of the best, as well as earliest and most widely read analyses of the syndicalist nature of mature industrialism and of the natural predominance of the large corporation within it, was provided in 1902 in a wry but essentially fatalistic study, *Our Benevolent Feudalism*, by William J. Ghent. Ghent thoroughly understood the essential feature of the new order: through its coordination of technology, capital, and labor, it could produce enough to provide plenty for everyone. But with the insight that provided the imagery of his title, he also realized that an economic, or political and social, decision by the giants would affect every citizen to a sizable degree. While he concluded that the new system was too powerful to be destroyed and supplanted, and was likely to be moderately benevolent, he nevertheless pinpointed a central problem suggested by his analogy with feudalism: How were the vassals and the serfs of the new system to enforce the reciprocal obligations of the lords? This became a major issue that was never satisfactorily resolved. . . .

VARIOUS APPROACHES TO THE PROBLEM OF THE CORPORATION POLITICAL ECONOMY

As they emerged from the Depression of the 1890's and the Spanish-American War into an era of peace and greater domestic prosperity, Americans faced several problems in organizing and institutionalizing the new political economy of the large corporation. Some concerned domestic affairs and would have existed even if the new political economy had never been criticized by domestic radicals or foreign rivals. Others were more directly related to the difficulties of maintaining the overseas economic expansion which began in the late 1890's (playing an important part in recovery from the depression) and was considered vital to the system. Part of those foreign-policy problems were endemic to the expansionist effort itself. The rest grew out of the opposition to American expansion manifested by conservative and liberal—as well as radical—leaders of foreign countries. Since all of those aspects of reality continued to exist past the middle of the century, it is apparent that any discussion of them has to be conceived in terms of decades rather than years (or a few special events).

At home, Americans had to devise ways of maintaining the sustained functioning of the large corporation; not only was it *the* unit of economic production, and hence of welfare, but because of its vast interconnections throughout the rest of the system its failure would mean social and political crisis. They also had either to develop a pattern of politics that would institute and maintain a democratic process of decision-making among the various functional and syndicalist elements of the system (*and within them*), or they had to evolve and accept a sophisticated class-conscious leadership that would take command of the system and run it on the principles of equity and long-range

objectives. Finally, and regardless of the choice between these alternatives, the society faced the necessity of constructing a philosophy appropriate to an interrelated system in which the individual was clearly not the key figure that he had been during the age of laissez nous faire.

Despite many assertions to the contrary, these features of the new reality were not unique to the United States. Nor were American reactions as different as observers have claimed. Some Americans became reactionaries who wanted to restore laissez faire as it had existed in the 1850's or 1870's. Radicals of various persuasions proposed socialism, labor syndicalism, or anarchism. Interest-conscious corporation leaders, who composed the largest bloc of conservative spokesmen, accepted the new system and argued, in keeping with the precedents of their outlook, that the corporation should be allowed to run its world within broad limits. Liberals (reformers, as they will subsequently be called) likewise accepted the basic features of the new order and sought to balance its various elements and moderate its inequities. And a small coalition composed of descendants of the colonial feudal gentry, others who identified with that tradition and heritage, and a small group of corporation leaders who very slowly developed the class-conscious outlook of a new industrial gentry sought to balance and sustain the system through control of the new corporation economy and the national government.

Though this political and philosophical spectrum is anything but novel, it might be argued that American reformers have been almost unique in the intensity of their commitment to private property.* To an extensive degree, the reformers—like the conservatives and reactionaries—have defined Man, and individual men, as creatures

*The development of Western European socialists raises doubts about the uniqueness of even this attitude. They have steadily moved toward the position taken up by American reformers at the turn of the century. Even Britain's Labour Party has produced little beyond the American warfare-welfare state.

of, and dependent upon, property. More property rather than more thought has been the key to wealth and welfare in their world. They have not been callous, and their efforts have improved society. The nature of their position, not a judgment of their accomplishments, is the issue. And to borrow the wonderfully perceptive term of Professor George Mosse, American reformers have been socialists of the heart. They have tried to take for their own purposes Marxian socialism's magnificent reassertion of the ideal of a Christian commonwealth, and a few of its practical tools, without taking its commitment to social property. Therein lies the most persistent and persuasive influence of the frontier experience itself, and of the frontier thesis of American (and world) history advanced in the 1890's. It was fundamentally and extensively anti-intellectual in its direct impact and long-range results. Having defined everything good in terms of a surplus of property, the problem became one of developing techniques for securing more good things from a succession of new frontiers. The alternative, that of defining the good society in nonproperty terms, was dismissed as leading to the horrors of socialism in which the individual is destroyed because he has no property. Walter Lippmann caught the essence of such socialism of the heart as early as 1914. "There has been no American policy on the trust question," he explained: "there has been merely a widespread resentment."

Despite all the assertions about old and new orders, and about various fundamental changes that are claimed to have occurred, the essence of American history throughout the twentieth century has been the continuing attempt to resolve the dichotomy between a set of ideas developed in the 1890's and a reality to which they have proved ill-adapted. American leaders have been grappling with one central issue: how to transform a political economy created and dominated by the large corporation into a true social system—a community—without undercutting private property, without destroying the large corporation, and while fur-

ther handicapped by the anti-intellectual consequences of the frontier experience (and the frontier interpretation of history) which offered a surplus of property as a substitute for thought about society. Having at bottom not much more to guide them than the frontier conception of democracy as a bundle of rights, and lacking any rigorous and sophisticated theory of mutual and interrelated duties, obligations, and responsibilities which combine to make a society, Americans have been repeatedly confronted by the harsh fact that the corporation leaders know more about managing the central and dynamic element of the system than any other group.

By and large, therefore, leaders of the large corporation have exerted a preponderant influence in the nation's basic decisions. But even this group has been severely limited in its grasp of the mechanics of the system and by the narrowness of its interest-conscious outlook, which emphasizes the importance of private property in its corporation form. The resulting pattern of unstable, lurching, oscillating, and inequitable development was a poor performance judged even by the assumptions, criteria, and claims of the system, to say nothing of the organization and results that would have been possible if the effort had been directed more rationally according to priorities set by a different scale of values. This inferior record benefited the reformers and the class-conscious gentry in two principal ways. It provided them with after-the-failure chances to moderate some of the more glaring weaknesses. And this caretaker function placed them in a relatively more favorable light and at the same time created the impression that they had a dynamic and basically effective philosophy and program. But in fact they have *on their own* never done more than restore the system to a level of performance that existed before the periodic crisis. In every instance, further development has been achieved only with assistance from the interest-conscious corporation community, and through the kind of hothouse economic boom that always accompanies a war in which a country suffers neither serious indirect losses nor direct physical damage. . . .

THE FURTHER DEVELOPMENT OF AMERICAN SYNDICALISM

As such functional differences suggest, another aspect of the new reality that confronted American leaders, and caused them great difficulties, was the strong propensity of the system to develop in a syndicalist pattern. Now syndicalism is usually thought of in connection with revolutionary labor movements and assumed to be a violent proletarian outlook. This interpretation confuses the group in modern industrial society which has usually, though by no means always, or even most effectively, embraced and acted upon the idea with the outlook itself. Syndicalism is in essence a philosophy derived from two basic values: function and efficiency. Arguing that an industrial system operates through a division of labor organized by function and in groups rather than through individuals who handle many jobs, syndicalists conclude that such a pattern should be accepted, encouraged, and rationalized. Political representation should arise within each segment and be coordinated at the top in the national government. Individuals would thus participate in the relevant decisions and at the same time enjoy a sense of community and purpose within their particular group that would replace the alienation of an individual lost in a highly organized society.

As in Europe, overt syndicalism first appeared within the ranks of labor. Founded in 1905 under the leadership of Daniel DeLeon, William Haywood, and Eugene Debs (who resigned two years later), the Industrial Workers of the World presented a militant challenge to the established leadership of the corporation system. Organizing western miners, itinerant workers in agriculture and construction, and eastern textile laborers, it practiced a tough, violent kind of unionism dedicated to changing the existing order. The fear that it might penetrate the automobile industry seems to have played a part in Ford's introduction of the Five Dollar

Day. On a more general level, the IWW unquestionably served as a spur to corporation leaders and business-union spokesmen to evolve some pattern of accommodation within the established system.

While they were openly scared of and antagonistic toward the IWWs kind of labor syndicalism, American leaders nevertheless adapted the principles of that philosophy to their own conservative objectives. Theodore Roosevelt repeatedly analyzed society within that framework, as did Herbert Croly and later Progressives whose slogans, the New and Fair Deals, were merely rather unimaginative variations of the Square Deal. Even more significantly, the corporation leaders who struggled to transform their interest-conscious outlook into a class consciousness developed their thought almost wholly within the syndicalist approach. Hanna was merely one of the first to use the tool, as in his advice to the farmers to organize trusts of their own.

In later years, men like Bernard Baruch, Owen D. Young, and Swope developed and extended the same analysis. But Herber Hoover was the crucial figure in the evolution of the approach. Describing society as composed of three major groups—labor, capital, and the government—he struggled to balance and control the units so that they would not drive the system toward fascism (business control), socialism (labor dominance), or the tyranny of bureaucratic government. All such men, from Theodore Roosevelt through Hoover and later theorists, recognized that the central problem was to find some ideal that would generate the self-discipline and public spirit essential to maintaining equity.

To some extent, the theologian Reinhold Niebuhr ultimately provided a philosophy appropriate to the need. Combining selected portions of Catholicism and Calvinism, and then adding a generous leaven of Freud, pragmatism, and the frontier interpretation of American history, Niebuhr constructed a *Weltanschauung* that explained and justified the limited achievement of the Progressive Movement on the grounds that utopia was impossible, and that a more dynamic outlook would in any event produce one of the dangers outlined by Hoover. But nationalism was the main driving force of whatever unity and purpose the system exhibited, and it was largely the negative kind of nationalism directed against other countries and ideas.

One such foreign challenge was itself syndicalist in nature. As a basic component of both the fascist movement in Italy and the hard core of national socialism in Germany, syndicalism provided the leaders of both parties and countries with many of their central ideas and programs. Since they resorted to terror in establishing and maintaining the approach, and distorted it in other ways, the essential characteristics common to American and European syndicalism are generally missed or discounted. Although there was widespread use of intrigue and violence against American labor, the foreign methods created a difference of degree that in the end produced a difference in kind. The Progres-sive Movement did not become fascist or nazi. The initially favorable response to Mussolini, and even to Hitler, manifested by many corporation leaders and other Americans should not be interpreted in that light.

What is significant, however, is the extent to which a syndicalist analysis and approach underlay the programs of all three countries. Even American labor, which vigorously criticized fascism from the outset, did so on the ground that it favored business almost exclusively, not that the syndicalist approach was wrong. And not only did it support the National Industrial Recovery Act, which was openly compared to Italian fascism by New Deal spokesmen, but it continued to frame its own programs within the syndicalist outlook. In the end, of course, the particular nationalisms which were used to coordinate and unite each respective system in a corporate whole came into conflict and produced American involvement in World War II.

The End of Politics, American Style

5   The New Politics of Conviction

Grant McConnell

Until recently, one of this country's major sources of national pride has been the quality of its political life. By contrast with the tumultuous and often downright bloody ways of foreigners, our pattern of politics here has been generally orderly and on the whole sensible and practical. Forgetting the period of the Civil War, we can claim that the results of our national elections, whatever their incidents of absurdity and general noisiness, have been accepted by the losers as a matter of course, and that sportsmanship has characterized the attitude of the winners. The national government has not suffered the turnover of regimes that has bedeviled other countries—in fact the term "regime" has an alien ring in this country—and there has been no succession of first, second, third, fourth, and fifth "republics." Here is but one republic, *the* republic, and we all know what we mean when we pledge allegiance to it. And like "regime," "class struggle" and "ideology" are foreign terms and, we remain convinced, foreign experiences.

Looked at over the past two centuries, American politics may be characterized as a system designed and adapted to the settlement or adjustment of *economic* conflicts.* That is not quite all there is to it but, in gen-

eral, the great bulk of the work of government has been to deal with competing claims for the material goods of the world. That it would be so was specifically foreseen by that most perceptive of all American political thinkers, James Madison. In his most celebrated passage, he wrote that the great problem of government had been "faction," an evil which found its most common and durable source in the unequal distribution of property, which in turn created distinct interests in society—a landed interest, a manufacturing interest, a mercantile interest, a moneyed interest, and so on. In one degree or another this understanding of the problem of government has been shared by other thinkers, from Calhoun through Charles Beard and down to more recent times. In one degree or another most of us have believed that politics is a reflection of economics.

And to a considerable degree we have been right about American politics. The bulk of the important work of American government has been economic: development of railroads, subsidies for this or that interest, regulation of competition, distribution of land, etc. The statement of one senator to a freshman colleague near the turn of this century, "Young man, tariffs are the whole of politics; study them," was only an exaggeration of the reality. More recently, we have extended the work of government to other groups than those originally favored—to industrial workers—and now we are at least doing some thinking and talking about the

Reprinted with permission from *The Nation* (April 8, 1968).

*Where McConnell says "economic," Schaar (in selection 3) said "private," with *almost* the same meaning.—Ed.

poor. The "what" of "Politics, Who Gets What . . . " has very largely been economic.

In recent years, however, a new wind seems to have been blowing in America. Our politics has been taking on a new note, marked by an attitude that at times can be characterized only as mean and hateful. The name-calling we hear is not new; the *manners* of American politics in the nineteenth century were probably worse than those of today, and it wouldn't take much research to turn up evidence of attitudes toward FDR in his time quite as bitter as some of those now directed at LBJ. Not long ago some observers were proclaiming the breakdown of America in a final conflict of classes. Perhaps it is possible to recall that time with equanimity now, because we know the outcome: it wasn't a really fundamental class struggle and it didn't result in breakdown. But I doubt that we are justified in assuming from this that events are certain to turn out all right in the future.

Everyone is aware of the evidence. We are in the midst of a large war whose legitimacy and necessity are denied with passion by a very considerable segment of the American people. Large numbers of individuals, including some conspicuously excellent citizens, openly advocate courses of resistance to the war that go beyond the bounds of law. Many of the young, again conspicuously including a large number of the best, are heeding the call to resistance. Negroes—or black people, as militants now insist the correct term to be—increasingly scorn the ideal of integration and are groping for some formula of apartheid of their own. After the death and destruction of several long hot summers, we are preparing, on the testimony of the president himself, for more. While rumors fly as to the stocking of firearms, some public officials take actions seemingly calculated to aggravate the situation. Just recently the sheriff of Cook County, Illinois, began enrolling gun enthusiasts in a vigilante gang.

Justifications are offered for all this activity. The society is corrupt from top to bottom; we are all alienated; it is time for direct action; we must fight back or "they" will take over. For both sides, liberals are the worst enemy.

It is tempting to perceive these discontents as the product of two issues, the war in Vietnam and the racial crisis. It is easy to demonstrate what a host of evils are either rooted in or made worse by the conflict in Southeast Asia. As for the rest of our difficulties, a great many seem to come down to questions of race. Certainly as a practical matter, we can formulate no better agenda than to deal effectively with these two topics.

However, if we seek to understand the full sweep of our situation, this reduction of the problem to two items is not adequate. Note that in the past external war has been a means of rallying the nation and of quieting signs of internal discord. This has been true even of some of our most unsavory wars, of which we have had rather a number. Vietnam is having quite the contrary effect. And the racial crisis, while more intense today than in the past century, has existed below the surface for longer than a century. Indeed, it is arguable that the eruption of great discord on matters of war and race represents a moral advance in America. But the point to be made here is that even on these two scores our present troubles arise from something additional.

A perspective can be gained on this point by looking at the style of politics developed by some of the less preoccupying and less dramatic issues of the day. Look, for example, at the pattern of politics of what may be called the environmental issues. Consider the struggles to achieve clean air and water; consider also the bitterness of the fights over the protection of scenic and wilderness areas, the redwoods, the Grand Canyon, and so on. Think also of the utter intransigence of the student leaders who demand "freedom" and "participation" on some campuses. What is at the root of this very general change?

We are certainly too close to the events to give more than a partial and tentative answer to this question. With that caution, my answer in brief is that we are just now beginning to confront the important problems of governing this country. The fact is, economics is no longer the single overriding issue of American political life.

One of the most interesting phenomena of the post-World War II period is the recent articulation in this country of a body of political doctrine that celebrates the American scheme of politics. This doctrine now seems to go by the name of "pluralism," a tag partly adopted by those who have formulated it and partly pinned on by their opponents. The term is borrowed from a now largely forgotten body of English and European thought and is misleading in some ways. Moreover, the doctrine by no means is to be regarded as a complete political theory. It has had, nevertheless, much popularity until quite recently. It is an important bit of evidence in its own right.

Perhaps the outstanding quality of American political life, as the pluralists see it, is pragmatism. American politics is not ideological. Its outstanding virtues are compromise and tolerance. Americans do not seek to murder one another with politics. When they get into political contests they do not insist that the losers be executed or exiled. At moments of succession, losers smile gamely and settle down to ordinary life—and are allowed to. After a noisy bit of verbal hair-pulling, "deals" are quietly made—bargains in which nobody entirely loses, and which are subject to review and readjustment. Nobody ever gets all he wants and nobody is left without hope that next time he will do better.

This is in marked contrast with European politics. There they have had a real and bitter class struggle. There they had the Russian Revolution with all mass slaughter and hatreds unleashed. There they have had fascism, again with slaughter and hatred. And why? Because they have never learned the American attitude which looks not to utopia and the distant tomorrow but to the here and now. There has always been something millennial in European thinking. By contrast, Americans restrict themselves to what they can do now—maybe not something that will utterly transform our lives, but something practical and available. And, in the process,

they *have* transformed their lives and left Europe behind.

The American lesson has been learned by virtually all segments of society. In fact, one of the best and earliest formulations came from organized labor. Samuel Gompers and his early colleagues in the AFL came to this outlook as a kind of revelation. One-time Marxists, driven to escape from Europe and still clinging for a while to the precepts of that doctrine, they eventually saw that, in America at least, great strides were possible if workers would simply concentrate on three matters: wages, hours, and working conditions. By avoiding grandiose goals or "ultimate ends," by turning their backs on the class struggle, they could fit themselves into American life and in time come to enjoy a standard of living about which their European brothers could only dream.

Industrial relations in America are in some respects a paradigm of American political life. With parties free of ideology, directed simply to the winning of regular elections; with undisciplined legislatures devoting themselves to the trifling concerns of pork-barrel politics—yes, even playing relatively harmless games of boodle—American politics has lacked the sting and danger of politics elsewhere. Public affairs have not always been neat or even wholly admirable, but America has reaped the enormous benefit of domestic peace on a continental scale.

This leaves much to be said of pluralism as a doctrine, but it is the part that calls for our attention here. What is its validity? Within some limits, it has much. The seemingly chaotic and meaningless character of our political parties *has* given major benefits. The party system has been open to a variety of groups. Its failure to dominate legislatures has permitted a vast number of petty bargains that in sum have given satisfaction to elements that might otherwise have taken to building barricades in the streets. Perhaps most important, this general looseness and seeming triviality have allowed energetic entrepreneurs and workers the freedom and incentive to build an expanding economy while simply seeking their own individual, immediate, and mundane ends. Not wasting too much time on the division of what goods there are, they have gone on to make so many more goods that nearly everybody gets more than he had before.

There are qualifications to this, of course. Some people are still poor. Moreover, American politics has not been quite as free from ideology and bitterness as I have just made out. In industrial relations, for example, there has been a good deal more class struggle than we like to remember, and it has been marked with genuine violence. What is important to note, however, is that where genuine battles have been fought, the issues have not been wages, hours, or working conditions. Rather, the issue has been legitimacy of the unions—i.e., recognition. Once recognition has been won, strikes could occur (even with a bit of violence) without very great disturbance or danger to the political order. It is a remarkable fact that few people today can name the largest strike in American history, althought it occurred only a few years ago. That steel strike of 1959 simply did not raise any fundamental issue.

The most impressive fact of this whole record is that the system has worked. America is a great success story in that such a vast and powerful nation has emerged from enormously diverse elements. But the next most striking fact is that the benefits which the system has allocated have largely been economic and material. These benefits have been the coins with which the acquiescence of different groups in the making of a nation has been bought. And with every passing year our common capacity to make this kind of payment has increased. It would seem obvious that Americans have been getting what they wanted.

And yet . . . something is false here and we all sense it. All history may be the history of class struggles—in America perhaps not of classes in the Marxist sense but of "classes" in much greater numbers and drawn on a much smaller scale. Nevertheless, we know intuitively that men care deeply about other things than material advantage. In other societies the record is plain that nonmaterial,

even abstract issues have been the important ones. Nonmaterial values were strongly cherished in ancient Athens. Art occupied an important place in the life of Florence in its great period. Men have valued military glory. For centuries, religion was at the heart of political life. Important as the economic component of politics has always been it is simply wrong to say that economics lies at the heart of all politics or that men in fact always and invariably place material values first.

Madison and Beard were on firm ground insofar as they assessed the reality of the political life of their own times and the times near to them. American politics has been largely about material things, and it has been arranged structurally so that this should be so. But in its preoccupation with economics America has been successful, enormously successful, perhaps dangerously successful. The figures on this success are beyond rational appreciation. Who can assign any real meaning to a GNP of $700 billion or $800 billion? Consider also the general calm that greets the current proposal for a negative income tax. This scheme asserts that the trouble with the poor is that they don't have enough money; the solution, accordingly, is to *give* them money. This notion, which not long ago would have shaken most Americans to their boots, occasions some controversy, but it is clear that as a nation we could afford it easily and nobody is deeply troubled by the idea.

The change implied here is not easy to grasp. To attempt to assess its importance, consider a psssage J. M. Keynes wrote in the terrible year of 1930. It appears in an article entitled "Economic Possibilities for our Grandchildren":

I draw the conclusion that, assuming no important wars and no important increase in population, the economic problem may be solved, or be at least within sight of solution, within a hundred years. This means that the economic problem is not—if we look into the future—the permanent problem of the human race. . . . [This] is startling because, if instead of looking into the future, we look

*into the past we find that the economic prob-
lem, the struggle for subsistence, always has
been hitherto the primary, most pressing
problem of the human race . . . not only of the
human race, but of the whole of the biological kingdom from the beginnings of life in its
most primitive forms.*

*Thus we have been expressly evolved by
nature—with all our impulses and deepest
instincts—for the purpose of solving the economic problem. If the economic problem is
solved, mankind will be deprived of its traditional purpose.*

*Will this be a benefit? If one believes at all
in the real values of life, the prospect at least
opens up the possibility of benefit. Yet I think
with dread of the readjustment of the habits
and instincts of the ordinary man, bred into
him for countless generations, which he may
be asked to discard within a few decades.*

*Thus for the first time since his creation
man will be faced with his real, his permanent problem—how to use his freedom from
pressing economic cares, how to occupy the
leisure which science and compound interest will have won for him, to live wisely and
agreeably and well.*

Is it too much to say that we are beginning
to see, at least in the United States, the realization of this prophecy? Poverty and hunger
still stalk large parts of the world. Keynes's
proviso—no major wars and no increase of
population—has not been met, and as a result much of the earth is in a sorry economic
condition and still has a sorry prospect. In
America, nevertheless, the prophecy is visibly in the process of realization.

If this is true in any substantial degree, we
are in trouble. It is marvelous and wonderful
trouble if we look back to the depression
days when Keynes chose to be so exasperat-
ing. But recall that Keynes warned of what
we would be in for when the change came.
He mentioned some of the prospective moral
difficulties; there are also prospective political difficulties.

If we are on the way to solution of the economic problem, clearly economic matters
will lose their former urgency. As Keynes

pointed out, other preoccupations will rise to
the surface, and these will be important ones
—and important in an ultimate sense. We
shall probaby find, indeed we are already beginning to find, that they are more difficult to
solve, politically less tractable.

Consider the advantages of dealing with
an economic politics. Once a society is past
the condition in which it must continually
fear famine, once it is beyond a pervasive
terror of economic failure, a wide range of
bargains, deals, and accommodations opens
up. Men may compete with one another for
the goods of the world, but they have almost
endless room for settling their contests. As
Gompers and his associates discovered, if
one forgets ultimate things, immediate
things become available. By ignoring shib-
boleths like "control of the means of production," workers can have better wages, hours,
and working conditions—and can have them
now. If a union will not try to challenge the
boss's ownership of his factory, it can get
him to agree to a wage increase. The union
leader asks for an increase of 50¢ and hour.
The boss offers an increase of 10¢. After
some haggling, perhaps after a rather harmless strike, the two sides settle on 20¢. Good
fellowship is renewed; everybody is satisfied
for a while. If the satisfaction passes, the process can be run through again. And the process works: it works quite beautifully.

But consider what happens when I begin
to suspect that you are attacking my religion.
If you seem to be trying to suppress my
forms of worship on the ground that you
think them immoral, I am going to resist you
bitterly and there will be no compromise between us. As a moral person, I must lay
things, perhaps even my life, on the line. And
you do the same. That is a formula for the
most savage kind of politics, the sort that led
to centuries of really terrible warfare in the
past. Remembering that history, the founding fathers carefully took religion out of politics and established the principle of religious
toleration. We have done our contending
about economics, and by comparison it has
been mere squabbling. In a money fight,
sooner or later, you sit down with your oppo-

nent and bargain; in a religious fight, you must destroy him.

To some degree, the same applies to most issues of principle, that is, to most issues that are not primarily economic. If, for example, you are a black man and concerned with human dignity, the time may come when you are prepared to kill or be killed. Or if you are white and determined to protect the purity of your women from the vilest of threats, you may do the same. If you are convinced that a given war is simple murder, you may defy the laws and spit on the flag. However, if you are a patriot of the elemental sort, you may hurl yourself upon the defilers of the flag.

These are extreme examples, and yet we see them before us today. But there is more to the potential change in political priorities than just these two appalling issues of war and race. Americans are beginning to have time and energy for other, less conspicuous issues. Conservation, for example, used to mean sensible care not to waste natural resources of wood, minerals, etc.—concern for the economic resources. Today it means the intangibles of scenery, wilderness, threatened species like the whooping crane. One of the great political phenomena of recent years is the rapid growth of the new conservation movement. Individuals in all walks of life and of all political allegiances are banding together in some parts of the country to defend and protect such values. Many of these individuals are good solid middle-class citizens, clean-cut and without beards (although some of the beards are joining up too). Yet they often behave without regard to the conventions and niceties of traditional American politics, tending to ignore the appeals to be reasonable and to make bargains. Last year, there was bitter resistance to a scheme to put a big dam in the Grand Canyon. The statement of a leading conservationist sums up the matter very precisely: "It's the *Grand Canyon* they are talking about!" Here no compromise is possible. For the moment that dam project is in abeyance, but if it is ever built in any form it will not be because the conservationists struck a bargain. For them, any appeal to compromise is

without meaning, and while they may conceivably be defeated, they can hardly be expected to accept their defeat in a spirit of good fellowship. When the Grand Canyon is filled with a fluctuating reservoir, when the 2,000-year-old redwoods and the whooping crane are gone, something final will have happened, and nothing offered in return will pay for it.

If these and similar issues come in the future to be the preoccupying problems of politics and bring about a general change in the quality of political life, it still remains to be asked why haven't they been more conspicuous in the past. Part of the answer, the major part, is that hitherto we have simply found the economic and material problems more urgent. But why did they continue to be more urgent in the United States even past the time when most people had more than enough to eat? In different times and places in the nonaffluent past, nonmaterial concerns have been thought more urgent. Probably much of the answer to this lies in the American commitment to equality; we have not been satisfied to relax our headlong rush for production and consumption of goods until most of the population among whom political power is diffused has had a substantial margin over sheer animal necessity.

But there is more to the answer than that. We have structured our political life *as though* economics were the substance of politics. We have framed things politically so as to treat nonmaterial problems as though they were economic, material, and bargainable issues. The fiction works—up to a point. Thus we have been able to bargain with political counters of appointive jobs for immigrant ethnic groups and so in time have brought their members into full membership in our republic of producers and consumers. The process has worked far better than might have seemed possible if its basis had been made explicit in the beginning. But today we are having doubts that it will work with Negroes, our largest, oldest, and least assimilated ethnic group.

Beyond that, the general system of an economic politics is necessarily founded on some means of suppressing the nonmaterial and principled issues that can prove so divisive. We have found different ways to do just that—and have certainly paid a price in the inculcation among too many individuals of the belief that only material matters are serious. However, it is probably untrue that Americans at large are really committed to such belief. There is a tough, questioning spirit among Americans which belies the assertions of foreign critics that we are a wholly materialistic people. And the solution to this paradox of an at least partially nonmaterialistic people behaving politically as though life were wholly an economic matter goes back, I believe, to the fact that our political system has been devised to favor such behavior. Specifically, the pattern of decentralization and devolution of political life has on the whole offered better prospect of selfish and material than unselfish and nonmaterial rewards. In general, the tactics available to small communities are appropriate to small and immediate ends. These, in turn, are most probably, in the American culture at least, material and economic. With issues of principle, say social justice for men of all races, left in the hands of localities or private firms, what remains open is getting and spending. With so much political power defined into the hands of Arizona, the task of defending the Grand Canyon in all its natural and wasteful splendor is far more difficult than it would be if the decision were put up to the nation as a whole. The American people have a far smaller per capita money stake in damming the Canyon's potential kilowatts than do the people of Arizona.

But now we are rich beyond the dreams of yesterday. For many individuals, greater wealth has a sharply diminishing attraction. The large generation of college age has no memory of general depression. It is beginning to be free of "those pseudo-moral principles which have hagridden us for two hundred years, by which we have exalted some of the most distasteful of human qualities into the position of the highest virtues," once again to use the words of Keynes. And the division of America into a multitude of small constituencies as decreed in the political system which has served us so well in the past is also changing. Instead of the constituencies of states, towns, and firms, we are perhaps being divided into opposing camps to contest values of a more fundamental sort. And just because the values are more fundamental, the quality of our political life may be becoming more tense, more bitter, and more dangerous.

It would be a mistake to leap to the conclusion that the quality of political life we may see in the future will be worse than what we have known so far. My own view is that probably in an ultimate sense it will be better. But I am sure it will be more difficult.

III

The Basic Structure of
Power, Interest, and Policy

We in the United States eat more and live more comfortably, on the average, than any other large nation in history or the contemporary world, and we increase our consumption of calories and consumer goods every year. We give college degrees to more of our young adults every year. We spend billions of our annual public income to produce new scientific and technological discoveries. We reward the highly educated groups in the population —especially professional and managerial types—by increasing their buying power at the expense of poorly educated groups—particularly elderly people living on pensions, unskilled and service workers, poor farmers, and nonwhite people.

We are also a very tolerant nation. We tolerate as a nation quite a few facts that we find intolerable as individuals. We let ten million of our fellows go to bed hungry every night, even though there is more than enough food to feed every person in the country and the government spends billions of our public income each year to keep large farmers and farm corporations from producing more. We let more newborn babies die, out of each thousand born, than do several European countries that are much less rich than we. We tolerate a rate of fatal accidents among underground miners that is four times higher than in most West or East European countries. We tolerate a private economy which was able to provide a new job for only one out of every five people added to the working-age population from 1950 to 1969 (the rest were in schools, in the army, employed by the government, or employed in jobs that were directly due to military expenditures), which produces unemployment at a higher rate than most West European countries, which discriminates strongly against people of color, and in which the distribution of income has not changed for twenty years and is more unequal than in most other noncommunist, advanced industrial countries. And we tolerate a level of pollution and a quality of ugliness in our physical and natural surroundings that is not only annoying and depressing but actually dangerous to the physical and mental health of those people who cannot escape it.

Another of the things we do as a nation is to spend millions of dollars of our public income employing police to—among other things—protect this distribution of power and privilege from attempts to change it. And as a result we keep close to half a million people (of whom proportionately far more are nonwhite than there are nonwhites in the whole population) in prisons, year in and year out. (Isn't it sensible, when you stop to think about it?—More nonwhites are in prison because nonwhites are more hurt by the existing distribution of power and privilege and so make more attempts to change it in their favor; lacking power, their attempts are often illegal, and they get caught by the police that white people employ to protect their advantages.)

Another of the things we do is to spend billions of dollars of our public income overseas on military goods, and to invest billions of dollars of corporation income in foreign countries, even though our government and university economists know that the effect of that spending and investing (given the rest of our economic behavior and the government's economic policies) is to make the prices we pay as consumers higher than they would otherwise be. We "regulate" business so that railroads, the utility and telephone monopolies, and airline companies receive billions of dollars *more* than they would without this kind of regulation; we have a "progressive" tax system that according to government figures does *not* change the distribution of income from what it is before taxes are paid; we subsidize a variety of private businesses with billions of dollars of our public income; and we prevent foreign businesses from selling their goods in this country at their own low cost in order to protect our corporations, thereby forcing ourselves as consumers to pay higher prices. It is notorious, of course, that we spend well over half of our public income on military programs, and more of our public income on space programs than on housing programs even though six million of our dwellings are grossly substandard. And another of the things we do as a nation is to send our men, machines, and money to foreign countries to influence events there; our attempts at influence are serious enough to involve killing hundreds of thousands of people and destroying vast areas of countryside, when we meet with resistance.

Why do we as a nation do these things? Why do we not do other things?

A few years ago, Marc Pilisuk and Thomas Hayden wrote an article called "Is There a Military-Industrial Complex Which Prevents Peace?"* Their answer was not a simple "yes" or "no." They wrote,

Our concept is not that American society contains a ruling military-industrial complex. Our concept is more nearly that American society is *a military-industrial complex. It can accommodate a wide range of factional interests . . . . What it cannot accommodate is the type of radical departures needed to produce enduring peace.*

In order to understand what Pilisuk and Hayden are getting at, we must first recognize the falsity of the three other popular explanations for our twenty-five years of "cold war." First, the Cold War has *not* been due solely to our need to defend against the continuing threat of military aggression by the Soviet Union and China. Not that there has been no threat by those two nations—there has been and is—but the threat is recognized by all serious analysts and scholars to be economic, political, and ideological, *not* military. It is not possible rationally to deny that there must be something *inside* our nation that is significantly responsible for continuing such Cold War policies as spending over 60 per cent of our public income on military and military-related projects.

Second, our continuing Cold War policies have not been caused by a unified ruling group whose power has been so great as to dominate the nation and whose goals have included perpetuating the Cold War. Of course, at first it sounds plausible to say that continued Cold War spending must be due to the power and interests of the military and of the corpora-

*Marc Pilisuk and Thomas Hayden, "Is There a Military-Industrial Complex Which Prevents Peace?," *Journal of Social Issues,* 21 (1965), pp 67–99.

tions that profit from doing business with the military. But then we must ask: can it be true that this small group of people has virtually dictatorial power over us, and that they consciously use their overwhelming power to prevent peace? (That question must be asked, because *that* degree of power and *that* sort of goal are implied by the statement that a ruling group or power elite has deliberately caused our Cold War policies.) Merely to pose the question in such stark terms is to suggest the answer. No, the military and military-related corporations are not that dominant, and are not consciously united on that goal. The fact is that civilians in the government often overrule the military. The most powerful corporations could get along without such huge defense budgets, and the economy has suffered as a result of the Vietnam War. The corporations that really depend on the military budget are undeniably influential, but hardly powerful enough by themselves to dictate policy to Washington. And these various corporations, and the various subgroupings within the military, usually conflict with each other on matters of "defense" policy. Moreover, it is safe to say that some of the military and most of the powerful corporations do *not* have as a *goal* the prevention of international peace.

But third, our continuing Cold War policies are not at all the result of a balance of countervailing powers, or an adjustment of competing interests, between the pro-Cold War and anti-Cold War factions of our society. There are certainly plenty of powerful interests that get satisfied by our Cold War policies, but to do this they do *not* have to win out in a serious power struggle against the people and interests that would be satisfied by a national policy of nonintervention in the affairs of foreign nations and drastically reduced military expenditures. Because the fact is that there are *no* powerful interests in our society that are *opposed* to our Cold War policies! There is no civilian-military conflict among the powerful, for example, because the civilians at the top of our government (in the Department of Defense, the Central Intelligence Agency, the State Department, the key advisory positions in the White House, and the President) are just as often advocates of "hawkish" or "militaristic" policies as are the uniformed military. As Pilisuk and Hayden point out, counterinsurgency (relatively smallscale actions aimed at preventing guerrilla forces from building strength), the most popular type of military operation in the defense establishment for use in Third World nations, was developed mainly by civilians like McGeorge Bundy, Robert Kennedy, W. W. Rostow, and Robert McNamara —and in opposition to some of the uniformed military. Likewise, there is no serious conflict of interest between "war profiteers" and corporations in the "peace economy" because there are almost no major corporations that do not profit in some way from our Cold War policies. Just consider those groups and institutions that are usually recognized as the most powerful in our society—the political parties, the national government itself, the associations of business corporations, the AFL-CIO, the universities, the news media, the agricultural associations, and so on. These organizations are all dominated or run by men in basic agreement with our Cold War policies, although there are of course a handful of dissenters. Where would any powerful opposition come from?

In the process of dismissing these three false accounts of our continuing national Cold War policies, the outlines of Pilsuk and Hayden's explanation have become clear. They argue that our nation is dominated by bureaucratic power centers, of which the most important are the military, the major corporations, and the federal government (including the two major political parties). Within these power centers there is no significant opposition to our Cold War policies, and some of these power centers' basic interests benefit from those policies. It follows that opposition to those Cold War policies is weak—that is, is not to be found in any major institutional power centers— and so is unable to change or modify those policies.

Pilsuk and Hayden go on to explain that the reason why those institutional power centers are so dominant, and the reasons why they share a consensus on our Cold War policies, is that almost everyone in the country shares certain beliefs which indirectly justify the maintenance of both those institutions and those policies. (Recall the discussion of our constitutional principles and institutions in Part I.) These beliefs are:

1. A nation should act realistically and pragmatically, satisfying its interests as effectively as possible, and sacrificing principle to efficacy where necessary (so that military means may be used when nonviolent means might be less effective—which is quite often).

2. The institution of private property (particularly the principle that property may be used for purposes that are not decided collectively by an entire community) must be defended.

3. Our form of government is preferable to any other kind of government.*

To say that our nation is dominated by bureaucratic power centers is not to say that those bureaucracies emerge victorious whenever they get caught in a struggle to the death with some people or organizations that do not dominate; such a struggle never occurs. Rather, these institutions dominate in the sense of having an effectively unchallenged right to satisfy their basic interests before any other interests get attention. And these organized interests have this "right" because so few people and organizations in our society think they should not have it, and act on that thought. The point of

---

*Pilsuk and Hayden also point out that these beliefs alone, even aside from the Cold War policies they justify, must prevent any lasting international peace because they fly in the face of certain things that would have to be done in order to achieve and maintain such a peace. These tasks include: the transition of our economy into a nondefense economy, which would have to be planned and managed by a central bureaucracy, violating (2) and possibly (3) above; resolution of certain situations, such as American corporations dominating foreign economies, which cannot be accomplished peacefully and satisfy (2) and (3); and a reduction in the disparity of living standards between the richer and poorer nations, which cannot be accomplished without a degree of centralized control over the "underdeveloped" economies that would violate (2) and harm economic interests of the United States.

saying that the most important bureaucratic power centers are the major corporations, the military, and the federal government and major political parties is to stress this fact that those organizations' interests get priority over other interests, and that the effects of satisfying those interests are more fundamental and far-reaching than satisfying the other interests.

Charles E. Wilson, former secretary of defense and a top corporation executive, described this fact (that our national priorities are to satisfy the key interests of the dominant institutions) by saying "what's good for General Motors is good for the country." In fact, given the way our economy and society are now, that is true—27,000 small businesses and hundreds of thousands of jobs would go down the drain if GM stopped expanding and making its profits, and the stock market would go into a tailspin. Moreover, in fact, almost all Americans agree with Wilson's blooper; it was a controversial statement only in the sense that people who agreed with it in principle ("Of course GM shouldn't be forced to go bankrupt or be nationalized") wanted to argue how far it should be applied in practice ("18 per cent is just too high a profit rate").

It is because the key interests of the major corporations, the military, and the federal government and major political parties have priority that I have called the effects of satisfying them "our national priorities." "Economic growth," "technological progress," and "national security" are indeed goals that everyone takes for granted, as the context inside of which we will worry about other issues.* This is the reason why I have referred to the wheeling and dealing, bargaining for a bigger share of the national pie, and horse-trading among separate and opposed interests that takes place within the constraints imposed by our national priorities as "the politics of accommodation." Most of what we usually see as politics—the politics of civil rights, labor, agriculture, prices and taxes, health care, pollution control, education, poverty, and so on—is in fact an accommodation to our national priorities. The selections by Lowi and McConnell in the section on "The Politics of Accommodation," as well as those in the section on "The National Priorities," show some of the consequences of this accommodation—consequences, that is, of satisfying the major interests of the dominant bureaucratic power centers.

I said in Part I that power is *ultimately* rooted in human emotions and habits. But it will not do to leave the question of how certain bureaucracies dominate our society with the mere observation that their interests are effectively unchallenged. After all, few people want to fight in a war, to pay more for a car than it costs to make it, or to be put out of work by automation (three things required by our national priorities). Obviously, power in our society is hardly a matter of traditional customs or spontaneous feeling. The

*The three phrases are in quotes as a reminder that what we call "economic growth," for example, is not at all the *only kind* of economic growth possible, but is rather a euphemism for a process that would more accurately be described as "continued corporate expansion." Thus one might be opposed to "national security" without being opposed to national security.

power we see exercised is shaped and focused by tools of violence, by our laws, by our system of interdependent socioeconomic interests, by the existence of enormous bureaucratic organizations, and by the distribution of wealth and skill among the population. In other words, a demand that we as a nation do a particular thing (say, to continue the war or get out of it, to ignore pollution or prevent it, to encourage "benign neglect" or to stop racial oppression, or whatever) will be powerful to the extent that the people making the demand have control over tools of violence, can use the laws or make new ones, have control over bureaucratic organization, and possess great wealth and skill, and to the extent that the demand complements important other socioeconomic interests.

Most of these ingredients of power should be familiar. A good illustration of how they work was the struggle over "People's Park" described in selection 14 in Part IV. But the notion of our system of interdependent, complementary socioeconomic interests may need some clarification. Two points are involved. First, an "interest" is both a demand and a performance. "The farm interest," for example, is a demand upon the rest of the nation (that farmers get paid well for their work), and is inextricably tied up with the production of food for the rest of the nation. The interests of the aerospace industry involve both the demand that government spend money on space programs, and the production of planes, missiles, electronic equipment, and so on. A system of interests is interdependent when the demands of any one interest are, in effect, for the performances of the other interests. The aerospace industry is powerful partly because it is interdependent with other important interests—certain local governments, certain labor unions, certain other industries, and the federal government—all of whose own interests require the performance of the aerospace industry, and thereby make them willing to grant its demands. Secondly, interests are complementary if their demands can be met simultaneously by a single policy. For example, the three branches of the armed services, for all that they squabble over their respective shares of the military budget, have complementary interests in that they all benefit from a large defense budget. Defense contractors, for all that they complete among each other for specific contracts, have complementary interests in keeping those contracts coming.

Now it's possible to explain in a few words what the title of this part means: "the basic structure of power, interest, and policy" is the whole pattern, the whole set of interrelationships between the dominant bureaucratic power centers, their interdependent and complementary interests, and the important things we do as a nation.

But there is still one question that these notes must answer. What sense does it make to talk about the interests of the government? If there are elections, then aren't the "interests of the government" the same thing as the interests of the majority of voters? The answer to this latter question, as selection 10 shows, is that what we do as a nation is not and cannot be in any direct, specific way the result of elections. But if the interests of the government are not what a majority of voters want, then what are they? The answer is that elected officials have an interest in doing what they see as proper and necessary in order to win elections. Bureaucratic officials, like the personnel in all bureaucracies, have an interest in strengthening their organization and in accomplishing the tasks their organizational roles set for them. Politicians and government bureaucrats do have interests, then, and these interests are not necessarily at all the same as the will of the people.

If the interests of the government are not necessarily the same as the will of the people, however, neither are they necessarily *just* the same as those of the major corporations or the military. It is true that today the basic interests of major corporations never clash with the government, and that the "party of the common man," to say nothing of the Republicans, has moved a long way toward a meeting of minds with the dominant sector of industry. But, on the other hand, during the New Deal in the 1930's there were few businessmen who doubted that the government's policy of assisting radical unions to organize and bargain with employers over wages and working conditions was a direct threat to their interests. In retrospect, of course, it is possible to see that the New Deal, far from being the socialistic menace that it appeared to the Chamber of Commerce at the time, actually "saved" and "modernized" American capitalism. But this fact does not mean that the government was *unable* to do anything other than "save" the private economy (by forcing business to act in its long-run rather than short-run interests). The fact that the New Deal government did not move toward socialism was hardly because it knuckled under to the power of business. Rather, the government could not have moved very far toward socialism and still satisfied its *own* interests (for example, strengthening the "New Deal coalition" by appealing to labor, big city machines, intellectuals, ethnic groups, and the South).

In other words, *if* there were a major political party dedicated to a radical restructuring of our entire pattern of power, interest, and policy, supported enthusiastically by a large majority of the people, and with control over most of the elective offices in the government, such a party's government would be able to act in spite of the domination by corporate and military interests. But, on the other hand, precisely the dominance of the present government (including the two major parties), the corporations, the military—and of all the lesser bureaucratic power centers that are part of the basic structure with them—precisely that dominance makes it extremely unlikely that the "if" conditions can be achieved, at least in the near future. (In the introduction to Part VI there is more careful discussion of this question.) At present, as the following selections show, the interests of the government and major politicians are thoroughly intertwined with those of the other dominant bureaucracies.

But the fact that our government has a will of its own does not mean that "we, the people" are not involved significantly in deciding what our national policies will be. It should be clear that our beliefs and our own private interests make us the supporters or willing accomplices of our nation's basic structure of power, interests, and policy. (After all, already even in the 1950's almost 60 per cent of all paid workers were employed by the biggest 1 per cent of business firms; over ten million people depended on government for some form of welfare in 1968; 5 per cent of all the jobs in the country and 10 per cent of all the jobs in manufacturing, in 1967, depended on Defense Department spending. If those 1 per cent of corporations, the Defense Department, and the welfare agencies formed a political party and ran for office, their dependents would be a large majority of the voting population!) Now that we have arrived a the point where it is possible to account for our national policies in terms of this basic structure, it may be tempting to say that the "power structure" does everything, and "the people" are helpless, unwilling victims. We may be the victims, but we are mostly pretty helpful, willing victims.

The National Priorities

6   What Is Our Government There For?

Ralph Miliband

This is the only selection in Parts I–V by a non-American, and the only one that describes other countries than the United States. But precisely because of the comparative approach taken by Miliband (and in spite of occasional British-isms in his language—for example, his use of the word "governments" in the first sentence where we would say "administrations"), he is able to reveal some important facts about American politics that we often fail to see. Particularly, Miliband argues, we usually ignore the profound significance of things we take for granted—things such as the private ownership of property and the nondemocratic nature of our government. When we stop taking such things for granted and examine their significance, says Miliband, then we begin to grasp the fundamental facts of political power and policy in a nation such as the United States.—Ed.

At first sight, the picture is one of endless diversity between succeeding governments, and indeed inside each of them—as also between governments of different countries. Presidents, prime ministers, and their colleagues have worn many different political labels (often wildly misleading) and belonged to many different parties, or occasionally to none.

Excerpted from Chapter 4, "The Purpose and Role of Governments," in *The State in Capitalist Society* by Ralph Miliband, © 1969 by Ralph Miliband, Basic Books, Inc., Publishers, New York. (Permission to republish in Canada granted by George Weidenfeld & Nicolson, Ltd., London.) Footnotes have been renumbered, and a few have been omitted.

This diversity of views, attitudes, programs, and policies, on an infinite number of subjects, is certainly very striking and makes for live political debate and competition. And the impression of diversity and conflict is further enhanced by the insistence of party leaders, particularly at election time, on the wide and almost impassable, or actually impassable, gulf which separates them from their opponents and competitors.

The assertion of such profound differences is a matter of great importance for the functioning and legitimation of the political system, since it suggests that electors, by voting for one or other of the main competing parties, are making a choice between fundamental and incompatible alternatives, and that they are therefore, as voters, deciding nothing less than the future of their country.

In actual fact, however, this picture is in some crucial ways highly superficial and mystifying. For one of the most important aspects of the political life of advanced capitalism is precisely that the disagreements *between those political leaders who have generally been able to gain high office* have very seldom been of the fundamental kind these leaders and other people so often suggest. What is really striking about *these* political leaders and political officeholders, in relation to each other, is not their many differences, but the extent of their agreement on truly fundamental issues—as they themselves, when occasion requires, have been wont to recognize, and as large numbers of people among the public at large, despite the political rhetoric to which they are subjected, recognize in the phrase "politicians are all the same."[1] This is an exaggeration, of course. But it is an exaggeration with a solid kernel of truth, at least in relation to the kind of men who tend to succeed each other in office in advanced capitalist countries. Marxists put the same point somewhat differently when they say that these men, whatever their political labels or party affiliations, are bourgeois politicians.

The basic sense in which this is true is that the political officeholders of advanced capitalism have, with very few exceptions, been agreed over what Lord Balfour, in a classical formulation, once called "the foundations of society," meaning above all the existing economic and social system of private ownership and private appropriation—Marx's "mode of production." Balfour was writing about Britain, and about the Whig and Tory administrations of the nineteenth century. But his point applies equally well to other capitalist countries, and to the twentieth century as well as to the nineteenth.

[1] As witnessed, for instance, by the number of people in countries like Britain and the United States who, when asked whether they believe that there are important differences between the main competing parties, tend to answer in the negative.

For it is no more than a matter of plain political history that the governments of these countries have mostly been composed of men who, beyond all their political, social, religious, cultural, and other differences and diversities, have at least had in common a basic and usually explicit belief in the validity and virtues of the capitalist system, though this was not what they would necessarily call it; and those among them who have not been particularly concerned with that system, or even aware that they were helping to run a specific economic system, much in the way that they were not aware of the air they breathed, have at least shared with their more ideologically aware colleagues or competitors a quite basic and unswerving hostility to any socialist alternative to that system.

However, even if we leave out for the present the particular role of formally socialist power-holders, it must be stressed again that this basic consensus between bourgeois politicians does not preclude genuine and important differences between them, not only on issues other than the actual management of the economic system, but on that issue as well.

Thus, it has always been possible to make an important distinction between parties and leaders, however committed they might be to the private enterprise system, who stood for a large measure of state intervention in economic and social life, and those who believed in a lesser degree of intervention; and the same distinction encompasses those parties and men who have believed that the state must assume a greater degree of responsibility for social and other kinds of reform; and those who have wished for less.

This quarrel between strong interventionists and their opponents has been and remains a perfectly genuine one. No doubt, no serious politician—however bourgeois and convinced of the virtues of private enterprise—would now wish or be able to dismantle the main structure of state intervention; and indeed it is often the most capitalist-oriented politicians who see most clearly how essential that structure of intervention has become to the maintenance of capitalism. Even so, sufficient differences endure about the desirable extent, the character and the incidence of intervention, to make the debate around such questions (and around many other ones as well) a serious and meaningful one, upon whose outcome depends much which affects many aspects of public policy and many individual lives. From this point of view at least, competition between these men is by no means a complete sham.

But the fact nevertheless remains that these differences and controversies, even at their most intense, have never been allowed by the politicians concerned to bring into question the validity of the "free enterprise" system itself; and even the most determined interventionists among them have always conceived their proposals and policies as a means, not of eroding—let alone supplanting—the capitalist system, but of ensuring its greater strength and stability. To a much larger extent than appearance and rhetoric have been made to suggest, the politics of advanced capitalism have been about different conceptions of how to run the *same* economic and social system, and not about radically different social systems. *This* debate has not so far come high on the political agenda.

This consensus between political officeholders is clearly crucial. The ideological dispositions which make the consensus possible may not, because of various counterpressures, finally determine how governments will act in every particular situation. But the fact that governments accept as beyond question the capitalist context in which they operate is of absolutely fundamental importance in shaping their attitudes, policies, and actions in regard to the specific issues and problems with which they are confronted, and to the needs and conflicts of civil society. The general commitment deeply colors the specific response, and affects not only the solution envisaged for the particular problem perceived, but the mode of perception itself; indeed, ideological commitment may and often does prevent perception at all, and makes impossible not

only prescription for the disease, but its location.

However, political officeholders themselves do not at all see their commitment to capitalist enterprise as involving any element of class partiality. On the contrary, they are the most ardent and eloquent exponents of the view of the state, and of themselves, as above the battles of civil society, as classless, as concerned above all to serve the whole nation, the national interest, as being charged with the particular task of subduing special interests and class-oriented demands for the supreme good of all. In their thoughts and words, Hegel's exalted view of the state as the embodiment and the protector of the whole of society, of its higher reason, and of its permanent interests, lives again—particularly when they rather than their opponents are in office. "I belong to everyone and I belong to no one," General de Gaulle said shortly after coming to power in 1958, and it would be absurd to doubt that this is indeed how the general does see himself—far, far above the interests of lesser men, be they capitalists, wage-earners, farmers, shopkeepers, the sick, the poor, the young, or the old. Other political leaders may not find it easy to present themselves in quite such grandiose terms; but they do their best, and see themselves in much the same guise as the general does, even when they appear to others to exhibit the most blatant class bias in their policies and actions.

That most political leaders in positions of power do hold this view of their office, and of themselves, with sincerity and conviction need not, in general, be doubted. Indeed, to dismiss their proclamations of freedom from class bias as mere hypocrisy leads to a dangerous underestimation of the dedication and resolution with which such leaders are likely to pursue a task of whose nobility they are utterly persuaded. Men so persuaded are not easily deflected from their purpose by appeals to reason or sentiment or evidence, particularly when matters of great moment are at stake.

Opponents of capitalism believe it to be a system whose very nature nowadays makes impossible the optimum utilization of resources for rational human ends; whose inherent character is one of compulsion, domination, and parasitical appropriation; whose spirit and purpose fatally corrode all human relations; and whose maintenance is today the major obstacle to human progress.

Bourgeois politicians and governments view the system in precisely opposite terms —as most closely congruent with "human nature," as uniquely capable of combining efficiency, welfare, and freedom, as the best means of releasing human initiative and energy in socially beneficient directions, and as providing the necessary and only possible basis for a satisfactory social order.

Anyway, why speak of "capitalism" at all, with its emotive and propagandistic evocations of a system which no longer *really* exists, and which has been replaced by an "industrial system" in which private enterprise, though still the essential motor of the economy, is now much more "responsible" than in the past, and whose purposes are now in any case closely supervised by the democratic state?

"Liberal democracy," Robert Lynd wrote twenty-five years ago,

has never dared face the fact that industrial capitalism is an intensely coercive form of organization of society that cumulatively constrains men and all of their institutions to work the will of the minority who hold and wield economic power; and that this relentless warping of men's lives and forms of association becomes less and less the result of voluntary decisions by "bad" men or "good" men and more and more an impersonal web of coercions dictated by the need to keep "the system" running.[2]

This is even more true than when it was first written; but the governments which manage "liberal democracy" are mostly composed of men who *cannot* see the system in this guise, who attribute the deficiencies in it which they perceive as separate and specific "problems," remediable within its confines—

[2]Foreword to R. A. Brady, *Business as a System of Power*, 1943, p. xii.

in fact *only* remediable within its confines. This is what makes it possible for politicians who are, in this fundamental respect, extreme doctrinaires to claim that theirs is an essentially empirical, undogmatic, pragmatic, *practical* approach to affairs.

Given their view of that system, it is easy to understand why governments should wish to help business in every possible way, yet do not at all feel that this entails any degree of bias toward particular classes, interests, and groups. For if the national interest is in fact inextricably bound up with the fortunes of capitalist enterprise, apparent partiality toward it is not really partiality at all. On the contrary, in serving the interests of business and in helping capitalist enterprise to thrive, governments are really fulfilling their exalted role as guardians of the good of all. From this standpoint, the much-derided phrase "What is good for General Motors is good for America" is only defective in that it tends to identify the interests of one particular enterprise with the national interest. But if General Motors is taken to stand for the world of capitalist enterprise as a whole, the slogan is one to which governments in capitalist countries do subscribe, often explicitly. And they do so because they accept the notion that the economic rationality of the capitalist system is synonymous with rationality itself, and that it provides the best possible set of human arrangements in a necessarily imperfect world.

In this sense, the attitude of political officeholders to businessmen as a class or as a social type is of relatively minor importance. Their circle of relations, friends, former associates, and acquaintances is much more likely to include businessmen than, say, trade-union leaders; and the favorable view they take of capitalist enterprise is also likely to make them take a sympathetic view of the men who run it. Thus President Eisenhower in 1952 [said]:

I believe in our dynamic system of privately owned businesses and industries. They have proven that they can supply not only the mightiest sinews of war, but the highest standard of living in the world for the greatest number of people. ... But it requires some-

one to take these things and to produce the extraordinary statistics that the United States with 7 per cent of the world's population produces 50 per cent of the world's manufactured goods. If that someone is to be given a name, I believe that his name is the American businessman.[3]

Political leaders in countries less steeped in the business creed are not often quite so naively gushing; and even in the United States, presidents have on occasion taken a less enthusiastic view of those whom one of them (admittedly long ago, and not very seriously) denounced as "malefactors of great wealth." It may well be, indeed, that many political leaders have taken a very poor view of this or that section of business, or even considered business as an inferior activity, from which they felt themselves far removed.

All this, however, is of no serious consequence, given a fundamental commitment to the system of which businessmen are an intrinsic and major part. Because of that commitment, and because of their belief that the national interest is inextricably bound up with the health and strength of capitalist enterprise, governments naturally seek to help business—and businessmen. Thorstein Veblen once wrote that "the chief—virtually sole—concern of the constituted authorities in any democratic nation is a concern about the profitable business of the nation's substantial citizens."[4] This is quite true, but not necessarily or at all because of any particular predilection of the "constituted authorities"

for substantial citizens. The concern goes with the general commitment.

The first and most important consequence of the commitment which governments in advanced capitalist countries have to the private enterprise system and to its economic rationality is that it enormously limits their freedom of action in relation to a multitude of issues and problems. Raymond Aron has written that "il va de soi qu'en régime fondé sur la propriété des moyens de production, les mesures prises par les législateurs et les ministres ne seront pas en opposition fondamentale avec les intérêts des propriétaires."[5] This proposition, he comments, is too obvious to be instructive. It *should* perhaps be obvious. But it does not appear to be so to most Western political scientists who view the state as free from the inherent bias in favor of capitalist interests which Professor Aron's proposition implies.

That bias has immense policy implications. For the resolution, or at least the alleviation, of a vast range of economic and social problems requires precisely that governments *should* be willing to act in "fundamental opposition" to these interests. Far from being a trivial matter, their extreme reluctance to do so is one of the largest of all facts in the life of these societies. Were it to be said about a government that though faced with a vast criminal organization it could not be expected to act in fundamental opposition to it, the observation would not be thought uninstructive about its character and role. The same is true of the proposition which Professor Aron so casually puts forward and tosses aside.

On the other hand, that proposition tends to obscure a basic aspect of the state's role. For governments, acting in the name of the state, have in fact been compelled over the years to act against *some* property rights, to erode *some* managerial prerogatives, to help

[3]S. E. Harris, *The Economics of Political Parties,* 1962, p. 5. On coming to office, President Johnson put the same point somewhat differently but, it may be surmised, with no less feeling: "We think we have the best system. We think that where a capitalist can put up a dollar, he can get a return on it. A manager can get up early to work and with money and men he can build a better mousetrap. A laborer who is worthy of his hire stands a chance of getting attention and maybe a little profit-sharing system, and the highest minimum wages of any nation in the world." (R. Evans and R. Novak, *Lyndon B. Johnson: The Exercise of Power,* 1966, p. 347.)

[4]T. Veblen, *Absentee Ownership,* 1923, pp. 36–37.

[5]("It's obvious that in a system based on the ownership of the means of production, measures taken by the legislators and the executive branch will not be in fundamental opposition to the interests of the owners,") R. Aron, "Classe Sociale, Classe Politique, Classe Dirigeante," in *Archives Européennes de Sociologie,* 1:2 (1960), pp. 272–273.

redress *somewhat* the balance between capital and labor, between property and those who are subject to it. This is an aspect of state intervention which conservative writers who lament the growth of "bureaucracy" and who deplore state "interference" in the affairs of society regularly overlook. Bureaucracy is indeed a problem and a danger, and the experience of countries like the Soviet Union has amply shown how greatly unrestrained bureaucratic power can help to obstruct the creation of a socialist society worthy of the name. But concentration upon the evils of bureaucracy in capitalist countries obscures (and is often intended to obscure) the fact that "bureaucratic" intervention has often been a means of alleviating the evils produced by unrestrained private economic power.

The state's "interference" with that power is not in "fundamental opposition" to the interests of property: it is indeed part of that "ransom" of which Joseph Chamberlain spoke in 1885 and which, he said, would have to be paid precisely for the purpose of *maintaining* the rights of property in general. In insisting that the "ransom" be paid, governments render property a major service, though the latter is seldom grateful for it. Even so, it would not do to ignore the fact that even very conservative governments in the regimes of advanced capitalism have often been forced, mainly as a result of popular pressure, to take action against *certain* property rights and capitalist prerogatives.

As against this, however, must be set the very positive support which governments have generally sought to give to dominant economic interests.

Capitalist enterprise . . . depends to an ever greater extent on the bounties and direct support of the state, and can only preserve its "private" character on the basis of such public help. State intervention in economic life in fact largely *means* intervention for the purpose of helping capitalist enterprise. In no field has the notion of the "welfare state" had a more precise and opposite meaning than here: there are no more persistent and successful applicants for public assistance than the proud giants of the private enterprise system.

Nor need that assistance be of a direct kind to be of immense value to capitalist interests. Because of the imperative requirements of modern life, the state must, within the limits imposed upon it by the prevailing economic system, engage in bastard forms of socialization and assume responsibility for many functions and services which are beyond the scope and capabilities of capitalist interests. As it does so, however, what Jean Meynaud calls "the bias of the system" ensures that these interests will automatically benefit from state intervention. Because of the private ownership and control of a predominant part of economic life, Professor Meynaud writes:

All the measures taken by the state to develop and improve the national economy always end up by being of the greatest benefit to those who control the levers of command of the production distribution sector: when the state cuts tunnels, builds roads, opens up highways, or reclaims swamps, it is first of all the owners of the neighboring lands who reap the rewards. . . . the concept of the "bias of the system" makes it also possible to understand that the measures taken to remedy the derelictions, shortcomings, and abuses of capitalism result ultimately, where successful, in the consolidation of the regime. It matters little in this respect that these measures should have been undertaken by men sympathetic or hostile to capitalist interests: thus it is that laws designed to protect the workers and directed against their exploitation by employers will be found useful to the latter by inducing them to make a greater effort to rationalize or mechanize the productive process.[6]

Governments may be solely concerned with the better running of "the economy." But the description of the system as "the economy" is part of the idiom of ideology, and obscures the real process. For what is

[6]J. Meynaud, *Rapport sur la Classe Dirigeante Italienne,* 1964, pp. 190–191.

being improved is a *capitalist* economy; and this ensures that whoever may or may not gain, capitalist interests are least likely to lose.

The "bias of the system" may be given a greater or lesser degree of emphasis. But the ideological dispositions of governments have generally been of a kind to make more acceptable to them the structural constraints imposed upon them by the system; and these dispositions have also made it easier for them to submit to the pressures to which they have been subjected by dominant interests.

Taxation offers a ready illustration of the point.... [T]he economic system itself generates extremely powerful tendencies toward the maintenance and enhancement of the vast inequalities of income and wealth which are typical of all advanced capitalist societies. Given that economic system, no government can achieve redistributive miracles. But the limits of its powers in this field are nevertheless not finally fixed—despite the system's tendencies to inequality and the fierce opposition of the forces of wealth to redistributive taxation. And the fact that taxation has not, over the years, affected more deeply than it has the disparities of income and wealth in these societies must to a major extent be attributed to the attitude of governments toward inequality, to the view they take of the conflicting claims of the rich and the poor, and to their acceptance of an economic orthodoxy which has, at any particular moment of time, declared additional burdens on the rich to be fatal to "business confidence," "individual initiative," the propensity to invest, etc.

The same considerations apply to government intervention in "industrial relations," the consecrated euphemism for the permanent conflict, now acute, now subdued, between capital and labor.

Whenever governments have felt it incumbent, as they have done more and more, to intervene directly in disputes between employers and wage-earners, the result of their intervention has tended to be disadvantageous to the latter, not the former. On innumerable occasions, and in all capitalist countries, governments have played a decisive role in defeating strikes, often by the invocation of the coercive power of the state and the use of naked violence; and the fact that they have done so in the name of the national interest, law and order, constitutional government, the protection of "the public," etc., rather than simply to support employers, has not made that intervention any the less useful to these employers.

Moreover, the state, as the largest of all employers, is now able to influence the pattern of "industrial relations" by the force of its own example and behavior: that influence can hardly be said to have created new standards in the employer-employee relationship. Nor could it have been expected to do so, given the "businesslike" spirit in which the public sector is managed.

Governments are deeply involved, on a permanent and institutionalized basis, in that "routinization of conflict" which is an essential part of the politics of advanced capitalism. They enter that conflict in the guise of a neutral and independent party, concerned to achieve not the outright defeat of one side or the other but a "reasonable" settlement between them. But the state's intervention in negotiations occurs in the shadow of its known and declared propensity to invoke its powers of coercion, against one of the parties in the dispute rather than the other, if "conciliation" procedures fail. These procedures form, in fact, an additional element of restraint upon organized labor, and also serve the useful purpose of further dividing the trade-union ranks. The state does interpose itself between the "two sides of industry"—not, however, as a neutral but as a partisan.

Nor is this nowadays only true when industrial disputes actually occur. One of the most notable features in the recent evolution of advanced capitalism is the degree to which governments have sought to place new and further inhibitions upon organized labor in order to prevent it from exercising what pressures it can on employers (and on the state as a major employer) in the matter of wage claims. What they tend to achieve, by such means as an "incomes policy," or by deflationary policies which reduce the demand for labor, is a *general* weakening of the bargaining position of wage-earners. Here, too, the policies adopted are proclaimed to be essential to the national interest, the health of the economy, the defense of the currency, the good of the workers, and so on. And there are always trade-union leaders who can be found to endorse both the claims and the policies. But this does not change the fact that the main effect of these policies is to leave wage-earners in a weaker position vis-a-vis employers than would otherwise be the case. The *purpose,* in the eyes of political officeholders, may be all that it is said to be; but the *result,* with unfailing regularity, is to the detriment of the subordinate classes. This is why the latter, in this as in most other instances, have good reason to beware when the political leaders of advanced capitalist countries invoke the national interest in defense of their policies—more likely than not they, the subordinate classes, are about to be done. Wage-earners have always had to reckon with a hostile state in their encounter with employers. But now more than ever they have to reckon with its antagonism, in practice, as a direct, pervasive, and constant fact of economic life. Their immediate and daily opponent remains the employer; but governments and the state are now much more closely involved in the encounter than in the past.

Quite naturally, this partiality of governments assumes an even more specific, precise, and organized character in relation to all movements, groupings, and parties dedicated to the transformation of capitalist societies into socialist ones. The manner in which governments have expressed this antagonism has greatly varied over time, and between countries, assuming here a milder form, there a harsher one; but the antagonism itself has been a permanent fact in the history of all capitalist countries. In no field has the underlying consensus between political officeholders of different political affiliations, and between the governments of

different countries, been more substantial and notable—the leaders of all governmental parties, whether in office or in opposition, and including nominally "socialist" ones, have always been deeply hostile to the socialist and militant left, of whatever denomination, and governments themselves have in fact been the major protagonists against it, in their role of protectors and saviors of society from the perils of left-wing dissidence.

In this instance too, liberal-democratic and pluralist theorists, in their celebration of the political competition which prevails in their societies, and in their insistence on the political neutrality of the state, quite overlook the fact that the governments of advanced capitalist societies, far from taking a neutral view of *socialist* competition, do their level best to make it more difficult. In some countries, for instance federal Germany, Communist and other left-wing parties and organizations are suppressed altogether, and membership made a crime punishable by law; in others, such as the United States, left-wing organizations, of which the Communist Party is only one, operate in conditions of such harassment as to narrow rather drastically, in their case, the notion of free political competition.

Nor is the state's hostility less marked in other countries, though it may assume different forms—for instance electoral manipulation as in France and Italy for the purpose of robbing their Communist parties of the parliamentary representation to which their electoral strength entitles them; the engineering of bias in the mass media, insofar as lies in the considerable and growing power of governments; and also episodic but quite brutal repression of left-wing dissenters.

Governments, in other words, are deeply concerned, whatever their political coloration, that the "democratic process" should operate within a framework in which left-wing dissent plays as weak a role as possible.

The argument is not whether governments should or should not be neutral as between conservative and anticonservative ideologies, movements, parties, and groups. That question is not susceptible to resolution in terms of such imperatives. The argument is rather that the governments of advanced capitalist countries have never been thus neutral, and that they have for the most part used the state power on the conservative as against the anticonservative side. And the further argument is that in so doing they have, whatever other purposes they might have wished to serve, afforded a most precious element of protection to those classes and interests whose power and privileges socialist dissent is primarily intended to undermine and destroy. Those who believe in the virtues of a social order which includes such power and privileges will applaud and support governmental partiality, and may even ask for more of it. Those who do not will not. The important point is to see what so much of political analysis obscures, often from itself, namely that this is what governments, in these countries, actually do.

The argument so far has centered on some of the main *internal* consequences which flow from the commitment of governments to the capitalist system. But the *external* consequences of that commitment are no less direct and important.

Here, perhaps even more than in other fields, the purposes which governments proclaim their wish to serve are often made to appear remote from specific economic concerns, let alone capitalist interests. It is the national interest, national security, national independence, honor, greatness, etc. that is their concern. But this naturally includes a sound, healthy, thriving economic system; and such a desirable state of affairs depends in turn on the prosperity of capitalist enterprise. Thus, by the same mechanism which operates in regard to home affairs, the governments of capitalist countries have generally found that their larger national purposes required the servicing of capitalist interests; and the crucial place which these interests occupy in the life of their country has always caused governments to make their defense against foreign capitalist interests, and against the foreign states which protect *them,* a prime consideration in their conduct of external affairs.

7   What Is Our Economy Good For?

Paul A. Baran and Paul M. Sweezy

The following selection is only a part of Baran and Sweezy's argument. Their whole position can be summarized (though of course not adequately explained) in a series of propositions. Any economy based on private control over production will either repeat ever-more-serious cycles of overproduction followed by depression, or else will produce more than can be consumed by businesses and households. Because the American economy is dominated in each industry by a handful of giant corporations, and because the government is committed to economic policies that will prevent serious depression, the American economy is producing more than it can consume. This surplus must be "absorbed" (i.e., gotten rid of) somehow, or else it will produce precisely the depression whose avoidance was the reason for the creation of a surplus in the first place; if the surplus ever came onto the market, it would immediately cause a fall in prices and a drop in employment, leading to depression. The major ways that the economic surplus is absorbed are: increasing the investment done by corporations; increasing the level of consumption "artifically" through advertising, psychologically manipulative marketing techniques, etc.; increasing the spending done by governments on nonmilitary projects; and increasing the spending done by the government on the military and other foreign projects. For various reasons (some of which are explained below in the following selection), the last method of "surplus absorption" is more and more appealing to the people who make important economic decisions. Even in combination, however, these attempts to stave off economic collapse are bound to fail in the long run.

This argument is worth taking seriously as perhaps the first attempt in English to extend Marx's theory of capitalism to the new conditions of postwar American business. But the selection that follows deals with only a small part of the whole theory, the part that describes how our economic surplus is "absorbed" by civilian government and by military and foreign spending. The crux of this part of Baran and Sweezy's argument is their claim that "civilian" spending—on social welfare, education, poverty, and so forth—is unable to increase as much as it should (in terms of what our society needs), and that the part of the surplus that cannot be absorbed by our limited civilian government spending will therefore have to go into military and imperialistic spending if we are to avoid another Great Depression.

One possible misunderstanding should be clarified. Baran and Sweezy are not arguing that there is absolutely no way to have our government spend money on socially worthwhile projects and stop spending on military projects. They are just saying that without some very basic changes there is no way to improve this situation. Those changes, in Baran and Sweezy's eyes, must result in the control of our economy being shifted from private hands to publicly responsible hands—or, in other words, in a new way of setting our national priorities.—Ed.

... what does determine the limits on the expansion of civilian spending? The answer is the particular interests of the individuals and groups which comprise the oligarchy and the way these interests are affected by the various types of spending. . . .

In the case of almost every major item in the civilian budget, powerful vested interests are soon aroused to opposition as expansion proceeds beyond the necessary minimum. This occurs whenever a significant element of competition with private enterprise is involved, but it is also true of other items where competition with private enterprise is largely or even wholly absent.

There are many urgent social needs which government can satisfy only by entering into some form of competition with private interests. River-valley development, for example, an area in which private enterprise could never hope to operate effectively, is essential for flood control, water conservation, rebuilding eroded soils, etc. But it also produces electric power which competes with private power and thus provides a yardstick by which the performance of the private power monopolies can be measured. For this reason, river-valley development is bitterly opposed not only by the utilities themselves but also by the entire Big Business community. The history of the Tennessee Valley Authority affords eloquent testimony to the effectiveness of this opposition. TVA had its origin in the government's need for nitrates during World War I. A dam, hydroelectric

Reprinted from Chapters 6 and 7 ("The Absorption of Surplus: Civilian Government" and ". . .: Militarism and Imperialism") of *Monopoly Capital* by Paul A. Baran and Paul M. Sweezy, by permission of Monthly Review Press. Copyright © 1966 by Paul M. Sweezy. Footnotes have been renumbered and some have been omitted.

generating facilities, and a nitrate plant were built at Muscle Shoals, Alabama, to satisfy strictly military requirements. During the 1920's, a campaign to turn Muscle Shoals into a broad river-valley development scheme was led by Senator Norris of Nebraska; but, in this period of capitalist prosperity, nothing came of it, and even the original investment was allowed to deteriorate in idleness. It was only during the "Hundred Days" after Roosevelt's inauguration in 1933—a period of near-panic for the moneyed oligarchy—that Norris's determined efforts were crowned with success. And the oligarchs have been regretting their moment of weakness ever since. From their point of view, the trouble with TVA was that it was a tremendous success. It gave the American people their first glimpse of what can be achieved by intelligent planning under a governmental authority equipped with the powers necessary to carry out a rational program. To cite only one of its achievements, by the later 1950's a typical household in the TVA area was paying only half as much for its electricity and consuming twice as much as the national average. And on a worldwide scale, TVA had become a symbol of the New Deal, a light showing others the way to democratic progress. Under these circumstances, the oligarchy did not dare destroy TVA outright. Instead, it organized a long-range campaign of unremitting criticism and harassment destined to hedge TVA in, curtail its functions, force it to conform to the norms of capitalist enterprise. And this campaign has achieved considerable successes: TVA has never been allowed to realize anything like its full potential. Nevertheless, its popularity with the people of the seven-state area in which it operates has protected it from being gutted and perverted from its original aims. The greatest triumph of the anti-TVA campaign, therefore, has been its total success in keeping the principle of the multipurpose river-valley authority from being applied to any of the other numerous river valleys of the United States where it could so richly further the people's welfare. The need for more TVA's is easily demonstrable to any rational person; during the 1930's and later, expanded government outlays on river-valley development would frequently have made excellent sense as a partial solution to the problem of inadequate surplus absorption. But what Marx called the Furies of private interest, having been thoroughly aroused, easily repelled any further encroachment on their sacred domain.[1]

Public housing, potentially a vast field for welfare spending, is another activity which encroaches upon the realm of private enter-

[1] In the light of this record, there is something peculiarly repulsive about the way the oligarchy repeatedly cites TVA as proof of the United States' devotion to progressive goals in the underdeveloped countries of the world. Secretary of State Rusk, seeking to persuade Latin American governments to join in destroying the historic achievements of the Cuban Revolution, told the Punta del Este meeting of foreign ministers in January, 1962: "Years of thought and work and debate were required to prepare America for the necessary steps of self-help and social reform. I remember well the bitter resistance before Franklin D. Roosevelt was able to win support for the Tennessee Valley Authority, that immense network of dams and power stations and fertilizer factories and agricultural extension offices which has wrought such miraculous changes in our South. But a succession of progressive leaders, determined to bring about social change within a framework of political consent, carried through an alliance for progress' within the United States." (*New York Times,* January 26, 1962.) If TVA has wrought such miracles, why has this great "succession of progressive leaders" never succeeded in getting even one more river-valley authority established? (It is interesting that the Secretary of State, in this meeting of North, Central, and South American countries, apparently saw nothing inappropriate in referring to the United States simply as "America.")

prise. A really effective low-cost housing program would necessarily call for extensive building in open spaces, which abound in most cities in the United States. But this is precisely what the powerful urban real-estate interests are against. On the rock of this opposition, all attempts to launch a serious attack on the twin problems of insufficient and inadequate housing have foundered. . . .

River-valley development and public housing are but two examples of government activities which trespass upon the territory of private interests. In all such cases, since private interests wield political power, the limits of government spending are narrowly set and have nothing to do with social needs— no matter how shamefully obvious. But it is not only where there is competition with commercial enterprise that such limits are imposed: the same thing happens in areas like education and health where direct competition is either nonexistent or of relatively minor importance. Here too the opposition of private interests to increased government spending is soon aroused; and here too the amounts actually spent bear no relation to demonstrable social need. . . .

. . . How can it happen that even modest increases in federal aid to education are so often turned down?

The answer, in a nutshell, is that the educational system, as at present constituted, is a crucial element in the constellation of privileges and prerogatives of which the moneyed oligarchy is the chief beneficiary. This is true in a triple sense.

First, the educational system provides the oligarchy with the quality and quantity of educational services which its members want for themselves and their offspring. There is no shortage of expensive private schools and colleges for the sons and daughters of the well-to-do. Nor are the public schools of the exclusive suburbs and exurbs starved of funds, like the schools which serve the lower-middle and working classes in the cities and the countryside. The educational system, in other words, is not a homogeneous whole. It consists of two parts, one for the oligarchy and one for the rest of the population. The part which caters to the oligarchy is amply financed. It is a privilege and a badge of social position to go through it. And the very fact that it serves only a small part of the population is precisely its most precious and jealously guarded feature. This is why any attempt to generalize its benefits is bound to be stubbornly fought by the oligarchy. This is also perhaps the most basic reason for the strength of the opposition to expanded programs of federal aid to education.

Second—the other side of the same coin—that part of the educational system which is designed for the vast majority of young people must be inferior and must turn out human material fitted for the lowly work and social positions which society reserves for them. This aim of course cannot be achieved directly. The egalitarianism of capitalist ideology is one of its strengths, not to be lightly discarded. People are taught from earliest childhood and by all conceivable means that everyone has an equal opportunity, and that the inequalities which stare them in the face are the result not of unjust institutions but of their own superior or inferior natural endowments. It would contradict this teaching to set up, in the manner of European class-divided societies, two distinct educational systems, one for the oligarchy and one for the masses. The desired result must be sought indirectly, by providing amply for that part of the educational system which serves the oligarchy while financially starving that part which serves the lower-middle and working classes. This ensures the inequality of education so vitally necessary to buttress the general inequality which is the heart and core of the whole system. No special arrangements are needed, however, to achieve this force-feeding of one part of the educational system and starving of the other. The private schools and colleges are in any case well provided for, and the established system of local control and financing for public schools automatically results in extremely unequal treatment for the suburban and ex-urban public schools in contrast to the urban and rural schools. What is crucial is to pre-vent this delicate balance from being upset by massive federal invasion, with the enormous taxing and spending powers of the national government being used to implement the educational reformers' age-old ideal of equal and excellent educational opportunity for all. Here we have a second compelling reason for the oligarchy to keep government spending to a minimum in an area which reason tells us could beneficially absorb a large proportion of society's surplus product.

The third sense in which the educational system supports the existing class structure is complementary to the first two. Every viable class society must provide a method by which brains and talent from the lower classes can be selected, used by, and integrated into the upper classes. In Western feudal society, the Catholic church provided the necessary mechanism. Competitive capitalism made it possible for able and aggressive lower-class boys to ascend a purely economic ladder into the oligarchy. Monopoly capitalism has effectively blocked this channel of upward mobility: it is now rarely possible to start a small business and build it up into a big one. A substitute mechanism has been found in the educational system. Through low-tuition state universities, scholarships, loans, and the like, boys and girls who are really able and ambitious (desirous of success, as society defines it) can move up from the inferior part of the educational system. Accepted into the better preparatory schools, colleges, and universities, they are given the same training and conditioning as upper-class young people. From there the road leads through the corporate apparatus or the professions into integration in the upper-middle, and occasionally the higher, strata of society. The superficial observer, having heard the slogans about equal opportunity, may see evidence here that the educational system works to undermine the class structure. Nothing could be further from the truth. The ideal of equal opportunity for all could be realized only by abolition of the special privileges of the upper classes, not by making these privileges available to a select group from the lower classes. This simply strengthens the class structure by infusing new blood into the upper classes and depriving the lower classes of their natural leaders. And these are the objectives that are actually served by currently fashionable educational reforms, including such modest increases in federal aid as the oligarchy is prepared to put up with. Any serious attempt to meet the real educational needs of a modern technologically and scientifically advanced society would necessitate a totally different approach—including a commitment of resources on a scale that no dominant oligarchy intent on preserving its own narrow privileges would even dream of.

It would be possible to run through the gamut of civilian spending objects and show how in case after case the private interests of the oligarchy stand in stark opposition to the satisfaction of social needs. Real competition with private enterprise cannot be tolerated, no matter how incompetent and inadequate its performance may be; undermining of class privileges or of the stability of the class structure must be resisted at any cost. And almost all types of civilian spending involve one or both of these threats. There is just one major exception to this generalization in the United States today, and it is very much the type of exception which proves the rule: government spending on highways.

There is no need here to detail the importance of the automobile to the American economy. We need only say that the main business of several of the largest and most profitable corporations is the production of motor vehicles; the petroleum industry, with some ten corporations having assets of more than a billion dollars, makes most of its profits from the sale of gasoline for use in motor vehicles; several other major monopolistic industries (rubber, steel, glass) are crucially dependent on sales to automobile makers or users; more than a quarter of a million persons are employed in the repair and servicing of automobiles; and countless other businesses and jobs (trucking, motels, resorts, etc.) owe their existence, directly or indirectly, to the motor vehicle. This complex

of private interests clustering around one product has no equal elsewhere in the economy—or in the world. And the whole complex, of course, is completely dependent on the public provision of roads and highways. It is thus only natural that there should be tremendous pressure for continuous expansion of government spending on highways. Counterpressures from private interests do exist—notably from the railroads, hard hit by the growth of highway transportation, but the railroads have been no match for the automobile complex. Government spending on highways has soared; limitations posed by state and local finances have been overcome by increasingly liberal federal grants-in-aid. And today highways are second only to education as an object of civilian government spending.[2]

This fact does not in itself prove that spending on highways has gone beyond any rational conception of social need. What does prove it—dramatically and overwhelmingly—is the frightful havoc which has been wreaked on American society by the cancerous growth of the automobile complex, a growth which would have been impossible if government spending for the required highways had been limited and curtailed as the oligarchy has limited and curtailed spending for other civilian purposes. Cities have been transformed into nightmares of congestion; their atmosphere is fouled by disease-bearing pollutants; vast areas of good urban and rural land are turned into concrete strips and asphalt fields; peaceful communities and neighborhoods are desecrated by the roar and stench of cars and trucks hurtling past; railroads, which can move goods and passengers efficiently and unobtrusively, lose traffic and correspondingly raise rates in a vicious circle which threatens the very exis-

[2]In 1957, total government purchases of goods and services for civilian purposes came to $40.4 billion. Of this $13.6 or 33.7 per cent went for education and $7.2 billion or 17.8 per cent for highways—the two items together accounting for more than half of civilian government spending. See F. M. Bator, *The Question of Government Spending*, pp. 26–29.

tence of commuter service for our biggest cities; urban rapid-transit systems are at once starved and choked, so that getting around the downtown area of New York, Chicago, and dozens of other metropolises becomes an ordeal to which only the necessitous or the foolhardy will submit. And the usual remedy for this increasingly frightful and frightening state of affairs? More highways, more streets, more garages, more parking areas—more of the same poison that is already threatening the very life of an increasing urbanized civilization. And all this is made possible by lavish grants of public funds, eagerly sought and approved by an oligarchy of wealth which fights tooth and nail against every extension of those public services which would benefit the great body of their fellow citizens. Nowhere is the madness of American monopoly capitalism more manifest, or more hopelessly incurable.

The New Deal managed to push government spending up by more than 70 per cent, but this was nowhere near enough to bring the economy to a level at which human and material resources were fully employed. Resistance of the oligarchy to further expansion in civilian spending hardened and held with unemployment still well above 15 per cent of the labor force. By 1939 it was becoming increasingly clear that liberal reform had sadly failed to rescue United States monopoly capitalism from its own self-destructive tendencies. As Roosevelt's second term approached its end, a profound sense of frustration and uneasiness crept over the country.

Then came the war, and with it salvation. Government spending soared and unemployment plummeted. At the end of the war, to be sure, arms spending was cut back sharply; but owing to the backlog of civilian demand built up during the war (compounded of supply shortages and a massive accumulation of liquid savings), the downturn associated with this cutback was relatively mild and brief and soon gave way to an inflationary reconversion boom. And the boom was still going strong when the Cold War began in earnest. Military spending reached its postwar low in 1947, turned up in 1948, received a tremendous boost from the Korean War (1950–1953), declined moderately during the next two years, and then in 1956 began the slow climb which continued, with a slight interruption in 1960, into the 1960's. As a percentage of GNP, the variations of military spending have followed a similar pattern, except that there was very little change from 1955 to 1961.

... The difference between the deep stagnation of the 1930's and the relative prosperity of the 1950's is fully accounted for by the vast military outlays of the 1950's. In 1939, for example, 17.2 per cent of the labor force was unemployed and about 1.4 per cent of the remainder may be presumed to have been employed producing goods and services for the military. A good 18 per cent of the labor force, in other words, was either unemployed or dependent for jobs on military spending. In 1961 (like 1939, a year of recovery from a cyclical recession), the comparable figures were 6.7 per cent unemployed and 9.4 per cent dependent on military spending, a total of some 16 per cent. It would be possible to elaborate and refine these calculations, but there is no reason to think that doing so would affect the general conclusion: the percentage of the labor force either unemployed or dependent on military spending was much the same in 1961 as in 1939. From which it follows that if the military budget were reduced to 1939 proportions, unemployment would also revert to 1939 proportions.

Why has the oligarchy, which keeps such a tight rein on civilian spending, become in the last two decades so openhanded with the military? ...

[In their next nine pages, which are omitted here, Baran and Sweezy argue that the United States has a need for a large and expanding military budget, and that this need cannot be explained merely as the response to the USSR.]

The American oligarchy's need for a huge military machine must be sought elsewhere than in a nonexistent threat of Soviet aggression. Once we recognize this and free our minds of the cant and confusion generated by the oligarchy's ideological and propagandistic distortions, we shall soon discover what we are looking for: the same implacable hatred of socialism, the same determination to destroy it, that has dominated the leading nations of the capitalist world from the time the Bolsheviks seized power in November 1917. The central purpose has always been the same: to prevent the expansion of socialism, to compress it into as small an area as possible, and ultimately to wipe it off the face of the earth. What has changed with changing conditions are the methods and strategies used to achieve these unchanging goals. . . .

We cannot leave this subject of the need for military strength without inquiring into the causes of capitalist hostility to the existence of a rival world socialist system. If, as some people seem to think, this hostility is based largely on irrational prejudices and fears, like the sedulously cultivated belief in Soviet aggressiveness, then there would seem to be at least a chance that in time more rational views might come to prevail. In that case, peaceful coexistence and disarmament could be looked upon not as propaganda slogans in the struggle between the two systems but as realizable goals. On the other hand, if the prejudices and fears are, as so often happens, simply masks for deep-rooted interests, then we would have to assess the outlook differently.

First, we must dispose of one very common argument purporting to prove that the spread of socialism is a mortal threat to the existence of the capitalist system. It is often said that capitalism cannot exist without foreign trade and that every advance of socialism means a constriction of capitalism's trading area. Hence, the argument continues, for the leading capitalist countries, even if they are not threatened by powerful internal socialist movements, the struggle against socialism is quite literally a struggle for survival. Put in this form, the reasoning from capitalist interests involves a non sequi-

tur. It is true that capitalism is inconceivable without foreign trade, but it is not true that socialist countries are unwilling or unable to trade with capitalist countries. Hence the spread of socialism, taken by itself, does not imply any reduction of the trading area open to the capitalist countries. One can even go further. Bourgeois economists never tire of repeating that the more industrially developed a country is, the greater its potential as a trading partner. Since underdeveloped countries industrialize more rapidly under socialism than under capitalism, the leading capitalist countries, on this argument, should welcome the spread of socialism in the underdeveloped parts of the capitalist world. That they do not but instead resist it tooth and nail must be explained on other grounds.

The problem is in reality much more complex and can only be fruitfully posed in quite different terms. Capitalist governments do not, in general, trade with each other. Most trade in the capitalist world is carried on by private enterprises, mainly by large corporations. What these corporations are interested in is not trade as such but profits: the reason they and the governments they control are opposed to the spread of socialism is not that it necessarily reduces their chances of importing or exporting (though of course it may), but that it does necessarily reduce their opportunities to profit from doing business with and in the newly socialized area. And when account is taken of the fact that for corporations in the leading capitalist countries, profit rates from doing business with and in the less developed and underdeveloped countries are generally higher than domestic profit rates, the reason for the vehemence of opposition to the spread of socialism in precisely those areas will be appreciated.

We advisedly use the general term "doing business with and in" rather than the more limited "buying from and selling to." The international relationships and interests of the typical giant corporation today are likely to be diverse and extremely complex, much more so than mere exporting or importing. There is perhaps no better way to make this clear than by summarizing the worldwide scope and character of what is unquestionably the leading United States "multinational corporation"—Standard Oil of New Jersey. The facts and figures which follow are taken from official publications of the company.

In terms of dollar assets, Jersey Standard is the largest industrial corporation in the United States, the total at the end of 1962 amounting to $11,488 million. Aggregate revenues for the same year were $10,567 million and net income (profit) $841 million. It is only when these figures are broken down geographically, however, that the crucial importance of foreign operations becomes clear. As of the end of 1958, the percentage distribution of assets and profits by regions were as follows:

	Assets	Profits
United States and Canada	67	34
Latin America	20	39
Eastern Hemisphere	13	27
Total	100	100

While two-thirds of Jersey's assets were located in North America, only one-third of its profits came from that region. Or to put the point differently, Jersey's foreign investments were half as large as its domestic investments but its foreign profits were twice as large as its domestic profits. The indicated profit rate abroad is thus four times the domestic rate.

That Jersey's operations are truly worldwide can be gathered from the facts that in 1962 the company sold its products in more than a hundred countries and owned 50 per cent or more of the stock in 275 subsidiaries in 52 countries. . . . Summarizing by regions, we find that Jersey had 114 subsidiaries in the United States and Canada, 77 in Europe, 43 in Latin America, 14 in Asia, 9 in Africa, and 18 elsewhere.

The tremendous variety and scope of Jersey's foreign operations might lead one to suppose that over the years the company has been a large and consistent exporter of capital. Nothing could be further from the truth. Apart from a small initial export of capital many years ago, the expansion of Jersey's

foreign assets has been financed from the profits of its foreign operations. Moreover, so great have been these foreign profits that after all foreign expansion needs have been taken care of, there have still been huge sums left over for remittance to the parent company in the United States. . . .

Up to World War II, it would have been correct to treat Standard Oil as a sort of exception—a very important one, to be sure, exercising tremendous, and at times even decisive, influence on United States world policy. Nevertheless in the multinational scope and magnitude of its operations not only was it far ahead of all the others; there were only a handful which could be said to be developing along the same lines. Many United States corporations of course had large interests in import and export trade, and quite a few had foreign branches or subsidiaries. In neither respect, however, was the situation much different in 1946 from what it had been in 1929. Indeed, direct foreign investments of United States corporations actually declined from $7.5 billion to $7.2 billion, or by 4 per cent, between these two dates. Most of the giant corporations which dominated the American economy in those years were, in the words of *Business Week*, "domestically oriented enterprises with international operations" and not, like Standard Oil, "truly world oriented corporations."

A big change took place during the next decade and a half. To quote *Business Week* again, "In industry after industry, U.S. companies found that their overseas earnings were soaring, and that their return on investment abroad was frequently much higher than in the U.S. As earnings abroad began to rise, profit margins from domestic operations started to shrink. . . . This is the combination that forced development of the multinational company." As a result, of course, foreign direct investments of American corporations shot up—from $7.2 billion in 1946 to $40.6 billion in 1963, a more than fivefold increase in the years since World War II. Parallel to this growth in foreign investments has gone an increase in the sales and profits of foreign branches and subsidiaries. In manufacturing (excluding petroleum and mining), sales of such affiliates amounted to $ 18.3 billion in 1957 (the first year for which figures are available) and to $28.1 billion in 1962, an increase of 54 per cent in six years. ...

So much for the American oligarchy's *need* for a military establishment. We must next examine the effect of satisfying this need on the private interests of the members of the oligarchy, and on the stability and cohesiveness of the country's class structure.

It was argued at some length ... that most governmental activities designed to satisfy collective needs involve either competition with private interests or injury to the class position and privileges of the oligarchy, and that for these reasons opposition is quickly aroused and rapidly reinforced as these activities are extended. The result is that roadblocks are encountered long before socially rational and desirable goals have been attained. How is it with government activities in the military sphere?

To begin with, it is obvious that the building up of a gigantic military establishment neither creates nor involves competition with private enterprise. There are no private military establishments with a vested interest in keeping the government out of their preserves and the military plays the role of an ideal customer for private business, spending billions of dollars annually on terms that are most favorable to the sellers. Since a large part of the required capital equipment has no alternative use, its cost is commonly included in the price of the end product. The business of producing arms is therefore virtually risk-free, in spite of which the allowable profit rates include a generous margin for a mythical risk factor. And the fact that military procurement officers often look forward to lucrative employment with arms manufacturers after retirement from the service hardly makes for strictness in their dealing with suppliers.

The results of this system were well illustrated in testimony before the Senate Investigations Subcommittee dealing with the profitability of the Boeing Company, one of the country's largest airplane manufacturers:

Mr. Nunnally [staff accountant] testified that Boeing's government contracts for work on the Bomarc, B-52 and B-54 bombers, KC-135 tanker and other projects had totaled $ 11,818,900,000 since 1951. He said the company's costs on the work had totaled $ 10,911,200,000, leaving gross profits of $907,700,000.

He said a year-by-year measurement of the profits against the company's net investment (net worth plus all borrowed capital) showed profit percentages ranging from 108.6 per cent in 1953 to 36 per cent in 1951 and 1960.

Mr. Nunnally said Boeing's profit as measured by the company's net worth averaged 74.38 per cent before payment of taxes and 35.68 per cent after taxes on its government contracts and 19.05 per cent after taxes on its combined government and commercial business.

He said this was "almost double" the 10.73 per cent average net profit for all manufacturing industries in the United States computed by government regulatory agencies against net worth in the same years.

Overall data on the profitability of arms production have never, to our knowledge, been compiled, and it is possible that Boeing is a specially favored corporation. Be that as it may, there is no doubt that supplying the military is universally regarded as good business: all corporations, big and little, bid for as large a share as they can get. The private interests of the oligarchy, far from generating opposition to military spending, encourage its continuous expansion.

The class interests of the oligarchy work in the same direction. Whereas massive government spending for education and welfare tends to undermine its privileged position, the opposite is true of military spending. The

reason is that militarization fosters all the reactionary and irrational forces in society, and
inhibits or kills everything progressive and
humane. Blind respect is engendered for authority; attitudes of docility and conformity
are taught and enforced; dissent is treated as
unpatriotic or even treasonable. In such an
atmosphere, the oligarchy feels that its moral
authority and material position are secure.
Veblen, more than any other social scientist,
appreciated the importance of this social
function of militarism:

*The largest and most promising factor of
cultural discipline—most promising as a cor-
rective of iconoclastic vagaries—over which
business principles rule is national politics.
... Business interests urge an aggressive national policy and businessmen direct it. Such
a policy is warlike as well as patriotic. The
direct cultural value of a warlike business
policy is unequivocal. It makes for a conservative animus on the part of the populace.
During wartime, and within the military organization at all times, civil rights are in abeyance; and the more war and armaments the
more abeyance. Military training is a training
in ceremonial precedence, arbitrary command, and unquestioning obedience.... The
more consistent and the more comprehensive this training, the more effectually will
the members of the community be trained
into habits of subordination and away from
that growing propensity to make light of personal authority which is the chief infirmity of
democracy. This applies first and most decid-
edly, of course, to the soldiery, but it applies
only in less degree to the rest of the population. They learn to think in warlike terms of
rank, authority, and subordination, and to
grow progressively more patient of en-
croachments on their civil rights.... Habitua-
tion to a warlike, predatory scheme of life is
the strongest disciplinary factor that can be
brought to counteract the vulgarization of
modern life wrought by peaceful industry
and the machine process, and to rehabilitate
the decaying sense of status and differential*

*dignity. Warfare, with the stress on subordi-
nation and mastery and the insistence on
gradations of dignity and honor incident to a
militant organization, has always proved an
effective school in barbarian methods of
thought.*

These generalizations, presumably based
at least in part on Veblen's observations during the Spanish-American War, have been all
too convincingly confirmed by the events of
the past two decades when what President
Eisenhower, in his poignant Farewell Address, called the military-industrial complex
was rising to dominance in American life.
Civil liberties indeed fell into abeyance, and
dissent from global policies of imperialism
and antisocialism became identified with
communism and hence with treason to the
nation.

It would be misleading to leave the impression that only the oligarchy has favored the
steady increase in military spending during
these years. If one assumes the permanence
of monopoly capitalism, with its proved incapacity to make rational use for peaceful and
humane ends of its enormous productive potential, one must decide whether one prefers
the mass unemployment and hopelessness
characteristic of the Great Depression or the
relative job security and material well-being
provided by the huge military budgets of the
1940's and 1950's. Since most Americans,
workers included, still do assume without
question the permanence of the system, it is
only natural that they should prefer the situation which is personally and privately more
advantageous. And in order to rationalize
this preference, they have accepted the official ideology of anticommunism which appears to justify an unlimited expansion of the
military establishment as essential to national survival.

Against this background it is easy to understand why there has been so little political
opposition in recent years to expanding military budgets. In a Congress normally characterized by fierce fighting among lobbies and

pressure groups, a majestic unanimity emerges as soon as a request is made for additional billions for the armed services, with congressmen vying with one another for the honor of proposing the largest increases.

The people's representatives in their enthusiasm even pay little attention to the strictly military rationality of how the money is spent. "My own experience in the Senate," says William Proxmire, Democratic senator from Wisconsin, "has shown me the painful inability of our democracy to resist the momentum of excessive spending and waste that accompanies our vast military establishment." And he gives a graphic illustration, the Senate's reaction to strong urging by Secretary of Defense McNamara against spending more on B-52 and B-58 bombers than the President had already requested:

Only three senators joined me in voting for my amendment, which would have eliminated this appropriation. In the Senate debate, we had made an overwhelming case against spending more than half a billion dollars in this way. Yet some 95 per cent of the senators voting that day rejected the logic of the case, rejected the advice of the president, the secretary of defense and his aides, and voted to appropriate the funds. This was more money than was spent in that year by the federal government for medical research; more than was spent for all federal housing programs; more than the budgets allocated to the U.S. Forest Service, the National Park Service, and the Fish and Wildlife Service combined.[3]

No wonder Senator Proxmire concludes that "as a rationalization for federal expenditure, national defense has few peers. Programs that wouldn't get a second look from Congress flit through if they are attached to an armed forces appropriation." The views of Proxmire, reputed to be one of the more

liberal members of the Senate, might be discounted as likely to be exaggerated. This would hardly apply to Senator Richard B. Russell of Georgia, a conservative southerner, chairman of the Senate Armed Services Committee, and often described as the most powerful individual in the Congress. Here is Senator Russell in a colloquy on the Senate floor with Senator Proxmire:

There is something about preparing for destruction that causes men to be more careless in spending money than they would be if they were building for constructive purposes. Why that is so I do not know; but I have observed, over a period of almost thirty years in the Senate, that there is something about buying arms with which to kill, to destroy, to wipe out cities, and to obliterate great transportation systems which causes men not to reckon the dollar cost as closely as they do when they think about proper housing and the care of the health of human beings.[4]

A more devastating condemnation of a whole social order would be hard to imagine. Nor, as we have seen, are the reasons so mysterious as Senator Russell seems to think. The Cold War, the well-known Harvard economist Sumner Slichter explained in 1949, "increases the demand for goods, helps sustain a high level of employment, accelerates technical progress and thus helps the country to raise its standard of living. . . . So we may thank the Russians for helping make capitalism in the United States work better than ever." And a few months later *U.S. News & World Report,* published by the ultraconservative David Lawrence, spelled out the same idea with brutal candor:

Government planners figure they have found the magic formula for almost endless good times. . . . Cold War is the catalyst. Cold War is an automatic pump primer. Turn a spigot, the public clamors for more arms

---

[3]"Spendthrifts for Defense," *The Nation* (Aug. 25, 1962), p. 63.

[4]*Ibid.,* pp. 65–66.

spending. Turn another, the clamor ceases. Truman confidence, cockiness, is based on this "Truman formula." Truman era of good times, President is told, can run much beyond 1952. Cold War demands, if fully exploited, are almost limitless.

U.S. News & World Report was still saying the same thing in 1954. Following news that the United States had exploded the world's first hydrogen bomb, it commented: "What H-bomb means to business. A long period . . . of big orders. In the years ahead, the effects of the new bomb will keep on increasing. As one appraiser put it: 'The H-bomb has blown depression-thinking out the window.'"

Here at last monopoly capitalism had seemingly found the answer to the "on what" question: On what could the government spend enough to keep the system from sinking into the mire of stagnation? On arms, more arms, and ever more arms.

Yet it somehow has not worked out quite this way. The Cold War intensified; the military budget, after a dip at the end of the Korean War, resumed its upward trend. But a sort of creeping stagnation set in all the same.

Why was the military budget not expanded still further? If $50 billion is not enough, why not $60 billion? The Congress, we know, has shown itself ready to vote whatever military appropriations are asked of it, and more. Why did the president not gear his requests to the requirements of a prosperous economy? Why were growth rates allowed to lag, profit margins to sag, unemployment to mount? Evidently, even the amount of military spending is not a perfectly free variable through manipulation of which the leaders of the oligarchy can maintain the right head of steam in the economic engine. Here too, it seems, obstacles and contradictions are in operation. . . .

The Politics of Accommodation

8   Agriculture: The New Feudalism

Theodore J. Lowi

Agriculture is that field of American government where the distinction between public and private has come closest to being completely eliminated. This has been accomplished not by public expropriation of private domain—as would be true of the nationalization that Americans fear—but by private expropriation of public authority. That is the feudal pattern: fusion of all statuses and functions and governing through rigid but personalized fealties. In modern dress, that was the corporativistic way, which has been recently revived in a slightly revised form by the French Right. It is also the pluralist way, the way of the so-called Left in the United States. However, the best definition is one which puts the reader in the very presence of the thing.

THE PRESENT ESTATE
OF AGRICULTURE

On December 18, 1963, President Johnson summoned a conference of the leaders of major agriculture interests and interest groups. These representatives were asked to formulate a program by which they and their supporters could be served and regulated. The president's call for an agriculture congress was followed on January 31 with a

Reprinted from *The End of Liberalism* by Theodore J. Lowi. By permission of W. W. Norton & Company, Inc. Copyright © 1969 by W. W. Norton & Company, Inc.

Farm Message. In the message the president proposed the establishment of a bipartisan commission to investigate the concentration of power in the food industry and "how this greatly increased concentration of power is affecting farmers, handlers and consumers. . . ." Such investigations are always popular in farm states in helping spread the blame for high prices despite large subsidies. As one administration spokesman explained, "We're not making a whipping boy out of anybody, but we're receiving repeated charges that certain retailers are setting market prices and it is clear that some chains do have large concentrations of market power." In the same message the president also called for new legislation to strengthen farmer cooperatives, to encourage their expansion through merger and acquisition, and to provide them with further exemptions from the antitrust laws.

The summoning of an agriculture congress was a call to agriculture to decide for itself what it wants from government. The president's attack in his Farm Message on concentration of market power, coupled with his proposals for expanded and stronger farm cooperatives, was obviously not an attack so much on concentration itself as on the intervention of nonagricultural power into strictly agricultural affairs.

That agricultural affairs should be handled strictly within the agricultural community is a basic political principle established before the turn of the century and maintained since then without serious reexamination. As a result, agriculture has become neither public nor private enterprise. It is a system of self-government in which each leading interest controls a segment of agriculture through a delegation of national sovereignty. Agriculture has emerged as a largely self-governing federal estate within the federal structure of the United States.

President Johnson recognized these facts within three weeks of his accession when he summoned the conference of agricultural leaders. The resulting concession to agriculture's self-government was the wheat-cotton bill of 1964. Because cotton supports were too high, the cotton interests wrote a bill providing for a subsidy to mills of six to eight cents a pound in order to keep them competitive with foreign cotton and domestic rayon without touching the price supports. On the other hand, wheat supports were too low because wheat farmers in the 1963 referendum had overwhelmingly rejected President Kennedy's plan to provide some federal regulation along with supports. The wheat section of the new act called for a program whereby wheat farmers would voluntarily comply with acreage reduction for subsidies of up to seventy cents a bushel but without the federal supply regulations. The press called this a major legislative victory for Mr. Johnson. But the victory really belonged to organized cotton and wheat and testified to the total acceptance by the president, press, and public of the principle that private agriculture interests alone govern agriculture. It is a sturdy principle; its inheritance by President Johnson was through a line unbroken by personality or party in the White House. For example, in one of President Kennedy's earliest major program messages to Congress, on March 16, 1961, he proposed:

The Soil Conservation and Domestic Allotment Act . . . should be amended to provide for the establishment of national farmer advisory committees for every commodity or group of related commodities for which a new supply adjustment program is planned [as proposed in the same message]. Mem-

bers of the committees would be elected by the producers of the commodities involved or their appropriate representatives. In consultation with the Secretary of Agriculture, they could be charged with the responsibility for considering and recommending individual commodity programs. . . .

In order to insure effective farmer participation in the administration of farm programs on the local level, the Secretary of Agriculture is directed to revitalize the county and local farmer committee system and to recommend such amendments as may be necessary to safeguard such farmer participation.

ORIGINS IN ECONOMICS AND TACTICS

The reasons for agricultural self-government are deep-rooted, and the lessons to be drawn from it are vital. For a century agriculture has been out of joint with American economic development. Occasional fat years have only created unreal expectations, making the more typical lean years less bearable. As industries concentrated, discovered the economics of scale and how to control their markets, agriculture remained decentralized and subject to the market. As industries showed increasing capacity to absorb technology and to use it to increase profit, agriculture took on technology only with net debt. Profit from increased productivity was either neutralized with lower prices or absorbed by the processing, distributing, and transporting industries interposed between agriculture and its markets. After the Civil War America's largest and most basic industry was never for long out of trouble. At the beginning of World War I, for example, net farm income was $3.6 billion. By 1919, it was $9.3 billion; but two years later it was back down to $3.7 billion. It rose slowly to $6.1 billion in 1920–1930 and had fallen off to $1.9 billion by 1932. At a higher level, these fluctuations have beset agriculture since World War II as well. The only things stable about agriculture have been (1) its declining relative importance in the census and in the economy, (2) the reverence it enjoys in the American mythology, and (3) the political power it possesses despite (1) and largely because of (2).

Organized agriculture was early to discover the value of political power as a counterweight to industrial wealth. The land grant and homesteading acts were followed by governmental services in research, quarantine, and education. But continuing distress despite governmental support led to bolder demands. First the movement was for a redistribution of wealth and power toward agriculture. As a debtor class, farmers saw inflation as the solution; William Jennings Bryan was one of many spokesmen for cheaper money and easier credit. Farmers also sought government regulation of those economic forces they had identified as the causes of their problems. The monopolies, the railroads, the grain merchants and other processors, the banks, and the brokers were to be deprived of market power by dissolution or by severe restraints upon the use of that power. Finally farmers sought solutions by emulating the business system: almost simultaneously they hit upon the cooperative to restrain domestic trade, and international dumping over high tariff walls to restrain international trade.

All these mechanisms failed the farmers. The blunderbuss—inflation of the whole economy—failed both for want of enough legislation and because more and more of the national debt was held by the industrial rich. Regulation of industry failed for want of will and power to administer it; a governing elite opposed to inflating the business system could not be expected to dismantle it. International dumping never was given the test; Coolidge and Hoover vetoed the Smoot-Hawley tariff bills that would "make the tariff work for agriculture." The cooperative movement did not fail; it simply did not succeed on a large enough scale.

By a process of elimination, organized agriculture turned then to another way: *the regulation of itself.* In the Democratic Party of 1930 and the Democratic Party philosophy, to be called the New Deal, agriculture found

an eager handmaiden. And in the modest government assistance programs of the pre-New Deal period the appropriate instrumentalities and precedents were found. After the 1932 election all that remained was to ratify in legislation the agreements already reached. The system created then has remained with only a few marginal additions and alterations. Bitter political conflicts within the agriculture community have been fought out over the margins, but on the system itself there is almost total consensus among the knowledgeable minority and total apathy and ignorance among the nonagricultural majority.

The principle of self-regulation might have taken several forms, the most likely one being a national system of farm representation within a farmer's type of NRA. Instead, a more elaborate and complicated system of "cooperation" or local self-government developed largely for constitutional reasons. There was already experience with local districts in the Extension Service that had become a proven way for the federal government to get around the special constitutional problem of regulating agriculture. Agriculture was the most "local" of the manufactures the government was attempting to reach. The appearance if not the reality of decentralizing federal programs through local, farmer-elected committees helped to avoid straining the interstate commerce clause and to escape the political charge of regimentation.

Eventually, many separate programs were created within the government-agriculture complex. Each constituted a system in and of itself. The programs were independently administered and often had conflicting results. But underneath all the complexity of parity, forestry, conservation, electrification, education, extension, and credit there was a simple principle: it amounted to the loan of governmental sovereignty to the leadership of a private sector to accomplish what other sectors could accomplish privately. Agriculture was so decentralized and dispersed that private, voluntary agreements to manipulate markets were obviously too difficult to reach and impossible to sustain. Therefore it was not going to be possible to emulate business. So, in a travesty of the Declaration of Independence, to secure these rights governments were instituted among farmers. Administrative agencies were created to facilitate agreements, and, once reached, public authority was expected to be employed where necessary to sustain them.

THE SYSTEM: BUILDING ON LOCAL COMMITTEES

The prototype, the Federal Extension Service, is "cooperative" in the sense that it shares the expense of farm improvement with the states, the land-grant colleges, the county governments, and the local associations of farmers. The county agent is actually employed by the local associations, which are required by law. In the formative years, the aid of local chambers of commerce was enlisted; the local association was the "farm bureau" of the chamber. In order to coordinate local activities and to make more effective claims for additional outside assistance, these farm bureaus were organized into state farm bureau federations. The American Farm Bureau Federation, formed at the Agriculture College of Cornell University in 1919, was the offshoot. A filial relationship between farm bureau, land-grant college, and the Extension Service continues to this day. This transformation of an administrative arrangement into a political system has been repeated in almost all agriculture programs since that time. The Extension Service exercises few sanctions over the states and colleges, which in turn leave the localities alone. All are quick to scream "federal encroachment!" at the mere suggestion that the Department of Agriculture should increase supervision or investigation, or that it should attempt to coordinate extension programs with other federal activities.

As other agriculture programs came along, most were similarly organized. Any inconsistency of purpose or impact among programs has been treated as nonexistent or beyond the jurisdiction of any one agency. The Soil Conservation Service operates through its soil conservation districts, of which there were 2,936 in 1963, involving 96 per cent of the nation's farms. These districts are actually considered units of local government, and each is in fact controlled by its own farmer-elected committee, which is not to be confused with other farmer associations or committees. Agreements between the farmer and the Service for acre-by-acre soil surveys, for assistance in instituting soil-conserving practices, and for improving productivity are actually made between the farmer and the district committee. Enforcement of the agreements is handled also by the district committee.

Additional aid to the farmer channels through the cooperatives, which are in turn controlled by farmer-elected boards. Four out of five farmers belong to at least one co-op. The Farmer Cooperative Service touches the farmer only through the boards of directors of the cooperatives as the boards see fit.

When the stakes get larger the pattern of local self-government remains the same. Price support, the "parity program," is run by the thousands of farmer-elected county committees of farmers, which function alongside but quite independent of the other local committees. Acreage allotments to bring supply down and prices up are apportioned among the states by the Agricultural Stabilization and Conservation Service. (The ASCS is the lineal descendant, thrice removed, of the AAA.) State committees of farmers apportion the allotment among the counties. The farmer-elected county Stabilization and Conservation Committees receive the county allotment. The county committees made the original acreage allotments among individual farmers back in the 1930's, and they now make new allotments, bring about any adjustments and review complaints regarding allotments, determine whether quotas have been complied with, inspect and approve storage facilities, and act as the court of original jurisdiction on violations of price-support rules and on eligibility for parity payments. The committees are also vitally important in campaigning for the two-thirds-

vote acceptance of high price-support refer-
enda. Congress determines the general level
of support, and the secretary of agriculture
proclaims the national acreage quotas for ad-
justing supply to guaranteed price. But the
locally elected committees stand between
the farmer and the Congress, the secretary,
the ASCS, and the Commodity Credit Corporation.

In agriculture credit, local self-government
is found in even greater complexity. The
Farmers Home Administration (FHA, but not
to be confused with Federal Housing Administration) and the Farm Credit Administration
are, in essence, banks; and as banks they are
unique. Credit extended by the FHA is almost
entirely controlled by local FHA farmer committees. There is one per county, and again
these are not to be confused with the other
committees. The much larger Farm Credit
Administration, an independent agency
since 1953, was within the Department of
Agriculture from 1938 until 1953 and was
autonomous before that. But its departmental status is irrelevant, because it also operates through local farmer control. There is
not one but three "bodies politic" within the
FCA. (1) Membership in the mortgage loan
"body politic" requires the purchase of stock
in a local land-bank association. Broad participation is so strongly desired that it has
been made mandatory. The farmer-borrower
must purchase an amount of voting stock
equal to 5 per cent of his loan in one of the
750 land-bank associations. (2) In the short-
term loan "body politic," 487 separate production credit associations own virtually all
the stock, and the farmer-owners or their representatives pass upon all requests for loans
with their respective districts. It is a point of
pride in the FCA that ownership and control
of these banks has passed from government
to local, private hands. (3) The third "body
politic" within the FCA is the cooperative system, controlled by elected farmer-directors
and operated by credit available from the
FCA's Central Bank for Cooperatives and its
32 district Banks for Cooperatives.

THE TEN SYSTEMS AND POLITICS

Taking all the agriculture programs within or
closely associated with the Department of
Agriculture, there are least ten separate, autonomous, local self-governing systems.
These account for the overwhelming proportion of government activities, expenditures,
and capital transactions in the field of agriculture. In fiscal 1962, $5.6 billion of the
total $6.7 billion Department of Agriculture
expenditures were administered through
one or another of these self-governing systems. In calendar 1962, an additional $5.8
billion in loans were handled similarly. This
$11.4 billion constitutes a rather large pro-
portion of the total of federal activity in the
domestic economy, and the local and district
farmer committees constitute the vital element in the administration of the $11.4 bil-
lion. To the individual farmer, the local
outpost of each of these systems is the Department of Agriculture, perhaps the government itself. Loyalty is always most likely to
focus upon the spot where authoritative decisions are made.

Due to the special intimacy between federal agriculture programs and private agriculture, each administrative organization
becomes a potent political instrumentality.
Each of the self-governing local units
becomes one important point in a definable
political system which both administers a
program and maintains the autonomy of that
program in face of all other political forces
emanating from other agriculture systems,
from antagonistic farm and nonfarm interests, from Congress, from the secretary, and
from the president.

The politics of each of these self-governing
programs is comprised of a triangular trading pattern, with each point complementing
and supporting the other two. The three
points are: the central agency, a congressional committee or subcommittee, and the
local or district farmer committees. The latter
are also usually the grass-roots element of a
national interest group.

The classic case is extension. The Extension Service at the center of this system is supported in Congress by the long-tenure "Farm Bureau" members of the agriculture committees, particularly in the Senate. The grass-roots segment is composed of the Farm Bureau Federation and the local extension committees around which the Farm Bureau was originally organized and to which the bureau continues to contribute assistance. Further interest-group support comes from two intimately related organizations, the Association of Land-Grant Colleges and Universities and its tributary, the National Association of County Agricultural Agents.

Another such triangle unites the Soil Conservation Service with Congress primarily through the Subcommittee on Agriculture of the House Committee on Appropriations, through which SCS managed to double its appropriations between 1940 and the early postwar years while severely limiting the related activities of the FHA and the old AAA and its successors. The third point is the local soil conservation districts, which speak individually to the local congressman and nationally to Congress and the president through the very energetic National Association of Soil Conservation Districts. The SCS draws further support from the Soil Conservation Society of America (mainly professionals) and the Izaak Walton League of America (formerly Friends of the Land, mainly urban well-wishers).

Similar but much more complex forms characterize the price-support system. The Agriculture Stabilization and Conservation Service ties into Congress through the eight (formerly ten) commodity subcommittees of the House Agriculture Committee and the dozens of separately organized interest groups representing each of the single commodities. (Examples: National Cotton Council, American Wool Growers Association, American Cranberry Growers Association.) These in turn draw from the local price-support committees.

As in geometry and engineering, so in politics the triangle seems to be the most stable type of structure. There is an immense capacity in each agriculture system, once created, to maintain itself and to resist any type of representation except its own. These self-governing agriculture systems have such institutional legitimacy that they have become practically insulated from the three central sources of democratic political responsibility: (1) Within the Executive, they are autonomous. Secretaries of agriculture have tried and failed to consolidate or even to coordinate related programs. (2) Within Congress, they are sufficiently powerful within their own domain to be able to exercise an effective veto or to create stalemate. (3) Agriculture activities and agencies are almost totally removed from the view of the general public. Upon becoming the exclusive province of those who are most directly interested in them, programs are first split off from general elective political responsibility. (Throughout the 1950's, for example, Victor Anfuso of Brooklyn was the only member of the House Committee on Agriculture from a nonfarm constituency.) After specialization there is submersion.

9　Labor Unions' "Autonomy"

Grant McConnell

Until 1932 the politics of labor exhibited a consistency, almost a purity, of pattern unmatched in other major segments of American politics. Preservation of the autonomy of the established national (officially, "international") unions was central. Union autonomy was to be defended against employers, government, and even labor's own federation. It implied emphasis upon job control, concentration upon hard economic issues of immediate concern to the unions' constituencies, reliance upon the unions' own economic strength, and rejection of "politics," whether this was taken to mean partisanship or the seeking of legislation. All these were pursued in the name of liberty and were continually and rigidly defended as pragmatism. . . .

The arrival of the New Deal provided a vast impetus for what has generally been interpreted as a redirection of American unionism. The first sign was the inclusion of Section 7(a) in the National Industrial Recovery Act. This guaranteed the right of employees "to organize and bargain collectively through representatives of their own choosing." The Act had the support of the AFL, and President Green of the Federation followed it up with a letter to affiliates calling on them to take advantage of this "revolutionary" measure by organizing.[1] The opening effort was to be a great organizing campaign in Detroit, but the campaign turned out to be less than energetic.

At this moment no greater issue faced the labor movement than its own size. Depres-sion-born unemployment had reduced its ranks dramatically since the beginning of crisis in 1929; by the time the low point had been reached, the membership rolls totaled less than three million members. Few of the mass-production industries had any organization at all, despite the growth of the automobile, rubber, oil, and similar industries in the period of prosperity just preceding. The problem was actually of long standing and was in one sense merely aggravated, though on a large scale, by the Depression. At the end of World War I, organized labor had had a membership approximately twice its size in 1930; the decline had been steady throughout the 1920's. Reasons for the decline were complex. Certainly one was that the membership at the close of World War I was swollen by the nearly automatic organization accorded under wartime contracts; some portion of this at least could reasonably be expected to fall away. Another was the "American Plan" campaign of employers (the open shop with public relations touches).

Whatever the strength and importance of these influences on union organization, a substantial part of the explanation for the decline in membership lay in the outlook of the AFL unions themselves. On the face of things, this outlook was characterized chiefly by lack of aggressiveness, if not outright defeatism, illustrated by the Federation's half-hearted efforts to establish unions in the automobile industry. . . .

In a large sense what had happened to the AFL during the years between World War I and the Depression was that its constituency had narrowed. The constituency when the AFL was formed had been very broad, at least in the sense that virtually all workers for wages were regarded as organizable ulti-

Reprinted from *Private Power and American Democracy* by Grant McConnell. By permission of Random House, Inc. Copyright © 1966 by Alfred A. Knopf, Inc.

[1]Philip Taft, *Organized Labor in American History* (New York: Harper & Row, 1964), pp. 418, 419.

mately into separate national unions. This goal, however, was vague; the cold reality of the labor movement was that it consisted of established unions for the most part based on the skilled crafts. What Michels has called the conservative basis of organization soon dominated these organizations, and no body in the official labor movement was capable of making the vision of the large constituency of wage workers a reality. The responsibility of labor leaders was to a variety of much narrower constituencies. These constituencies did extend beyond the actual membership of the various unions, but even so a great mass of workers were left without organizations to which they might have had recourse. The Industrial Workers of the World had been an exception, but this frightening organization had been effectively smashed in the antiradical repression after World War I. The AFL, as the example of the automobile workers suggests, was the remaining possible matrix of organization, but its loose federal form prevented it from taking vigorous action. In effect, the automobile workers and others in mass-production industries were outside its constituency. Moreover, many of the workers over whom the established unions had once asserted jurisdiction and the right of ultimate organization were by 1932, in any realistic view, also outside the actual union constituencies.

There was a close, though not always easily visible, connection between the shrinkage of organized labor's constituency and its reliance upon economic methods. Except in municipalities, labor had not followed the examples of business and agriculture in establishing its own parts of public government. Representation of a kind, it is true, had long existed in the federal government. Pressure from the Knights of Labor in the late 1870's had resulted in formation of a Bureau of Labor. From its beginning, this agency was devoted to the gathering of statistics and other information, first from a vantage point in the Department of the Interior and then in the Department of Commerce and Labor. The AFL succeeded in gaining separate departmental status for labor in 1913, but the new

department's powers did not develop in the same manner as those of its counterparts elsewhere in government. One reason was that the first secretary, William Wilson, was a former United Mine Workers official and was deeply committed to the doctrines of voluntarism.[2] Thus, for example, he felt it would be wrong for Congress to give his own office greater power in industrial disputes, arguing that legislation to this end would give "to the Secretary of Labor the power he should not have—power to organize, direct, and concentrate public opinion so as to compel the employer to give conditions he does not want to give or the employee to accept conditions he does not want to accept. Both of them are wrong and should never be incorporated in the laws of the U.S."[3] Moreover, to Secretary Wilson labor meant organized labor, even when this amounted to only 6 per cent of the working class. . . .

Despite the doctrinaire "pragmatism" of organized labor, passage of the Norris-LaGuardia Act and the National Industrial Recovery Act released (or at least was followed by) a burst of new organizing activity. This was most notable in the United Mine Workers, a union which long before had fought and won the issue of industrial unionism within the AFL. It had a membership long

[2][McConnell uses this term (which was first used in this sense by the founder of the American Federation of Labor, Samuel Gompers) to describe the outlook of most AFL leaders from the 1880's on, an outlook that is—as he shows elsewhere in his book—very close to the orthodox business doctrine of laissez faire. This outlook was centered on "a very loud and persistent appeal for liberty" of a particularly American variety—namely, as the absence of compulsion from the state for certain kinds of private association (like trade associations, agricultural associations, labor unions, etc.). Coupled with this hostility to the state and to political action was the belief in small units of association as the essence of democracy, and the dislike of law and legal authority. (Compare this outlook with the description in the introduction to Part VI of typical American notions of freedom.)—Ed.]

[3]Quoted in John Lombardi, *Labor's Voice in the Cabinet* (New York: Columbia University Press, 1942), p. 65.

accustomed to risk and hardship and so, perhaps, was more open than others to rough and drastic measures. It was also endowed with leadership of an unusual caliber. Even before President Roosevelt signed the NRA, John L. Lewis was conferring with his lieutenants over plans for a great new organizing campaign. Lewis and his aides took vigorous part in formulating the NRA code for the coal industry, from which the first of a succession of agreements emerged. The union achieved the check-off, as well as other benefits. A new spirit of aggressiveness animated the organization and its rolls grew dramatically.[4] The Amalgamated Clothing Workers under Sidney Hillman and the International Ladies' Garment Workers under David Dubinsky also caught the note of opportunity and mounted organizational campaigns.

For all the clarity with which these signs pointed to a new era in labor history, the really great breach in voluntarism came with passage of the Wagner Act in 1935. This Act had directed continuity with the now-defunct NRA. Nevertheless, it went far beyond that little-lamented experiment, at least insofar as labor was concerned. In providing a solid administrative structure for carrying out the public policies that employees had the right to organize and that collective bargaining was the proper method of regulating industrial relations, the Wagner Act created the basis for an entirely new unionism, one which could assume that government was not only not hostile but was actively assisting labor organization. The Act's requirement that employers engage in bargaining and the enumeration of unfair labor practices by employers spelled out its meaning in considerable detail. For the first time at the national level labor unions had a genuine handle on government. . . .

The agency of government to which organized labor now could have recourse, the National Labor Relations Board, was thoroughly unlike the Department of Labor. It was modeled at least in part on the ICC, the FTC, and the other independent regulatory commissions. Thus it might have been expected that

in time the agency would serve labor as some of the other independent agencies served their own clienteles, and indeed, for a number of years the NLRB appeared to be doing just this. Given the long-standing hostility of many employers to collective bargaining and to any avoidable dealing with unions, and given the Wagner Act's injunctions against expressions of this hostility, the Board made many decisions against employers and in favor of labor.[5] This apparent partisanship, however, was simply what was required under the policy of the Wagner Act; it was not favoritism of the order that developed from the discretion given some of the other independent agencies. Moreover, it was implicit in the Board's structure from the beginning that once employers generally came to accept the policies of the Wagner Act the Board would prove to be less a partisan of labor than it appeared in its early days. In actuality, the Board had a double constituency—management as well as labor. This reality, however, was some time in appearing.

The other great change that affected labor during the New Deal era was the vast increase in organized labor's constituency. Industrial unionism was obviously the key to organization of the big mass-production industries as yet largely untouched by unionism. But the craft unions of the AFL were bitterly antagonistic to this sort of mass organization. Their hostility was doctrinaire and rigid, but it was not wholly irrational. Its rationality had two bases. First, change in the constituent foundation of any organization is profoundly disruptive to that organization, not least to the security of its leadership—a truth as clear today to state legislators faced with reapportionment as in the 1930's it was to unions threatened with a flood of newcomers. Second, a very real tactical advantage accrued to organizations with small constituencies and limited objectives. Thus,

[5]It is worth observing that the NLRB has a considerably higher reputation than some of the other independent regulatory agencies. See, for example, Henry J. Friendly, *The Federal Administrative Agencies* (Cambridge, Mass.: Harvard University Press, 1962), pp. 36–52.

[4]See Taft, *op. cit.,* pp. 424–432.

a union with a relatively small number of skilled craftsmen could demand—and get—substantial economic benefits from an employer who also used the services of a large number of unskilled workers. The cost to him of granting a rather large increase of wages, say, to the small skilled group would be minor in proportion to the cost of enduring a strike that would close down his entire plant. The situation might be quite different if he were confronted with a possible strike for relatively small benefits for a large number of workers. Obviously, however, enjoyment of this tactical advantage depended on the existence of a small constituency in the union and its holding to very narrowly construed objectives, however extreme these might be in degree.

The rise of the Committee for Industrial Organization (later renamed the Congress of Industrial Organizations) was the major feature of a near-revolution within the labor movement. For all the prominence of personalities in the formation of the CIO it is difficult to imagine how except by revolutionary means (revolutionary, that is, in the context of existing labor organization) the constituency of organized labor could have been enlarged on the scale it was. Nevertheless, it is notable that increase of membership occurred not only in the CIO, but in the AFL and the independent unions as well. Total union membership, which in 1930 was 2,900,000 rose to 4,300,000 in 1935 and to 8,500,000 in 1940; of this last figure, 4,900,000 members were in AFL unions and 2,800,000 were in CIO unions.[6] The explanation for this dramatic growth obviously cannot be simple. The energy that went into organizing campaigns was an essential fact. Behind this, however, was the fact that the CIO leaders had burst asunder the chains that existing AFL organization and ideology had bound about the labor movement.[7] Related to this was the great change in the attitude and action of government, specific in the influence

of the Wagner Act and the NLRB, but also general in the widespread impression that the national administration was favorable to labor organization. And at nearly every point in labor history at which union membership has changed markedly, the help or hindrance of government has been intimately connected.[8] ...

... Since 1932 it has been axiomatic that "labor" is Democratic. The commitment, although clear, was informal during the 1930's, but in 1944 the CIO formed the Political Action Committee for the explicit purpose of reelecting Franklin Roosevelt. In 1948 the PAC had the assistance of Labor's League for Political Education (AFL) in campaigning for Truman's reelection. Official commitment of both AFL and CIO came when both endorsed Adlai Stevenson in 1952. The merger of the two federations brought the creation of the Committee for Political Education, which was active in the 1960 presidential campaign on behalf of John Kennedy. Organized labor spent substantial sums raised by special contributions on these elections. Thus, through the 1950's the national political committees of the AFL, the CIO, and of ten individual unions spent a total of between $1,500,000 and $1,750,000 in each election.[9] By 1962, President George Meany of the AFL-CIO was asserting, "Political action is labor's most important activity at this time."[10] On the face of things, the abandonment of the strictures of voluntarism against partisan politics would seem to be complete.

Nevertheless, some important qualifications to any such conclusion must be made. First, some labor leaders retain Republican affiliations. (Whether the Goldwater candi-

[6]Florence Peterson, *American Labor Unions* (New York: Harper & Row, 1962), p. 43.
[7]See Walter Galenson, *The CIO Challenge to the AFL* (Cambridge, Mass.: Harvard University Press, 1963).
[8]See Philip Ross, "The Role of Government in Union Growth," *Annals of the American Academy of Political and Social Science* (November 1963), pp. 75–85.
[9]Alexander Heard, *The Costs of Democracy* (Chapel Hill: University of North Carolina Press, 1960), p. 182.
[10]Quoted in J. David Greenstone, *Labor Politics in Three Cities: Political Action in Detroit, Chicago and Los Angeles.* Unpublished doctoral dissertation, University of Chicago, 1963, p. 1.

dacy in 1964 has seriously changed this situation remains to be seen.) Neither the federation nor individual unions levy political tests, and it is unthinkable that they would try. Second, it remains official doctrine that labor should be nonpartisan—even in political education. The first constitutional convention of the AFL-CIO in 1955 affirmed "labor's traditional policy of avoiding entangling alliances with any other group and of supporting worthy candidates regardless of their party affiliation."[11] Third, it is at least arguable that organized labor's commitment to the Democratic Party is the product of labor's political weakness rather than of any fundamental decision to support the Democrats. Thus it can be said that ever since the New Deal era labor has had no alternative to support of the Democratic Party, and that so long as existing labor legislation is on the books it must seek friends in public office. Given the powers of the National Labor Relations Board, for example, the stake of union organizations in the character of appointments to the Board is great, and only one party can be regarded as friendly to the labor movement. Given labor's inability to isolate the NLRB from influences other than its own, the choice of remaining aloof from partisan politics is not open.

Ultimately, the political weakness of organized labor lies in the unions' inability to control the votes of their members. This was dramatized by labor's effort to defeat Senator Taft in 1950, a venture which met overwhelming failure. Additional evidence has made it plain that members' loyalty to unions does not extend to automatic acceptance of union-approved candidates.[12] Campaigns by labor have indeed had some local successes. The United Auto Workers, for example, have acted very aggressively in Michigan politics, and have probably played a larger political role than other unions. Their success, however, was in no small degree the consequence of the fact that the UAW was able to

[11]Quoted in Taft, op. cit., p. 617.
[12]For example, Angus Campbell, et al., The American Voter (Ann Arbor: University of Michigan Survey Research Center, 1960), p. 325.

act in the absence of a developed party structure and to serve the functions of a party in a city where the union bulks unusually large. Even in this situation, however, the union has had to compromise and has had some failures. A recent comparison of the political pattern in Detroit with those in other cities suggests that unions are less able to act effectively in political campaigns where strong party machinery already exists.[13] . . .

Much of the argument that a fundamental change in the character of the American labor movement has occurred since 1933 must rest on the characteristics exhibited by the unions that have developed and grown large in this period, particularly the unions of the former CIO. Understandably, the smaller craft unions can be expected to behave along the old lines of voluntarism. A craft union with a small membership cannot hope to act effectively in politics or be expected to forego the tactical advantages of concentrating its energies on the narrow economic interests of the craft. On the whole, unions of this sort have continued to exhibit the traits of what Robert Hoxie termed "business unionism"—that is, voluntarism.[14]

The union with the best claim to vitality based upon ability to increase its membership is the Brotherhood of Teamsters. Whereas most major unions have lost members since 1955, the Teamsters have made marked gains, despite opprobrium heaped on them by congressional committees, the press, and the general leadership of the labor movement. The union's growth in membership is the product of the special position of power deriving from the fact that very few articles of commerce or industry do not at some time move by truck, and also from the

[13]Greenstone, op cit., Chap. 3.
[14]Robert F. Hoxie, Trade Unionism in the United States (New York: Appleton, 1921), pp. 45, 46. Joseph Shister has rather aptly distinguished business unionism from today's "social unionism," which is more concerned with public policy and has a broader outlook. He notes that the latter requires a large membership base. "Unresolved Problems and New Paths for American Labor," Industrial and Labor Relations Review (April 1956).

remarkable view of its jurisdiction contained in the Teamsters' constitution. That document specifies a long list of worker groups and then adds, "and other workers where the security of the bargaining positions of the above classifications requires the organization of such other workers."[15] It might be expected that this nearly all-encompassing jurisdictional claim would lead to the making of broad social demands and to political action, but the Teamsters have been intensely particularistic and have largely avoided political action.

The explanation is that this is a "business union" par excellence. Its leadership has always emphasized wages, hours, and working conditions. No other union has demonstrated so decisively that such a narrow range of interests is compatible with an intensive accumulation and exercise of power. Its broad constitutional claim of jurisdiction is a reflection of the union's almost obsessive concern to protect its outposts and then its outposts' outposts. A consequence is that to guard its own security the Brotherhood of Teamsters often appears more willing to collaborate with employers than with other unions. Certainly it seems true that the union is moved far less by any idea of solidarity than by the logic of its own power as an autonomous organization.

The notoriety of the Brotherhood of Teamsters rests primarily on a long series of investigations which have revealed an intricate set of relationships between the union's leaders and underworld figures and business ventures of dubious morality and legality. These ventures and relationships have been traced in hearings and reports of ponderous length; the McClellan Committee hearings alone ran to 58 volumes.[16]   The stories

brought forth in these investigations of sweetheart contracts, paper locals, dubious loans and partnerships made national headlines for many months, and inevitably the outcome was legal pursuit of the presumed evildoers.[17] The whole thing made splendid newspaper copy, but it obscured the issues of genuine public importance.

These issues revolved around the problem of business unionism itself. Certainly not all business unions are corrupt or engage in the practices the Teamsters have been charged with. Nevertheless, the particular forms of enterprise of which this union has been accused are rather clearly the particular pathology of business. Other aspects of the Teamsters' business unionism are more important, if less sensational. Certainly the union's propensity to collaborate with business in restrictive practices is more important than any collaboration in corrupt arrangements for the enrichment of leaders, however serious these may be. Perhaps the classic example of restrictive practice dates from the days when Dave Beck was head of the Western Conference of Teamsters. By refusing to make deliveries to Seattle filling stations which Beck regarded as "excessive," the Teamsters eliminated "cutthroat competition" in the business and earned the good will of established units in the industry.[18] The union presumably made gains of some substance for its members in return. It is less clear that this type of arrangement ("Dave Beck's little NRA") has served the public well.

Although the Teamsters have been avowedly nonpolitical in accordance with the best precepts of voluntarism, the union has not been especially hostile to the use of government when it has seemed that particular governmental powers might serve its interests and the interests of its industry. Thus, while former President Daniel Tobin of the Teamsters disapproved of the labor provisions of the NRA, he liked those of its fea-

[15]The entire clause is quoted in Robert D. Leiter, *The Teamsters Union* (New York: Bookman Associates, 1957), pp. 61, 62.

[16]The Committee assembled a large shelf of hearings under the title *Investigation of Improper Activities in the Labor or Management Field*, 85th Cong., 1st and 2nd Sess. (1957, 1958). For a list of other hearings on Teamsters affairs, see Leiter, *op. cit.*, pp. 287–289. Even this is not complete.

[17]The spirit of the campaign to trap James Hoffa can be seen in Robert F. Kennedy, *The Enemy Within* (New York: Harper, 1960).

[18]Cf. Leiter, *op. cit.*, pp. 49, 50.

tures designed to fix rates and trade practices. The union, moreover, has sought governmental regulation of small owner-operators of trucks who have not been under union contracts. The Teamsters have been in considerable agreement with the American Trucking Association, and it is clear that their common goal is a reduction in the scale of operations of independents.[19] Indeed, at one point Beck expressed a complaint reminiscent of complaints sometimes made by business leaders:

We feel as if we are orphans in this industry. We are the only transportation industry in America without its own regulatory body. The railroads have the Interstate Commerce Commission. The airlines have the Civil Aeronautics Board, and ships have the Maritime Board. Yet our industry must be regulated by the railroad-dominated Interstate Commerce Commission.[20]

James Hoffa, Beck's successor as Teamster president, has continued the policy of collaboration with trucking firms and promotion of organization among truckers themselves. He has not achieved the sort of governmental regulation longed for by Beck, but this may be in large part because he has even more reason than Beck to be personally distrustful of government. However, the Teamsters' power under his regime has grown by rigid adherence to the voluntaristic principles of economic action, autonomy, support of the industry, and strict limitation of interest to the narrow constituency.[21]

The Brotherhood of Teamsters, however, can be regarded as unique in various ways. It has singular advantages deriving from the strategic position of its industry. Its membership may be more given to cynicism than many others. Its tradition is deeply rooted in voluntarism, and it has a web of relationships with industry of unusual complexity and long

standing. Accordingly, it may not be the most significant union in which to seek evidence of the trend of things in the labor movement.

The United Mineworkers of America has contributed to the development of the labor movement to a degree perhaps greater than any other union. It fought out and won the issue of industrial unionism more than two decades before that issue was confronted by labor as a whole. When that time did come, the Mineworkers provided in John L. Lewis and Philip Murray the two greatest leaders in the reconstitution of the movement. This union also provided a large part of the money that made the CIO a reality. Under Lewis's leadership the UMW became an important political force, although its influence was diminished by the later estrangement of Lewis from Franklin Roosevelt. It is an organization that might well be expected from its record to be in the vanguard of any movement away from labor's traditional voluntarism.

Developments of the postwar era do not fulfill such expectations. Since the late 1940's the coal mining industry has been mechanized to a degree that amounts to a technological revolution, a revolution the union has not only permitted, but has actively fostered. One of the consequences is a sharp decline in the number of coal miners. These, the backbone of the union, numbered approximately 400,000 in 1948. Within ten years their number had been reduced by half, and the decline continues.[22] The UMW has won a remarkable financial return in its Welfare and Retirement Fund for its cooperation in mechanizing the industry. This fund, supported by a rising levy on each ton of coal mined, quickly rose to magnificent proportions and supported an impressive system of welfare benefits. Although it later encountered difficulties, it created benefits on a scale seldom rivaled and won repeated skirmishes with the American Medical Association.

Even more impressive, the UMW provided the leadership that has brought prosperity to

[19] *Ibid.,* pp. 138–159.

[20] J. B. Gillingham, *The Teamsters Union on the West Coast* (Berkeley: University of California, Institute of Industrial Relations, 1956). p. 40.

[21] See Paul Jacobs, *The State of the Unions* (New York: Atheneum, 1963), pp. 5–70.

[22] Cf. J. B. S. Hardman, "John L. Lewis, Labor Leader and Man: An Interpretation," *Labor History* (Winter 1961), p. 21.

the industry itself. The great increase in mechanization of the mines has been the major factor in this prosperity, but in union and management eyes alike the union-fostered organization of the industry has been equally important. The UMW has held that the industry's central problem has been excess capacity—the counterpart of the problem of too many miners. With organization in both industry and union, excess of both capacity and miners has been eliminated in recent years, with a resultant increase in both profits and wages.

The union has saved itself from what otherwise might have become a disastrous situation. It has earned the praise of coal operators as the industry's savior. But it has also earned the curses of the more than 300,000 miners of the Appalachian coal areas who have been forced out of work in a fifteen-year period.[23]   Large numbers of these miners remain in the valleys once dominated by the now abandoned mines. It is thoroughly believable that the UMW acted in a manner best calculated to insure its survival. The miners who remain in its constituency enjoy prosperity that their fathers might have found difficult to believe. But the choices made by the union to narrow its constituency and to collaborate with (even to force organization among) the coal operators are clearly in the mainstream of voluntarist tradition. For the union it is an old tradition; the conspicuous political ventures of the 1930's suggested more of a break than actually occurred in the union's economic policy.[24]

Somewhat the same impulsions have been apparent in another union which would seem at least superficially to have a thoroughly different character: the International Longshoremen and Warehousemen's Union. This union developed in the 1930's from a split-off from the International Long-

[23]Cf. A. H. Raskin, "The Obsolescent Unions," *Commentary* (July 1963), p. 23.

[24]The UMW has consistently sought restriction of output. Cf. Morton S. Baratz, *The Union and the Coal Industry* (New Haven, Conn.: Yale University Press, 1955), pp. 69–74.

shoremen's Association, and under the highly aggressive leadership of Harry Bridges soon transformed the situation of West Coast longshoremen. Where before they had been subjected to the degrading insecurity of the shape-up (as longshoremen continued to be on the East Coast), hiring was placed on an impartial basis through union-operated hiring halls. Wages and working conditions improved markedly, but only after bitter struggles with employers. Bridges was attacked as a communist in a series of legal campaigns that today seem difficult to believe. Everything about the union seemed tinged with ideology, and it earned a reputation as a radical organization. Employers seemed bent on its utter destruction.

Nevertheless, after the Soviet Union entered World War II, the union undertook to support prosecution of the war and established a record of cooperation as marked as its previous seemingly implacable hostility to capitalism. From the cooperation with employers that developed in this period there gradually emerged a pattern of collaboration with employers. This collaboration did not occur immediately, but after an ideological crusade against Bridges and the ILWU in the late 1940's by employers and the United States government collapsed, the plan for an accommodation between union and employers developed. This plan, like that of the United Mineworkers, involved acceptance by the union of mechanization on the docks and gradual reduction of the union's rolls. A substantial price was exacted by the ILWU from the employers, but the essential facts were that the union and the employers reached a long-term settlement and that one of its conditions was the union's agreement to the deliberate contraction of its constituency. The results were highly favorable to those who remained within the constituency, but were admittedly different for those who were now outside. Bridges, the notorious radical, explained in a statement of remarkable candor: "You can't go getting mad at the employer because under our system he's in business to make profits. So you have to try to work out a solution within the system, and ours is admittedly a pretty selfish solution."[25]

A prominent feature of each of these narratives is the attainment of fundamental agreement between union and industry for the common enjoyment of benefits gained in some degree at the expense of those outside their joint constituency. Collaboration on this basis has been no less possible for a combative organization like the Mineworkers and an ideologically colored union like the West Coast longshoremen than for a business-minded union like the Teamsters. All have arrived at positions of remarkable similarity in this respect—suggesting that differences of ideology and style may be superficial. The record of another union, the United Steelworkers, however, indicates that this explanation is inadequate.

The steel industry has been widely regarded, rightly or wrongly, as peculiarly and fundamentally important to the general economy. For this reason and also because steel is unqestionably of central importance in wartime, government has been repeatedly and heavily involved in the industrial relations of steel—an involvement deriving as well from fear of inflation and of the consequences of protracted strikes. Nevertheless, industrial relations in steel since the end of World War II have followed a pattern in which industry and union have engaged in one bitter dispute after another and settlements have featured higher wages, higher prices, and defeat for the government. This pattern began in 1946, when a post-strike settlement resulted in dissolution of the public machinery for controlling inflation. There were no strikes in 1947 or 1948, but increased wages were followed by increased prices; results in 1949 after a 45-day strike were similar. There was no strike in 1950, but in 1951 and 1952, during the Korean War, a particularly sharp contest between union and industry resulted first in disruption of economic stabilization machinery, and then in its destruction. Feeling ran high between the two contending parties. The union was convinced the industry should have no price increase, but was determined to have higher wages for itself. In the outcome the wage increase was accompanied by a price increase generally regarded as larger than necessary to meet the cost of the wage increase. A strike by the union enforced both demands in the situation.[26] So the pattern continued for the rest of the decade; its culmination was the largest single strike in American history, that of 1959.[27]

The degree to which results of the frequently hostile relationships in steel were similar to those of the often friendly arrangements in the industries mentioned earlier is remarkable. . . .

[26]Cf. Grant McConnell, *The Steel Seizure of 1952.* (Published by the University of Alabama Press, University, Ala., 1960, for the Inter-University Case Program.)

[27]For an account of this general history see *Collective Bargaining in the Basic Steel Industry* (Washington, D.C.: U. S. Department of Labor, 1961), Appendix A. This volume is usually known as "The Livernash Report" after E. Robert Livernash, who directed its preparation.

[25]Burton H. Wolfe, "The Strange Twilight of Harry Bridges—A Labor Leader Turns Business-man," *Harper's* (March 1964), p. 79.

Is This Structure Democratic?

10   The Truth about Political Parties and Elections

Thomas R. Dye and L. Harmon Zeigler

Can masses hold elites responsible through elections? Over half a million governmental officials are chosen through the ballot in America, but the extent of popular control of government through elections is undetermined. Although voters help to select the men who occupy prominent positions in government, voters do not order troops to Vietnam, or enact civil rights laws, or write tax legislation; and the effect of elections on these and other actions by governmental elites is unclear. The ballot is widely considered a panacea for social ills, but there is little evidence that voters can directly affect public policy through the exercise of their franchise.

In order for elections to serve as mandates, and for voters to exercise influence over public policy through elections, four conditions would need to be fulfilled: (1) Competing candidates would offer clear policy alternatives; (2) voters would be concerned with policy questions; (3) majority preferences on these questions could be ascertained in election results; (4) elected officials would be bound by the positions they assumed during the campaign.

... we shall contend that none of these conditions are fulfilled in American politics

From *The Irony of Democracy: An Uncommon Introduction to American Politics* by Thomas R. Dye and L. Harmon Zeigler. Copyright © 1970 by Wadsworth Publishing Co., Inc., Belmont, Calif. 94002. Reprinted by permission of the publisher.

and, consequently, that voters cannot exercise direct control over public policy. First of all, the parties do not offer clear policy alternatives. Both parties agree on the major direction of public policy; they disagree only over the *means* of implementing public policy. Therefore, the voters cannot influence public policy by choosing between the parties.

Moreover, voter decisions are not motivated primarily by policy considerations. For a mandate to be valid, the electorate must make informed, *policy-oriented* choices; but traditional party ties and candidate personalities are more influential in most voting decisions than are policy questions. When voters cast their ballot because of traditional party ties, their party loyalty dilutes their influence over policy.

Even if the voters were primarily concerned with policy questions, it would be difficult to ascertain majority preferences on these questions from the election results. Victory for the party of a candidate does not necessarily mean that the voters support that party's programs. For one reason, voters are inconsistent in their policy preferences, and they frequently misinterpret or pay little attention to the policy preferences of a candidate. Generally a candidate's voters include not only advocates of his position but also some who oppose his position, as well as some who vote for him for other reasons. Moreover, a popular majority may really be composed of many policy minorities. How is

117

a candidate to know which of his policy positions resulted in his election? It is unlikely that his election can be interpreted as a mandate for *all* of his policy positions.

Finally, in order for voters to exercise control over public officials through elections, it would be necessary for elected officials to be bound by their campaign pledges. Needless to say, campaign pledges are frequently ignored by elected officials.

The Vietnam War provides an interesting illustration of the difficulties in controlling public officials through elections. In 1964, President Johnson's victory over Barry Goldwater was widely attributed to a popular desire for military restraint and avoidance of escalation. In the campaign, Goldwater presented a more "hawkish" image than President Johnson, who projected an image of restraint and responsibility toward American involvement in Vietnam. Yet detailed examination of voter opinion suggests that hawks and doves among the voters did not divide themselves into supporters of Goldwater and Johnson respectively. Actually, Johnson won the support of a majority of both hawks and doves. While 63 per cent of those favoring withdrawal from Vietnam voted for the president, so did 52 per cent of those favoring "a stronger stand even if it means invading North Vietnam." Johnson also won 82 per cent of those who prefer to keep our soldiers in Vietnam, but try to end the fighting. Thus, opinion surveys suggest that Johnson's victory was *not* a mandate for any particular policy in Vietnam.

Of course, once elected, Johnson violated his implied pledge to avoid escalation of the war. True, it is not clear that Johnson was going against the wishes of the voting majority, since they had given no explicit command on Vietnam, but the president did pursue a policy at variance with his election campaign image. Goldwater could rightly claim that Johnson was pursuing policies that he had earlier criticized Goldwater for proposing.

Thus, the 1964 elections did not provide the voters with an opportunity for influencing the direction of policy in Vietnam. Even though the candidates provided reasonably clear policy alternatives, there is no evidence that the voters were concerned primarily with the question of the Vietnam War in their voting decisions, or that the election of Johnson clearly revealed a majority preference for military restraint. And, in any case, Johnson did not keep his campaign pledges about Vietnam policy.

If elections do not provide a means for voters to exercise direct control over public policy, what is the purpose of elections? Elections are primarily a symbolic exercise for the masses to help tie them to the established order. Political scientist Murray Edelman agrees that voters have little effect on public policy and contends that elections are primarily "symbolic reassurance." According to Edelman, elections serve to "quiet resentments and doubts about particular political acts, reaffirm belief in the fundamental rationality and democratic character of the system, and thus fix conforming habits of future behavior."[1] Even though electoral participation does not permit the masses to determine public policy, it nonetheless gives them a feeling that they play a role in the political system.

The second function of elections is to give the masses an opportunity to express themselves about the conduct of the public officials who have been in power. Elections do not permit the masses to direct *future* events, but they do permit the masses to render judgment about *past* political conduct. For example, in 1968, voters could not choose a specific policy by voting for Nixon. They had no way of knowing what policies Nixon would follow in Vietnam, because Nixon did not set forth any specific proposals regarding that conflict. But the voters *were* able to express their discontent with Johnson's handling of the war by voting against a continuation of the Democratic administration. As Gerald Pomper explains:

The voters employ their powerful sanction retrospectively. They judge the politician after he has acted, finding personal satisfac-

[1]Murray Edelman, *The Symbolic Uses of Politics* (Urbana: University of Illinois Press, 1964), p. 17.

tions or discontents as the results of these actions. ... The issue of Viet Nam is illustrative. ... For their part, critics of the war did not emphasize their own alternative policies, but instead concentrated on retrospective and adverse judgments. ... Declining public support of the war brought all major candidates to promise its end. The Republican Party, and particularly Richard Nixon, joined in this pledge, but provided no specific programs, instead seeking the support of all voters inclined to criticize past actions.[2]

... Pomper also asserts that the voters' restospective judgment on past administrations may have an impact on the behavior of current and future elected officials. Pomper contends, rather optimistically, that even though the voters have no *power* over government, they nonetheless have an *influence* on government. He accepts Carl Friedrich's definition of influence: "Influence flows into the human relation whenever the influencer's reaction might spell disadvantage and even disaster for the actor, who foresees the effect the action might have and alters more or less in accordance with his foresight."[3] Pomper contends that because "politicians might be affected by the voters in the next election, they regulate their conduct appropriately."[4]

But he fails to say how elected officials are supposed to know the sentiments of voters on policy questions in order to "regulate their conduct appropriately." As we shall see, most voters do not have an opinion that can be communicated to elected officials; and elected officials have no way of interpreting voters' policy preferences from electoral results. By ousting the Democratic administration from power in 1968, were the voters saying they wanted a military victory in Vietnam? Or were they saying they wanted a negotiated peace and compromise with the Viet Cong?

[2]Gerald Pomper, *Elections in America: Control and Influence in Democratic Politics* (New York: Dodd, Mead, 1968), pp. 255–256.
[3]Carl Friedrich, *Man and His Government* (New York: McGraw-Hill, 1963), pp. 199–201.
[4]Pomper, *op. cit.*, p. 254.

Perhaps all that we can really say is that the retrospective judgment that voters can render in an election helps to make governing elites sensitive to mass welfare. Elections do not permit masses to decide what should be done in their interests, but they do encourage governing elites to consider the welfare of the masses. Knowing that a day of reckoning will come on election day, elected officials strive to make a good impression on the voters in the meantime.

The existence of the vote does not make politicians better as individuals; it simply forces them to give greater consideration to demands of enfranchised and sizeable groups, who hold a weapon of potentially great force. ... The ability to punish politicians is probably the most important weapon available to citizens. It is direct, authoritative, and free from official control.[5]

It has been argued that elections have a third function—that of protecting individuals and groups from official abuse. John Stuart Mill wrote: "Men, as well as women, do not need political rights in order that they might govern, but in order that they not be misgoverned."[6] He went on:

Rulers in ruling classes are under a necessity of considering the interests of those who have the suffrage; but of those who are excluded, it is in their option whether they will do so or not, and however honestly disposed, they are in general too fully occupied with things they must attend to, to have much room in their thoughts for anything which they can with impunity disregard.[7]

Certainly the long history of efforts to insure Negro voting rights in the South suggests that many concerned Americans believed that if Negroes could secure access to the polls, they could better protect themselves from official discrimination. Some major steps in the struggle for voting rights

[5] *Ibid.*, pp. 254–255.
[6]John Stuart Mill, *Considerations on Representative Government* (Chicago: Regnery, Gateway edition, 1962), p. 144.
[7] *Ibid.*, pp. 130–131.

were the abolishment of the "white primary" in 1944; the Civil Rights Acts of 1957, 1960, 1964, and 1965, all of which contained provisions guaranteeing free access to the polls; and the Twenty-fourth Amendment to the Constitution which eliminated poll taxes. But the high hopes stirred by the development of new law were often followed by frustration and disillusionment when Negroes realized that their problems could not be solved through the electoral process alone. No doubt William R. Keech is correct when he asserts that the vote is a symbol of full citizenship and equal rights, which may contribute to Negro self-respect.[8] But it is still open to question how much Negroes can gain through the exercise of their vote. In the North, Negroes have voted freely for decades, but conditions in the urban ghettos have not been measurably improved through political action. In signing the Voting Rights Act of 1965, President Johnson said:

The right to vote is the most basic right, without which all others are meaningless. It gives people—people as individuals—control over their own destinies. . . . The vote is the most powerful instrument ever devised by man for breaking down injustice and destroying the terrible walls which imprison men because they are different from other men.

But the Negro experience in both the North and the South suggests that the ballot cannot eliminate discrimination, much less enable men to "control their own destinies." It is probably true that men can *better* protect themselves from government abuse when they possess and exercise their voting rights, but the right to vote is not a guarantee against discrimination. . . .

There is a great deal of truth to the "Tweedledum and Tweedledee" image of American political parties. American parties do, in fact,

[8]William R. Keech, *The Impact of Negro Voting: The Role of the Vote in the Quest for Equality* (Chicago: Rand McNally, 1968), p. 3.

subscribe to the same fundamental political ideology. Both the Democratic and Republican parties have reflected prevailing elite consensus on basic democratic values—the sanctity of private property, a free enterprise economy, individual liberty, limited government, majority rule, and due process of law. Moreover, since the 1930's both parties have supported the public-oriented, mass-welfare domestic programs of the "liberal establishment"—social security, fair labor standards, unemployment compensation, a graduated income tax, a national highway program, a federally aided welfare system, countercyclical fiscal and monetary policies, and government regulation of public utilities. Finally, both parties have supported the basic outlines of American foreign and military policy since World War II—international involvement, and anticommunism, the Cold War, European recovery, NATO, military preparedness, selective service, and even the Korean and Vietnam Wars. Rather than promoting competition over national goals and programs, the parties reinforce societal consensus and limit the area of legitimate political conflict. . . .

Any comparison of leaders and followers among the Democratic and Republican parties should take into account the uniquely decentralized and informal characteristics of the American party system. Unlike European mass-membership parties, American parties are not "organizations" in the sense normally understood by that term. To be a "Democrat" or a "Republican" involves no greater commitment to the organization than supporting, occasionally, the nominees of that party.

There is, of course, a party organization, consisting of the formally chosen leadership, informal power-holders (who do not hold government or party office), and the party activists who contribute their time and money and consequently acquire the right to make decisions in the name of the party. However, neither political party is structurally hierarchical. Both are decentralized to the extent that no chain of command from national through state to local levels can be said to exist. But the structure of power within the activist group in each party is not especially relevant to our concern. Rather, we are interested in interaction *between* this group and the overwhelming majority of Democrats and Republicans, who do not involve themselves in formulation of party objectives or the selection of candidates (except in primaries) but merely accept or reject the product offered to them by the party activists. For all but a tiny portion of the participants in the political system, the major political act is that of a consumer. The association with the party is entirely passive.

It is somewhat of an irony that the parties, as the agents of democratic decision-making, are not themselves democratic in their structures. One of the most sweeping indictments of political parties on this count comes from Roberto Michels, whose "iron law of oligarchy" leads him to conclude that "every party . . . becomes divided into a minority of directors and a majority of directed."[9]   However, the organizational characteristics of American parties supply few relevant data to either support or refute Michels' assertion. There is, indeed, an active minority, but there is no passive majority because the party in the electorate, the masses, are not really members of the party. The party as an organization is composed of those persons who exercise varied degrees of influence within the activists' cadre. Sorauf describes American parties in this way:

Despite recent trends, the American parties remain largely sketetal, "cadre" party organizations, manned generally by small numbers of activists and involving the great masses of their supporters scarcely at all. . . . By the standards of the parties of much of the rest of the world, American party organization continues to be characterized by its

unusual fluidity and evanescence, by its failure to generate activity at non-election times, and by the ease by which a handful of activists and public officeholders dominate it.[10]

The evidence suggests that American parties, within the activists' cadre, are not a perfect fit for Michels' model, for party activists are neither as homogeneous nor as numerically small as his model requires. A more appropriate analytic construct would appear to be one developed by Harold Lasswell and Abraham Kaplan, and most recently employed by Samuel Eldersveld—the "stratarchy."[11]   a stratarchy is a hierarchical structure best described as a flat-topped pyramid, in which power resides at the top level (just as it does with conical-shaped hierarchies), but in which there are a number of persons occupying that level. In the case of American party stratarchies, those who are at the top level—the activists—are both numerous and heterogeneous. Power is diffused among them rather than centralized. The exception to this rule is a few large city political machines, such as those found in Chicago, Pittsburgh, and Philadelphia; these political machines are tightly and hierarchically controlled.

Although the other extreme—virtual disorganization—is more typical of both parties, big city machines play a more pivotal role in the organization of the party than would be suggested by their numbers alone. Their influence is more evident in the Democratic Party and is particularly manifest during the nomination of the presidential candidate. The power of the political machines is largely a consequence of the fact that there is no national party organization, and thus the national party is no more than a coalition of state and local parties that assembles every

[9]Roberto Michels, *Political Parties: A Sociological Study of the Oligarchical Tendencies of Modern Democracy* (New York: Dover Publications, 1959; originally published in English in 1915), p. 32.

[10]Frank J. Sorauf, *Party Politics in America* (Boston: Little, Brown, 1968), pp. 79–80.

[11]Harold D. Lasswell and Abraham Kaplan, *Power and Society* (New Haven, Conn.: Yale University Press, 1950), pp. 219–220; and Samuel J. Eldersveld, *Political Parties: A Behavioral Analysis* (Chicago: Rand McNally, 1964), pp. 9, 98–117.

four years to nominate a presidential candidate. In such a bargaining process, a cohesive local political organization can play a key role. For instance, Mayor Richard Daley of Chicago can deliver almost all the votes of the Illinois delegation.

In essence, power in American parties tends to rest in the hands of those who have the time and the money to make it a full-time, or nearly full-time, occupation. Party activists —consisting of no more than 3 or 4 per cent of the adult population—can decide what product is to be offered to political consumers (the party in the electorate). Beyond this, there is little interaction between the party in the electorate and the party activists. The crucial question is, therefore, who are the party activists? We know . . . that the activists are strongly ideological and committed to the norms of the democratic decision-making process. Since these characteristics describe the upper socioeconomic groups, it is not surprising to discover that party activists are of relatively high socioeconomic status, and come from families with a history of party activity. The highest socioeconomic levels are found in the highest echelons of the party organization. As Sorauf notes, "the parties . . . attract men and women with the time and financial resources to be able to afford politics, with the information and knowledge to understand it, and with the skills to be useful in it."[12]

It is, of course, true that—reflecting the basis of support among the party in the electorate—Democratic activists are of somewhat lower socioeconomic status than their Republican counterparts. The activists of both parties are somewhat representative of their clientele. Nevertheless, the socioeconomic status of both Democratic and Republican activists is above the average for the area they represent. This distinction between elite and mass, then, is especially characteristic of American political parties.

But what does it matter whether or not the parties are democratic in structure? If the competition between parties is similar to the

[12]Sorauf, op. cit., p. 94.

competition between businesses, the structural characteristics of each group of producers are not very important. Each competitor, democratic or not, has the primary function of satisfying his customers. For instance, it is of no concern to the average consumer that he does not have a voice in determining the type of electric toaster manufactured by the General Electric Corporation. If he does not like this toaster, he can always buy one from Sunbeam or Westinghouse or any one of a number of competitors.

Unfortunately, this analogy is not especially apt for American political parties. The political alternatives offered by parties are much more constricted than are the alternatives offered in business. The voter cannot choose from a number of competing products, but is limited to a choice between two. If the voter finds the product of one competitor unsatisfactory, he must accept the single alternative or decline to become a consumer. Given the consensual nature of American parties, the range of alternatives is quite narrow.

Further, it is difficult for consumers to force the producers to change their product. At first glance, it would seem easy to become an activist in a party and change the agenda-setting personnel. At most levels of political participation, this is superficially quite simple. State legislatures generally require that the party machinery be "open," so anyone can become an activist. Indeed, thousands of party positions are unfilled. However, gaining control of the political party apparatus takes longer than the normally short-term commitment that even more active portions of the citizenry are willing to make. Also, challenges to the dominant group of activists are generally focused around a candidate such as Eugene McCarthy, and such a strategy is futile, since the majority of delegates to the national conventions are not selected in primaries but are chosen by party organizations. Thus, a relatively small number of party leaders can control the decisions of a large proportion of the delegates to the national conventions. The choice of a nominating convention will be, therefore, the choice of the party activists who have long-term commitments to the party, rather than the choice of those activists who are occasionally mobilized by a particular candidate. Only on the rare occasions when temporarily mobilized activists encounter the power of the permanent activists are we able to see the extent to which the parties are the property of the small cadre willing to commit themselves to politics as an avocation.

IV

The Shape of
American Public Life

Americans like to believe that politics is a bit dirty. We may never have read any of the works of the British historian Lord Acton, but we accept his saying that "power corrupts, absolute power corrupts absolutely." We find it easy to hear that politics is "really" a matter of power, of "who gets what, when, how." Our readiness to observe politics from this muckraking point of view suggests the depth of our disillusionment with our own politics. But this view is crippling. It's like being cynically "sophisticated" after being disappointed, and saying with a wise look that religion is just the opiate of the masses and a tool of the ruling class. In other words, our muckraking, "sophisticated" view of politics is crippling because it blinds us. It prevents us from seeing a lot of what politics can be, and might be for us.

Part III of this book described American politics in power terms, and the picture there was probably fairly familiar. But this part describes our politics in a more unusual way. In fact, some of the selections that follow might not seem to be about important political matters at all, if it weren't for the discussion in Part I about the nature of politics. These articles describe an Air Force court-martial trial, how policemen feel about their job, the customs and folkways of United States senators, the behavior of the University of California in the Battle of People's Park in Berkeley, and the campaign tactics of Richard Nixon in 1968. Such subjects may not seem very connected with real power or with who gets the most of the real wealth or of the other things there are to get. Nor are most of them concerned directly with the key governmental institutions—the presidency, the congressional committees, the Department of Defense, and other executive bureaucracies. So from our customary perspective these articles might seem politically trivial at best, and possibly biased or distorted as well.

But the perspective that makes these subjects look trivial is our muckraking, "sophisticated" view of politics. When I said that this conventional view blinds us, I meant that it can make articles such as these seem politically trivial or biased. To find these articles trivial is to take a position analogous to the person who, believing that religion is the opiate of the masses and nothing more, fails to find accounts of the saints' religious experience revealing about the nature of religion. What these articles do is to describe aspects of our politics that we don't ordinarily see.

To see how articles on "Justice," "Community," and "Leadership" can reveal significant things about the way we are governed, it may be helpful to recall the definition of politics given in Part I: *politics is the interactions among people who are attempting to achieve or prevent certain possibilities for their community.* This definition suggests, first, that *politics will always involve conflict*—will always involve people dealing with their important differences—since people will always have, more or less profoundly, different visions for their futures. In Part I it was shown that any nation's version of justice is, in fact, the principles that guide and justify its own way of handling actual and potential conflict. So to think about "American justice" is to think about the principles we Americans customarily follow in dealing with our differences. Of course, we are different in many ways, and we know various ways of dealing with conflict. The single article on justice by Larner cannot describe all of our conflicts and all of our ways of dealing with conflict. On the other hand, it is not necessary to look only at top-level, newspaper-headline events in order to study how we deal with our conflicts. It is possible, and easier, to see our version of justice by looking at ordinary public affairs, rather than by trying to untangle the "way of dealing with conflict" from everything else that goes into great affairs of state (which affairs, anyway, are difficult for us to understand because we are used to having them described in the oversimplified, stereotyped reports we read in the "news"). The article by Larner on a military court-martial trial is intended to reveal one of the most important versions of American justice operating in a relatively ordinary situation, one we can all hope to understand well enough to realize how another method of dealing with conflict might produce radically different outcomes. Larner's description of this bureaucratic (mechanical, formalistic) version of justice should be read in connection with the analysis in Part I of the relations between personal troubles and social-constitutional issues using the illustration of bureaucracy, with Schaar's critique of bureaucratic equality in his selection in Part II, and with the readings in the following Part V.

The definition of politics also suggests that democratic *politics will always involve collective action:* the formation of subcommunities which are united in their pursuit of a particular future that they want to achieve or prevent for their community, and the interaction of these collectives as they struggle to define the direction the whole community will take. Part I has already defined "community" as the feelings and relationships that enable a collection of people to say "we" about themselves. The two articles that follow on the American version of community deal with the sorts of feelings and relationships that typically exist when Americans act collectively. In other words, since self-government for a community or a nation is by definition a collective endeavor, these articles describe some of the sorts of feelings and relationships that prevent Americans from governing themselves well, and that distort our self-government. Again, just as with "justice," there are many kinds of "community" in the United States. The articles included here describe two typical kinds of American community—an exclusive group or subcommunity related hostilely to the larger society, and a conformist, private-oriented, rule-run social body with many of the features of a bureaucracy. And again, it is important to consider these pictures in light of some of the other selections in this book, especially the three in "In the Beginning . . ." in Part II, and the articles on ideology and control mechanisms in Part V.

Finally, the definition I gave of politics suggests that *politics will always involve a community's moving in certain directions,* a suggestion that raises the questions of "Who directs?" and "Why do such people direct the community?" And a nation's source of direction is by definition found in its (version of) leadership. So the two articles on "Leadership" are about the kinds of people who direct our society, and the ways in which they exercise direction. Put in other words, these selections describe the qualities that bind together the directors and the directed in our society, the values embodied in authority-holders and authoritative institutions that make them able to move the nation in certain directions without effective opposition. If it is true that leadership teaches people who they are and how they can behave, it is also true that people are simply not led by a leadership they don't actually need. So the selections on "leadership" can be seen as describing something significant about *both* leaders and followers in our society—namely, how they relate to and how they affect each other in the process of achieving or preventing certain possible futures for our nation. As described in the selections by Wolin and Schaar and by McGinniss, our leaders teach us—and depend on us—to be obedient and passive, and to accept their assumption that the world is competitive, violent, and without any meaning aside from the satisfaction of private interests and the preservation of established routines and patterns. Such bureaucratic and antipolitical leadership is probably familiar to most readers of this book, but it will take on added significance when considered in the context of Part II's description of our traditions, Part III's analysis of the effects of power, and Part V's discussion of the limits on everyday lives in our society.

But it may still seem that justice, community, and leadership are matters of *process,* and that what really matters in politics is *results.* Certainly our conventional view of politics (that it is a matter of who gets the most of what there is to get) denies that there is much significance in the quality of *how* results are produced. This traditional view, which may be shared by most readers of this book, holds that what matters politically is the power to win or get what you want. Results, then, are simply caused by power. And to get different results, "obviously," one changes the power structure. But this view—which can be held both by those who are satisfied with the present results of our politics and by those who are discriminated against by, and dissatisfied with, the present results of our politics—is incorrect. Politics is not, can never be, simply a matter of the powerful getting what they want. There is always some sort of process, some interaction among people, involved in arriving at the state of affairs we call a result. In fact, a result is properly seen as merely one stage in an ongoing process; we come to think only of results because, in our country, the process is so very often the same that we take it for granted. But power has to be exercised through some process; it cannot be simply and directly transformed into desired results, as can, say, money. The exercise of power must always depend upon the ways in which people interact with each other. And any process of human interaction involving power is shaped by the expectations people have about how conflict is dealt with, about whether and how collective action can take place, and about the special qualities of the people who exercise leadership. Therefore, the conclusion follows logically, any exercise of power (any political result) must depend in part upon the things I am calling a nation's version of justice, community, and leadership.

In short, referring once again to the definition of politics as the interactions among people as they attempt to achieve or prevent things for their community, the following selections are about the typical nature and quality of political interactions in America. To be able to achieve different results than those now produced by our political interactions (which were described in Part III), then, it will not be enough simply to change the power structure. We will also have to change the quality of our political processes. That is, we will have to find better ways of dealing with differences than those Larner describes, to learn other ways of acting collectively and publicly than those Kempton and Matthews describe, and to demand better qualities from our leaders (a demand which at the same time requires better from ourselves) than those described by Wolin and Schaar and by McGinniss.

"Justice"

11   The Court-Martial of Captain Noyd

Jeremy Larner

Once upon a time there was a blue-eyed, baseball-playing American boy who grew up straight as an arrow in Wenatchee, Washington, married his college sweetheart, and became a pilot in the U.S. Air Force. Dale Noyd, in fact, was the only member of the Washington State ROTC class of '55 to be offered a regular commission; and he accepted. After several years of training, Dale Noyd was assigned to three years of duty as a tactical fighter pilot in Woodbridge, England, flying in a combat group with what the Air Force calls a "nuclear delivery capability."

According to testimony at his court-martial, Captain Noyd's character and performance as a pilot were rated very highly. On July 30, 1959, while flying his F-100D over the Mediterranean, Noyd noticed a malfunction in his flight control system causing a full right rudder deflection. His flight leader radioed him to press his ejection button and abandon his aircraft. Noyd, however, attempted a landing with his left wing drooping 20 degrees from the horizontal. He managed to get his plane on the ground, but it veered sharply to the right and plunged off the runway. Noyd blew his left tire, and the plane swerved back on the runway, saving the government approximately a quarter of a million dollars. For this he was given a medal and a recommendation, by a squadron com-

mander who could hardly have guessed that nine years later his country would be spending thousands of dollars to put Noyd in Leavenworth for refusing to aid the war in Vietnam.

After his service in England, Noyd's hitch was up and he could have left the Air Force. He chose instead to take three years of graduate school at government expense, studying experimental psychology at the University of Michigan, and thereby obligating himself for six additional years in the service. Friends from Ann Arbor remember him as an efficient student, extremely intelligent, decent and sincere, but somewhat rigid personally and conservative in manner and belief. In three years he practically finished his work for the Ph.D., and moved on to the "Department of Psychology and Leadership" at the Air Force Academy in Colorado, where he taught such courses as "Management and Leadership," "Motivation," and "Marriage."

According to his lawyer at the court-martial, Dale Noyd in the fall of 1966 had a "religious experience" which made him "no longer the same man as he was when he accepted his commission." Probably whatever happened had started back in Ann Arbor, where Noyd in 1964 bought his first folk record and began to read Camus and Sartre. One of his friends believes that, later on, "Dale was very disappointed when he realized he couldn't make the Air Force Academy into a liberal-arts college." At any rate, he did indeed become a different man, a man who now despises the fact that he once played baseball, and puts down the pleasure of flying a plane as a temptation to an infantile sense of power.

The new man knew very well that as of June 1967 he would have to leave the Academy and would probably be assigned to combat flying in Vietnam. So in December of 1966 he sat down and composed with his customary thoroughness a letter resigning his Air Force commission. In it he explained that he was no pacifist; he believed there are times when men must fight "to deter or repel totalitarian aggression." But he could not bring himself to participate in "a war that I believe to be unjust, immoral, and which makes a mockery of both our Constitution and the Charter of the United Nations—and the human values which they represent."

Captain Noyd admitted that talk about Vietnam tended to become "simplistic and obfuscated by clichés and slogans." Nevertheless, he attempted in his resignation to set forth a political history of the U.S. involvement. One can image the astonishment of his commanding officer, as he read an analysis of "the principal considerations of our foreign policy" over the past twenty years! But Noyd didn't stop there. He considered the question of moral responsibility as an aspect of personal identity. Discussing modern cynicism, he concluded that "The Zeitgeist that encourages this cynicism is understandable —men such as Jaspers, Russell, and Camus speak of the feelings of impotence that accompany the vastness and complexity of modern society." Noyd was having none of that feeling if he could help it; he explained that he could not for the sake of his own well-being "ground" himself (by claiming injury or mental incapacity) or seek an assignment other than in Southeast Asia. His resignation seemed the only choice that represented "an honest confrontation of the issues.". . . Which may have made it the last such confrontation in the whole long case it set in motion.

For Noyd's resignation was refused. Far from confronting the issues he raised, the Air Force merely whisked him out of the Academy and made him housing officer at Cannon Air Force Base near the little town of Clovis, New Mexico. At Cannon, Noyd performed so well as housing officer that he was made squadron commander for a short time —till the story got out over the wire services and the base commander heard from the Pentagon. Meanwhile Noyd had filed an application as a conscientious objector, on the grounds that the war violated his humanist beliefs. Since Air Force regulations are not clear as to *selective* objection, Noyd's application was rejected on the grounds that he was not a "universal pacifist."

At this point Noyd, having written hundreds of letters and made scores of contacts, went into federal court with the American Civil Liberties Union in an attempt to force the Defense Department to honor his resignation or to grant him CO status. The court ruled it did not have jurisdiction, that Captain Noyd had not exhausted his "administrative remedies" within the service. The district court was upheld on appeal and the Supreme Court refused to hear the case. But by this time Noyd had gathered to his side a battalion of lawyers and divinity school professors, who had filled up a fat book of testimony. He wrote out another CO application, to call the new testimony to Air Force attention. His new application, which was printed in the *Humanist* magazine, quoted Tillich, Buber, David Muzzey, Teilhard de Chardin, Camus, Huxley, Fromm, Potter, Russell, Pike, Lippmann, Cummings, Lamont, Dewey, and others. He also wrote an essay titled "Ontogeny of the Military Beast," a psychosociological analysis of the motives of the Vietnam fighter pilot. On the first page of the typescript is an explanation that Captain Dale Noyd has been court-martialed, with term and place of sentence left blank.

So Dale Noyd was probably not surprised when the Air Force ordered him out of his noncombatant housing office and assigned him to retrain on the current F-100. In the next few months the Pentagon squandered a good deal of time and money making Dale Noyd into a jet combat flight instructor. Even then, they could have ordered him back to

Europe—and he would have gone. Instead, on December 4, 1967, his squadron commander handed him an order to train a student pilot who would probably be sent to Vietnam. The commander prefaced his order by reading Noyd a little speech not unlike the statement a precinct cop is supposed to read to a suspect to advise him of his rights and privileges. With equal spontaneity, Noyd refused—and the stage was set for the court-martial at Cannon in March of 1968.

The trial begins in a stuffy little room at the end of a long corridor in the long wooden infirmary. Noyd sits at a table with his five lawyers, cheerful, intent, taking in every word, his blond hair never losing its comb grooves. The nine court officers look down from a raised pine-paneled jury box which stretches the length of a side wall. Having been ordered to listen, they listen with obvious effort. Six of the nine have been to Southeast Asia, most of them as pilots. All but two have seen combat.

As for us visitors, we're hungry for combat of our own. We yearn to see a drama in which the final guilt will be assigned and acknowledged. We think that Dale Noyd is going to test for us whether an individual can stand up as the Nuremberg trials said he should and say sorry, no thanks, this war is politically and morally wrong. But we learn very quickly that Dale Noyd's political and moral beliefs will not be examined by the U.S. Air Force. One must be a conscientious objector on religious grounds only, not philosophical or moral.

So the case has to be built around Noyd's "humanism." The ACLU has come weighted with evidence as to the religious profundity of Noyd's beliefs, replete with what his chief counsel keeps referring to as "distinguished theologians." But the Air Force is willing to accept rather casually that Noyd is personally religious. The point to them, as the legal officer (or judge) keeps making clear, is whether or not Dale Noyd knowingly violated an order. If he did, he is guilty, and that is all there is to it. The defense counsel wants to prove the order was "unlawful," because by law the Air Force should have accepted Noyd's CO application. The prosecution ob-

jects; objection sustained. The court will not discuss the question of selective objection.

Most of the next four days are spent with the defense and prosecution huddled around the law officer's dais, discussing what evidence can and cannot be admitted. As soon as the defense touches on Noyd's beliefs, the prosecutor objects, the court is dismissed, and all parties are called to the bench. It soon emerges that Noyd will be guilty as charged unless he can claim that his refusal of the order was not intentional—that it was based on a form of "compulsion." The compulsion, according to Noyd's defense, came from his "religious conscience."

"Sir," objects the gum-chewing major who handles the prosecution, "this raises a question as to whether the defendant is *sane!*"

And so it does. "I told you yesterday," says the law officer to the glowering defense counsel, "that moral compulsion falling short of rendering him mentally incapable would be insufficient defense. I am not going to permit any evidence on religious scruples."

Noyd is thus in a paradoxical position. Though he is sane enough to have scruples about Vietnam, he can establish his innocence only by pleading insanity. Captain Noyd is reminded of *Catch-22*, in which Captain Yossarian is sane enough to want to ground himself. If he were truly insane, Yossarian would want to fly. But then and only then could he qualify for grounding.

Finally, after much out-of-court consultation, the defense counsel works out the wording of certain questions he will be permitted to put to Noyd on the nature of his "compulsion."

COUNSEL: *When you received the order, were you capable of obeying?*
NOYD: *Because of my humanist beliefs, I could not.*
COUNSEL: *Then your state of mind was such that you were incapable of obeying?*
NOYD: *No, I could not.*
COUNSEL: *What was your state of mind?*
NOYD: *Because of these beliefs, the order would have been a flagrant violation, would have destroyed these beliefs. I simply could not obey that order.*

COUNSEL: *Would you state to the court the nature of such beliefs?*
OBJECTION. SUSTAINED. ...

Then comes a lieutenant colonel in his early forties, a man once a colleague of Noyd's at the Academy but who has in the meantime spent a year in Vietnam and is now in Florida instructing "psychological counterinsurgents." The Vietnamese called him Montgomery Clift: he had the same mad, startled stare, the nervous grimace, even the scar. It turns out he is a member of the Mormon priesthood. "Is Noyd a religious man?" they ask him. "Very much so." Questioned about Noyd's integrity, he rates him "in the upper one per cent of all the men I have ever known."

Later I see this man in the hall, standing by himself and watching the others unhappily. "I was *angry*," he says softly, "angry at the establishment—and at my own impotence. By establishment I mean what the hippies mean—all the regulations and institutions that keep us from really discussing the important issues. That's what's happening in this trial."

"But what would you have liked to say?"
"That Dale Noyd has more integrity than any man I've ever met!"
"Then you agree with him!"
"That's not the point. I don't agree with him. But I'm frustrated with the whole U.S. legal system, which is based more on winning than on getting at the truth. It's run by the stereotype, and the stereotype doesn't fit. Believe me, most of these men are very disturbed by Noyd. But there's only just so much input they can take on this issue. When he challenges them he raises doubts as to *the uniform they wear*—do you realize what I mean?—the assumption that they are part of something that is collectively right. Then something clicks off."

We talk longer but it is hard for us to talk. I cannot entirely grasp the shape of his anguish. I wonder what it means to teach counterinsurgency, how he felt at being in Vietnam. He tells me stories of Vietcong tor-

ture and terror. I understand each separate thing he says, but I do not know how he hangs it all together. One urgent insight after another comes tumbling from this man in his neat blue uniform, as I nod and repeat and smile and nod. After a time it becomes clear that there is going to be no connection between the different thoughts he thinks and thinks and thinks. He steps back, watching me nervously, as if he might say one thing more.

Dale Noyd is back on the stand for a final attempt at clarification. He speaks as always with speed and precision, as if the words that come to him are the only words possible. "When I was up against that order, I could not obey that order. I feel that the decision occurred one and a half years before, and from that point on I knew I would do what I must do. Did I have a choice? I don't know. But I felt as if I didn't. I knew I just couldn't. If I could have changed everything I was, then I could have obeyed. If there was a decision, it was a long time ago."

Every eye is on him: there is a sense of awe in the courtroom. Noyd has stuck to his guns, refused to cop an insanity plea. But the catharsis will not come—something doesn't work. By stressing the power of his "beliefs," Noyd has involved himself in an existential contradiction. If he was totally bound to a prior decision, he had given up his moral freedom. In the terms of the moral philosophers of whom his defense is constantly reminding us—Luther, Thomas More, Camus—Noyd's refusal to obey loses its full significance if it is not absolutely conscious and voluntary.

As the court adjourns, Noyd sees that his wife has begun to weep. "What's with *you*?" he smiles. She is laughing at herself through her tears. Noyd pats her on the back and they walk off arm-in-arm to their car as a crowd of photographers gives way before them. They do not care for self-pity, and their matter-of-fact bravery is so impressive that it almost overcomes the trial itself. But it doesn't fit, the trial doesn't mean what they think. ...

There is a little banquet that night at the

local Holiday Inn. The ACLU is having a party for its historical-precedent-setting client, and its lawyers sit in somber discussion at the end of the table. The rest of us are having a peculiar time explaining who we are to one another. "This is a pretty strange group," remarks Noyd, looking up and down with satisfaction. . . . One can see his special delight in presenting a young professor from Michigan State, "my far-out leftist friend." The professor has a little wet mouth inside his beard which is always explaining how things really are. "Dale hasn't changed a bit," the mouth is saying. "He was always a conservative. That's why we get along—right, Dale?"

"Right!" Dale laughs, squints, looks over his shoulder.

"It's the liberals who have put Dale in this position, just like it's the liberals who are doing the killing in Vietnam. I think the time has come when radicals can make alliances with conservatives. We both believe in pulling out our troops and minding our own business, we both believe in building up the blacks inside the ghetto. And we both understand that liberalism is the main enemy."

Dale's brother and wife listen gravely. Like half the Air Force officers, Gus Noyd wears a cornered crew cut showing skin on top. His wife runs a catering service in her spare time and turns over the profits to the Wenatchee hospital. They are scared of Lyndon Johnson, worried about the trial, lonely for their children, and immensely proud of Dale Noyd. But the mouth smiles to itself as it explains to them, because they don't know that they are the enemy.

I wander into the bar with the Air Force men, who are baffled and depressed. To a man they disagree with Noyd. Though they are bothered by the war, the trial doesn't shake them. They see it mostly as the last sad confirmation that their old friend Dale is stepping into a different world, a world of people who talk in abstractions about things they have not seen and cannot know, a world of people who sit around thinking they are better than other people. "Why does Dale need signs?" they want to know. "Why does he

need that Joan Baez poster in his hall?" "I have books too," says a teacher from the Academy, "but I don't have to shove them down your throat.". . .

I remember Montgomery Clift: "There is only so much input they can take." They are upset, whether they know it or not, and they show it constantly. All the younger men, for instance, love *Catch-22*. They love it, they think, because it exposes the bureaucratic ballups of the Air Force. If it weren't for administrative bungling, they continue, we might be doing better in Vietnam.

That's not the main problem, I try to say, but I am drowned out by a violent argument. The president of the junior class has taken on a colonel who was a "political warfare adviser" in Vietnam. They are arguing about "individualism" versus "the collective society," each so contemptuous that the two parts of the argument never touch. The colonel says, "There couldn't be a military without subordination of the individual." Most of the others agree, but the young lieutenant demands to know *what* he is to be subordinated to, and proposes instead a model of "bonded individuals," among whom goals are chosen by consensus. The lieutenant reminds the colonel of his twenty-year-old son, with whom the colonel has no "rapport." "I don't want that kind of rapport," says the colonel. "Because then"—his face insinuating wisdom—"I'd have to advise him.". . .

The next day the prosecuting attorney holds up two fists. "Which is going to take precedence," he demands, "the belief of a man of religious conscience—or an order given by a superior officer?" If individual belief takes precedence, "that would allow each man to become a law unto himself. . . . If you get right down to the nuts and bolts and the nitty-gritty, that order was lawful and was disobeyed."

The ACLU man talks heavily and at great length comparing Noyd again to Luther, staking out his place "in the annals of our history." A Catholic priest lawyer harangues the court on the nature of conscience. But the court gets down to the nuts and bolts: Captain Noyd is found guilty of willfully disobeying an order.

Sentencing will not take place till the next day, after the defense has had a chance to present more witnesses in its claim for "extenuation and mitigation." Dale Noyd celebrates his last night of freedom by having his friends over for lasagna, and playing them Aretha Franklin and Simon and Garfunkel.

The final day opens with the good-humored theologian, who is now allowed to testify to the nature and quality of Noyd's religious feelings. Speaking simply and modestly, he explains Paul Tillich's definition of religion as "total commitment": "If you want to know a man's religion, find what he centers around, where his courage lies." Addressing himself to the president of the court, he praises him for having said on the trial's first day that a soldier must obey orders. That is an example of total commitment. Dale Noyd had also another commitment, and therefore he was caught between two worlds.

The officers are visibly impressed. One major, who has spent the trial half-dozing in suety boredom, suddenly lights up.

MAJOR: *By your definition, what you are is your religion? Any decision I make is my religion?*

THEOLOGIAN: *The risk decisions, the imperatives. You may be a deeply religious man.*

MAJOR: (WITH THE GRACE OF ENLIGHTENMENT UPON HIS BROW) *Then the military life may be a religion!*

THEOLOGIAN: *Yes. One religion may have men deeply involved one way, and another in another way. And at times religious faiths may come in conflict.*

MAJOR: *And that's what we have here.*

THEOLOGIAN: *Apparently.*

MAJOR: (IN AWE) *It's hard to explain.*

LAW OFFICER: (INTERRUPTING) *I think the court should confine itself to questions.*

MAJOR: *No, but it's very interesting. It's not the military against his religion. It's the conflict of two different religions.*

LAW OFFICER: (FIRMLY) *I think I'll renew my previous suggestion.*

MAJOR: (SHEEPISH SMILE)

And thereafter even the prosecutor refers to the case as "a religion butting heads against a religion." And when he holds up his fists again he says that the court "must decide which of these religions must fall away and leave the other standing."

And so it comes to pass in the little town of Clovis, New Mexico, that as a result of an act of "religious conscience," an Air Force officer was hit with the revelation that the military is a religion. From the look of beatitude which passed in that moment across his face, it may be assumed that he went forth and from that day onward napalmed in the holy spirit.

As for Captain Noyd, he received a year's hard labor, loss of pay and allowances, and dismissal from the service. . . .

"Community"

12   Cops: Protectors of the Community, or of Their Own?

Murray Kempton

"Women were thus endlessly absorbent," Lambert Strether came to decide, "and to deal with them was to walk on water." Policemen constitute the only other oppressed minority that has earned the same high compliment, having, like women, developed the subtlest implements to attack and repel while vividly retaining a legitimate sense of inquiry.

These works* are peerings into a cave. Eliot Asinof offers us the case of Laurence Butcher, a Bedford-Stuyvesant Negro who was beaten by two policemen after having refused to pay them off. He then bravely entered upon a struggle for judicial redress, and ended with the reward of a conviction for disorderly conduct. Chevigny's "study" is less, thank God, a study than an intimate memoir of his career as a lawyer provided by the New York Civil Liberties Union for victims of false arrest. Both books are informed equally by passion and common sense and are thus essential to understanding the policeman's means of defense. . . .

The youthful work of William A. Westley . . . help[s] us to understand not only how

   *This article was originally published as a review of several books on the police, especially E. Asinof, *People vs. Butcher*, P. Chevigny, *Police Power*, and W. A. Westley, *The Police*.

policemen act but but how they *feel*. In 1950 Westley was a graduate student under Joseph Lohman at the University of Chicago. Lohman, a criminologist who was to become a sheriff and then again an academician, got him access to the police department of a "midwestern industrial city" which he calls "X." There he was able to interview eighty-five of the city's 180 policemen at great length and with that ingenuity which alone makes length useful.

His findings were reduced to doctoral form but never published. They survive in photostat in the library of the John Jay College of Criminal Justice in New York and nowhere else I know of: an example of policemen's preference that their intimacies neither be published nor perish.

Sixty-two of Westley's eighty-five police subjects felt that the public hated them. "We are," one said, "only 140 against 140,000."

These policemen liked children ("approving innocents to be guided and taught"). They respected the respectable ("In the better districts, the purpose is to make friends of the people and get them to like you"). But they were armed against the slums ("Those people understand and respond only to force").

Westley asked fifty of them what they thought of Negroes. Thirty-eight had an unfavorable opinion; twenty-two of the fifty thought that the Negro is biologically inferior. Sixty per cent of the sample explained

Negro crime as a taint of the Negro character; "lazy, irresponsible by nature" (25 per cent of the whole); "savages" (19 per cent); "born criminals, love crime" (8 per cent); "lacks sense of morals" (6 per cent); "mentally underdeveloped" (3 per cent). By all evidence from which surmise is possible, Westley's City X sounds like Gary, Indiana, which suggests that Mayor Richard Hatcher inherited a police force nearly half of whose members, after serious reflection, had once judged him their biological inferior.

Westley tested a few of his subjects by posing a question approximately like this:

On a two-man radio patrol, you arrest a drunk. In searching him, you find $500 on his person. You drive him to the precinct; your partner sits in the back with the prisoner. When you arrive, the $500 is missing. Only your partner could have stolen it. Upon recovery, the drunk files a complaint against both you and your partner. Would you testify against your partner?

Eleven of the fiteen patrolmen confronted with this hypothesis answered that they would perjure themselves rather than tell the truth about their partner.

When seventy-four policemen were asked when they would think themselves justified in roughing a citizen up, the most frequent reply, volunteered by more than a third, was "Disrespect." An outrage to one's own dignity was offered as an excuse for the use of force more than three times as often as outrage against society, represented by cases involving "hardened criminals" (5 per cent), "people you know are guilty" (3 per cent), or "sex criminals" (3 per cent). None mentioned self-defense. Altogether 66 per cent of the subjects felt that rough treatment was justified in cases where it is absolutely unlawful.

What Westley explored then was the mind of a garrison, formed most of all by the sense of the outsider as enemy, and with a concept of law entirely its own and unrelated to the theoretical concepts of the general community:

When these men are confronted with the alternative of breaking the law by perjury, most of them break the law. [To them] the

law is subordinate to secrecy. Sixty-six per cent believe in [police] violence for illegal but group ends.

Eleven of twelve policemen said that they would overlook enforcement of the statutes against vice, gambling, and shoplifting if their chief told them to. All these incidences of duty subordinated to the needs of the group bring Westley to this plausible conclusion:

When enforcement of the law conflicts with the ends of the police, the law is not enforced. When it supports the ends of the police, they are fully behind it. When it bears no relation to the ends of the police, they enforce it as a matter of routine.

Policemen, like Black Panthers, draw their social cohesion not from the school but from the experience of the streets: they are formed by the "rejection and hostility of the public and the warmth and fraternity of the force itself." All the younger patrolmen in Westley's sample remember two common moments of initiation: they were embarrassed at being so conspicuous in the uniform and all the older policemen tried to help them. The rites of passage into the force seem singularly easy; all the recruits had expected hazing and none had suffered the smallest burden of it. Being thus warmly accepted, they are glad to accept instruction in the wisdom of the experienced, which seems to have two major principles: (1) "What happens between you and I is strictly between you and I. You shouldn't talk about police work off duty." (2) "It is not good for public relations in the police department to arrest too many people."

"The police as a social group," Westley concludes,

possess collective ends arising out of their feeling that the community is hostile to them and their experience as a social stereotype. . . . Their vehicle of self-protection is the rule of silence—secrecy. That of attack is the emphasis on the maintenance of respect for the police.

The rule of defense by secrecy best explains the habit even of police departments as sophisticated as New York City's of burdening their patrolmen with clerical work from which they ought, in all logic, to be relieved by civilians. An Albany senior officer explained ... that if "you get a civilian in here, to him it's just a job. He'll learn things and start blabbing them around. You get a lot of sensitive stuff in police work and you have to know how to keep your mouth shut." ... Nothing is more sensitive than the internal privacies of the police force itself. Any police department's diffidence toward outsiders arises from the condition that they are not trained to silence.

When the *Times* began to discourse on the subject of police corruption, the New York Police Department's Bureau of Internal Affairs started its own investigation. This curious process seems to have been limited to summoning the few policemen indicated from prior experience as the sort who complain about corruption and having them depose on the record that they had never said any such thing to the *Times.* At one such confrontation, the inspector-in-charge turned on his tape recorder and asked the suspect if he knew anything about police corruption. He answered that he certainly did and would now proceed to give instances. Thereupon the inspector-in-charge turned off the tape recorder and announced that the hearing was adjourned.[1]

In this case, the senior officers of the de-

[1]After their nonpublication, Westley presented his findings, in abridged form in articles in *Social Policy* and *The American Journal of Sociology.* They seem to have been repeatedly cited since.... Westley's stature, in any case, comes not just from his ability to perceive but from his unique opportunity to get in. Gary's police chief seems to have made the mistake of ordering his force to talk candidly to Westley. That mistake has not since been repeated; and these eighty-five policemen seem to remain as the only ones whose attitudes have been subject to the observation of a precise and sensitive scholar. The rule of secrecy ever since has made it impossible for Westley, modest as his claims to authority are, to be superseded. A $100,000 grant from the Ford Foundation to study the mind of the New York policeman has reportedly remained unspent for two years now because the department refuses to cooperate.

partment showed themselves not so much bothered by corruption as bothered by the intrusion of outsiders complaining about it. Their primary impulse was to hold back a siege, to repel the *Times,* and to discover traders with that enemy. The garrison mind which directed the resulting scene is, of course, Westley's central subject. ...

The procedures of the Bureau of Internal Affairs, of course, reflect the assurance, which emerges from almost any long conversation with a policeman, that everything is a conspiracy. Westley does not mention this occupational weakness for conspiracy theories, but he does provide one explanation for it. The policeman, Westley says, thinks of himself as having only a single source of social prestige: "He knows what's going on." What is going on, of course, is seldom worth talking about; but social need eventually drives the policeman to pride in "knowing" something he could at best hope only to imagine.

Even those few members of the New York department who testify against corruption cannot, being policemen, concede the possibility that it exists because their superiors are merely slothful and tolerant; they insist that it is a system managed by the highest officers on the force. Their conviction that all life is a conspiracy has survived even after they rebel against so many other canons of the police ethic.

It also survives social enlightenment. A friend tells of a conversation some years ago with Sanford Garelik, now president of the City Council and a former chief inspector, who owed his rise to his delicate and sometimes sincere solicitude for liberal opinion. My friend recalls Garelik talking rather wistfully about the sound and commendable social concerns of the Students for a Democratic Society. It was only a pity, he said, that they were getting all that money from Peking.

The rule that the police attack to maintain respect for themselves is Chevigny's subject and Asinof's. Many of Chevigny's clients were persons who had argued with policemen and been arrested either for disorderly conduct or, in cases where the officer had been aroused enough to work them over, for resisting arrest. The etiquette in matters of enforcing respect seems indeed so stylized as to impel the enforcers to instruct Chevigny early on in his stewardship. He had a client arrested for disorderly conduct who claimed to have been beaten.

"Counselor," said the arresting officer in an injured tone, "we never laid a hand on him. You can tell that. If we had, he would have been charged with resisting arrest, isn't that right?"

Chevigny, without ever losing his sense of engagement, is judicious enough to make us grateful that clients so unfortunate could at least be lucky enough to have had an attorney so sensible. He is capable even of occasionally liking a policeman and he is sensitive to their mystery:

One thoroughly puzzled woman who complained of being manhandled in a welfare center by a policeman told me that the officer had later brought her lunch and said he would like to drop the charges, but he dared not because she might sue the city.

His description of the system, painful as it is, can even occasionally induce in us a detestable and ignominious feeling almost of being entertained. For example:

If there was no crime but rather a personal dispute with the policeman, then the defendant must be charged with disorderly conduct and resisting arrest. Other, more serious charges become something of a matter of taste. Experienced men tend to add other charges, in order to increase the pressure for a plea to guilty to one of the charges.

I once heard two transit policemen arguing in the hallway outside the courtroom after one of my clients had refused to plead guilty to disorderly conduct in exchange for a dismissal of a charge of resisting arrest. The more experienced of the two was saying, "You see? He wouldn't take it. I told you you should have charged him with felonious assault."

Asinof's chronicle of the operation of these techniques in the horrors visited upon Lau-

rence Butcher presents an extreme beyond the run of cases so soberly described by Chevigny. Butcher was the son of a striving Georgia family; his course when young was normal in its errancy—statutory rape, a numbers conviction, a disorderly conduct arrest for crap shooting—until he thought he had found his way as proprietor of a grocery store in Bedford-Stuyvesant.

It was a failing enterprise; and his only chance to stay afloat was to keep it open on Sundays. That resort, he and the police were united in the mistake of thinking, was a violation of the Sabbath closing law. On the first Sunday, he was summoned and paid a five-dollar fine. For a while thereafter, according to his version of events, two radio patrolmen visited him every Sunday and he paid them each two dollars as a tolerance fee.

One Sunday, with his affairs at their worst, he told the patrolmen, "I'm not giving you nothing." They called their sergeant, and Butcher, by now past all caution, announced that the three could just serve him a summons and get out of his store. He was thereafter beaten and pistol-whipped. He spent twelve days in the hospital, unconscious for the first two, and handcuffed to his bed. He emerged charged with felonious assault on an police officer.

Butcher's family had the good fortune to find Conrad Lynn to represent him. Three witnesses agreed to testify for him. The neighborhood had been so intensely agitated that there had been fears of a riot. But by the time Butcher came out, the normal order of events had asserted itself; his store, a shrine in the early hours, was robbed of its poor stock a few days afterward. The Bedford-Stuyvesant Community Corporation would not grant him a rehabilitation loan; at length he had to give up and sell its husk for $700. One of his witnesses moved away, leaving no address. The police offered to reduce the charge against him to mere disorderly conduct; he refused and demanded a swift trial. The district attorney of Kings County did not prosecute the case until eighteen months after the event.

On the morning the trial began, Assistant District Attorney Sheldon Greenberg solicited a corridor conference with Lynn, Butcher's counsel, and offered to permit the defendant to plead guilty to disorderly conduct and then be released.

I told him that I would inform my client of this, but I didn't think he would go for it [Lynn said afterward]. He was an innocent man and he insisted on complete expression of his innocence. ... [Greenberg] said he thought it would be a mistake for me if we didn't accept this deal. He said he could fix it so we wouldn't win, sounding as if there was no question about if.

I replied that we were going to trial anyway. He shook his head sadly and said something about how he didn't want a decent young man like my client to go to prison for this. I guess he was trying to make me feel responsible.

On trial, Butcher listened to the two patrolmen and their sergeant recite their common version of how, alone in his store, he had attacked three armed policemen. On the day before his defense began, he and his wife-to-be went to pick up his last two corroborating witnesses, a father and his son. "However no one was home. At least no one answered the door. They rang persistently for over ten minutes without success." Butcher went off to search for the father at work and the son at school; neither could be found. Somehow there is nothing in all Asinof's story quite so sad as his account of those pathetic pilgrimages. When they were over, Butcher had no witness except himself.

He did no worse than a citizen with a few minor convictions can expect to do when there are three witnesses against him, and those policemen. District Attorney Greenberg could make free play with his skills upon an object so lonely as this; by the time he had finished, Lynn knew the risk his client bore if the case went to the jury. Butcher had a record, such as it was; and, if he should be convicted, Judge Joseph Corso would have little option but to sentence him to six months in prison. The district attorney's bargain held until the case went to the jury; if Butcher would plead guilty to disorderly conduct, the felony charge would be expunged. The morning before the judge was to charge

the jury, Lynn advised his client that it would be best to take the plea.[2]

So Butcher surrendered and pleaded guilty. Both the judge and the district attorney were especially intense about making the record deny any pressure of circumstance as a factor in Butcher's recantation:

"Are you pleading guilty because you are in fact guilty?" the judge demanded.

"Yes, I am," the defendant replied.

"You are not doing it because of fear of anything else?"

"No, I'm not."

"You're doing it because you are in fact guilty?"

"Yes. Yes."

Laurence Butcher had lost his store and some of his health; but the experience had gained him, for the moment, a status of equality before the law: he was, by force of circumstance, another perjurer for the prosecution. That happens to be the only felony Laurence Butcher is known ever to have committed; its commission, plain to the district attorney and probably suspected by the judge, was not cause for his going to prison but the reason for his staying out.

Butcher was only a peculiarly tormented victim of the custom by which prosecutors collude in what they know is a general policy of perjury among the police. Chevigny provides us with both any number of lesser examples and a final definition:

The Criminal Court is not viewed [by policemen] as a tribunal for the determination of fact, but as a sort of administrative adjunct

[2]This was a gesture of honor which might seem extraordinary to the majority which accepts the strictures of respectable lawyers on radical ones. Lynn is a proud Marxist-Leninist. He had spent infinitely more time on this case than his fee could remotely compensate. He took it, he candidly admits, because he had been waiting a long time for a strong case against a policeman. Of the three courses before him, only the guilty plea ought to have disappointed Lynn: if the jury had acquitted, he would have beaten the police department; if the jury convicted, he could, as a revolutionary, point to a thundering instance of iniquity. Even so, he thought only of Butcher.

to the police station for the purpose of obtaining desirable results. Lying is a litigation tool, much like investigation.

This finding, hardly a surprise to prosecutors, makes particularly curious District Attorney Frank Hogan's recent public estimate that there are no more than a thousand corrupt policemen on the force. His tone seems rather blithe when you consider that this figure represents almost 3 per cent of the whole force and a much more sizable proportion of those whose duties offer a chance to take bribes. But catching crooks is hardly the responsibility of the district attorney alone; and we should never complain when he has the dignity to speak of criminals outside his net without the rancor of frustrated vengeance.

The district attorney does seem, however, to have overlooked an obligation which is his alone, the obligation, that is, to present no witness to a jury whose testimony is not absolutely believed by the prosecutor. But we could hardly expect Mr. Hogan to worry much that corrupt policemen might perjure themselves as state witnesses: he must already know that even the honest ones habitually lie under oath. That mendacity is indeed a great help to Mr. Hogan's work. Very few convictions of numbers runners would be possible in New York unless the arresting officer swore to a description of his search methods which not only managed to fit every test of the Supreme Court but was also a lie so formalized by now as not to vary a syllable from case to case.[3]

Yet, grateful as we ought to be for the small glimpses, the shafts of light on this corner or that which three of these writers afford us, the cave remains dark. To fish among policemen is to draw a haul whose only meaning seems to be its contradiction; all that can be caught is the nonrevelatory anecdote.

The current issue of the student newspaper of John Jay College carries a column on the duty of students to care about their responsibilities to the victims of society. It is very much the sort of thing you find in college newspapers these days.

We are [it says in part] now insensitive to the teeming huddled masses which our "Lady of Liberty" is sworn to protect. . . . Our politics vary from the absurd to the surrealistic incarnation of the theory of the "might makes right" concept. We accommodate and vacillate to this "power theory" so frequently that we cannot distinguish our free and willful acts from those which have been dictated to us by our own greedy ambitions. What ever became of "honor," where has our manhood gone? Perhaps those two noble beings are lying in the same pawnshop where we have pledged respect, duty, and responsibility.

This was signed by Raymond Wood, a New York City police detective. In 1965, Robert Collier and two others of the only four known members of the Black Liberation Front were arrested for having plotted to blow up the Statue of Liberty. The other member was an undercover police patrolman who seems to have brought whatever purpose there was to the vagrant musings of the cell, and made such arrangements for this *attentat* as could remotely be called practical.

This patrolman used police funds to rent the car in which he drove Collier to pick up the dynamite; the department even paid for the dynamite; Collier and the others were arrested while they were allegedly rehearsing the plan of assault which the patrolman had drawn up for them. One day Walter Bowe, one of the defendants, had come in and said that he had seen the Statue of Liberty that day and would certainly like to blow that old bitch's head off; the patrolman had answered "Why not?" and was thereafter manager of the project.

The patrolman, of course, was Raymond Wood. His service then is not remembered nor are his words now set forth as irony, but just as mystery.

On the night of Martin Luther King's assassination, one student patrolman entered his classroom at John Jay drunk, stood up,

[3]In fairness, Chevigny finds Hogan increasingly sensitive to police abuse and much less tolerant of its necessary lies than most judges.

raised his hand, and proclaimed, in tones of heavy derision, "A toast to our fallen leader." He was wearing his pistol even while off-duty, as department regulations require. He interrupted the lecture with similar displays of taste until the instructor finally managed to quiet him. Afterward, having a beer with the other student policemen, the instructor remarked that he found this a rather disturbing situation, since the demonstrator was armed and drunk. "Don't worry, Professor," a student policeman answered. "We had him covered."

The Seventy-first Precinct in Brooklyn's Crown Heights seems to suffer the city's highest incidence of random gunfire upon policemen. There have been at least four cases of sniping, the latest in the summer. Two policemen were crippled from an ambush in August, two years ago. The imagination travels to the Crown Heights precinct as to an armed camp; yet when I visited the neighborhood recently its streets had that sylvan quiet with which Brooklyn maintains so much of its power to surprise us. The precinct house was so quiet that the entrance of a Tactical Patrol Force officer with his prisoner seemed almost an intrusion, like a fist through the window, an invasion of the comfortable by the aroused. Occasionally, when the TPF brings in a prize, a patrolman regularly assigned to the precinct will offer the arrestee a friendly greeting, having likely arrested him many times before. Special anti-crime patrols have the function of clearing the streets of the same persons the regular patrolmen used to arrest but sensibly ceased bothering with.

Captain Daniel Berman, the precinct's commander, was at a meeting of its Community Council at the Jewish War Veterans clubhouse. It turned out to be a forum for happy problems; most Negroes in attendance were Jamaicans and home owners.

Their complaints about the police were limited to a lack of diligence in enforcing the alternate side street parking regulation. After the evening ended Captain Berman brought over Patrolman James Rigney, one of the precinct's two community relations officers, to meet me.

"You ought to talk to Jim," the Captain said. "He's been sniped at twice." He spoke like a host who, while grateful for the decorum of the evening, understands that a foreign guest might like a little more spice.

Patrolman Rigney said his windshield had been shot out in the summer of 1968 and his patrol car demolished by a shotgun last summer. He had been unhurt except for scratches and he had decided that his second assailant hadn't even known he was shooting at a policeman, being quite past any sense of reality and unrelated to the urban war.

"The community couldn't have been nicer," Patrolman Rigney said. "The department offered me a transfer but I wanted to stay. My wife kept asking why I stayed in that crazy neighborhood. I told her it's not crazy; these people are really trying not to let this city deteriorate them. But then I guess it's my community; I live in Rockaway, but, with college, I spend more time here than I do at home."

He wasn't entirely sure that the snipings had been altogether bad. "They've made us understand that the best way of combatting these things is to be more friendly with people." He paused, as policemen seem so often to do, as if some interior desk officer had fed them the signal of duty to the garrison. "I'm not saying that all patrolmen feel this way. But I do."

The one thing you must learn never to expect from any policeman is the thing you expected.

13 The Folkways of a Real American Political Community

Donald Matthews

Reading only the selection by Kempton, one might think that the problem with American community is simply that we don't have any. But of course we do. And by all accounts, one of the most significant communities in America is the body of one hundred United States senators. The point of the following selection is not merely to show some influences on the behavior of senators, or some factors that contribute to a senator's legislative effectiveness. What Matthews is describing here is the kind of community that Americans form, in those rare situations when some sort of real community does come into existence. What is perhaps most striking about Matthews' subtle and informed account (which is as accurate today as it was when written) is the way that the senators' "folkways" almost seem calculated to turn what might have been a serious public forum into a cross between a bureaucratic organization, a cocktail party, and a marketplace!—Ed.

The Senate of the United States, just as any other group of human beings, has its unwritten rules of the game, its norms of conduct, its approved manner of behavior. Some things are just not done; others are met with widespread approval. "There is great pressure for conformity in the Senate," one of its influential members said. "It's just like living in a small town."

What are the standards to which the senators are expected to conform? What, specifically, do these unwritten rules of behavior say? Why do they exist? In what ways do they influence the senators? How, concretely, are they enforced? What kinds of senators obey the folkways? Which ones do not, and why?

These are difficult questions for an outsider to analyze. Only those who have served

Reprinted from Donald Matthews, *U.S. Senators and Their World* (Chapel Hill: University of North Carolina Press, 1960), by permission of the publisher. Footnotes have been renumbered and some have been omitted.

in the Senate, and perhaps not even all of them, are likely to grasp its folkways in all their complexity. Yet, if we are to understand why senators behave as they do, we must try to understand them.

APPRENTICESHIP

The first rule of Senate behavior, and the one most widely recognized off the Hill, is that new members are expected to serve a proper apprenticeship.

The freshman senator's subordinate status is impressed upon him in many ways. He receives the committee assignments the other senators do not want. The same is true of his office suite and his seat in the chamber. In committee rooms he is assigned to the end of the table. He is expected to do more than his share of the thankless and boring tasks of the Senate, such as presiding over the floor debate or serving on his party's Calendar Committee. According to the folkways of the

144

Senate, the freshman is expected to accept such treatment as a matter of course. . . .

The freshman who does not accept his lot as a temporary but very real second-class senator is met with thinly veiled hostility. For instance, one old-timer tells this story:

When I came to the Senate, I sat next to Senator Borah. A few months later, he had a birthday. A number of the older men got up and made brief, laudatory speeches about it. Borah was pleased. Then a freshman senator —one who had only been in the chamber three or four months—got to his feet and started on a similar eulogy. He was an excellent speaker. But between each of his laudatory references to Borah, Borah loudly whispered, "That son-of-a-bitch, that son-of-a-bitch." He didn't dislike the speaker, personally. He just didn't feel that he should speak so soon.

Even so, the veterans in the Senate remark, rather wistfully, that the practice of serving an apprenticeship is on the way out, and, to some extent, they are undoubtedly correct. The practice seems to have begun well before the popular election of senators and the exigencies of the popularly elected official have placed it under considerable strain. As one very senior senator, whose service extends back almost to the days before popular election, ruefully explained: "A new senator today represents millions of people. He feels that he has to do something to make a record from the start."

This judgment is also colored by the tendency in any group for the old-timers to feel that the young generation is going to hell in a handbasket. To the present-day freshmen in the Senate, the period of apprenticeship is a very real and very confining. As one of them put it, "It reminds me a little of Hell Week in college." Indeed, the nostalgic talk of the older senators regarding the unhappy lot of the freshman in the good old days is one way the senior senators keep the younger men in their place. One freshman Democrat, for example, after completing a floor speech found himself sitting next to Senator George, then the dean of the Senate. Thinking that he should make polite conver-

sation, the freshman asked the Georgia patriarch what major changes had taken place in the Senate during his long service. Senator George replied, "Freshman didn't use to talk so much." . . .

SPECIALIZATION

According to the folkways of the Senate, a senator should not try to know something about every bill that comes before the chamber nor try to be active on a wide variety of measures. Rather, he ought to specialize, to focus his energy and attention on the relatively few matters that come before his committees or that directly and immediately affect his state. "When you come to the Senate," one administrative assistant said, "you have to decide which street corner you are going to fight on."

In part, at least, senators ought to specialize because they must: "Thousands of bills come before the Senate each Congress. If some senator knows the fine details of more than half a dozen of them, I've never heard of him." Even when a senator restricts his attention to his committee work, the job is more than one man can do. "I belong to twelve or thirteen committees and subcommittees," a leading senator says. "It's physically impossible to give them all the attention I should. So I have picked out two or three subcommittees in which I am especially interested and have concentrated on them. I believe that this is the usual practice around here."

The relatively few senators who have refused to specialize agree. One of these, a relatively young man of awesome energy, says, "I'll be perfectly frank with you. Being active on as wide a range of issues as I have been is a man-killing job. In a few years I suspect that I will be active on many fewer issues. I came down here a young man and I'm gradually petering out." The limit of human endurance is not, however, the only reason for a senator to specialize. By restricting his attention to matters concerning his committee work and his home state, the senator is concentrating on the two things he should know best. Only through specialization can he know more about a subject than his colleagues and thus make a positive contribution to the operation of the chamber. . . .

Moreover, modern legislation is complex and technical, and it comes before the Senator in a crushing quantity. The committee system and specialization—in a word, a division of labor within the chamber—increase skill and decrease the average senator's work load to something approaching manageable proportions. When a senator refuses to "go along" with specialization, he not only challenges the existing power structure but also decreases the expert attention which legislative measures receive.

COURTESY

The Senate of the United States exists to solve problems, to grapple with conflicts. Sooner or later, the hot, emotion-laden issues of our time come before it. Senators as a group are ambitious and egocentric men, chosen through an electoral battle in which a talent for invective, righteous indignation, "mud-slinging," and "engaging in personalities" are often assets. Under these circumstances, one might reasonably expect a great deal of manifest conflict and competition in the Senate. Such conflict does exist, but its sharp edges are blunted by the felt need—expressed in the Senate folkways—for courtesy.

A cardinal rule of Senate behavior is that political disagreements should not influence personal feelings. This is not an easy task; for as one senator said, "It's hard not to call a man a liar when you know that he is one."

Fortunately, a number of the chamber's formal rules and conventions make it possible for him to approximate this ideal—at least so far as overt behavior is concerned. The selection of committee members and chairmen on the basis of their seniority neatly by-passes a potential cause of grave dissension in the Senate. The rules prohibit the questioning of a colleague's motives or the criticism of another state. All remarks made on the floor are, technically, addressed to the presiding officer, and this formality serves as a psychological barrier between antagonists. Senators are expected to address each other not by name but by title—

Earle C. Clements does not disagree with Irving M. Ives, but rather the Senior Senator from Kentucky disagrees with the Senior Senator from New York.

Sometimes the senators' efforts to achieve verbal impersonality become ludicrous in their stilted formality. For example:

MR. JOHNSON OF TEXAS: *The Senator from Texas does not have any objection, and the Senator from Texas wishes the Senator from California to know that the Senator from Texas knew the Senator from California did not criticize him. . . .*[1]

Few opportunities to praise publicly a colleague are missed in the Senate. Senators habitually refer to each other as "The distinguished Senator from _____" or "The able Senator from _____." Birthdays, anniversaries, reelection or retirement from the Senate, and the approach of adjournment are seized as opportunities for the swapping of praise. Sometimes, on these occasions, the sentiment is as thick as Senate bean soup. For example, the following recently took place on the Senate floor and was duly printed in the *Record:*

MR. JOHNSON OF TEXAS: *Mr. President, if the Senate will indulge me, I should like the attention of members of both sides of the aisle for a bipartisan announcement of considerable importance. It involves the minority leader, the distinguished Senator from California* [MR. KNOWLAND].

For many years, I have been closely associated with the Senator from California. Like every member of this chamber—on either side of the aisle—I have found him to be able, patriotic, courteous, and thoughtful.

But I wonder how many colleagues know that he is also a five-time winner in the contest for the proudest granddaddy in the Senate?

His fifth victory was chalked up last Monday when Harold Jewett II discovered America. Anybody who has found buttons lying on the floor in front of the minority leader's desk in the past few days can know now that they popped right off Bill Knowland's shirt. . . .

[1] Except when otherwise noted, this and the following quotations are taken from the *Congressional Record.*

In private, senators are frequently cynical regarding this courtesy. They say that "it doesn't mean a thing," that it is "every man for himself in the Senate," that some of their colleagues "no more should be senators than I should be Pope," that it is "just custom." Senator Barkley's advice to the freshman senator—if you think a colleague stupid, refer to him as "the able, learned, and distinguished senator," but if you *know* he is stupid, refer to him as "the *very* able, learned, and distinguished senator"—is often quoted.[2] Despite its blatant hypocrisy, the practice persists, and after serving in the Senate for a period of years most senators grow to appreciate it. "You discover that political self-preservation dictates at least a semblance of friendship. And then before you know it, you really *are* friends. It is rather like the friendships that might develop within a band of outlaws. You all hang together or you will hang separately."

Courtesy, far from being a meaningless custom as some senators seem to think it is, permits competitors to cooperate. The chaos which ensues when this folkway is ignored testifies to its vital function.

RECIPROCITY

Every senator, at one time or another, is in a position to help out a colleague. The folkways of the Senate hold that a senator should provide this assistance and that he be repaid in kind. The most important aspect of this pattern of reciprocity is, no doubt, the trading of votes. Occasionally this is done quite openly in the course of public debate. The following exchange, for example, took place during the 1956 debate on acreage allotments for burley tobacco:

MR. LANGER [North Dakota]: *We don't raise any tobacco in North Dakota, but we are interested in the tobacco situation in Kentucky, and I hope the Senator will support us in securing assistance for the wheat growers in our State.*

MR. CLEMENTS [Kentucky]: *I think the Senator will find that my support will be 100 per cent.*

[2]Alben W. Barkley, *That Reminds Me* (Garden City, N.Y.: Doubleday, 1954), p. 255.

MR. BARKLEY [Kentucky]: *Mr. President, will my colleague from Kentucky yield?*

MR. CLEMENTS: *I yield.*

MR. BARKLEY: *The colloquy just had confirms and justifies the Woodrow Wilsonian doctrine of open covenants openly arrived at.* [Laughter].

Usually, however, this kind of bargain is either made by implication or in private. Senator Douglas of Illinois, who tried unsuccessfully to combat this system, has analyzed the way in which a public works appropriation bill is passed.

. . . This bill is built up out of a whole system of mutual accommodations in which the favors are widely distributed, with the implicit promise that no one will kick over the applecart; that if Senators do not object to the bill as a whole, they will "get theirs." It is a process, if I may use an inelegant expression, of mutual backscratching and mutual logrolling.

Any member who tries to buck the system is only confronted with an impossible amount of work in trying to ascertain the relative merits of a given project; and any member who does ascertain them, and who feels convinced that he is correct, is unable to get an individual project turned down because the senators from the State in which the project is located, and thus is benefiting, naturally will oppose any objection to the project; and the other members of the Senate will feel that they must support the Senators in question, because if they do not do so, similar appropriations for their own States at some time likely will be called into question.

Of course, *all* bills are not passed as the result of such implicit or explicit "deals." . . .

INSTITUTIONAL PATRIOTISM

Most institutions demand an emotional investment from their members. The Senate of the United States is no exception. Senators are expected to believe that they belong to the greatest legislative and deliberative body in the world. They are expected to be a bit suspicious of the President and the bureaucrats and just a little disdainful of the House. They are expected to revere the Senate's personnel, organization, and folkways and to champion them to the outside world.

Most of them do. "The most remarkable group that I have ever met anywhere," "the most able and intelligent body of men that it [has] been my fortune to meet," "the best men in political life today"; thus senators typically describe their colleagues. The Senate as an institution is usually described in similar superlatives.

A senator whose emotional commitment to Senate ways appears to be less than total is suspect. One who brings the Senate as an institution or senators as a class into public disrepute invites his own destruction as an effective legislator. One who seems to be using the Senate for the purposes of self-advertisement and advancement obviously does not belong. Senators are, as a group, fiercely protective of, and highly patriotic in regard to, the Senate.

This, after all, is not a great deal different from the school spirit of P.S. 34, or the morale of a military outfit, or the "fight" of a football team. But ... its political consequences are substantial, for some senators are in a better position than others to develop this emotional attachment. ...

All this would be very "interesting" but not particularly important to serious students of politics if the Senate folkways did not influence the distribution of power within the chamber.

The senators believe, either rightly or wrongly, that without the respect and confidence of their colleagues they can have little influence in the Senate. "You can't be effective," they said over and over again, "unless you are respected—on both sides of the aisle." The safest way to obtain this respect is to conform to the folkways, to become a "real Senate man." Those who do not run a serious risk. "In the Senate, if you don't conform, you don't get many favors for your state. You are never told that, but you soon learn." ...

In order to test this hypothesis, a crude index of "Legislative Effectiveness" was constructed for the Eighty-third and Eighty-fourth Congresses by calculating the proportion of all public bills and resolutions introduced by each senator that were passed by the Senate. While such an index does not pretend to measure the over-all power or influence of a senator, it does seem to reflect his efficiency as a legislator, narrowly defined. To the extent that the concept as used on Capitol Hill has any distinct meaning, "effectiveness" seems to mean the ability to get one's bills passed.

The "effectiveness" of the conforming and nonconforming senators is presented in [the accompanying table]. The less a senator talks on the Senate floor, and the narrower a senator's area of legislative interest and activity, the greater is his "effectiveness." Conformity to the Senate folkways does, therefore, seem to "pay off" in concrete legislative results.

FLOOR SPEAKING, ... SPECIALIZATION, AND LEGISLATIVE EFFECTIVENESS
(83RD AND 84TH CONGRESSES)

Level of Floor Speaking	Index of Legislative Effectiveness			
	High	Medium	Low	
High	0%	33%	67%	100% (9)
Medium	3%	68%	29%	100% (31)
Low	15%	59%	26%	100% (39)
Index of Specialization				
High	23%	69%	8%	100% (13)
Medium	10%	62%	28%	100% (29)
Low	8%	51%	41%	100% (39)

"Leadership"

14   The Battle of People's Park:
A Case Study in Bureaucratic Leadership

Sheldon S. Wolin and John H. Schaar

Shortly before 5:00 A.M., on Thursday, May 15, 1969, a motley group of about fifty hippies and "street-people" were huddled together on a lot 270 x 450 feet in Berkeley. The lot was owned by the Regents of the University of California and located a few blocks south of the Berkeley campus. Since mid-April this lot had been taken over and transformed into a "People's Park" by scores of people, most of whom had no connection with the university. Now the university was determined to reassert its legal rights of ownership. A police officer approached the group and announced that it must leave or face charges of trespassing. Except for three persons, the group left and the area was immediately occupied and surrounded by about 200 police from Berkeley, Alameda County, and the campus. The police were equipped with flak jackets, tear gas launchers, shotguns, and telescopic rifles. At 6:00 A.M. a construction crew arrived and by mid-afternoon an eight-foot steel fence encircled the lot.

At noon a rally was convened on campus and about 3,000 people gathered. The president-elect of the student body spoke. He started to suggest various courses of action that might be considered. The crowd responded to the first of these by spontane-

ously marching toward the lot guarded by the police. (For this speech, the speaker was charged a few days later with violating numerous campus rules, and, on the initiative of university officials, indicted for incitement to riot.) The crowd was blocked by a drawn police line. Rocks and bottles were thrown at the police, and the police loosed a tear gas barrage, scattering the crowd. Elsewhere, a car belonging to the city was burned. Meanwhile, police reinforcements poured in, soon reaching around 600. A rock was thrown from a rooftop and, without warning, police fired into a group on the roof of an adjacent building. Two persons were struck in the face by the police fire, another was blinded, probably permanently, and a fourth, twenty-five-year-old James Rector, later died. Before the day was over, at least thirty others were wounded by police gunfire and many more by clubs. One policeman received a minor stab wound and six more were reported as having been treated for minor cuts and bruises.

Meanwhile, action shifted to the campus itself, where police had herded a large crowd into Sproul Plaza by shooting tear gas along the bordering streets. The police then formed small detachments which continuously swept across the campus, breaking up groups of all sizes. Tear gas enfolded the main part of the campus and drifted into many of its buildings, as well as into the surrounding city. Nearby streets were littered with broken glass and rubble. At least six buckshot slugs entered the main library and three .38 caliber bullets lodged in the wall of a reference room in the same building. Before the day ended, more than ninety people had been injured by police guns and clubs.

Under a "State of Extreme Emergency" proclamation issued by Governor Reagan on February 5 in connection with the "Third World Strike" at Berkeley late last winter and never rescinded, a curfew was imposed on the city. Strict security measures were enforced on campus and in the nearby business districts, and all assemblies and rallies were prohibited. The proclamation also centralized control of the police under the command of Sheriff Frank Madigan of Alameda County.

Roger Heyns, the chancellor of the university, saw none of this, for he had left the previous day for a meeting in Washington. His principal vice chancellor had gone to the regents' meeting in Los Angeles. The regents took notice of the events by declaring, "It is of paramount importance that law and order be upheld." The governor said that the lot had been seized by the street-people "as an excuse for a riot." A Berkeley councilman called the previous use of the lot a "Hippie Disneyland freak show."

The next day, May 16, 2,000 National Guardsmen appeared in full battle dress, armed with rifles, bayonets, and tear gas. They were called into action by the governor, but apparently the initiative came from local authorities acting in consultation with university administrators. Helicopters weaved back and forth over the campus and city. Berkeley was occupied. (The next day one helicopter landed on campus and an officer came out to ask that students stop flying their kites because the strings might foul his rotors. A collection was promptly taken and the sky was soon full of brightly colored kites.)

During the next few days a pattern emerged. Each day began quietly, almost like any other day, except that people awoke to the roar of helicopters and the rumble of transports. As university classes began (they had never been officially cancelled), the guardsmen formed a line along the south boundary of the campus. The guard and the police would cordon off the main plaza and station smaller detachments at various points around the campus. Gradually the students crowded together, staring curiously at the guardsmen and occasionally taunting them. The guard stood ready with bayonets pointed directly at the crowd. This stand-off would continue for an hour or two, and then the police would charge the crowd with clubs and tear gas. The crowd would scatter, the police would give chase, the students and street-people would curse and sometimes hurl rocks or return tear-gas canisters, and the police would beat or arrest some of them.

On Tuesday, May 20, the pattern and tempo changed. Previously the police had sought to break up gatherings on the campus, so now the protesters left the campus and began a peaceful march through the city. This was promptly stopped by the police. The marchers then filtered back to campus and a crowd of about 3,000 assembled. The group was pressed toward the plaza by the police and guardsmen and, when solidly hemmed in, was attacked by tear gas. A little later a helicopter flew low over the center of the campus and spewed gas over a wide area, even though the crowd had been thoroughly scattered. Panic broke out and people fled, weeping, choking, vomiting. Gas penetrated the university hospital, imperiling patients and interrupting hospital routines. It caused another panic at the university recreation area, nearly a mile from the center of campus, where many people, including mothers and children, were swimming. The police also threw gas into a student snack bar and into an office and classroom building.

The next day, May 21, was a turning point. More than 200 faculty members announced their refusal to teach; a local labor council condemned the police action; some church groups protested; and the newspapers and television stations began to express some criticism. Controversy arose over the ammunition which the police had used the previous Thursday. Sheriff Madigan was evasive about the size of birdshot issued, but the evidence was clear that buckshot had killed James Rector. The tear gas was first identified as the normal variety (CN) for crowd disturbances, but later it was officially acknowledged that a more dangerous gas (CS) was also used. The American army uses CS gas to flush out guerrillas in Vietnam. It can cause projectile vomiting, instant diarrhea and skin blisters, and even death, as it has to the VC, when the victim is tubercular. The Geneva Conventions outlaw the use of CS in warfare.

On the same day the chancellor issued his first statement. He deplored the death which had occurred, as well as "the senseless violence." He warned that attempts were being made "to polarize the community and prevent rational solutions," and he stated that a university has a responsibility to follow "civilized procedures." Heyns made no criticism of the police or National Guard tactics: the same day a guardsman had thrown down his helmet, dropped his rifle, and reportedly shouted, "I can't stand this any more." He was handcuffed, taken away for a physical examination, and then rushed off to a psychiatric examination. He was diagnosed as suffering from "suppressed aggressions."

In Sacramento, where a deputation of Berkeley faculty members was meeting with the governor, aggression was more open. The governor conceded that the helicopter attack might have been a "tactical mistake," but he also insisted that "once the dogs of war are unleashed, you must expect things will happen. ..." Meantime, the statewide commander of the guards defended the gas attack on the grounds that his troops were threatened. He noted that the general who ordered the attack had said, "It was a godsend that it was done at that time." The commander regretted the "discomfort and inconvenience to innocent bystanders," but added: "it is an inescapable by-product of combatting terrorists, anarchists, and hardcore militants on the streets and on the campus."

The next day, May 22, a peaceful march and flower-planting procession began in downtown Berkeley. With little warning, police and guardsmen converged on the unsuspecting participants and swept them along with a number of shoppers, newsmen, people at lunch, and a mailman, into a parking lot, where 482 were arrested, bringing the weeks's total near 800. As those arrested were released on bail, disturbing stories began to circulate concerning the special treatment accorded to "Berkeley types" in Santa Rita prison.

These stories, supported by numerous affidavits and news accounts submitted by journalists who had been bagged in the mass arrest, told of beatings, verbal abuse and humiliation, physical deprivations, and refusal of permission to contact counsel. Male prisoners told of being marched into the prison yard and forced to lie face down, absolutely motionless, on gravel and concrete for several hours. The slightest shift in posture, except for a head movement permitted once every half-hour, was met with a blow to the kidneys or testicles. On May 24 a district court judge issued an order restraining Sheriff Madigan's subordinates from beating and otherwise mistreating the arrestees taken to Santa Rita prison.

Despite all the arrests, the shotguns, gas, and clubs, the protesters have thus far shown remarkable restraint. Although both police and guards have been targets of much foul language and some hard objects, nothing remotely resembling sustained violence has been employed against the police; and the guard has been spared from all except verbal abuse. At this writing, the only damage to campus property, other than that caused by the police, has been two broken windows and one flooded floor.

After the mass arrests, the governor lifted the curfew and the ban on assemblies, saying "a more controlled situation" existed. But he warned that no solution was likely until the troublemaking faculty and students were separated from the University. "A professional revolutionary group," he said, was behind it all. Charles Hitch, the president of the

University of California, issued his first statement. (Much earlier, his own staff issued a statement protesting campus conditions of "intolerable stress" and physical danger.) The president ventured to criticize "certain tactics" of the police, but noted that these "were not the responsibility of university authorities."

In a television interview, the chancellor agreed with the president, but added that negotiations were still possible because "we haven't stopped the rational process." A published interview (May 22) with the principal vice chancellor found him saying, "Our strategy was to act with humor and sensitivity. For instance, we offered to roll up the sod in the park and return it to the people. . . . We had no reason to believe there would be trouble." Meanwhile the governor was saying, "The police didn't kill the young man. He was killed by the first college administrator who said some time ago it was all right to break laws in the name of dissent."

The governor also accused the president of the university, a former assistant secretary of defense and RANDsman, of "trying to weasel" to the side of the street-people. Two days later the governor refused the request of the Berkeley City Council to end the state of emergency and recall the guard—requests, it might be added, that the university itself had not yet made. At this time the mayor of Berkeley suggested that police tactics had been "clumsy and not efficient," to which Sheriff Madigan retorted: "If the mayor was capable of running the city so well without problems we wouldn't be here. I advise the mayor to take his umbrella and go to Berkeley's Munich. . . ."

On Friday, May 23, the Faculty Senate met. It listened first to a speech by the chancellor in which he defined the occupation of the lot as an act of "unjustified aggression" against the university, and declared that the "avoidance of confrontations cannot be the absolute value." He said that the fence would remain as long as the issue was one of possession and control, and, pleading for more "elbow room," he asserted that the faculty

should support or at least not oppose an administrative decision once it had been made. The faculty then defeated a motion calling for the chancellor's removal (94 voted for, 737 against, and 99 abstained). It approved, by a vote of 737 to 94, a series of resolutions which condemned what was called "as irresponsible a police and military reaction to a civic disturbance as this country has seen in recent times."

The resolutions demanded withdrawal of "the massive police and military presence on campus"; the "cessation of all acts of belligerency and provocation by demonstrators"; and investigation by the attorney general of California and the Department of Justice; and the prompt implementation of a plan whereby part of the lot would become "an experimental community-generated park" and the fence would be simultaneously removed. The faculty also resolved to reconvene in a few days to reassess the situation.

There is where events now stand (May 26). But pressures from all sides are increasing. A student referendum, which saw the heaviest turnout in the history of student voting, found 85 per cent of the nearly 15,000 who voted favoring the use of the lot as it had been before the occupation. The students also voted to assess themselves $1.50 each quarter to help finance an ethnic studies department previously accepted by the university but now foundering. As of this writing, college students from all over the state are planning direct protests to Governor Reagan. Leaders of the protesters are preparing for a huge march against the fence on Memorial Day. The governor remains committed to a hard line. All the issues remain unsettled.

What brought on this crisis? Like many of its sister institutions, the Berkeley campus has been steadily advancing its boundaries into the city. Back in 1956 it had announced its intention to purchase property in the area which includes the present disputed lot. Owing to its lack of funds, very little land was actually purchased. Finally, in June 1967, the monies were allocated and the university announced that ultimately dormitories would be build on the land, but that in the interim it would be used for recreation.

The lot itself was purchased in 1968, but no funds were then available for development. Undoubtedly the university was aware of the disastrous experience of other academic institutions which had attempted to "redevelop" surrounding areas. In fact, a short time ago the university announced, with much fanfare, its intention to mount a major attack on the problems of the cities. Despite these professions, the university's treatment of its own urban neighbors has consisted of a mixture of middle-class prejudice, esthetic blindness, and bureaucratic callousness.

The victims in this case, however, have not been so much the blacks as another pariah group, one whose identity is profoundly influenced by the university itself. For many years, Telegraph Avenue and "the south campus area" have constituted a major irritant to the university, the city fathers, and the business interests. It is the Berkeley demimonde, the place where students, hippies, dropouts, radicals, and runaways congregate. To the respectables, it is a haven for drug addicts, sex fiends, criminals, and revolutionaries. Until the university began its expansion, it was also an architectural preserve for fine old brown-shingle houses and interesting shops. It is no secret that the university has long considered the acquisition of land as a means of ridding the area not of substandard housing, but of its human "blight." The disputed lot was the perfect symbol of the university's way of carrying out urban regeneration: first, raze the buildings; next let the land lie idle and uncared for; then permit it to be used as an unimproved parking lot, muddy and pitted; and finally, when the local people threaten to use and enjoy the land, throw a fence around it.

Around mid-April, a movement was begun by street-people, hippies, students, radicals, and a fair sprinkling of elderly free spirits to take over the parking lot and transform it. Many possibilities were discussed: a child-care clinic; a crafts fair; a baseball diamond. Soon grass and shrubs were planted, playground equipment installed, benches built, and places made for eating, lounging, and occasional speech-making. About 200 people were involved in the beginning, but soon the park was intensively and lovingly used by children, the young, students and street-people, and the elderly. A week after the park began, the university announced its intention to develop a playing field by July 1, and the park people responded by saying that the university would have to fight for it. Discussions followed, but not much else. The university said, however, that no construction would be started without proper warning and that it was willing to discuss the future design of the field.

On May 8 the chancellor agreed to form a committee representing those who were using the lot as well as the university. But he insisted as "an essential condition" of discussions about the future of the land that all work on the People's Park cease. In addition he announced certain guidelines for his committee: university control and eventual use must be assured; the field must not produce "police and other control problems"; and no political or public meetings were to be held on the land. Suddenly, on May 13, he announced his decision to fence in the area as the first step toward developing the land for intramural recreation. "That's a hard way to make a point," he said, "but that's the way it has to be. . . . The fence will also give us time to plan and consult. Regretfully, this is the only way the entire site can be surveyed, soil-tested, and planned for development . . . hence the fence."

Why did it have to be this way? Because, as the chancellor explained, it was necessary to assert the university's title to ownership. Concerning the apparent lack of consultation with his own committee, he said that a plan could not be worked out because the park people had not only refused to stop cultivating and improving the land, but they had "refused to organize a responsible committee" for consultative purposes. In addition, he cited problems of health, safety, and legal liability, as well as complaints from local residents.

The first response came from the faculty chairman of the chancellor's committee. He declared that the chancellor had allowed only two days (the weekend) for the committee to produce a plan and that the "university didn't seem interested in negotiations." On May 14 a protest rally was held and the anarchs of the park, surprisingly, pulled themselves together and formed a negotiating committee. Although rumors of an impending fence were circulating, spokesmen for the park people insisted that they wanted discussion, not confrontation.

On May 15, the day immediately preceding the early morning police action, the chancellor placed an advertisement in the campus newspaper inviting students to draw up "ideas or designs" for the lot and to submit them by May 21. The ad was continued even after the military occupation. On May 18, three days after the occupation had begun, the chancellor announced that there would be "no negotiations in regard to the land known as People's Park," although discussions might go on "while the fence is up anyway." His principal vice chancellor, in an interview reported on May 22, stated that the university had not turned down a negotiating committee.

He also noted—and this was after the helicopter attack—that "the fence was necessary to permit the kind of rational discussion and planning that wasn't possible before." Once more the faculty chairman had to protest that he had not been informed of meetings between the administration and representatives of the People's Park and that the chancellor had consistently ignored the committee's recommendations. However, the principal vice chancellor had an explanation for this lack of consultation: "I guess that's because the chancellor didn't want him to get chewed up by this thing."

Why did the making of a park provoke such a desolating response? The bureaucratic nature of the multiversity and its disas-

trous consequences for education are by now familiar and beyond dispute. So, too, is the web of interdependence between it and the dominant military, industrial, and political institutions of our society. These explain much about the response of the university to the absurd, yet hopeful, experiment of People's Park.

What needs further comment is the increasingly ineffectual quality of the university's responses, particularly when its organizational apparatus attempts to cope with what is spontaneous, ambiguous, and disturbingly human. It is significant that the Berkeley administration repeatedly expressed irritation with the failure of the park people to "organize" a "responsible committee" or to select "representatives" who might "negotiate." The life styles and values of the park people were forever escaping the categories and procedures of those who administer the academic plant.

Likewise the issue itself: the occupants of the park wanted to use the land for a variety of projects, strange but deeply natural, which defied customary forms and expectations, whereas, at worst, the university saw the land as something to be fenced, soil-tested, processed through a score of experts and a maze of committees, and finally encased in the tight and tidy form of a rational design. At best, the most imaginative use of the land which the university could contemplate was as a "field-experiment station" where faculty and graduate students could observe their fellow beings coping with their "environment." In brief, the educational bureaucracy, like bureaucracies elsewhere, is experiencing increasing difficulty, because human life is manifesting itself in forms which are unrecognizable to the mentality of the technological age.

This suggests that part of the problem lies in the very way bureaucracies perceive the world and process information from it. It was this "bureaucratic epistemology" which largely determined how the university responded to the People's Park. Bureaucracy is both an expression of the drive for rationality and predictability and one of the chief agencies in making the world ever more rational and predictable, for the bureaucratic mode of knowing and behaving comes to constitute the things known and done themselves.

Now this rational form of organizing human efforts employs a conception of knowledge which is also rational in specific ways (cf. Kenneth Keniston's analysis in *The Uncommitted: Alienated Youth in American Society* [reprinted in Part V]). The only legitimate instrument of knowledge is systematic cognition, and the only acceptable mode of discourse is the cognitive mode. Other paths to knowledge are suspect. Everything tainted with the personal, the subjective, and the passionate is suppressed, or dismissed as prejudice or pathology. A bureaucrat who based his decisions upon, say, intuition, dialectical reason, empathic awareness, or even common sense, would be guilty of misconduct.

The bureaucratic search for "understanding" does not begin in wonder, but in the reduction of the world to the ordinary and the manageable. In order to deal with the world in the cognitive mode, the world must first be approached as an exercise in "problem-solving." To say there is a problem is to imply there is a solution; and finding the solution largely means devising the right technique. Since most problems are "complex," they must be broken down by bureaucrats into their component parts before the right solution can be found. Reality is parsed into an ensemble of discrete though related parts, and each part is assigned to the expert specially qualified to deal with that part. Wholes can appear as nothing more than assemblages of parts, just as a whole automobile is an assemblage of parts. But in order for wholes to be broken into parts, things that are dissimilar in appearance and quality must be made similar.

This is done by abstracting from the objects dealt with those aspects as though they were the whole. Abstraction and grouping by common attributes require measuring tools that yield comparable units for analysis: favorite ones are units of money, time, space, and power; income, occupation, and party affiliation. All such measurements and comparisons subordinate qualitative dimensions, natural context, and unique and variable properties to the common, stable, external, and reproducible. This way of thinking becomes real when campus administrators define "recreation" in fixed and restrictive terms so that it may accord with the abstract demands of "lead-time." In a way Hegel might barely recognize, the Rational becomes the Real and the Real the Rational.

When men treat themselves this way, they increasingly become this way, or they desperately try to escape the "mind-forged manacles," as Blake calls them, of the bureaucratic mentality and mode of conduct. In the broadest view, these two trends increasingly dominate the advanced states of our day. On the one side, we see the march toward uniformity, predictability, and the attempt to define all variety as dissent and then to force dissent into the "regular channels" —toward that state whose model citizen is Tocqueville's "industrious sheep," that state whose only greatness is its collective power.

On the other side we see an assertion of spontaneity, self-realization, and do-your-own-thing as the sum and substance of life and liberty. And this assertion, in its extreme form, does approach either madness or infantilism, for the only social institutions in which each member is really free to do his own thing are Bedlam and the nursery, where the conditions may be tolerated because there is a keeper with ultimate control over the inmates. The opposing forces were not quite that pure in the confrontation over the People's Park, but the university and public officials nearly managed to make them so. That they could not do so is a comforting measure of the basic vitality of those who built the Park and who have sacrificed to preserve it.

But this still does not account for the frenzy of violence which fell on Berkeley. To understand that, we must shift focus.

Clark Kerr was perceptive when he defined the multiversity as "a mechanism held together by administrative rules and powered by money." But it is important to understand that the last few years in the university have seen more and more rules and less and less money. The money is drying up because the rules are being broken. The rules are bring broken because university authorities, administrators and faculty alike, have lost the respect of very many of the students. When authority leaves, power enters—first in the form of more and tougher rules, then as sheer physical force, and finally as violence, which is force unrestrained by any thought of healing and saving, force whose aim is to cleanse by devastation.

Pressed from above by politicians and from below by students, the university administration simultaneously imposes more rules and makes continual appeals to the faculty for more support in its efforts to cope with permanent emergency. It pleads with the faculty for more "elbow room," more discretionary space in which to make the hard decisions needed when money runs short and students run amuck. That same administration is right now conducting time-and-motion studies of faculty work and "productivity." Simultaneously, both faculty and administration make spasmodic efforts to give the students some voice in the governance of the institution. But those are always too little, too late, too grudging.

Besides, as soon as the students get some power, unseemly things happen. Admit the blacks on campus and they demand their own autonomous department. Give the students limited power to initiate courses and they bring in Eldridge Cleaver and Tom Hayden. The faculty sees student initiative as a revolting mixture of Agitprop and denial of professional prerogatives. The administration sees it as a deadly threat to its own precarious standing within the university and before the public. The politicians see it as concession to anarchy and revolution. The result is more rules and less trust all around —more centralization, bureaucratization, and force on one side, more despair and anger on the other.

Under these conditions, the organized system must strive to extend its control and reduce the space in which spontaneous and unpredictable actions are possible. The subjects, on the other hand, come to identify spontaneity and unpredictability with all that is human and alive, and rule and control with all that is inhuman and dead. Order and liberty stand in fatal opposition. No positive synthesis can emerge from this dialectic unless those who now feel themselves pushed out and put down are admitted as full participants. But that is not happening. More and more, we are seeing in this country a reappearance of that stage in the breakdown of political societies where one segment of the whole—in this case still the larger segment—determines to dominate by force and terror other segments which reject and challenge its legitimacy.

This dynamic largely accounts for the crushing violence and terror that hit Berkeley. When spontaneity appeared in People's Park, it was first met by a restatement of the rules governing possession and control of land. When that restatement did not have the desired effect, the university failed to take the next step dictated by rule-governed behavior—seeking an injunction. Nor did it take the step which would have acknowledged itself as being in a political situation—talking on a plane of equality and acting in a spirit of generosity with the other parties. Instead, it regressed immediately to the use of physical measures. In the eyes of the administration, the building of People's Park was an "unjustified aggression," and the right of self-defense was promptly invoked.

Once force was called into play, it quickly intensified, and the university cannot evade its share of responsibility for what followed. He who wills the end wills the means; and no university official could have been unaware of the means necessary to keep that fence standing. But the administrators did not quite understand that their chosen agents of force, the police, would not limit their attention only to the students and street-people, who were expendable, but would turn against the university and the city as well.

Ronald Reagan reached Sacramento through Berkeley because, in the eyes of his frightened and furious supporters, Berkeley is daily the scene of events that would have shocked Sodom and revolutionary Moscow. All this came into intense focus in the behavior of the cops who were on the scene.

The police were numerous and armed with all the weapons a fertile technology can provide and an increasingly frightened citizenry will permit. Their superiority of force is overwhelming, and they are convinced they could "solve the problem" overnight if they were permitted to do it their own way: one instant crushing blow, and then license for dealing with the remaining recalcitrants. All the troublemakers are known to the police, either by dossier and record or by appearance and attitude. But the police are kept under some restraints, and those restraints produce greater and greater rage.

The rage comes from another source as well. Demands for a different future have been welling up in this society for some years now, and while those demands have not been unheard they have gone unheeded. Vietnam, racism, poverty, the degradation of the natural and man-made environment, the bureaucratization of the academy and its active collaboration with the military and industrial state, unrepresentative and unreachable structures of domination—all these grow apace. It seems increasingly clear to those who reject this American future that the forces of "law and order" intend to defend it by any means necessary. It becomes increasingly clear to the forces of law and order that extreme means will be necessary, and that the longer they are delayed the more extreme they will have to be.

Those two futures met at People's Park. It should be clear that what is happening this time is qualitatively different from 1964 and the Free Speech Movement. The difference in the amount of violence is the most striking, but this is largely a symptom of underlying differences. In 1964, the issues centered around questions of civil liberties and due process within the university. The issues now are political in the largest sense.

The appearance of People's Park raised questions of property and the nature of meaningful work. It raised questions about how people can begin to make a livable environment for themselves; about why both the defenders and critics of established authority today agree that authority can be considered only in terms of repression, never in terms of genuine respect and affection. These questions cannot be evaded. Those who honestly and courageously ask them are not imperiling the general happiness but are working for the common redemption.

It is increasingly clear that legitimate authority is declining in the modern state. In a real sense, "law and order" *is* the basic question of our day. This crisis of legitimacy has been visible for some time in just about all of the nonpolitical sectors of life—family, economy, religion, education—and is now spreading rapidly into the political realm. The gigantic and seemingly impregnable organizations that surround and dominate men in the modern states are seen by more and more people to have at their center not a vital principle of authority, but a hollow space, a moral vacuum. Increasingly, among the young and the rejected, obedience is mainly a matter of lingering habit or expediency or necessity, but not a matter of conviction and deepest sentiment.

The groups who are most persistently raising these questions are, of course, white middle-class youth and the racial and ethnic minorities. The origins of protest are different in the two cases: the former have largely seen through the American Dream of meaning in power and wealth and have found it a nightmare; the latter have been pushed aside and denied even the minimal goods of the dream. But the ends of the protest are remarkably similar: both are fighting against distortions and denials of their humanity. Both reject the programmed future of an American whose only imperative now seems to be: more.

The people who built the park (there will be more People's Parks, more and more occasions for seemingly bizarre, perverse, and wild behavior) have pretty much seen through the collective ideals and disciplines that have bound this nation together in its conquest of nature and power. Having been victimized by the restraints and authorities of the past, these people are suspicious of all authorities and most collective ideals. Some of them seem ready to attempt a life built upon no other ideal than self-gratification. They sometimes talk as though they had found the secret which has lain hidden through all the past ages of man: that the individual can live fully and freely with no authority other than his desires, absorbed completely in the development of all his capacities except two—the capacity for memory and the capacity for faith.

No one can say where this will lead. Perhaps new prophets will appear. Perhaps the old faith will be reborn. Perhaps we really shall see the new technological Garden tended by children—kind, sincere innocents, barbarians with good hearts. The great danger at present is that the established and the respectable are more and more disposed to see all this as chaos and outrage. They seem prepared to follow the most profoundly nihilistic denial possible, which is the denial of the future through denial of their own children, the bearers of the future.

In such times as these, hope is not a luxury but a necessity. The hope which we see is in the revival of a sense of shared destiny, of some common fate which can bind us into a people we have never been. Even to sketch out that fate one must first decide that it does not lie with the power of technology or the stability of organizational society. It lies, instead, in something more elemental, in our common fears that scientific weapons may destroy all life; that technology will increasingly disfigure men who live in the city, just as it has already debased the earth and obscured the sky; that the "progress" of industry will destroy the possibility of interesting work; and that "communications" will obliterate the last traces of the varied cultures which have been the inheritance of all but the most benighted societies.

If hope is to be born of these despairs it must be given political direction, a new politics devoted to nurturing life and work. There can be no political direction without political education, yet America from its beginnings has never confronted the question of how to care for men's souls while helping them to see the world politically. Seeing the world politically is preparatory to acting in it politically; and to act politically is not to be tempted by the puerile attraction of power or to be content with the formalism of a politics of compromise. It is, instead, a politics which seeks always to discover what men can share—and how what they share can be enlarged and yet rise beyond the banal.

People's Park is not banal. If only the same could be said of those who build and guard the fences around all of us.

15   The Selling of the President, 1968:
A Case Study in Managed Leadership

Joe McGinniss

He was afraid of television. He knew his soul was hard to find. Beyond that, he considered it a gimmick; its use in politics offended him. It had not been part of the game when he had learned to play, he could see no reason to bring it in now. He half-suspected it was an Eastern liberal trick; one more way to make him look silly. It offended his sense of dignity, one of the truest senses he had.

So his decision to use it to become president in 1968 was not easy. So much of him argued against it. But in his Wall Street years, Richard Nixon had traveled to the darkest places inside himself and come back numbed. He was, as in the Graham Greene title, a burnt-out case. All feeling was behind him; the machine inside had proved his hardiest part. He would run for president again and if he would have to learn television to run well, then he would learn it.

Nixon gathered about himself a group of young men attuned to the political uses of television. They arrived at his side by different routes. . . .

Harry Treleaven, hired as creative director of advertising in the fall of 1967, immediately went to work on the more serious of Nixon's personality problems. One was his lack of humor: "Can be corrected to a degree," Treleaven wrote, "but let's not be too obvious about it. Romney's cornball attempts have hurt him. If we're going to be witty, let a pro write the words."

Treleaven also worried about Nixon's lack of warmth, but decided: "He can be helped

Reprinted with permission of Trident Press (a division of Simon & Schuster, Inc.) from *Harper's* (August 1969) and from the book *The Selling of the President 1968* by Joe McGinniss. Copyright © 1969 by Joemac, Incorporated.

greatly in this respect by how he is handled. . . . Give him words to say that will show his *emotional* involvement in the issues. . . . He should be presented in some kind of 'situation' rather than cold in a studio. The situation should look unstaged even if it's not."

Some of the most effective ideas belonged to Raymond K. Price, a former editorial writer for *The New York Herald Tribune,* who became Nixon's best and most prominent speechwriter in the campaign. Price later composed much of the Inaugural Address. In 1967, he concluded that rational arguments would "only be effective if we can get the people to make the *emotional* leap, or what theologians call 'leap of faith.'"

To do this, Price suggested attacking the "personal factors" rather than the "historical factors" which were the basis of the low opinion so many people had of Richard Nixon. "These tend to be more a gut reaction," he wrote, "unarticulated, nonanalytical, a product of the particular chemistry between the voter and the *image* of the candidate. *We have to be very clear on this point: that the response is to the image, not to the man. . . .*"

So there would not have to be a "new Nixon." Simply a new approach to television.

This was how they went into it. Trying, with one hand, to build the illusion that Richard Nixon, in addition to his attributes of mind and heart, considered "communicating with the people . . . one of the great joys of seeking the presidency," while with the other they shielded him, controlled him, and controlled the atmosphere around him. It was as if they were building not a president but an astrodome, where the wind would never blow, the temperature never rise or fall, and the ball never bounce erratically on the artificial grass.

And it worked. As he moved serenely through his primary campaign, there was new cadence to Richard Nixon's speech and motion; new confidence in his heart. And, a new image of him on the television screen, on live, but controlled, TV.

I first met Harry Treleaven on a rainy morning in June of 1968, in his New York office at Fuller and Smith and Ross, the advertising agency. Treleaven was small and thin. He had gray hair and the tight frowning mouth that you see on the assistant principal of a high school. He seemed to be in his middle forties. He looked like William Scranton. Treleaven, it turned out, did not work for Fuller and Smith and Ross. He worked for Richard Nixon. Fuller and Smith and Ross was only incidental to the campaign. An agency was needed to do the mechanics—buying the television time and the newspaper space—and this looked like a nice, quiet one that would not complain about not being permitted to do creative work. Treleaven had been born in Chicago and had gone to Duke University, where he was Phi Beta Kappa. After that, he moved to Los Angeles and worked on *The Los Angeles Times* and then wrote radio scripts. One night he and his wife were having dinner in a restaurant in Los Angeles with a couple he did not like. Halfway through the meal he turned to his wife.

"Do you like it here?"

"You mean the restaurant?"

"I mean Los Angeles."

"No, not especially."

"Then let's go."

And Harry Treleaven threw a $20 bill on the table and he and his wife walked out. He took a plane to New York that night and found a job with the J. Walter Thompson advertising agency. He stayed with Thompson eighteen years. When he left it was as a vice president. He did commercials for Pan American, RCA, Ford, and Lark cigarettes, among others.

Harry Treleaven was sitting on the beach at Amagansett one day in September of 1967, drinking a can of beer. A summer neighbor named Len Garment, who was a partner in the law firm where Richard Nixon worked, approached him. Harry Treleaven knew Garment from a meeting they had had earlier in the summer. Garment had vaguely mentioned something about Treleaven and the advertising needs of the Richard Nixon campaign. Now he was more specific. He offered Treleaven a job. Creative director of advertising. Treleaven would devise a theme for the campaign, create commercials to fit the theme, and see that they were produced with a maximum of skill.

Len Garment's office was on the third floor of Nixon headquarters, at Park Avenue and 57th Street. A man named Jim Howard, a public-relations man from Cleveland, was with him the day I came in. Jim Howard was talking to Wilt Chamberlain on the phone.

"Wilt, I *understand* your position but they just don't pay that kind of money."

Garment was a short, pudgy man, also in his middle forties, who once had played saxophone in a Woody Herman band. He had voted for John Kennedy in 1960. Then he met Nixon at the law firm. He was chief of litigation and he was making money but he hated the job. He found that Nixon was not so bad a guy and very smart. When Nixon asked him to work in the presidential campaign, he said yes. He had been practically the first person to be hired and now he was chief recruiter.

Jim Howard had been trying to get Wilt Chamberlain to appear on the Mike Douglas show for free. The idea was for Chamberlain to explain why Richard Nixon should be president. Chamberlain was the only Negro celebrity they had and they were trying to get him around. The problem was, the Douglas show did not pay. And Chamberlain wanted money.

Len Garment started to explain the Nixon approach to advertising. Or the Garment-Treleaven approach to advertising Nixon. "The big thing is to stay away from gimmicks," he said.

"Right," Jim Howard said. "Never let the candidate wear a hat he does not feel comfortable wearing. You can't sell the candidate like a product," he said. "A product, all you want to do is get attention. You only need 2 per cent additional buyers to make the campaign worthwhile. In politics you need a flat 51 per cent of the market and you can't get that through gimmicks."

Two weeks later, I met Frank Shakespeare. Treleaven, Garment (who this June became special consultant to the president in the area of civil rights), and Shakespeare made up what was to be called the media and advertising group. But of the three equals, Shakespeare was quickly becoming more equal than the others. He had come from CBS. He, too, was in his forties with blond hair and a soft, boyish face. When he was named director of the United States Information Agency, after Nixon's election, a *New York Times* profile reported that, although he had spent eighteen years at CBS, no one he worked with there could recall a single anecdote about him. He was working for free because his progress at CBS had been stalled when Jim Aubrey got fired. He had been one of Aubrey's boys. Now, it was said, he was trying to give his career some outside impetus. An association with the President of the U. S. could hardly hurt. . . .

"I am not going to barricade myself into a television studio and make this an antiseptic campaign," Richard Nixon said at a press conference a few days after his nomination. Then he went to Chicago to open his fall campaign. The whole day was built around a television show. Even when ten thousand people stood in front of his hotel and screamed for him to greet them he stayed locked up in his room, resting for the show.

Chicago was the site for the first of ten programs that Nixon would do in states ranging from Massachusetts to Texas. The idea was to have him in the middle of a group of people, answering questions live. Shakespeare and Treleaven had developed the idea through the primaries and now had it sharpened to a point. Each show would run for one hour. It would be live to provide suspense; there would be a studio audience to

cheer Nixon's answers and make it seem to home viewers that enthusiasm for his candidacy was all but uncontrollable; and there would be an effort to achieve a conversational tone that would penetrate Nixon's stuffiness and drive out the displeasure he often seemed to feel when surrounded by other human beings instead of Bureau of the Budget reports.

One of the valuable things about this idea, from a political standpoint, was that each show would be seen only by the people who lived in that particular state or region. This meant it made no difference if Nixon's statements—for they were not really answers— were exactly the same, phrase for phrase, gesture for gesture, from state to state. Only the press would be bored and the press had been written off already. So Nixon could get through the campaign with a dozen or so carefully worded responses that would cover all the problems of America in 1968.

Roger Ailes, the executive producer of the Mike Douglas show, was hired to produce the one-hour programs. Ailes was twenty-eight years old. He had started as a prop boy on the Douglas show in 1965 and was running it within three years. He was good. When he left, Douglas' ratings declined. But not everyone he passed on his way up remained his friend. Not even Douglas. Richard Nixon had been a guest on the show in the fall of 1967. While waiting to go on, he fell into conversation with Roger Ailes.

"It's a shame a man has to use gimmicks like this to get elected," Nixon said.

"Television is not a gimmick," Ailes said.

Richard Nixon liked that kind of thinking. He told Len Garment to hire the man. Ailes had been sent to Chicago three days before Nixon opened the fall campaign. His instructions were to select a panel of questioners and design a set. But now, on the day of the program, only six hours, in fact, before it was to begin, Ailes was having problems.

"Those stupid bastards on the set-designing crew put turquoise curtains in the background. Nixon wouldn't look right unless he was carrying a pocketbook." Ailes ordered the curtains removed and three plain, almost stark wooden boards to replace them. "The wood has clean, solid, masculine lines," he said.

His biggest problem was with the panel of questioners. Shakespeare, Treleaven, and Garment had felt it essential to have a "balanced" group. First, this meant a Negro. One Negro. Not two. Two would be offensive to whites, perhaps to Negroes as well. Two would be trying too hard. One was necessary and safe. Fourteen per cent of the population applied to a six or seven-member panel equaled one. Texas would be tricky, though. Do you have a Negro *and* a Mexican-American, or if not, then which?

Besides the Negro, the panel for the first show included a Jewish attorney, the president of a Polish-Hungarian group, a suburban housewife, a businessman, a representative of the white lower-middle class, and, for authenticity, two newsmen: one from Chicago, one from Moline.

That was all right, Roger Ailes said. But then someone had called from New York and insisted that he add a farmer. Roger Ailes had been born in Ohio, but even so he knew you did not want a farmer on a television show. All they did was ask complicated questions about things like parities, which nobody else understood or cared about. Including Richard Nixon. Besides, the farmer brought the panel size to eight, which Ailes said was too big. It would be impossible for Nixon to establish interpersonal relationships with eight different people in one hour. And interpersonal relationships were the key to success.

"This is the trouble with all these political people horning in," Ailes said. "Fine, they all get their lousy little groups represented but we wind up with a horseshit show."

There was to be a studio audience—three hundred people—recruited by the local Republican organization. Just enough Negroes so the press could not write "all-white" stories but not enough so it would look like a ball park. The audience, of course, would applaud every answer Richard Nixon gave, boosting his confidence and giving the impression to a viewer that Nixon certainly did

have charisma, and whatever other qualities they wanted their president to have.

Treleaven and his assistant, Al Scott, came to the studio late in the afternoon. They were getting nervous. "Nixon's throat is scratchy," Treleaven said, "and that's making him upset." Al Scott did not like the lighting in the studio. "The lights are too high," he said. "They'll show the bags under RN's eyes."

Then there was a crisis about whether the press should be allowed in the studio during the show. Shakespeare had given an order that they be kept out. Now they were complaining to Herb Klein, the press-relations man, that if three hundred shills could be bussed in to cheer, a pool of two or three reporters could be allowed to sit in the stands.

Shakespeare still said no. No *newspapermen* were going to interfere with his TV show. Klein kept arguing, saying that if this was how it was going to start, on the very first day of the campaign, it was going to be 1960 again within a week. Treleaven and Ailes went upstairs, to the WBBM cafeteria, and drank vending-machine coffee from paper cups. "I agree with Frank," Ailes said. "It's not a press conference."

"But if you let the audience in . . ."

"Doesn't matter. The audience is part of the show. And that's the whole point. It's a television show. Our television show. And the press has no business on the set.

"Goddam it, Harry, the problem is that this is an electronic election. The first there's ever been. TV has the power now. Some of the guys get arrogant and rub the reporters' faces in it and then the reporters get pissed and go out of their way to rap anything they consider staged for TV. And you know damn well that's what they'd do if they saw this from the studio. You let them in with the regular audience and they see the warm-up. They see Jack Rourke out there telling the audience to applaud and to mob Nixon at the end, and that's all they'd write about. You know damn well it is." Jack Rourke was Roger Ailes's assistant.

"I'm still afraid we'll create a big incident if we lock them out entirely," Treleaven said.

"I'm going to call Frank and suggest he reconsider."

But Shakespeare would not. He arranged for monitors in an adjacent studio and said the press could watch from there, seeing no more, no less, than what they would see from any living room in Illinois.

It was five o'clock now; the show was to start at nine. Ray Vojey, the makeup man borrowed from the Johnny Carson show, had arrived. "Oh, Ray," Roger Ailes said, "with Wilkinson, watch that perspiration problem on the top of his forehead."

"Yes, he went a little red in Portland," Ray Vojey said.

"And when he's off camera, I'd give him a treated towel, just like Mr. Nixon uses."

"Right."

Ailes turned to Jack Rourke, the assistant. "Also, I'd like to have Wilkinson in the room with Nixon before the show to kibitz around, get Nixon loose."

"Okay. I'll bring him in."

The set, now that it was finished, was impressive. There was a round blue-carpeted platform, six feet in diameter and eight inches high. Richard Nixon would stand on this and face the panel, which would be seated in a semicircle around him. Bleachers for the audience ranged out behind the panel chairs. Later, Roger Ailes would think to call the whole effect "the arena concept" and bill Nixon as "the man in the arena." He got this from a Theodore Roosevelt quote which hung, framed, from a wall of his office in Philadelphia. It said something about how one man in the arena was worth ten, or a hundred, or a thousand carping critics.

At nine o'clock, Central Daylight Time, Richard Nixon, freshly powdered, left his dressing room, walked down a corridor deserted save for Secret Service, and went through a carefully guarded doorway that opened on the rear of the set.

Harry Treleaven had selected tape from WBBM's coverage of the noontime motorcade for the opening of the show. Tape that showed Richard Nixon riding, arms outstretched, beaming, atop an open car. Hundreds of thousands of citizens, some who

had come on their own, some who had been recruited by Republican organizations, cheered, waved balloons, and tossed confetti in the air. One week before, at the Democratic convention, it had been Humphrey, blood, and tear gas. Today it was Nixon, the unifying hero, the man to heal all wounds. Chicago Republicans showed a warm, assured, united front. And Harry Treleaven picked only the most magical of moments for the opening of his television show.

Then the director hit a button and Bud Wilkinson appeared on the screen, a placid, composed, substantial, reassuring figure introducing his close personal friend, a man whose intelligence and judgment had won the respect of the world's leaders and the admiration of millions of his countrymen, this very same man who had been seen entering Jerusalem moments ago on tape: Richard Nixon. And the carefully cued audience (for Jack Rourke had done his job well) stood to render an ovation. Richard Nixon, grinning, waving, *thrusting,* walked to the blue riser to receive the tribute.

It was warmly given. Genuine. He looked toward his wife; the two daughters; Senator Ed Brooke, the most useful Negro he had found; Charles Percy, the organization man; and Senator Thruston Morton, resigned if not enthusiastic. They sat in the first row together.

He was alone, with not even a chair on the platform for company, ready to face, if not the nation, at least Illinois. To communicate, man to man, eye to eye, with that mass of the ordinary whose concerns he so deeply shared, whose values were so totally his own. All the subliminal effects sank in. Nixon stood alone, ringed by forces which, if not hostile, were at least—to the viewer—unpredictable.

There was a rush of sympathy; a desire— a need, even—to root. Richard Nixon was suddenly human: facing a new and dangerous situation, alone, armed with only his wits. In image terms, he had won before he began. All the old concepts had been destroyed. He had achieved a new level of communication. The stronger his statement, the stronger the surge of warmth inside the viewer.

Morris Liebman, the Jewish attorney, asked the first question: "Would you comment on the accusation which was made from time to time that your views have shifted and that they are based on expediencies?"

Richard Nixon squinted and smiled. "I suppose what you are referring to is: Is there a new Nixon or is there an old Nixon? I suppose I could counter by saying: Which Humphrey shall we listen to today?"

There was great applause for this. When it faded, Richard Nixon said. "I do want to say this: There certainly is a new Nixon, I realize, too, that as a man gets older he learns something. If I haven't learned something I am not worth anything in public life. ... I think my principles are consistent. I believe very deeply in the American system. I believe very deeply in what is needed to defend that system at home and abroad. I think I have some ideas as to how we can promote peace, ideas that are different from what they were eight years ago, not because I have changed but because the problems have changed.

"My answer is 'yes,' there is a new Nixon, if you are talking in terms of new ideas for the new world and the America we live in. In terms of what I believe in, the American view and the American dream, I think I am just what I was eight years ago."

Applause swept the studio. Bud Wilkinson joined in.

The farmer asked a question about farming. The Polish-Hungarian delivered an address concerning the problems of the people of Eastern Europe. His remarks led to no question at all, but no matter: Richard Nixon expressed concern for the plight of Eastern Europeans everywhere, including northern Illinois.

Then Warner Saunders, the Negro and a very acceptable, very polite one he seemed · to be, asked, "What does law and order mean to you?"

"I am quite aware," Richard Nixon said, "of the fact that the black community, when they hear it, think of power being used in a way that is destructive to them, and yet I think we have to also remember that the black community as well as the white community has an interest in order and in law, providing that law is with justice. ...."

John McCarter, the businessman, asked about Spiro Agnew. Nixon said, "Of all the men who I considered, Spiro Agnew had the intelligence, the courage, and the principle to take on the great responsibilities of a campaigner and responsibilities of vice president."

McCarter came back later wanting to know if Nixon thought the Chicago police had been too harsh on demonstrators in the streets.

"It would be easy," Nixon said, "to criticize Mayor Daley and by implication Vice President Humphrey. But it wouldn't be right for me to lob in criticism. I am not going to get into it. It is best for political figures not to be making partisan comments from the sidelines."

The show went on like that. At the end the audience charged from the bleachers, as instructed. They swarmed around Richard Nixon so that the last thing the viewer at home saw was Nixon in the middle of this big crowd of people, who all thought he was great.

Treleaven plunged into the crowd. He was excited; he thought the show had been brilliant. He got to Nixon just as Nixon was bending down to autograph a cast that a girl had on her leg.

"Well, you've got a leg up," Treleaven said.

Nixon stood up and grinned and moved away.

"Gee, that was sure a funny look he gave me," Treleaven said. "I wonder if he heard me. I wonder if he knew who I was." ...

Richard Nixon came to Philadelphia the next day: Friday. There was the standard downtown motorcade at noon. Frank Kornsey took the whole day off to stay home and write questions. "I got some beauties," he told Roger Ailes on the phone.

Ailes went to the studio at two o'clock in the afternoon. "I'm going to fire this director," he said. "I'm going to fire the son of a bitch right after the show. Look at this. Look at the positioning of these cameras. I've told him fifty times I want closeups. Closeups! This is a closeup medium. It's dull to shoot chest shots. I want to see pores. That's what people are. That's what television is."

He walked through the studio, shaking his head. "We won't get a shot better than waist-high from these cameras all night. That's 1948 direction. When you had four people in every shot and figured you were lucky you had any shot at all."

The audience filled the studio at seven o'clock. The panel was brought in at 7:15. Frank Kornsey was nervous. Roger Ailes offered him a shot of bourbon. "No thanks," he said. "I'll be all right." He tried to grin.

At 7:22 Jack Rourke stepped onto the riser. He was a heavy Irishman with a red face and gray hair. "Hello," he said to the audience. "I'm Frank Sinatra."

The Nixon family, David Eisenhower, and the governor of Pennsylvania came in. The audience applauded. This audience, like the others, had been carefully recruited by the local Republican organization. "That's the glee club," Jack Rourke said, pointing to the Nixons.

The director walked into the control booth at 7:24. "He's crazy," the director said, meaning Roger Ailes. "He has no conception of the mechanical limitations involved in a show like this. He says he wants closeups, it's like saying he wants to go to the moon." The director took his seat at the control panel and spoke to a cameraman on the floor. "Make sure you know where Mrs. Nixon is and what she looks like."

A member of the Nixon staff ran into the booth. "Cut the sound in that studio next door. We've got the press in there and we don't want them to hear the warm-up."

"Now when Mr. Nixon comes in," Jack Rourke was saying, "I want you to tear the place apart. Sound like ten thousand people. I'm sure, of course, that you'll also want to stand up at that point. So what do you say we try it now. Come on, stand up. And let me hear it."

"One forty-five to air," the director said in the control booth.

"Tell Rourke to check the sound level on the panel."

Jack Rourke turned to Frank Kornsey: "Ask a question, please. We'd like to check your microphone."

Frank Kornsey leaned forward and spoke, barely above a whisper. His list of "beauties" lay on a desk before him. He was still pale, even through his makeup.

"I was just wondering how Mr. and Mrs. Nixon are enjoying our wonderful city of Philadelphia," he said.

Pat Nixon, in a first-row seat, gave her tight, close-mouthed smile.

"No, they don't care for it," Jack Rourke said.

"Thirty seconds," came a voice from the control room. "Clear the decks, please, thirty seconds."

Then, at exactly 7:30, while a tape of Richard Nixon's motorcade was being played for the viewers at home, the director said, "Okay, cue the applause, move back camera one, move back one," and Richard Nixon stepped through a crack in a curtain, hunched his shoulders, raised his arms, wiggled his wrists, made V-signs with his fingers, and switched on his grin.

Jack McKinney, the talk-show host, was wearing his hairpiece for the occasion. Nixon turned to him first, still with the grin, hands clasped before him, into his fourth show now and over the jitters. Maybe, in fact, ready to show off just a bit. A few new combinations, if the proper moment came, to please the crowd.

"Yes, Mr. McKinney," he said.

Jack McKinney did not lead with his right but he threw a much stiffer jab than Nixon had been expecting: "Why are you so reluctant to comment on Vietnam this year when in 1952, faced with a similar issue in Korea, you were so free with your partisan remarks?"

Not a crippling question but there was an undertone of unfriendliness to it. Worse, it had been put to him in professional form. Nixon stepped back, a bit off balance. This sort of thing threatened the stability of the whole format; the basis being the hypothesis that Nixon could appear to risk all by going live while in fact risking nothing by facing the loose syntax and predictable, sloppy thrusts of amateurs. He threw up an evasive flurry. But the grin was gone from his face. Not only did he know now that he would have to be careful of McKinney, he was forced to wonder, for the first time, what he might encounter from the others.

The Negro was next. Warily: "Yes, Mr. Burress." And Burress laid Black Capitalism right down the middle, straight and soft. Nixon had it memorized. He took a long time on the answer, though, savoring its clichés, making sure his wind had come back all the way.

Then Frank Kornsey, who studied his list and asked, "What are you going to do about the *Pueblo*?" Beautiful. Nixon was honing this one to perfection. He had taken 1:22 with it in California, according to Roger Ailes's chart, but had brought it down to 1:05 in Ohio. Now he delivered it in less than a minute. He was smooth again, and grinning, as he turned to the liberal housewife, Mrs. Mather.

Was civil disobedience *ever* justified, she wondered. Nixon took a quick step backwards on the riser. His face fell into the solemnity mask. There were philosophic implications there he did not like. He could understand the impatience of those less fortunate than ourselves, he assured her, and their demand for immediate improvement was, indeed, healthy for our society in many ways. But—as long as change could be brought about within the system—and no, he was not like some who claimed it could not —then there was no cause, repeat, *no* cause that justified the breaking of a law.

But he knew he would have to watch her, too. The first line of sweat broke out across his upper lip.

The Young Republican from Wharton wanted to know how to bring the McCarthy supporters back into the mainstream, which was fine, but then the newsman from Camden asked if Nixon agreed with Spiro Agnew's charge that Hubert Humphrey was "soft on Communism."

He knew how to handle that one, but while sidestepping, he noted that this fellow, too, seemed unawed. That made three out of seven who were ready, it appeared, to mix it up. And one of them a good-looking articulate woman. And another, McKinney, who seemed truly mean.

It was McKinney's turn again: Why was Nixon refusing to appear on any of the news confrontation shows such as *Meet the Press?* Why would he face the public only in staged settings such as this, where the questions were almost certain to be worded generally enough to allow him any vague sort of answer he wanted to give? Where the presence of the cheering studio audience was sure to intimidate any questioner who contemplated true engagement? Where Nixon moved so quickly from one questioner to the next that he eliminated any possibility of follow-up, and chance for true discussion . . .?

"The guy's making a speech!" Frank Shakespeare shouted in the control booth. Roger Ailes jumped for the phone to Wilkinson on stage. But McKinney was finished, for the moment. The question was, had he finished Nixon, too?

"I've done those quiz shows, Mr. McKinney. I've done them until they were running out of my ears." There was no question on one point: Richard Nixon was upset. Staring hard at McKinney he grumbled something about why there ought to be more fuss about Hubert Humphrey not having press conferences and less about him and *Meet the Press*.

It did not seem much of a recovery but in the control room Frank Shakespeare punched the palm of one hand with the first of the other and said, "That socks it to him, Dickie Baby!" The audience cheered. Suddenly, Nixon, perhaps sensing a weakness in McKinney where he had feared that none existed, perhaps realizing he had no choice, surely buoyed by the cheers, decided to slug it out.

"Go ahead," he said, gesturing. "I want you to follow up."

McKinney came back creditably, using the word "amorphous" and complaining that viewers were being asked to support Nixon for President on the basis of "nothing but a wink and a smile" particularly in regard to Vietnam.

"Now, Mr. McKinney, maybe I haven't been as specific . . ." and Nixon was off on a thorough rephrasing of his Vietnam nonposition, which, while it contained no substance —hence, could not accommodate anything new—sounded, to uninitiates, like a public step forward. The audience was ecstatic. Outnumbered, two hundred forty-one to one, McKinney could do nothing but smile and shake his head.

"Be very careful with McKinney," Shakespeare said, bending over Roger Ailes. "I want to give him a chance but I don't want him to hog the show."

"Yeah, if he starts making another speech I'll call Bud and—"

But Shakespeare was no longer listening. He was grappling with a cameraman who had come into the control booth and begun to take pictures of the production staff at work.

"No press," Shakespeare said, and when the man continued shooting his film, Shakespeare began to push. The cameraman pushed back as well as he could, but Shakespeare, leaning hard, edged him toward the door.

Meanwhile, Frank Kornsey, consulting his written list again, had asked, "What do you intend to do about the gun-control law?" Then, quickly the others: Are you writing off the black vote? What about federal tax credits . . . water and air pollution? And then the Camden newsman, whose name was Flynn, asking about Nixon's action in 1965 when he had called for a removal of a Rutgers history professor who had spoken kindly of the Vietcong—on campus.

Nixon assured Mr. Flynn that academic freedom remained high on his personal list of privileges which all Americans should enjoy, but added, "There is one place where I would draw the line. And that is, I do not believe that anyone who is paid by the government and who is using government facilities—and Rutgers, as I'm sure you are aware,

Mr. Flynn, is a state institution—has the right to call for the victory of the enemy over American boys—while he is on the campus."

But now McKinney gathered himself for a final try: "You said that the Rutgers professor 'called for' the victory of the Vietcong, but as I recall he didn't say that at all. This is what I mean about your being able, on this kind of show, to slide off the questions. Now the facts were—"

"Oh, I know the facts, Mr. McKinney. I know the facts."

Nixon was grinning. The audience poured forth its loudest applause of the night. Bud Wilkinson joined in, full of righteous fervor. Of course Mr. Nixon knew the facts.

McKinney was beaten but would not quit: "The facts were that the professor did not 'call for' the victory—"

"No, what he said, Mr. McKinney, and I believe I am quoting him *exactly,* was that he would 'welcome the impending victory of the Vietcong.' "

"Which is not the same thing."

"Well, Mr. McKinney, you can make that distinction if you wish, but what I'll do is I'll turn it over to the television audience right now and let them decide for themselves about the semantics. About the difference between 'calling for' and 'welcoming' a victory of the Vietcong."

He was angry but he had it under control and he talked fast and hard and when he was finished he swung immediately to the next questioner. The show was almost over. McKinney was through for the night.

"Boy, is he going to be pissed," Roger Ailes said as he hurried down from the control room. "He'll think we really tried to screw him. But critically it was the best show he's done."

Roger Ailes went looking for Nixon. He wound up in an elevator with Nixon's wife. She was wearing a green dress and she did not smile. One thought of the remark a member of the Nixon staff had made: "Next to her, RN looks like Mary Poppins."

"Hello, Mrs. Nixon," Roger Ailes said. She nodded. She had known him for months. "How did you like the show?" She nodded very slowly, her mouth was drawn in a thin, straight line.

"Everyone seems to think it was by far the best," Ailes said. "Especially the way he took care of that McKinney."

Pat Nixon stared at the elevator door. The car stopped. She got off and moved down a hallway with the Secret Service men around her. . . .

V

The Boundaries of
Life in the United States

The selections in this part of the book depict the kinds of lives that are lived in the United States. The basic argument behind these descriptions is simple. One: Life in the Great Society is significantly limited. Two: These limits are both cause and effect of the way we are, as a nation. Three: If we were different, as a nation, the limits that presently bound people's lives could be changed, for the better. The point is not merely that "you can't always get what you want"; the descriptions in these selections give an indication of what it is, typically, in our society that people can't be or do or have. These descriptions reveal some of the reasons for the limited lives in our society, reasons that often have very little to do with personal limitations at all. And these selections show that the boundaries of life in our society are intimately interconnected with the features of our society already discussed in Parts II, III, and IV.

A concrete illustration. I live on the east shore of San Francisco Bay, along with over a million other people. Every morning from Monday through Friday thousands of my neighbors get into thousands of cars at about the same time, and drive across the Bay Bridge to San Francisco (surely not the most pleasant way to start the day). Once there, most of them start work on jobs which are, aside from long habit, essentially alien to them, alien in that the person has not defined the job, does not control the work demanded by the job nor the tools used on the job, and does not own or control whatever product the job (together with other related jobs in the business or factory) produces. Then, after eight or so hours, everyone gets back in their cars or onto the buses, and the mass traffic tie-up of the morning is repeated as everyone returns home or heads for a bar or restaurant for an evening's fun, or perhaps goes to a second job or to night school in order to prepare themselves for better-paying jobs with more security or more interesting routines.

This picture implies some important limits on the sorts of lives these commuters can live. The effects of these limits can be described as: fragmentation, powerlessness, and meaninglessness. The separation of the world of work from the world of family and friends, for example, tends to produce a separation within the commuter's own personal world, a fragmentation or splitting of self into a self-on-the-job and a self-at-home. Both the conditions of work on the job and the dependence on a car for transportation involve the commuter in a relationship of powerlessness vis-à-vis his or her surroundings—dependent on the car, losing one hour each way in commute, unable to define or control the job, lacking any genuine connection with the product of the work. And the condition of being required to do things that make no sense in and of themselves, that one would never think of doing were one not in some way required to do them, leads eventually to a profound sense that more and more of life makes no sense, has no point or purpose, is meaningless.

Why do people live this way? Surely very few of these East Bay commuters would say that they *desire* any of the consequences I have just listed of some of the features of their workaday lives. But they would say, correctly, that they don't have much choice. That is, as long as they are living life in the Great Society, then they don't have much chance to live lives that are not powerless, fragmented, and meaningless.

Of course, every society limits somehow or other the lives its members can live. Yet in many societies those limits do not lead people to live in ways they really dislike. If all that these limits on our lives amounted to were merely the natural "socialization" or "acculturation" that every society gives its members, to enable them to get along with each other and live productively together, then why are so many people so tense, angry, and frustrated? Why the rising crime and suicide rate? Why the increasing use of psychiatrists and therapy groups? Why so many divorces, broken homes, and runaways? It's pretty obvious, I think, that my commuter neighbors in the East Bay do not waste two hours a day, make themselves dependent on a car (and unwittingly increase the already-alarming pollution), and separate their work lives from their family lives simply because they have been socialized to live that way. (They may have been socialized to *accept* living that way, but that's a totally different thing.) They all, I bet, grew up playing right near their homes, and had most of their friends either in the immediate neighborhood or from school. They may have been "socialized" to like driving a car, but that was for fun, not to commute. And their fathers and mothers, most of them, did not commute. So these people are *not,* now, living the sorts of lives that their socialization prepared them for. Then why do they do it?

The selections by Henry, Keniston, and Laing, I think, give part of the answer. For example, Henry uses the term "drivenness" to describe the sort of drive that forces Americans to pursue chimerical, will-o'-the-wisp goals— and thereby into lives they don't really want. Keniston describes some of the reasons why we are fragmenting our world and our lives more and more each generation. And Laing shows how we have been trained to be too obedient. But perceptive and accurate as these sketches are, they are only parts of the whole picture. For Henry, Keniston, and Laing make it begin to seem that the boundaries on our lives, the forces that drive and limit us, are *wholly psychological.* Although the reason for including this section on "The Dominant Ideology" is to stress the fact that *to an extent* our prison bars are inside our own heads, it is completely false to conclude that the whole problem is psychological, or to say with the Beatles that rather than making changes in the world "you've got to change your mind instead." American "drivenness," fragmentation, and super–obedience to impersonal authority, just to take those examples, are not *merely* psychological facts. They have their sources or reflections in the "invisible control mechanisms." And they are part and parcel of the sorts of things that the previous parts of this book have been talking about. You can see "drivenness," for example, in Slater's portrait of American character in Part II; in Baran and Sweezy's discussion in Part III of the way our economy keeps producing a surplus that we are forever trying to use up; and in McGinniss's description of President Nixon in Part IV.

In other words, the selections here relate to the previous selections so closely that they almost blend into each other. Part II was about the ways of feeling and thinking that have traditionally been American and about the social trends that produced our present condition of society; this part is about the same things, as they are in the present. The selections that follow on "the dominant ideology" describe the *result* of that clash between our traditional character and the social "modernization" process as they were described in Part II. And the section on the "Invisible Control Mechanisms" shows how that "modernization" process could happen even when so many people were opposed to it. Again, Part III was about the top of the power structure; this part is about the bottom parts of the structure of the whole society (the pattern of relationships and beliefs that holds all the groups, classes, and statuses together). Where Part III described interests, this part describes the ideology or belief system that defines and supports those interests. Where Part III talked about power so great that it dominates the whole society, this part describes how that power is created, sustained, and exercised over individual people in concrete situations. Finally, Part IV was about people's experiences of politics; this part is about people's social experiences in general. That is, whereas Part IV tried to describe the quality of our public life, this part tries to describe more broadly something of the quality of our everyday, workaday lives.

The connections between this part and the previous parts can be put another way. One often hears, nowadays, that our real problems are "technology," "mass society," "dehumanization," and "white middle-class culture." To either agree or disagree with such statements would be superficial; since this part is about those things, obviously I think they are important. But I have tried to emphasize how such things as "technology," "middle-class values," "mass society," and "alienation" cannot be understood without placing them in the historical, economic, and political context of the previous three parts.

To oversimplify drastically, but still indicate what I have in mind, what we call technology and mass society can be shown to be the visible effects of bureaucratic social organization and industrialism upon our pre-Civil War society (and these concepts were discussed earlier). What it is fashionable in some quarters today to sneer at as "middle-class values" are, in fact, the national traditions described in Part II. The alienation that one has heard more and more talk about in recent years is also, in part, a national tradition: recall how Slater's American was alienated from his surroundings and his neighbors, and even from himself insofar as he was unaware of what he was doing to himself. On the other hand, some of modern alienation is genuinely new, a result of the conflicts between our historical traditions and the changes that have occurred over the past hundred years. (But both of these latter two subjects were also discussed earlier.) In short, "technology" and "alienation" and so on are terribly important, but you don't understand what they are unless you see their interconnectedness with "the dried-up tradition," "the basic structure of power, interest, and policy," and "the shape of American public life."

This point is so important that it bears rephrasing from still another angle. Suppose you were asked to list some of our really important social problems. I imagine that you might include "racial struggle," "poverty," and "war," on one hand, and "alienation," "dehumanization," "the meaninglessness of life," and "mass society" (or other words that refer to such problems), on the other. That is, the usual way we think about our nation's problems is to separate out the "hard" from the "soft"—the material from the intangible, the violent from the subtle, the fact from the feeling—or, in terms of this book, Parts II and III from Parts IV and V (and a few selections in Part II). And after making this distinction between "hard" and "soft" problems, people usually call one or the other type of problem the "real" problem, and dismiss the other as "superficial." But if I am correct in stressing the connections between Parts II-III and Parts IV-V, then it is foolish to try to make that separation between our real problems and superficial problems, regardless of whether you think the real problems are "hard" or "soft."

Consider, for example, the racial situation in our society today. The "hards," white and black, usually claim that the real problem is white power and prejudice, reinforced by the nature of the economic system. Anyone who talks about how bad alienation and dehumanization have become in our society is likely to be accused of distracting attention from the real problem, and thereby weakening one side in the real struggle. But anyone who thinks that the racial struggle has little to do with alienation and dehumanization either does not understand those terms, or else does not understand what the racial struggle is all about. The only way someone can talk about "solving" the racial situation without simultaneously dealing with the facts of alienation and dehumanization is to ignore the social and personal context in which people of different races live in the United States today. This sort of abstract "solution" of the racial problem might indeed produce proportionate equality of white skins and black skins in all positions in the society. But such a "solution" would only *worsen* some of the actual life difficulties of black people, unless at the same time steps were taken to make sure that black people in those new positions could live as they want to. But such steps would be revolutionary, since even white people today have not taken them. This is what I mean by saying that a "solution" of the race situation that ignores the "soft" side of racial problems is no real solution at all.

But the reverse is also true. Anyone who thinks that the fundamental problems of our society are purely spiritual (a need for new values, for a religious reawakening, for putting meaning back into our lives) and not significantly connected with power, tradition, politics, and social structure simply does not understand that the spirit always lives in a body, that spiritual issues never come pure. We don't hear much about it today, but the evidence shows that Jesus was working with the anti-imperialist independence movement in Palestine at the same time as he did his preaching and worked his miracles. Martin Luther not only established a new form of Christianity, he also was largely responsible for the rise of the nation-state system. Gandhi was the key leader of the Indian mass movement for independence from the British at the same time that he became a traditional Hindu holy man, experimented with fasting and asceticism, and founded utopian religious communities. And so on.

Actually, the point being stressed here was implied in the selection by Williams in Part II. We have seen a good deal of change and reform in the United States in the twentieth century. We have been improving ourselves, you might say, to death. Why is it that we never seem to get anywhere? It is commonplace to observe that by now almost all of the "radical" demands of Populism and the early labor movement have become the law of the land; but to what avail? Can one seriously hold that two cars and a color TV set "balance" a state of mind verging on the neurotic and a style of life that drives its liver to the doctor? The fact that all these reforms were transformed, in their effects, by becoming bureaucratized and administered from above in not only proof, as Paul Goodman has said in many of his books, that means shape ends, that method is more important than content; it is also a demonstration that method *is* content. Or, that "soft" problems are *part of* "hard" problems, just as the introduction to Part IV showed that *process* cannot be separated from *results*. Concretely, when we as a nation chose to ignore the "soft" or political side of the question of labor-union organization, for example, and judged that what was really important was to have a powerful union movement that would protect jobs and raise wages (the "hard" or economic side), what we did was to ensure that more problems (both "hard" and "soft") would follow. Before long we had authoritarian, undemocratic union organization, and then corruption among some union leaders and collusion between many union leaders and management. Yet even though these problems were obviously results of our failure to deal with the "soft" side of the workers' movement—that is, results of the overcentralized and undemocratic form the unions quickly took—we still refused to take seriously the "soft" problems of the absence of self-government: social alienation, meaningless, and powerlessness. And by refusing to deal with them, naturally, we perpetuated them. They are still here.

There are of course other sorts of limits on the lives of Americans today besides the boundaries described in the following selections under the heading of "Invisible Control Mechanisms." There are elemental physical facts of life in city slums or in the isolation and poverty of an Appalachian farm. In addition to those absolute sorts of limitation, there are all the relative limits imposed on many people by unequal opportunity—relatively less education, relatively lower income, relatively poorer health, and so on. Also in this category go the limitations imposed by discrimination—religious, sexual, and racial. And finally, there are the sorts of limits imposed by actual fences, barbed wire, tear gas, and guns—that is, the limits imposed by the power to coerce compliance if ideology and invisible control mechanisms don't work to keep people within their assigned ruts. These are three obviously important kinds of boundaries on life in the Great Society that it is crucial to keep in mind, even though the following selections almost ignore them.

What the selections on "invisible control mechanisms" do show is that the kinds of everyday lives that many people lead in our society are not at all the result of their free choices (as we are taught), but are the result of the kind of society we have—the result of the way we are, as a nation. Many people are *made* to live their lives as they do: if they tried to live differently, they would be stopped or replaced by others who are more willing to be dominated. It might be a slight exaggeration to say that our society absolutely *requires* the existence of black ghettoes, a secretarial proletariat, and "dirty workers." But the selections by Tabb, Judith Ann, and Rainwater show persuasively that we would be living in a very different society from our own if we did not have economic racism, or sexual or class exploitation. And they also demonstrate clearly that there are powerful institutionalized forces in our society today that work to maintain these various forms of domination and exploitation.

The Dominant Ideology

16   Drivenness, Consumption, and Obsolescence

Jules Henry

Ours is a driven culture. It is driven on by its achievement, competitive, profit, and mobility drives, and by the drives for security and a higher standard of living. Above all, it is driven by expansiveness. Drives like hunger, thirst, sex, and rest arise directly out of the chemistry of the body, whereas expansiveness, competitiveness, achievement, and so on are generated by the culture; still we yield to the latter as we do to hunger and sex. Side by side with these drives is another group of urges, such as gentleness, kindliness, and generosity, which I shall call values, and in our culture a central issue for the emotional life of everyone is the interplay between these two. Values and drives—other than physiological drives—are both creations of the culture, but in the lives of Americans, and, indeed, of all "Western" men and women, they play very different roles. A value is something we consider good; something we always want our wives, husbands, parents, and children to express to us, to shower on us when we are gay, to tender to us when we are miserable. Love, kindness, quietness, contentment, fun, frankness, honesty, decency, relaxation, simplicity belong here.

Fundamentally, values are different from what I call drives, and it is only a semantic characteristic of our language that keeps the two sets of feelings together. To call both competitiveness and gentleness "values" is as confusing as to call them both "drives." Drives are what urge us blindly into getting bigger, into going further into outer space and into destructive competition; values are the sentiments that work in the opposite direction. Drives belong to the occupational world; values to the world of the family and friendly intimacy. Drives animate the hurly-burly of business, the armed forces, and all those parts of our culture where getting ahead, rising in the social scale, outstripping others, and merely surviving in the struggle are the absorbing functions of life. When values appear in those areas, they act largely as brakes on drivenness. Though the occupational world is, on the whole, antagonistic to values in this sense, it would nevertheless be unable to function without them, and it may use them as veils to conceal its underlying motivations.

In our own culture the outstanding characteristic of promotable executives is drive.[1] It is no problem at all to locate jobs requiring an orientation toward achievement, competition, profit, and mobility, or even toward a higher standard of living. But it is difficult to find one requiring outstanding capacity for love, kindness, quietness, contentment, fun, frankness, and simplicity. If you are propelled by drives, the culture offers innumera-

[1]C. Wilson Randle, "How to Identify Promotable Executives," *Harvard Business Review* (May–June 1956), pp. 123–134.

ble opportunities for you; but if you are moved mostly by values, you really have to search, and if you do find a job in which you can live by values, the pay and prestige are usually low. Thus, the institutional supports —the organizations that help the expression of drives—are everywhere around us, while we must search hard to find institutions other than the family which are dedicated to values.

Americans conceive of drive as a consuming thing, and in some people a drive may grow so strong that it engulfs the person who has it and those who come in contact with him. In the American conception, drives can become almost like cannibals hidden in a man's head or viscera, devouring him from inside. Urged on by drive, the American then may consume others by compelling them to yield to his drivenness. Values are merely ideas about good human relations, and though they do give people direction, they lack the compelling power of drives because they do not have institutional support. Americans get heart attacks, ulcers, and asthma from the effects of their drives, and it seems that as exotic cultures enter the industrial era and acquire drive, their members become more and more subject to these diseases.[2]

A phenomenon that is important to an understanding of our culture and, indeed, of the contemporary world is the underlying assumption of the modern world that one does not really know what one thinks one knows; that it is likely, on close investigation, to turn out to be wrong. This assumption of probable error inherent in all decisions helps create a condition of uncertainty, so that the torment of always being possibly wrong, or at least of not having the "best" answer to any of life's problems, becomes a dominating characteristic of modern life. Uncertainty in contemporary culture feeds upon itself, for each new "truth" becomes a new error, and each new discovery merely opens the door to new uncertainties. If you put together in one culture uncertainty and the scientific method, competitiveness and technical inge-

[2] Dr. John Rees, director of the World Federation for Mental Health, personal communication.

nuity, you get a strong new explosive compound which I shall call *technological drivenness*.

Among the first to describe the driven quality of industrial society was David Ricardo, whose central discovery was that it is driven by its productive forces to a constantly spiraling expansion and change. Unless the reality of this process and its capacity to drive the culture inexorably is understood, the fate and the dilemma of the American people are not comprehensible.

The vast natural resources of the United States made possible, though they did not determine, the coupling of great industrial development with technical creativity. Put to use in the laboratories of basic science, creativity results in new discoveries and inventions, which produce industries offering new products. Since they are new, demand for them must be stimulated, and the creation of new wants results in further industrial expansion; but since constant industrial expansion depletes and exhausts natural resources, scientists are paid to find new ones so that America itself will not become exhausted. The effort to increase productive efficiency is an expression of industrial growth, and that effort has pushed scientists, engineers, and inventors still further into research and discovery, with the result that still more industries have been born.

In view of all this, it is not surprising that the ideal American is an inexhaustible reservoir of drive and personality resources; one who, while not using up what he has, yet exploits his personality to the best advantage. To function inefficiently, to permit one's accomplishments to fall short of one's potentialities, is the same as using one's industrial capital inefficiently and is considered a symptom of neurosis.

The increase in the population of the United States and a rising living standard during nearly a century of rapid growth of productive facilities have helped solve the problem of the spiraling relationship between production and the need for an expanding market. Often primitive people cannot permit too many children to survive, for, given their technology, there simply is not enough to feed a large population in a harsh and niggardly environment. In America, until recently, the situation was the reverse: the productive machine seemed so efficient and nature so generous that a growing population appeared necessary to buy all that could be produced. Whereas in the Far East government officials might worry about overpopulation, in America even as late as 1961 the government welcomed every infant as a potential customer. Early in 1957:

A huge electric chart in the lobby of the Commerce Department building [in Washington, D.C.] registered the 170 millionth inhabitant of the United States. . . . Sinclair Weeks, Secretary of Commerce, was present to see the 170 millionth American chalked up. . . . "I am happy to welcome this vast throng of new customers for America's goods and services," he said. "They help insure a rising standard of living and reflect our prosperous times." [3]

And again in December 1961:

The population of the United States, as measured on the "census clock" in the Commerce Department lobby, reached 185,000,000 at 3:01 P.M. today.

Commerce Secretary Luther H. Hodges led a round of cheers as the numbers on the clock moved to that figure.

The growth of 5,000,000 since last year "gives some idea of the future needs of the country from the economic standpoint," he said. [4]

In 1962, however, the impending danger from automation, which had been hidden by government and industry in the economic closet for seven years,[5] could no longer be denied, for it was eliminating jobs so fast,

Automation and Technological Change, Hearings before the Subcommittee on Economic Stabilization of the Joint Committee on the Economic Report, 84th Congress, First Session (U.S. Government Printing Office, 1955).

[3] *New York Times,* February 16, 1957.
[4] *New York Times,* December 1961.
[5] The ritual of denial is embalmed in the classic

while the population was still growing, that chronic unemployment had become a persisting source of anxiety.

In America there is an asymmetry and imbalance among products, machines, wants, consumers, workers, and resources. It is never certain in our culture that a new product will be wanted or that an old one will continue in demand; on the other hand, there are always some economic wants that are unfulfilled. There is a continuous race between consumers and products: consumers must buy or the economy will suffer, and there must always be enough products to satisfy consumer demand. There must always be enough workers to man the machines, and there must always be just enough machines turning to absorb enough workers. Finally, there must always be enough raw materials to manufacture the needed goods, and the proper instruments must be produced in order to provide the raw materials necessary for manufacture. Unlike the ancient Greeks, the Americans have no gods to hold their world in equilibrium, and for this reason (and many others) America gives a visitor—and even a sensitive resident —the feeling of being constantly off balance, though many of our social scientists maintain that society is in equilibrium.

Imbalance and asymmetry, however, are necessary to America, for were the main factors in the economy ever to come into balance, the culture would fall apart. For example, if consumer wants did not outstrip what is produced, there would be no further stimulus to the economic system and it would grind to a halt and disintegrate. If there were ever a perfect balance between machines and workers to man them, then new industry would be impossible, for there would be no workers for the new machines, and so on. True equilibrium—balance, symmetry, whatever one wishes to call it—is poison to a system like ours.

In the United States, facilities for producing increasing quantities of products in constantly growing variety increase faster than the population, and since the lag must be taken up by the creation of needs, advertising became the messiah of this Era of Consumption, so well described by Riesman and Eric Fromm.

The fact that in stable cultures whatever is produced has a complementary need suggests the existence of a vast potential of human needs. For after all, if in stable cultures all over the world almost every object, however bizarre it may seem to us, is found to have a complementary need, it is only common sense to suppose that human beings have the potential for developing an enormous variety of needs. If the Ashanti of West Africa, for example, need golden stools, the natives of the South American jungles need curare, intoxicating drugs, dyed parrots, feather cloaks, shrunken heads, and flutes several feet long; if the Incas of Peru needed fields of flowers made of silver and gold and the Kwakiutl Indians needed totem poles, slat armor, engraved copper plates six feet square, and painted cedar boxes inlaid with mother of pearl, one can realize without even looking at Greece, Rome, Babylon, Egypt, and modern America that human beings have the capacity to learn to want almost any conceivable material object. Given, then, the emergence of a modern industrial culture capable of producing almost anything, the time is ripe for opening the storehouse of infinite need! But bear in mind that since our equation states that a necessary condition for cultural stability is perfect economic complementarity, it follows that lack of complementarity—a modern condition in which new objects are constantly seeking new needs, and new needs are constantly chasing after new objects—involves cultural *instability*. Meanwhile, we know that the storehouse of infinite need is now being opened in America. It is the modern Pandora's box, and its plagues are loose upon the world.

The following, from a full-page ad in *The New York Times,* illustrates the American preoccupation with creating new wants. Under the picture of a large, outstretched, suppliant hand at the top of the page appears, in capitals almost an inch high, the *first commandment* of the new era:

CREATE
  MORE
    DESIRE!

Now, as always, profit and growth stem directly from the ability of salesmanship to create more desire.

To create more desire . . . will take more dissatisfaction with time-worn methods and a restless quest of better methods! It might even take a penchant for breaking precedents.[6]

This formulation stands on its head the anthropological cliché that the function of culture is to satisfy a relatively fixed bundle of known needs, for in America, as elsewhere in industrialized cultures, it is only *the deliberate creation of needs* that permits the culture to continue. *This is the first phase of the psychic revolution* of contemporary life.

There is probably nothing to which industrialists are more sensitive in America than consumer desires, and in that respect there is a striking resemblance between the businessman watching consumers' wants and an anxious American mother watching her child eat. The slightest sign of a decline in consumer demand makes the business world anxious, but this very petulance in the consumer stimulates the manufacturer to throw new products on the market. The following gives the tone:

Merchants and manufacturers faced even with a slight increase in reluctance to buy must take steps to restimulate consumer appetite *for their goods. The tradition of American ingenuity will come to their aid. New fashions, new models of mechanical goods and new designs are all in the order of the day. . . .*

Even slight lags in consumer interest have brought new products to the market quicker than they might otherwise have been introduced. . . . In the automobile field the lag in sales appears to have stimulated development of the gas turbine cars that give prom-

[6] *New York Times,* July 12, 1949.

ise of more economical transportation and lower car prices.[7] [Emphasis supplied]

So if the reluctant consumer stops to count the change in his pocket, the businessman is there, eager to count it for him and to put it into his own pocket. If buying lags, the manufacturer lures the consumer with a new car style, color TV, or a pocket-size transistor radio. But this very reluctance to buy, though it troubles the manufacturer, propels him into new productive ventures, which in their turn give jobs to new hands, but also foster new troubles.

The second modern commandment, "Thou shalt consume!" is the natural complement of the first—"Create more desire!" Together they lead the attack on the key bastion of the Indo-European, Islamic, and Hebrew traditions—the impulse control system—for the desire for a million things cannot be created without stimulating a craving for everything. This is the second phase of the psychic revolution of our time—*unhinging the old impulse controls*. The final phase will be the restoration of balance at a new level of intergration.

The attack on the impulse control system, that is, on our resistance to inner cravings, is related then to technological drivenness. In its onward rush, technological drivenness eats up natural resources at such a rate that international combines must be formed to find and exploit new ones. It helps, through constantly increased advertising pressure, to lower the defenses against inner compulsions to express insatiable needs, while it harnesses human effort to the very machines that nourish the consuming appetites.

Born into a world where uncertainty was already a living principle, technological drivenness has intensified uncertainty by magnifying the economic imbalances on which it pivots, and the tension of uncertainty stimulates some to buy almost as a nervous man eats to calm himself. Industry, pressed by the drive for greater profits, by competition, and by the uncertainty of the market, commits

[7] *New York Times*, June 24, 1956.

ever larger sums to sales promotion. In the jargon of advertising in America, "education" means educating the public to buy, and "inspiration" means "inspired to buy."

As technological drivenness mines the earth of wealth, so it mines the desires of men; as the strip-shovel rips coal from the earth, as the pump sucks oil from the bed, so advertising dredges man's hidden needs and consumes them in the "hard sell." But without constant discovery and exploitation of hidden cravings, all of us would starve under the present system, for how would we be fed and clothed otherwise? Where would we be employed?

Were human wants to regress to a primitive level, there would be universal misery in America. No government could cope with the unemployment that would ensue, and at present there is no visible middle ground between the needs of the caveman and the cravings of space-man.

Meanwhile, advertising does not deserve all the (dubious) credit for destroying our impulse controls. After all, if they still served a social purpose we would keep them. If holding ourselves in check led to satisfaction in work, to a position of community respect, or to immortality, we would not let ourselves go so easily for fun and for the ever higher standard of living. But for most Americans, self-denial seems to lead nowhere any longer, for heaven has become detached from society, and for most people work is merely a dreary interlude between nourishing hours with one's family. Man in our culture has always bargained his impulses against higher goods —he has always sought to trade one day of abstinence against economic gain or against an eternity of supernatural blessings. But when the sacrifice of impulse release no longer assures rewards either on earth or in heaven, he will no longer keep his cravings under control unless he is punished, so that nowadays advertising merely opens the door to impulses clamoring to come out anyway.

The idea of obsolescence—or, better, "dynamic obsolescence"— has become such a necessary part of contemporary American thinking and life that it deserves a place, along with achievement, competition, profit, and expansiveness, among the drives. "Dynamic obsolescence" is the drive to make what is useful today unacceptable tomorrow; to make what fitted the standard of living of 1957 inappropriate even for 1960. It is the "new-car-every-year" drive. Technological drivenness is admirably served by dynamic obsolescence, for it compels us to throw away what we have and buy a newer form of the same thing or something entirely different. It is the technological complement to impulse release.

"Dynamic obsolescence" was formally installed as a cultural drive in a speech given by Mr. Harlow Curtice, president of General Motors, at the dedication of General Motors' wonderful new Research Center. No occasion could have been more appropriate for this historically unique phenomenon: the recognition and crowning of a new cultural drive. The only thing that was missing from the ceremony was a Miss Dynamic Obsolescence of 1956. Some excerpts from Mr. Curtice's speech on the occasion will give the tone:

Continuing emphasis on change, on a better method and a better product, in other words, on progress in technology, has been the major force responsible for the growth and development of our country. Some call this typical American progress "dynamic obsolescence" because it calls for replacing the old with something new and better. From this process of accelerating obsolescence by technological progress flow the benefits we all share—more and better job opportunities, and advancing standard of living—the entire forward march of civilization on the material side. . . .

The promotion of the progress of science and the useful arts is of crucial importance . . . [but] there is a far more vital consideration. I refer to the importance of technological progress in assuring the continuance not

only of American leadership in the free world, but of the democratic processes themselves.[8]

Dynamic obsolescence has thus become the American Fortuna, warm, fruity, and maternal, in whom all benefits abound.

In attempting to understand Mr. Curtice, I encounter two difficulties: I cannot decide who really is the leader in the world today; and I become lost in some of the implications of Mr. Curtice's words. For example, the emergence of India as a modern state seems to be the result of obsolescence not in the material, but rather in the social sense, for what became obsolete in India was British rule; and what is obsolescent is the caste system. On the other hand, the rise of India as a political power has become possible in large part also because the two grand power configurations (the Soviet Union and the United States) that are dynamic above all others in their (material) dynamic obsolescence confront each other in fear and trembling, and this gives India a chance. Thus, India's road to leadership-through-dynamic-obsolescence is indirect—but it is there, and the Oracle of Detroit is correct again.

Whatever role we wish to assign it in world affairs, however, there is no doubt that in American life dynamic obsolescence is fundamental and necessary. From the point of view of personality this means that one's human capacities are in danger of becoming obsolete, and every man and woman therefore stands in peril of waking up one morning to discover that he is, too. When the entire pattern of transportation changes and a thousand railroad stations are abolished overnight by one major road, then all the station masters, baggage clerks, and others

[8]Printed in " 'The Greatest Frontier'—Remarks at the dedication program, General Motors Technical Center," Detroit, May 16, 1956 (Public Relations Staff, General Motors, Detroit). I am grateful to Mrs. Sydney Slotkin for calling my attention to this speech and the remarks on obsolescence.

who manned them become obsolete;[9] when several large corporations merge into one, then many of the executives become unnecessary and obsolete;[10] and people's fear of becoming obsolete stirs hostility against Science, the paramount creator of obsolescence.

A few quotations from *Automation and Technological Change* will give the tone:

> ... *a radio poll in Detroit showed that listeners feared automation next to Russia.* ... [p. 247]
> ... *automation* ... *produces various sorts of fears in various sorts of individuals—fear of change, fear of technology itself, fear of displacement, fear of unemployment, fear of machines,* fear of science in general. [pp. 262–263] [Emphasis supplied]
> *We know of cases where some workers have gotten sick on the steps of the new [telephone company automated] toll center; others developed various illnesses which could be traced to fear of new work operations. We have been told of mature women crying in restrooms, improperly prepared for new methods and fearful of losing their jobs.* ... *The tragedy of the mature worker whose skill area suddenly disintegrates and is incorrectly retrained is profound.* [pp. 341–342]

As professors encounter their colleagues in the corridors of "progressive" American universities, they silently evaluate them as "obsolete" or "alive"; in order for a professor to stay "alive" in an American university that is not obsolescent, he must indeed change from year to year like an automobile, refrigerator, or washing machine.

The fear of becoming obsolete is so powerful that the sense of being useless is a common element in emotional crisis in America. However, this fear is rooted not only in the fear of obsolescence, but also in an industrial system that obliges too many people to do what they have so little interest in doing. In this respect America's industrial progress has made many people spiritually useless to themselves.

THE JOB AND THE SELF

Most people do the job they have to do regardless of what they want to do; technological drivenness has inexorable requirements, and the average man or woman either meets them or does not work. With a backward glance at the job-dreams of his pre-"labor force" days the young worker enters the occupational system not where he would, but where he can;[11] and his job-dream, so often an expression of his dearest self, is pushed down with all his other unmet needs to churn among them for the rest of his life. The worker's giving up an essential part of himself to take a job, to survive, and to enjoy himself as he may is the new renunciation, the new austerity: it is the technological weed that grows where the Vedic flower bloomed. What makes the renunciation particularly poignant is that it comes after an education that emphasized exploitation of all the resources of the individual, and which has declared that the promise of democracy is freedom of choice.

This renunciation of the needs of the self—this latter-day selflessness—is, paradoxically, a product of the most successful effort in human history to meet on a mass basis an infinite variety of material needs. The man who accepts such a renunciation does in-

[9]Front-page article, *New York Times*, August 21, 1956. I want to thank Mr. Richard Meier for calling my attention to the implications for obsolescence of this article.

[10]"National Job-Hunting Group Established to Aid Unemployed Executives over 40," *New York Times*, August 30, 1956. Between 1910 and 1950 the numbers of proprietors, managers, and officials declined by nearly 7 per cent *(Economic Forces in the U.S.A. in Facts and Figures*, U.S. Government Printing Office, p. 29) even though productive facilities and the gross national product have increased many times that.

[11]Gladys L. Palmer, "Attitudes toward Work in an Industrial Community," *American Journal of Sociology*, 43 (1957), pp. 17–26.

deed approach fulfillment of the wants the engines of desire-production have stirred within him, and whoever refuses to renounce his very self will get few of the material things for which he has been taught to hunger. The average American has learned to put in place of his inner self a high and rising standard of living, because technological drivenness can survive as a cultural configuration only if the drive toward a higher standard of living becomes internalized; only if it becomes a moral law, a kind of conscience. The operator, truck driver, salesclerk, or bookkeeper may never expect to rise much in "the firm," but he can direct his achievement drive into a house of his own, a car, and new furniture.

The massing of so much drive behind the living standard in our culture has brought it about that the very survival of our culture depends on a unique and fantastic material configuration created for us by technological drivenness, and to which the standard of living has been fastened psychologically by pressures from within and without.

As numberless selves have been ground up by the technological system, the popularity and usefulness of psychoanalysis have grown so that America is one of the most psychoanalytically minded countries on earth; and clinical psychology and learning theory have covered the country with practitioners—bad as well as good, of course. Though this flowering of psychology has much to do with the technological system, and though much of it has grown up either in order to speed the technology or to ameliorate its lethal effects, nevertheless, to the degree that psychology has expanded our understanding and deepened our sensitivity, it is a medicine wrung from the very system that inflicts wounds upon us.

Meanwhile, one should remember that the great rise in real income suggests that we have gotten what we paid for; but how far we have yet to go is suggested by an estimate that by 1965 half the babies born in New York City hospitals will be the offspring of "indigent parents."[12]

Along with the emotional problems they create, all cultures provide socially acceptable outlets or anodynes. In America some compensation for personality impoverishment is provided by the high-rising standard of living, but another available outlet is job change. More than half the American workers had from two to four jobs between 1940 and 1949, and in those ten years every worker shifted around an average of three times.[13] Beneath this continuous tidal movement in and out of jobs[14] lie deep narcissistic wounds whose pain the worker tries to ease by moving around, searching restlessly for the "perfect" job, as a sick man painfully shifts his body about in bed to find a more comfortable position. Of course, he never does. I have called this movement in and out of jobs tidal because it is a slow, never-ceasing trickle from many sources, from many industries and many occupations, and in the long run it has reached such proportions that millions are spent to analyze it, and some of the best brains in the land devote their lives to fascinated study of it. What keeps a worker on his job? Why does he move? Why does he *not* move if he doesn't? Are workers satisfied? If not, why not? What does "satisfied" mean? Can we measure the boundary line between satisfaction and dissatisfaction? So far, the mass study of "job attachment" shows that the American worker's involvement in his job is so insubstantial that it is next to impossible to define the term "attachment."

Meanwhile, industry is hostile to workers who move too often because it is costly to train new hands, and because a missing employee disturbs production. That is why American psychology considers frequent job

[12] *New York Times,* October 30, 1957.

[13] Gladys L. Palmer, *Labor Mobility in Six Cities* (New York: Social Science Research Council, 1954). It is to be regretted that later figures of equal comprehensiveness are not available.

[14] Professor Irvin Sobel reminds me that many semiskilled workers shift around from activity to activity within the same company at approximately the same level of skill. He tells me also that automation has now made even younger workers so apprehensive about job security that they move around less.

change as a symptom of emotional disturbance. It ought to be pointed out, however, in view of the fact that frequent job change is used routinely to diagnose emotional instability, that there are vast differences in the cultural pattern of job stability, for while over half the laborers had three or more jobs between 1940 and 1949, only two-fifths of the service workers had that many, and only a third of the professional workers.[15] At any rate, the man who changes jobs "too frequently" is simlpy manifesting in extreme the characteristic American tendency to job-flux.

Paradoxically, while it detests worker instability, industry must at the same time love it, for it is this very lack of involvement in, lack of loyalty to, the job that makes the rapid growth of industry possible. If a new factory making a new product is built, all that is necessary to get workers is to advertise, for the workers' lack of attachment to the jobs they have and their obstinate hope for better working conditions, a few cents more an hour, or a pleasanter boss, make it easy to attract them away from what they have to something new.[16] Were there firm and devoted attachment to the job, industrial growth would be much more difficult, for new enterprises would not be able to find trained workers if they loved it where they were. Since we require of most people that they be uninvolved in the institution for which they work, it follows that the ability to be uninvolved is a desirable quality in the American character. Meanwhile, since loyal workers are valued because every replacement cuts into profits, we have a paradoxical situation in which, since uninvolvement—"What do you give a damn, bub?"—is valued also, loyalty is obtained through higher wages, fringe benefits, and seniority. This emotionless connection that finally pins a worker to his job is called "attachment" in the ambiguous language of labor economics.

The recent social invention—the "coffee break"—fits this situation perfectly, for during the "break" the worker escapes from a task in which he has little or no interest, takes up his preferred and necessary role as consumer, and relaxes his impulse controls. In the uninvolved flirtations and sociability of the coffee break the worker can renew his self-esteem, badly battered through performance of the meaningless task, and assuage some of the anxiety and hostility stirred up by it. The coffee break is on-the-job therapy.

The fact that the majority have little or no involvement in the institutions for which they work means that work, which in most non-industrial cultures of the world is a strong and continuous socializing agency, is, in America, also desocializing. In the first place, for the overwhelming majority of Americans, the job itself—not the union or the associates on the job, but the institution in which they work—is precisely the mechanism that cuts them off from their most significant emotional involvements—family, friends, and Self; and in the second place, since the great majority of the tasks at which Americans work are routine, requiring little or no initiative and imagination,[17] most persons in the labor force never have the opportunity to develop, through work, characteristics that might contribute to the enrichment of society. Furthermore, the rising labor turnover since World War II[18] suggests that the pleasures of the "work group" have little binding force on the worker who wants to change.

To almost any American his working companions, however enjoyable, are inherently replaceable.[19] The comradely group a man has on one job can be replaced by a similar one on the next. The feeling of being replaceable, that others can get along without one, that somebody else will be just as good, is an active depressant in the American character.

By the Ice Age man had discovered that he could bind his fellows to him by sharing work

[15]Palmer, Labor Mobility in Six Cities.

[16]This applies especially to younger workers. As a unionized worker acquires seniority, he is less likely to change employers.

[17]Economic Forces in the U.S.A. in Facts and Figures, pp. 28–29.

[18]New York Times Magazine, May 19, 1957.

[19]Nancy C. Morse and Robert S. Weiss, "The Function and Meaning of Work," American Sociological Review, 20 (1955), pp. 191–198; also, Palmer, "Attitudes toward Work," loc. cit., and personal communication from Mr. Robert Weiss.

and its fruits. This discovery was so valuable that establishing solidarity through work and sharing became a stable human tradition, so that whether on an atoll in the South Pacific, in the jungles of South America, or in Arctic wastes, this aspect of early life has persisted. Since one of the many revolutions of industrial society has been the sweeping away of the unifying functions of work, work has lost its human meaning. Although it is true that on the job some pleasure is obtained nowadays in socializing, the hold of the worker's fellows on him is slight. This lack of deep positive involvement in the people with whom one spends most of his waking life derives in part from the fact that he does not work *for* the person he works *with,* for the fruits of activity are not shared among workers but belong to the enterprise that hires them.

Except for professionals and executives most Americans are emotionally involved neither in their occupation (what they do) nor in their job (the place where they do it).[20] What finally relates the average person to life, space, and people is his own personal, intimate economy: his family, house, and car. He has labeled his occupational world "not involved," and turned inward upon his own little world of family, hobbies, and living standard.

[20] *Fortune*'s study of executives reports a rapidly mounting turnover among them. See *The Executive Life* by the Editors of *Fortune*'s (New York: Doubleday, 1956). Professionals and executives care much about *what* they do, but have the characteristic American lack of loyalty to the organization for whom they do it.

17   Modernity: Divided Life + Fragmented Self = Anxiety

Kenneth Keniston

. . . The two trends I have so far discussed are closely related. The fragmentation of traditional tasks and the shattering of traditional community both involve differentiation, specialization, narrowing of scope, and increased demands for performance within a narrowed field. And behind both trends is a set of basic technological values about life, virtue, and efficacy. Did we not tacitly consent to these values, we would bridle at the social changes that increasingly implement

Reprinted from Chapter 9 of *The Uncommitted* by Kenneth Keniston. By permission of Harcourt Brace and Jovanovich, Inc. Copyright © 1960, 1962, 1965 by Kenneth Keniston.

them; in societies where men utterly reject these values, a technological society does not and cannot develop.

We usually think of technology, like science, as "objective," uninterested in ultimate values, and uninvolved with basic philosophical assumptions. Thus, to speak of the "values" of technology may seem a contradiction, for among the chief characteristics of technology is that it *has* no final values, that it is little concerned with the ultimate ends of life, and deals hardly at all with the whys, whats, and wherefores of human existence. But though technology lacks final values, it does specify instrumental values,

values about the procedures, techniques, processes, and modes which should be followed, values about "how to do it."

The question "How to do it?" of course admits many possible answers. Some societies have given highest priority to those techniques we term intuition, sensibility, revelation, and insight. In such societies, inner vision, fantasy, and communication with the Divine are the most cherished aspects of human experience. "Realism," whether in art, literature, domestic life, or personal experience is almost unknown: superstition, magic, myth, and collective fantasies abound. The favored instruments of knowledge in these societies are those we consider "nonrational": prayer, mysticism, intuition, revelation, dreams, inspiration, "possession." But in a technological society, these human potentials take second place: we distrust intuition and consider revelation a token of mental illness; and in everyday language "sensitivity" connotes the quality of being too easily offended rather than the capacity to experience deeply.

The preferred techniques of technology involve two related principles: that we *give priority to cognition,* and that we *subordinate feeling.* By "cognition," I mean men's capacities for achieving accurate, objective, practically useful, and consensually verifiable knowledge and understanding of their world; and by "priority" I mean to suggest that these capacities have increasingly become superordinate to other human potentials. Thus, feeling as a force of independent value—all of the passions, impulses, needs, drives, and idealisms which in some societies are the central rationales of existence—are increasingly minimized, suppressed, harnessed, controlled, and dominated by the more cognitive parts of the psyche. Feeling does not, of course, cease to exist; but insofar as possible, it is subordinated to the cognitive demands of our society.

The priority of cognition involves a series of other instrumental values and stratagems, which we consider applicable to the solution of all problems. Indeed, the very notion that

most difficulties in life are "problems" is one of the central assumptions of the technological outlook. We normally assume that the pitfalls along life's path can best be dealt with by treating them as cognitive difficulties whose solution involves the application of "know-how." Ours is a how-to-do-it society, and not a what-to-do society. For every discussion of the ethics of love, we have a dozen manuals in every drugstore on the "techniques" of love. For every discussion of the purposes of life, industry, and society, a thousand hours are spent in discovering how to sell soap, how to peddle the image of a politician, how to propagate the "American way of life." We approach even the question of national survival as a cognitive problem of how to ready ourselves to destroy the Russians efficiently should the need arise, and how to limit their effective capacity to destroy us. Our human troubles and tragedies are largely defined as "unsolved problems"; and our chief attention goes toward attempting to discover the proper cognitive techniques for solving them.

Thus our society characteristically dismisses "final questions" as either philosophically "meaningless" or—more commonly—as "irrelevant" to the pressing problems at hand. The man who insists on asking such questions is usually considered an obstructionist. Discussions of "why" and "what" are relegated to Sunday church-going, to neurotic adolescents, and to a few artists and dissidents whose views are occasionally reported, well behind the business news, in our national weeklies. Even the harassed middle-aged executives in modern manuals, who question "the meaning of it all," are allowed only a brief regression to adolescent philosophizing and a short sexual fling before being made to realize that selling codfish balls really can make sense after all. The relegation of ministers to their pulpits and intellectuals to their ivory towers effectively insulates the public from any potential gadfly who might raise embarrassing—and to many Americans, unanswerable—questions about ultimate purposes.

What, then, are the cognitive techniques

prescribed by our society for solving problems? First among these is to *analyze* the problems into manageable components. Life, tasks, problems, roles, and industrial goals are all said to consist of analytically distinct and separable components. Approaches to a problem that emphasize the continuity or irreducible wholeness of any phenomenon are deemed "merely" esthetic. Even human life is not seen as an organic whole but as a series of discrete, temporally contiguous events. American psychological theories stress isolated behavior patterns at the expense of continuous human processes; most industrial managers overlook the fact that men can often accomplish more working together than working separately on an assembly line. Despite the daily evidence of our senses that most functioning wholes are a great deal more than the sum of their parts, we often treat even society as a mere collection of individuals bound together by common laws, neglecting the obvious patterns of mutual interdependence that connect us all. To most Americans the term "synthetic" merely suggests bogus flowers or man-made fibers, and not the integrating potential of personality. We most value the "analytic," the "incisive," and the "sharp"—the qualities of intelligence which dissect, analyze, and break apart.

Analysis almost inevitably involves *reduction,* in that it attempts to reduce the large to the small, to divide unities into fractions, to locate the indivisible particles from which all else can be shown to be built. In practice, the impulse to reduce problems into smaller component parts often results in an implicit devaluation of what is analyzed. We attribute greater reality to the separate building blocks than to the finished edifice, perhaps because we assume that every whole is "merely" the sum of these building blocks. In psychology, this devaluation is seen in our countless daily assertions that apparently noble aspirations are "nothing but" rationalizations of other less admirable but more basic drives, that reason is a "mere" slave of powerful passions, that vision, idealism, and wisdom are "only" compensations for under-

lying blindness, corruption, and folly. Theories of learning frequently proclaim that human learning is essentially no different from animal learning—that Michelangelo in his studio is to the cheese-seeking rat merely as the large computer is to the small. Synthetic principles which might help explain wholeness, intactness, integration, and unity are rarely articulated.

Cognitive "problem-solving" also involves *measurement and comparison.* With the effort to reduce reality to basic building blocks goes the desire to find quantitative standards of comparison for apparently dissimilar entities. Money is one such standard: otherwise incomparable corporations or men share the fact that they make (or lose) money. But beyond this most visible yardstick of worth, our society abounds in other numerical comparisons: miles, horsepower, feet, IQ points, kilowatts, per cents, pounds, reams, grade averages, quires, and quartiles. On the scale of income, human worth can be measured (a $10,000-a-year-man); on the scale of IQ points, intelligence can be measured (an IQ of 106); and in percentages, we measure the heart of the nation (48 per cent approved of peace). And though measurement and comparison require overlooking differences in quality and individuality, this is a price we are willing to pay.

All of these characteristics of our technological values presuppose *empiricism,* a special view of reality that most Americans accept without question. In this metaphysic, what is "real" is external, sensory, and consensually validatable: "seeing is believing." Other cultures would of course have disagreed; for most men of the Middle Ages, Truth sprang not from the objective eye but from the divinely inspired soul. But for us, what is real and true is the visible, external, and scientifically verifiable; and the rest is "speculation," "mythical," "unverifiable," "merely a matter of opinion." Empiricism thus relegates the invisible world of poetry, art, feeling, and religion to a limbo of lesser reality, sometimes termed "fantasy gratifications" to permit men to repair the wounds incurred by their daily struggle in the "real world." American psychology sometimes reflects this empiricism by a discomfort at the invisible workings of the mind so extreme that it refers to thinking as "subverbal talking," or defines "reality factors" as those impinging on us from outside—as if fantasy, dream, and idealism were not "realities" as well. "Experience," a term which in principle includes everything that crosses consciousness, has come to mean "sensory experience"—"experience" of the "real world"—and we can suggest that human beings have other potentialities only by adding the awkward qualified "inner." Those who have overwhelming self-evident inner experiences are relegated to our mental hospitals, though other societies would have honored them as saints, seers, and prophets. Our gods are accuracy, realism, verifiability, and objectivity; while intuition, fantasy, and private illumination are considered useful only insofar as they lead to "objective" achievements or help dissipate the tensions created by the "real" world.

The triumph of cognition in a technological society thus involves a subordination of feeling. The techniques of cognitive problem-solving—analysis, reduction, measurement, comparison, and empiricism—are all non-emotional: they stress objectivity, they demand dispassionateness, they purport to be universally applicable to all situations. Emotion must be "kept in its place"—and this place is ideally somewhere away from public life, work, politics, or the economy. From an early age we are taught that strong feelings on the job cause trouble—unless they are about doing an efficient job, in which case they are desirable. Ideally, the "good worker" is cool, impersonal, always friendly and ready to listen to others but never "personally involved." He does not panic, he is not jealous, he neither loves nor hates his fellow workers, he does not daydream at work. When all goes well, his work goes "by the book": it lives up to or exceeds the standards established in his field. Even the desire for personal advancement—one feeling our society does admit—must be controlled if it threatens to interfere with the worker's performance: one does not wreck General Motors in order to become its president.

Men and women of course inevitably continue to have strong feelings about their livelihoods, and the people involved in them. But we early learn that these feelings are usually a "problem" to be "dealt with" in other ways —in our families, in recreation—and not "acted out" on the job. The vocabulary of deprecation is filled with terms to describe those who disobey the imperative against emotion: "prima donnas," "unstable" or "impulsive" types, "daydreamers," people who "act out." Whatever we really feel, we must *behave* as if we only felt a reasonable eagerness to do a good job, and in reward are called "dispassionate," "objective," "self-controlled," "level-headed," "rational," and "stable."

The subordination of feeling has several regular corollaries. One is the demand for *fairness and impartiality.* In all areas of public life we learn to "treat everyone the same." The highest principle of our legal code involves "equality before the law," and in work as in most other areas of public life men should be treated equally no matter who they are. There are still embarrassing lapses to this principle, especially in the case of dark-skinned Americans, but even here the growing pressure toward greater fairness is clear. In principle, equality means that we judge, punish, and reward people according to what they have done and not according to their birth, sex, age, race, or appearance. Only the family is exempt from the principles of fairness and impartiality, and then only because families cannot exist without a recognition of the inherent differences of gender and generation. Otherwise, the trend toward greater fairness, equality, and impartiality is unmistakable. Preferential treatment, nepotism, and favoritism are universally frowned upon, and expertise, competence, and proven achievements are the chief values of public life.

These requirements of our public world— that feeling be subordinated to the objective task at hand, that everyone be treated according to the same rules, and that a person's accomplishments should determine his rewards—run through much of American life. They are visible in the fragmented roles that determine our public behavior, they are implemented in the myriad organizations that have replaced traditional community, and they are closely related to the real needs of technology. To accomplish its primary goals—the systematic exploitation and cultivation of scientific knowledge to produce new objects of consumption—a technological society requires a highly cognitive outlook and a subordination of feeling to technological tasks. Technology and cognitive outlook have the same justification: if one wants to get things done, this is the way to do them—"facing facts gets results." The dreamer, the visionary, and the poet are thought to be of little use in the day-to-day working of technological society; personal expressiveness and "style" are of secondary value except as entertainment.

Even the areas where these cognitive and anti-emotional rules do not apply support the view that they take priority. For these other areas of life, family and leisure, are almost invariably relegated to a secondary role, termed outlets, recreation, havens, or exceptions to the basic rules of our social order. Implicitly or explicitly we view them as compensatory to the "real world"—they are the froth, frills, safety valves, and status symbols a technological society must allow itself. We pay reluctant obeisance to the need to "work off steam" built up by the emotional suppressions required in work; we allow "unproductive" people like young married women with small children to occupy themselves with arts and antiques; we study emotions scientifically to learn how better to subordinate them; and we even approve if our pianists beat the Russians on the concerto front of the Cold War. A rich society can afford its clowns and dreamers; and a cognitive society may need them as "outlets." But let a young man announce his intention of becoming a poet, a visionary, or a dreamer, and the reactions of his family and friends will unmistakably illustrate the values most Americans consider central.

Merely to deprecate these values would be to overlook their role in creating the many advantages of our technological society. Few of us would want to live in a society where partiality, unfairness, inequality, preferential treatment based on birth, arbitrarily applied whims, and uncontrolled passion ruled. But similarly, merely to praise the technological values of our society is to overlook the psychological demands these values entail, and thus to overlook their role in producing alienation.

SOCIAL FRAGMENTATION AND PSYCHOLOGICAL WHOLENESS

The trends I have discussed are familiar to anyone conversant with the mainstream of social criticism and analysis of technological societies. For almost a century sociologists have pointed to differentiation, fragmentation, specialization, "upgrading," the decline of intact community, and empiricism as important characteristics of societies like our own. But these analyses often stop short of considering the human impact of these social trends, and here we must continue beyond them, asking at what points the fragmentation of tasks, the shattering of community, and the ascendency of technological values subject individual Americans to the greatest psychological pressures.

The Burden of Choice—Our intellectual tradition has always held freedom of choice to be a positive value. If there has been any traditional "problem of freedom," it has been the problem of attaining the greatest possible freedom from social restraint. For centuries, our most vital political slogans have emphasized freedom from political, social, ideological, and, of late, psychological constraints on freedom. Some of the success of these political and ideological slogans has been accidental—increasing social fragmentation alone has meant an ever greater availability of life options. Whatever the reasons, the actual extent of choice in American society—and in democratic technological societies everywhere—has increased enormously in the past centuries. But though our political slogans continue to demand greater freedom, many Americans have come to experience this freedom as at best a mixed blessing and at worst an acute problem; the demand that one choose and make commitments in the face of an enormous variety of socially available options is increasingly felt as a heavy demand.

Consider the commitments that the average high school student must make in our fragmented society. For one, he must choose a *career*. From among literally tens of thousands of job possibilities, he must select *the one* which seems best suited to his talents, motives, needs, feelings, values, and background. And he must inevitably make this choice in relative ignorance of what most of these careers involve, yet fully aware that what they involve today may be quite different from what they will involve tomorrow. Whether he will be a plumber, a car-dealer, an engineer, a carpenter, a grocery man, an insurance man, a factory worker; whether he will go to college (and which college and to major in what), whether to seek fame or wealth or public service, whether he is talented enough for job A or too talented for job B, whether he has the motivation for job X or job Y—none of these questions admits an easy answer. Furthermore, at the same time or soon after, he must choose a *wife*. And this decision too can be difficult. When to marry? Now? Later? What kind of girl to marry? A beautiful girl? A practical girl? Intelligent? A good mother? And what kind of marriage to try to achieve? How many children to have? How much do you have to love someone to marry her? Many societies solve these problems with arranged marriages and ignorance of contraception; ours leaves them up to the individual.

But there is more: an American youth must also decide what he believes, where he will live, what style of life he will lead, how he will vote, what role he will play in which organizations, how he will spend his free time. Our society offers no "package deals" in which one choice takes care of most of the rest, no clear "blueprints for life" that an individual can take or leave as a whole. Each choice involves other choices; each commitment requires others; each decision is a preface to another new point of no return.

But of all the choices our society asks of us, the hardest is the "choice" of who to *be*, for this decision underlies the rest. To call it a "choice" is of course to make it sound more conscious and deliberate than it is; for most youths, "who to be" is hardly a matter of conscious reflection, but of unconscious selection and synthesis. Yet from outside, and over a long period, we can often see the slow development of an unspoken determination not be be like one's father but to be like some admired teacher; the gradual commitment to and cultivation of one set of capacities at the expense of other potentials; the evolution and strengthening of some psychological defenses and the wasting away of others. Most often, the battle of "who am I?" is consciously fought out on the battlegrounds of vocation, marriage, friendships, family size, home ownership, group membership, style of life, and a multitude of other specific choices. But to the individual, these specific commitments are important not only in themselves, but in their bearing on the deeper questions of personal identity.

"Freedom of choice" can be a problem only when there are real alternatives but no criterion for choosing among them. Were there a clear "rational" way to choose *the* one best career, it would solve the problem of choice. But of course no such standard exists: there are dozens of considerations; and so many careers exist, each changing so rapidly that no one can hope to know about more than a small fraction of them. Or if there were some simple way of choosing the *one* best spouse from among the millions available, "choosing a mate" would be little problem. Lacking such certainty, we must try to commit ourselves to vocations, people, and futures about which we cannot be sure.

Some young Americans can do just this: they can live without a guarantee that they have made the best or the only choice, and this capacity to make commitments *without* guarantees is a prime symptom of strength of character. But others—perhaps most young Americans—undergo a period of confusion beforehand, and often seek escapes from their freedom. We seldom recognize, for example, that "falling in love" is among other things a way of avoiding a reflective choice of a mate. In a situation where "rational" calculation is almost impossible, romantic love defines the choice of mate as an area where rational calculation is simply irrelevant: romantic love overwhelms the doubt, hesitation, and vacillation which must beset any man or woman who tries to decide "rationally" what he and his spouse will be like in forty years of marriage. So, too, "following in Dad's footsteps" can be a way of avoiding the difficult freedom that would follow from choosing *not* to be like Dad.

But the most common adaptation is to slide, not to decide—to limit one's choices by seizing only the opportunities that fall into one's lap, to choose the employer and the career which promises the most money, or to marry the first available girl with a nice personality and good figure. Sliding rather than deciding works best for those who have few inner obstacles to commitment, and for those at whose door opportunity knocks once, loudly, in the form of a remunerative employer or a nice pretty girl. It works less well for the underprivileged, the overprivileged, and for those who find commitment difficult. Opportunity knocks but lightly or not at all at the doors of the underprivileged, and it appears in threadbare clothes. And for the privileged, the talented and versatile, opportunities may knock too often and too loudly, appearing in guises so glittering and Protean that to choose between their beckonings is impossible. Furthermore, for those who distrust all commitments, no opportunity seems sufficiently attractive to overcome their distrust. The youths who live most easily with their freedom are the *moderately* talented, the moderately good-looking, the moderately ambitious, and the moderately capable. The stars, beauty queens, and the geniuses are often overwhelmed with offers; the paupers, the ugly, and the dull receive none; and the

alienated, whatever their talents, find all offers counterfeit.

For all these youths, as for the simply indecisive, the "freedom of choice" in our society constitutes a major human problem, which is ultimately the problem of identity. Ideally in America, commitment and self-definition go hand in hand during adolescence, so that each new commitment further clarifies identity and each clarification of identity permits new commitments. But the idea seldom occurs: for most youths indecision, vacillation, and doubt precede commitment and sometimes replace it. Having to choose, having to make commitments, is then experienced not as a joyous freedom but as a heavy burden.

The Meaning of Work—In most traditional societies, young men and women have had little choice as to their work: they worked *because* they were men and women; their work was their life; and work, play, and social life flowed over into each other. Under such circumstances, men rarely think or speak in terms of "work" (which implies something else which is "not work"); they merely speak of the tasks to be done, the catching of fish, the tilling of crops, the saying of Mass. All things run together; distinctions between sectors of life are meaningless: "I work because I am a man."

For most Americans, in contrast, "work" has vaguely unpleasant connotations. It is most frequently paired with words like "hard," or used in phrases like "all work and no play." Work is implicitly felt as something to be gotten out of the way. If we ask the average American why he works, he will answer, "To earn a living"; and this expression says much about the relationship of work and life. The goal of work is to earn the money necessary for "living" when one is not working. The purpose of work is to make possible *other* things (a "living") which are only possible after work. Implicitly, work is seen as a necessary instrumental evil without inherent meaning. Just as for the puritan, good work and good works were the way a man demonstrated his salvation—the pain of this life which guaranteed bliss in the next—

so for most Americans, work remains a mildly painful ordeal.

The reasons for our implicitly negative attitudes toward work can be inferred from the characteristics of most jobs. The fragmentation of tasks means that the individual's relationship to the total product or the total task is highly attenuated. As specialization proceeds, each worker finds himself assigned a smaller and smaller corner of a task; the whole job, the finished product, the whole person as client or patient recedes into the far distance. A sense of connection with a tangible accomplishment and a sense of personal responsibility for what one does are inevitably vitiated in our highly organized society where the Ford Motor Company, the Community Hospital, or DeVitale Homes, Inc., is responsible for the task. Even at upper levels of management, it takes considerable imagination for the executive to feel a personal relationship with, and to derive a sense of value from, his part in the production of iceboxes, soft drinks, insurance policies, or compact cars. Indeed, the reason high-level executives usually say they are relatively "satisfied" with their jobs may not be because these jobs are in fact more "meaningful," but merely because the executive's education, training, and conceptual ability gives him greater capacity to understand his tenuous relationship to his work.

The rising demands for performance on the job further affect a man's feeling about his job. In some highly skilled jobs, growing demands for training and skill may permit a feeling of personal competence which compensates for a tenuous relationship to the total task. The skilled surgeon, the senior machinist, the executive trained in organizational theory, industrial management, and human relations—all may be able to enjoy the use of their highly developed skills. But for many men, more demanding job requirements simply mean more taxing and exacting work, greater demands to "keep up" in order to succeed. Too few jobs challenge the heart, imagination, or spirit. On the contrary, most work enjoins a rigorous subordination of these feelings to the cognitive requirements of the job itself. It takes a very special kind of person to derive deep fulfillment from meeting the same exact specifications day after day, no matter how much skill these specifications require. The growing demands for precise and high-level skill, for a capacity to follow exact routines in an orderly way, to mesh without friction in large and highly organized firms, assembly lines, or sales offices often make work less rewarding to the individual despite his higher level of skill.

Nor do the cognitive demands of most jobs add to the meaningfulness of work. Most men and women cannot suppress emotion easily; they *do* have strong feelings about the work they do and the people they do it with, and the pressure to be cool, objective, and unemotional is a pressure to subordinate their deepest feelings. Inevitably, we find it hard to treat all our fellow workers the same way, since our feelings about them are never identical; and it is not easy to judge others only according to their "job-relevant" accomplishments, when in ordinary human relationships these are usually among the *least* determining factors in our feelings about them. Businessmen, like industrial workers, therefore traditionally arrive home tired from their work, full of pent-up feelings which their wives are exhorted to help them "release."

As a result, Americans mention "working for a living" a hundred times more often than they mention "living for their work." Even work that really does contribute to a socially useful product is often so organized that it yields little personal satisfaction. Most important of all, we have long since given up on work, long since stopped even expecting that work be "meaningful"; and if we enjoy our work, it is usually because of good working conditions, friends on the job, benevolent supervision, and above all because the "good living" we earn by working enables us to do other, really enjoyable things in our "spare" time. The phrases "meaningful work," "joy in work," "fulfillment through work" have an increasingly old-fashioned and quaint sound. Even our labor unions have given up any pressure for more meaningful work in favor of demands for less work and more fringe benefits and income to make "living" better instead. The loss of meaning in work goes far beyond the problems discussed by the youthful Marx, namely, the loss of worker's control over the means of production. It extends to the fragmentation of work roles, to the heavily cognitive demands made within work. Even when workers themselves own or control their factories, work often remains meaningless.

The spirit of work and the human qualities demanded by work inevitably colors the worker's conception of himself. In every society, men tend to identify themselves with what they exploit to earn their living: in our society, we often become identified with the machines we exploit to do our most onerous work. This identification is magnified by the parallel between the characteristics of good worker and good machine. Whether at high levels of management or on the most menial assembly-line tasks, the good worker is highly specialized, is expected to show few feelings, to operate "by the book," to be consistent, systematic, and precise, to treat all individuals impartially and unemotionally. A man operating under such a regime finds the most important parts of himself—his hopes, feelings, aspirations, and dreams—systematically ignored. Like a brilliant child with less brilliant contemporaries, he is forced to suppress the major portion of himself on the job —to have it ignored by others and, most dangerous of all, to ignore it himself. To be treated as if one were only part of a man— and to have to act as if it were true—is perhaps the heaviest demand of all.

Work therefore assumes a new significance in technological society. It requires a dissociation of feeling, a subordination of passion, impulse, fantasy, and idealism before cognitive problems and tasks. As breadwinners, most Americans neither find nor even seek "fulfillment" in their jobs. Work, split away from "living" by convention and tradition, becomes instrumental, a dis-

sociated part of life that makes possible, yet often vitiates, the rest of a "living." Yet to spend one's days at tasks whose only rationale is income and whose chief requirements are cognitive is another demand in our lives which makes our technological society less likely to inspire enthusiasm.

The Problem of Integration—We all marvel at the complexity of our society's organization and at the high levels of technological productivity it has achieved. But society which "works" well, as ours does in many ways, may nonetheless create great stresses on individuals by virtue of *how* it works. And no psychological adaptations are more burdensome than the maneuvers required to integrate individual life in a fragmented society. Men and women need a sense of coherence, integration, and wholeness; but to attain such personal wholeness in our technological society is not an easy task.

Consider once again the problem of identity. I have earlier emphasized two ways technological society intensifies this problem: first by requiring a multitude of choices for which "rational" criteria are not available; second by dissociating work from the rest of life and by destroying even the expectation that work might in itself be meaningful. But even if a young man has somehow made all of the necessary choices and accepted the fact that his work is merely a way of "earning a living," he still faces a third problem—how to integrate the pieces of his life so that he has some sense of being "of a piece."

The days are long past when a youth could choose to be a farmer, peasant, merchant, soldier, or seaman, and by this single decision resolve a variety of other questions: the kind of women he must marry, the place he must live, the things he must believe, the style and shape of his adult life. Moreover, those who seek to elevate one sector of life into the central principle of their existence have difficulty in doing so, for such an "integration" is in continual danger of collapsing by virtue of its incompleteness. Work in our society is not intended to satisfy most of our deeper feelings and needs. Those who seek a unifying principle in family and recreation —and this is the most common solution for middle-class Americans—also run the risk of one-sidedness, for our families are so arranged as to exclude any satisfaction of what Thorstein Veblen called "the instinct of workmanship." No matter how desperately we may seek an organizing principle for our lives in any single activity, belief, or affiliation, we are likely to be disappointed.

Thus, the only workable solution for most Americans is to attempt a unique integration of their own lives, an idiosyncratic synthesis of their disparate and divided activities, convictions, and commitments into a pattern that yields a sense of personal unity. This assignment is of course supported by the deep human need for psychic wholeness, which pushes all men in all societies toward integration and consistency. But it is continually frustrated by the dissociation of work and family, of cognition and feeling, of thinking and affect. Social fragmentation pushes toward psychic fragmentation: without institutions or ideals to support psychic wholeness, inner division is a continual danger.

Indeed, if an American persists in seeking a life where inner wholeness is reflected in the outer consistency of his daily activities, he is almost inevitably led to repudiate the life led by most Americans, with its careful dissocation of work, cognition, and public life from family, feeling, and fun. Those who insist upon or need outer consistency must instead usually choose—or create—a deviant role. The life of an alienated painter or writer promises, at least, that one's lifework and one's "living" will be united; some teachers manage to work at what they love and to love their work. At best such "deviant" vocations can join the spheres of family and fun with those of work and skill. These are, of course, the vocations most favored by the alienated—who as second choice also choose other integrated and old-fashioned lives where work and life are of a piece, like the "dairy farmer" mentioned by one student.

Most Americans are not, of course, ideologically alienated; but the problems that lead to alienation in a few are there for the many. Only a rare man or woman genuinely "solves" the problem of psychic integration short of choosing a deviant role. Furthermore, few men and women have the tenacity of purpose and strength of character to tolerate the dissociation of their outer lives without some feeling of inner fragmentation. When these few are with their families they are able to "shut off" the cognitive values and outlooks required in work; on the job they can dismiss the feelings they have at home; when having fun they can enjoy themselves without "working at it" or collapsing into self-indulgence. But to manage such a compartmentalization of self and life—and not to feel inwardly torn and confused—requires unusually great strength of character. And to feel that one truly "belongs" in our society takes a remarkable capacity to unify one's piecemeal "belongings" into a coherent inner sense of community.

Most of us lack these capacities. When asked the terrifying question "Who are you?" we can reply with a list of our social memberships, our roles, and even our personal characteristics. "Businessman, father of three, Rotarian, Methodist, Republican, homeowner, and decent man"—the list often contains only the unity of outer correlation, and leaves the speaker with a vague sense of being harried and harrassed, of having no vital center, of being only what he does and of doing things which have no relationship to each other or to the central self. And when asked where we really "belong," we usually avoid the question or respond with another list that itself testifies to not really belonging anywhere: "At home, with my family, in my office, with my friends." Even "home" is not the natal home you can't go home again to; and few of us really feel we "belong" in the apartment houses or suburbs where we live. We manage to live with all this—mostly because we must but partly because everyone else lives the same way. But in the dark hours of the night, how many men and women secretly feel a vague sense of inner disunity? How many wonder what ties their lives together? How many feel that at root they belong nowhere? For those who ask these questions, as for those who would but do not dare, our society has made wholeness hard. And though men can survive without a sense of inner wholeness or social community—and in our society they often must—a society that requires them to do so may fail to capture their deepest commitments.

ALIENATION AND TECHNOLOGICAL SOCIETY

The growing fragmentation of our technological society makes three heavy demands on individuals: that they choose without adequate criteria between the many social roles, "opportunities," and organizations that have been fractioned out of traditional society; that they work not because their work makes sense but merely to earn a "living" somewhere else with its proceeds; and that they somehow integrate—or live without being able to integrate—the fractured roles and organizations which fail to define and unify them. These demands are heavy ones; and among the common responses to them are to experience choice as a burden and seek an escape from freedom, to expect and therefore find no fulfillment and satisfaction in work, to feel psychologically divided and socially homeless. Moreover, like all heavy social demands, these are potentially alienating forces. In alienated youths like those we have studied, the demand to choose without criteria, to work only for a "living," and to

integrate one's life unaided—these demands cannot or will not be met: they help inspire a rejection of American society and a determination to find another way of life. And even for those who are not alienated, these demands can cause vacillation and indecision, a feeling of emptiness and lack of meaning, a sense of being inwardly divided and outwardly homeless.

In every society, new means of production, new inventions, and new technologies have always meant personal dislocation and uprootedness. In America, where technological refinement and development has become the dominating purpose of society, alienation follows from the qualities of technological society itself. Thus, the totalness with which the alienated reject the assumptions and practices of their society may be at least partly justified. Yet the alienated are both products of and rebels agains this society. They are its products in their refusal of freedom, in their rejection of commitment, and above all in their sense of psychic fragmentation. And they are rebels—albeit without a cause—in their negative definition of themselves as those who are *against*, in their rejection of the basic values of American society, and in their search for values based on feeling, passion, and sentience. And they are probably right in thinking that—for them at least—the only adequate life would be a life where external unity supports and encourages inner wholeness—and that such a life is hard to live in the mainstreams of American society.

18   A Modern Parable

R. D. Laing

The following is a simple morality tale from Yale University, an experiment conducted by Dr. Stanley Milgram.*

Dr. Milgram recruited 40 male volunteers who believed they were to take part in an experimental study of memory and learning at Yale University. The 40 men were between the ages of 20 and 50 and represented a wide range of occupations. Typical subjects were postal clerks, high school teachers, salesmen, engineers, and laborers. One subject had not finished elementary school, but some others had doctorate and other professional degrees.

The role of experimenter was played by a 31-year-old high school teacher of biology. His manner was impassive but he maintained a somewhat stern appearance during the experiment. The experimenter was aided by a mild-mannered and likable man, who acted as a "victim." The experimenter interviewed each volunteer and, with him, the "victim" masquerading as another volunteer. He told the two of them that the intention was to investigate the effects of punishment on learning, and in particular the differential effects of varying degrees of punishment and various types of teacher. The drawing of lots was rigged so that the volunteer was always the teacher and the "victim" was always the learner. The victim was strapped into an "electric chair" apparatus and elec-

Reprinted from "The Obvious" by R. D. Laing, in *To Free a Generation* (D. Cooper, ed.). Copyright © 1968 by The Institute of Phenomenological Studies, by permission of Deborah Rogers Literary Agency.
*As summarized in *New York Academy of Science,* 4 (1964), pp. 418–20. Milgram's original paper is: "Behavioral Study of Obedience," *Journal of Abnormal and Social Psychology,* 67 (1963), pp. 371–379.

trode paste and an electrode were applied. The teacher-volunteer was then taken into an adjacent room and placed before a complex instrument labeled "shock generator." The teacher-volunteer was given a 45-volt shock to demonstrate the apparent authenticity of the machine.

A row of 30 switches on the "shock generator" were labeled from 15 to 450 volts by 15-volt steps. In addition, groups of switches were labeled from "slight shock" to "danger: severe shock." Following instructions and in the context of a mock learning experiment, the teacher-volunteer was led to believe that he was administering increasingly more severe punishment to the learner-victim, who made prearranged responses. The learner-victim gave incorrect answers to three out of every four questions and received shocks as punishment for his errors. When the punitive shock reached the 300-volt level, the learner-victim—as had been prearranged—kicked on the wall of the room in which he was bound to the electric chair. At this point teacher-volunteers turned to the experimenter for guidance. The teacher-volunteer was advised to continue after a 5–10-second pause. After the 315-volt shock, the pounding was heard again. Silence followed. At this point in the experiment the teacher-volunteers began to react in various ways. But they were verbally encouraged, and even ordered in a firm manner, to proceed right up to the maximum level of voltage.

... Dr. Milgram states that contrary to all expectations 26 of the 40 subjects completed the series, finally administering 450 volts to the now silent "victim." Only 5 refused to carry on after the victim's first protest when 300 volts were apparently administered. Many continued, even though they experienced considerable emotional disturbance, as clearly shown by their spoken comments, profuse sweating, tremor, stuttering, and bizarre nervous laughter and smiling. Three subjects had uncontrollable seizures. The teacher-volunteers who continued the shock frequently voiced their concern for the learner-victim, but the majority overcame their humane reactions and continued as ordered right up to the maximum punishment.

One observer related: "I observed a mature and initially poised businessman enter the laboratory smiling and confident. Within 20 minutes he was reduced to a twitching, stuttering wreck, who was rapidly approaching a point of nervous collapse. He constantly pulled on his earlobe and twisted his hands.

At one point he pushed his fist into his forehead and muttered: 'Oh God, let's stop it.' And yet he continued to respond to every word of the experimenter, and obeyed to the end."

The conflict that the subjects faced in this experiment was between obeying an authority they trusted and respected, and doing something they felt to be wrong. The real-life situation is more horrible. There is, for many, perhaps no conflict at all. My guess is that *most* people feel guilty at *not* doing what they are told, even though they think it is wrong, and even though they mistrust those who give the orders. They feel guilty at trusting their own mistrust.

Invisible Control Mechanisms

19   The Political Economy of the Black Ghetto

William K. Tabb

The literature on residential segregation is extensive and unanimous in concluding that there is a high degree of black segregation in metropolitan areas in all parts of the country, and that there has been a remarkable stability of this segregation pattern since the 1930's. Although earlier data are poor, this situation probably existed before that time as well.[1] While legal restrictions have been struck down by the courts, informal collusion, combined with harassment and violence, has maintained patterns of segregation.

The suggestion that low income excludes blacks from better neighborhoods is not borne out by the evidence on income and race. In 1960 only 12 per cent of whites with incomes above the poverty level lived in poverty areas, while two-thirds of blacks who had incomes above the poverty level lived in poverty areas.[2] Numerous statistical studies have also concluded that socioeconomic differences do not adequately explain urban racial residence patterns. A. H. Pascal reports,

That segregation of nonwhites is widespread, intense, and of long duration in large American cities is the inescapable conclusion to be derived from the evidence presented. . . . [W]e can state that over 80 per cent of the nonwhite population of Chicago and over 50 per cent of the nonwhite population of Detroit would have to change its place of residence were segregation in these two metropolitan areas to be eliminated.[3]

Three conclusions emerge from these various studies. First, black-segregated residential patterns can be explained not by low income but by the working of "the exclusionary interests" ("real estate boards, suburban governments—that establish and maintain vast sanctuaries from Negroes and poor people").[4] Second, there is a great variety of available suburban housing. Studies show "a large supply of older low and moderate income housing already existing in many suburban communities. . . . *The existing suburban housing supply, in terms of housing cost, provides ample opportunity for de-*

[1] Karl E. Tauber and Alma F. Tauber, *Negroes in Cities* (Chicago: Aldine, 1965), especially pp. 78–95. See also David McIntire, *Residence and Race* (Berkeley, Calif.: University of California Press, 1960); and Chester Rapkin, "Price Discrimination against Negroes in the Rental Market," in *Essays in Urban Land Economics* (Los Angeles: Real Estate Research Program, University of California, 1966).

[2] U.S. Department of Health, Education and Welfare, *Toward a Social Report* (Washington, D.C.: Government Printing Office, 1969), p. 37.

[3] A. H. Pascal, *The Economics of Housing Segregation* (Santa Monica, Calif.: The Rand Corporation, 1967), p. 175.

[4] Alvin L. Schorr, *Explorations in Social Policy* (New York: Basic Books, 1968), p. 208.

segregation now."[5]   Third, government policies subsidize slumlords through lax or nonexistent code enforcement, thereby saving them millions of dollars; offer them generous tax treatment; and then pay them handsomely for their property when slums are bought under urban renewal. The economics of ghetto housing ensures that bad housing is profitable and that good housing cannot be maintained. There is a sort of Gresham's Law at work: bad housing drives out good; as neighborhoods deteriorate, further deterioration is induced.

This process continues because the owners of these buildings want to maximize their incomes. However, this fact does not indicate that slum housing in general is highly profitable. Given the unpleasantness and the risks involved, earnings may not be very good.[6] The point is rather that slum owners persist in their business because they make an adequate return, and that it is possible for the more disreputable and dishonest to do fairly well. Certainly the curtailment of existing practices through, for example, adequate code enforcement might bankrupt many marginally profitable operations. What profitably exists is the result of lack of law enforcement coupled with the existence of segregation.

The single most crucial factor in ensuring the profitability of slums is segregation. Timothy Cooney, a former city official in New York, gives a cynic's advice on "how to build a slum":

The importance of renting to minority families cannot be overemphasized . . . they are the key. . . . The all-white sections are essential to successful slum development. They must be maintained (until we decide to turn them into slums). The reason is obvious. With a "whites only" barricade (or other slums) surrounding our developing slum, there will be no escape for our selected tenants.[7]

Alvin Schorr describes the process in greater detail:

As buildings are subdivided, crowded, and more deteriorated, they become well-nigh impossible to maintain. However, it becomes impractical to try to maintain neighboring houses. They too become a profitable investment and slum development spirals. If the city steps in and tries to enforce codes strictly, some owners will be able to make no profit at all. They paid too high a price and counted on overcrowding. If it is suggested that the municipality take the houses over, paying for their reasonable value, it develops that this is less than the current owner paid for it. Why pick on him? Once begun, the cycle is not readily interrupted.[8]

Change is made still more difficult because government policy encourages slum formation and perpetuation.

HOUSING AND GOVERNMENT

On one level all that is required is an honest enforcement of the law. The burden of ensuring that there are no code violations could even be placed on the property owner by having "the Internal Revenue Service disallow all depreciation allowances, property tax deductions, and interest deductions on properties in designated 'high deterioration' zones within large cities unless the owners' tax returns are accompanied by certificates of full code compliance issued by local authorities."[9] But would such a plan work? The answer is no. There are already laws against discrimination in renting and sale of apartments and houses. There are laws to ensure

[5]Richard Langendorf, "Residential Desegregation Potential," *Journal of the American Institute of Planners* (March 1969). Emphasis in original.

[6]See George Sternlieb, *The Tenement Landlord* (New Brunswick, N.J.: Rutgers—The State University, Urban Studies Center, 1966).

[7]Timothy J. Cooney, "How to Build a Slum," *The Nation* (February 14, 1959), p. 141.

[8]Schorr, *Explorations in Social Policy*, p. 200.

[9]Anthony Downs, "Moving Toward Realistic Housing Goals," in Kermit Gordon (ed.), *Agenda for the Nation* (Washington, D.C.: The Brookings Institution, 1968) p. 171.

adequate plumbing and to enforce building codes, but the law is biased in favor of those who have some influence in the society. The blacks do not have such influence. Slum fires are so common that in some· areas the sick joke goes around which asks if one has heard about the new instant urban renewal program; for the night before for the third (or fifth) time this month there has been a major fire in the ghetto. After one such fire in Brooklyn, New York, a grand jury investigated a fifteen-block area. It found 3,122 code violations; before the survey only 567 violations had been filed.[10]   And of course little had been done about these 567. New York is not unique in its ratio of actual to reported violations. But because codes are often unclear, penalties slight, and enforcement staffs small, it is easier to ignore maintenance, not respond to warnings, and pay the small fine which eventually may be imposed, than to make repairs.

The hard fact is that profit-making incentives run counter—so far as the maintenance of housing is concerned—to the best interests of the poor. Tax laws and condemnation procedures combine with the peculiarly vulnerable situation of those who are poor to pay the most profit for the worst housing. Where enforcement is pitted day by day against the businessman's incentive to make profit, enforcement is bound to be in trouble.[11]

More than this, the whole system is predicated on the nonenforcement of the law. The code enforcement agencies could not possibly carry out their legal responsibility. If they did, landlords in large numbers would go bankrupt and tenants would be evicted as buildings were declared unfit for human habitation. Repair costs would in a great many instances prove more than the rental capacity of the building after repairs were made.

Just a modest step-up in enforcement activity under a new administration in New York City recently resulted in a rapid upsurge in the number of foreclosures, tax delinquencies, and vacate orders. When slumlords are pushed out, government has to house the minority poor. So the enforcement agencies use their powers gingerly and selectively, usually paying heed only when tenants have the tenacity or the "pull" to compel enforcement. In other words, slum profits depend on collusion between city agencies and landlords: in return for nonenforcement of the codes, the slumlord takes the blame for the slum and enables the city to evade the political ire of the ghetto.[12]

The culpability of government, if that is the proper phrase, goes much deeper than not enforcing housing codes. Federal government policies into the 1960's consciously encouraged segregation. The Federal Housing Administration, which insures millions of dollars of mortgages, for many years took the position that racial homogeneity was essential to a neighborhood's financial stability. It therefore placed higher valuations on properties in neighborhoods that were white than in those that were mixed. This policy served as a powerful inducement to segregation. After restrictive racial covenants in deeds were held to be unconstitutional, the FHA stopped insuring properties where such convenants applied. But it continued to tolerate discrimination, providing insurance where builders would not sell, mortgagors would not lend, and owners would not rent to Negroes. In 1962, President Kennedy issued an executive order reversing this policy. The order forbade discrimination in the sale or rental of all housing owned or financed by the government. But it applied only to future transactions; existing segregation was not disturbed.[13]   At the same time that the FHA was encouraging segregation, it was redistributing real income from general taxation to the nonpoor homeowners. Until August 1967, the FHA, by denying mortgage insur-

[10]Schorr, *Explorations in Social Policy*, p. 200.
[11]*Ibid.*, p. 198.

[12]Francis Piven and Richard Cloward, "Disrupting City Services to Change National Priorities," *Viet-Report* (Summer 1968), p. 28.
[13]Clair Wilcox, *Toward Social Welfare* (Homewood, Ill.: Irwin, 1969), p. 200.

ance programs to buyers in blighted areas (because such loan insurance was "economically unsound"), did not help blacks become homeowners in their own restricted housing markets. At the same time the white exodus was financed through FHA loans. As Michael Harrington has written,

It is one of the great postwar scandals that lavish, but discreet, subsidies have been provided for the homes of the middle class and the rich in the form of cheap, federally guaranteed credit, income tax deducations, and other genteel doles which effectively exclude everyone with incomes of less than $8,000 from the benefits.[14]

The extent of this perverse redistribution can be only crudely estimated. One study presents the following data for 1962. The federal government spent $820 million to subsidize housing for the poor (this total includes public housing, public assistance, and tax deducations). That same year at least an estimated $2.9 billion was spent to subsidize housing for middle- and upper-income families.[15] This sum includes only savings from income-tax deductions and so is a very conservative estimate of housing subsidies to the nonpoor. In his scheme to aid low-income people living in inadequate housing, Anthony Downs estimates that, assuming the federal government paid "only the marginal difference between the return demanded by the lenders and the amounts which households in inadequate units could afford to pay," subsidies amounting to $26 billion for the decade 1970–1980 (about the same amount spent on the space program in the decade 1960–1970) would be needed to do away with all substandard housing.[16] Such a plan would cost about the same amount as the subsidy that will be given to middle- and upper-income families in the same period.

[14]Michael Harrington, "Can Private Industry Abolish Slums?" *Dissent* (January-February 1968), p. 5.
[15]Schorr, *Explorations in Social Policy*, p. 208.
[16]Downs, "Moving toward Realistic Housing Goals," p. 161.

FEDERAL HOUSING POLICY

The artificially high demand for inferior ghetto housing results from segregation enforced through legal practices such as large-lot zoning which help keep lower-income (nonwhite) families out of suburbia, and illegal collusion, as when realtors refuse to sell to blacks. Ghetto housing is substandard because codes are not enforced and cannot be. The municipal property tax penalizes improvements and rewards poor maintenance. The use of earning power as a measure of determining value in condemnation procedures favors those who overcrowd their buildings. Capital-gains taxes and depreciation policies have improved somewhat but are still too generous to slum owners.

The two most important federal housing programs (after FHA-insured loans) are public housing and urban renewal. Both have been hamstrung by regulations to ensure that they cannot compete with, but can only complement, the workings of the private sector.

Public housing is built to be a badge identifying the poor. Projects are characterized by their ugliness and regimentation. In the minds of some, this is good. They are a warning against allowing the federal government to interfere. The same expenditure (about $25,000 a unit) could purchase a house in suburbia and a new car for the poor family, who then could live much like anybody else. Those who receive charity must carry the stigma of being public wards. In a class society part of one's evaluation of his own position as favorable stems from the distance between his income and standard of living and those of people who have less. This distance measures his success. Public housing must indicate the economic position of its residents.

Public housing has also failed in a quantitative sense, in that the number of units built has not begun to supply the demand of those qualifying for apartments. At the end of 1965 there were an estimated 600,000 units of public housing, with a waiting list of 500,000 families. There are about 8.5 million families who are eligible for public housing.[17] Because the waiting list is so long, many of those eligible do not bother to apply. At the same time public housing is not adding sufficiently to the housing stock, the supply of inexpensive housing is being diminished by urban renewal.

Urban renewal assembles large amounts of land and makes them available to private buyers at far less than they would have to pay on the open market. Poor families who reside in the renewal area are forced to relocate. Attempts are made to see that these families find standard housing at rents they can afford. However, if such housing were available, it is difficult to see why the people would have been living in slum housing. In any case, the supply of low-cost housing is diminished, pushing up rents, and making living more difficult for other low-income families looking for housing. The cleared land is then used to build middle- and upper-income housing or for industrial plants, or shopping centers.[18] In many cities urban renewal is called "Negro Removal," and many blacks see it as a land grab subsidized by the government and run by local real-estate interests.

There are federal housing policies which are designed to work in useful ways to help low-income people. One such program is rent supplements, under which the federal government pays the difference between what a family can afford to pay in rent (25 per cent of family income) and the rent a landlord can get on the free market. The family involved gets to live in adequate housing in a building with people of higher income and so is not stigmatized as "poor." The landlord receives adequate compensation, and the federal government's subsidy makes up the difference between what a family is able to pay and the cost of dwellings which meet minimum code standards. The program is obviously costly if subsidies go to very low-income families. Still, as incomes rise, subsidies diminish, and there is not the disincentive, as in public housing, where if a tenant's income rises beyond a certain point, he must move. Instead of government-run projects, rent subsidies leave housing rental to the private sector. However, the program is not doing well in Congress, perhaps because taxpayers do not like to see "the poor get something for nothing," especially when that something is being able to live in conditions similar to those they have worked hard to provide for themselves. Dick Netzer has suggested some further reasons why this may be so:

Partly, this may be because of the extent of subsidy; in part, the explanation may be opposition to the degree of racial integration implicit in a program that provides for people with very different incomes living in the same building. At any rate, the program has been encumbered with many restrictions, and the funds authorized for it have been minimal. The number of new housing units actually built under the program has been very small indeed.[19]

We could be hopeful and say that since this program only started in 1965 maybe it will gain support and be funded at meaningful levels. If so it would be unique.

[17]Pascal, *The Economics of Housing Segregation,* p. 6.

[18]See Jewell Bellush and Murray Hausknecht (eds.), *Urban Renewal: People, Politics and Planning* (Garden City, N.Y.: Doubleday, 1967); James Q. Wilson (ed.), *Urban Renewal: The Record and the Controversy* (Cambridge, Mass.: The M.I.T. Press, 1966); Charles Abrams, *The City Is the Frontier* (New York: Harper & Row, 1967); and Scott Greer, *Urban Renewal and American Cities (Indianapolis: Bobbs-Merrill, 1965).*

[19]Dick Netzer, *Economics and Urban Problems: Diagnoses and Prescriptions* (New York: Basic Books, 1970), p. 105.

20   The Secretarial Proletariat

Judith Ann

As a child, I had the highest ambitions for myself. I was bright in school and full of energy. I can remember at the age of about fifteen, feeling like the world was at my disposal; there was nothing I couldn't do once I turned my mind to it. I had my heart set on the Foreign Service—perhaps I'd be a United States senator—or else maybe a movie director—at any rate I always imagined myself in positions of power, with control over my environment, making creative decisions.

I went to college, although I wasn't sure I wanted to—I was so eager to take on the world that college seemed sort of a waste of time. Besides, although schoolwork came easily to me, I didn't like it. I was told I was "sensitive" and "perceptive"—nice things to be, and much more suitable for a girl than solid achievement. I swallowed that kind of claptrap, and found myself, as I grew older, actually getting less and less smart. By the time I was a sophomore in college, I was literally incapable of rigorous intellectual work. I attended most of my classes, because I enjoyed listening to the professors, but I didn't do any homework. The avid bookworm of my childhood became a complete nonreader. I didn't write a single paper that year, and even ceased making up excuses for not handing them in. I spent examination periods lost in sexual fantasies, daydreaming of the mythical Man who would rescue me from this misery and give meaning to my life. By the time I flunked out, I was beaten down and felt worthless. My childhood ambitions seemed like a joke.

I pulled myself together with the consolation that it didn't matter anyway if I flunked out. After all, I was only a girl—I couldn't be

drafted and there was no need really to plan a career; I resolved to take a job, any job, prove to the world that I was not really a failure, and in the meanwhile, devote my energies to husband-hunting. I went to live with my parents in Hartford, Connecticut, the insurance capital of the nation, and two days later I started work as a rater in an insurance company. The personnel manager was benevolent. I had done well on the intelligence tests, and I seemed sincere in my desire to mend my ways, and they really *wanted* to give me a good position, but young girls so often leave the company after a short time, and of course with my record of failure ...

Rating actually turned out to be one of the best jobs available to women in the company, except for secretaries and a few special categories of "clerical support." Raters, in fact, had exactly the same qualifications and background as underwriters, a prestigious group with a good deal of responsibility. The only difference in qualifications was that raters were women and underwriters were men. The floor I worked on sheltered both raters and underwriters. It was a large room with maybe seventy desks, all in rows. The underwriters, with telephones on each desk, were on one side of the room; raters, without telephones, were on the other side. A solid wall of high filing cabinets separated the two areas.

The working day was from 8:00 A.M. to 4:00 P.M. We had to be in our seats with our coats hung up by eight sharp, when a bell rang to start us to work. We were allowed to start cleaning up at about 3:35 and then we sat at clean desks with purses in hand from 3:45 to 4:00, when the bell rang again and we bolted the building. We had a short coffee break about half-way through the morning, and then 45 minutes for lunch. (The work day was thus officially 7¼ hours long; we were not paid for lunch period.) Since the whole floor went to lunch at the same time, it was easily and duly noted if you were even one minute late getting back. On paydays (every other Friday) we got an extra half-hour for lunch—a state law so that employees could go to the bank. Paydays were also special because of the "quarter pool." This was voluntary, of course, but each payday nearly every employee on our floor put a quarter in the pool and his name in the hat. I played the quarter pool every payday I was there, and although I never won, I spent a lot of time planning what I would do with the approximately fifteen dollars if I ever did win. The quarter pool, the World Series, and an astronaut voyage (a few people brought in transistor radios and were allowed to play them very quietly the morning of splash-down) were the only breaks in office routine.

We went to the ladies' room, in groups of two or three, twice a day, after coffee break and again in the middle of the afternoon. Talking (in low tones and small quantities) with co-workers was allowed only with neighbors directly to the side or front or back —even cater-corner was not permitted. (This rule applied to coffee break as well.) The atmosphere was similar to that of elementary school. We were even called "girls," not women, no matter what our ages. We had no rights, only duties. Each employee was allowed five sick days per year; after that you were docked—or fired. There was no severance pay.

The work itself was completely routinized, mindless toil. You got a stack of policies in the morning and you spent the day referring to a set of rate schedules and computing the rates on a calculator—an adding machine that also multiplies and divides. Your work was then checked by a co-worker and rechecked by the supervisor, and then sent out to the typists.

This isolation by hierarchy of the different levels of female clerical labor (secretaries, raters, typists, file clerks, in that order) was a very potent tool in the hands of management. By giving some units a sense of false

privilege and all units a feeling of rivalry with their sisters, we were effectively kept from any cross-unit solidarity or even sympathy, which would have been very threatening indeed to management.

Within the rating unit itself, however (and I suppose it was the same all over), there was a very warm feeling among the workers. Particularly the young unmarried raters developed strong friendships with each other and we often spent time together after working hours. We all hated our jobs, hated our supervisors, and spent long hours bitching about the conditions and plotting when and how we would quit. We also talked about what kind of jobs we would get instead—it was universally agreed that a small office with several men and only one or two girls would be a vast improvement over the rows and rows of women and the female supervisor that we now had to deal with. My friend Ann did leave while I was there. She went to an insurance agent's office. It was a small office, and she was clerical assistant to the three or four salesmen; in the insurance world, this was the creme de la creme of female employment, and the rest of us back at the old job were very envious.

The other subject we talked about even more consistently was men. Of course, we assumed that all this talk about future "better jobs" was only conditional on our single status, and it was our firm belief that at the end of all present suffering lay the final reward: marriage. We talked and thought about men constantly. If an unmarried underwriter looked at one of us cross-eyed, we would discuss the implications for an entire lunch hour. If one of us got a letter from a boy (usually in the Service or away at college) or, glory be, had a date, it provided us with conversation for days. Two or three of the girls were engaged and we discussed their wedding plans—and the terrifying, glorious "first night"—daily. We were all virgins, and the repressed sexuality of these vibrant young girls was almost tangible in the atmosphere. Since the work was so routinized, I found myself able to indulge in sexual fantasies eight straight hours a day—a vast improvement over the quality of my fantasies during exams at college, because, since here I could do my work at the same time, there was less anxiety attached to them. This is in fact one of the most oppressive aspects of female clerical work: since the working conditions were so bad and our daily life so dull, the only bright spots in our lives were our relationships or hoped-for relationships with men. We sought refuge from our oppression as working women in the male supremacist institutions of dating and marriage, and in escapist consumerism of make-up and pretty clothes. . . .

Because the young raters were "hard to handle" and had a high turnover rate (we had nothing to lose by job-hopping, and the myth of the "better job" kept us moving often), the company didn't like us much. There were continual rumors that soon they would stop hiring so many young women and instead hire older, more desperate women, who could be intimidated with greater ease and who would probably stay a long time. Management had good reason for wanting workers to stay a long time—that way they could get away with paying lower salaries. Several girls who had been working there for two years longer than me, and getting regular salary increases every six months, were still making less than my starting salary. I started at $60.00 a week; this was in 1965. We could not afford apartments, of course, and usually lived with our parents. Even so, expenses were high. Alice, who, like me, took home less than $50.00 a week, was making time payments on a second-hand car, and gave her parents $25.00 *a week* for room and board. When I protested to her that this seemed unfairly high, she replied that she didn't mind; her parents were saving her rent money in a special account to pay for her wedding. Alice was married that summer with a lovely wedding and got pregnant on her honeymoon; no one in the office ever heard from her after that.

I worked at the insurance company for six months, saving my money and making plans with a girlfriend to move to New York City, where I felt sure that my glamorous destiny would finally materialize. I was nineteen, and my work success (I was a very good rater) and the fact that I was about to leave my parents' home and protection had somewhat revived my basically independent spirit. Surely in New York, the most exciting city in the world, there would be an outlet for my creative energies. My old adolescent optimism surged. I was bursting to *do things,* to move, to grow, to be alive. A week after I arrived in New York, I found a job at a bank . . .

By the time I got to my third, and most recent, job (I am here discussing only my three major job experiences; I have also worked, for short periods, as a waitress, a flower-wrapper in a florist shop, a free-lance typist), I had begun to be conscious of women's oppression, and was involved in the political movement for women's liberation. It was therefore with a sharp sense of irony that I began work as a secretary in the editorial department of a leading bridal magazine. The more than $5 billion a year bridal industry, for which this magazine is a publicist and mainstay, is one of the largest institutionalized oppressors of women, since it reinforces the societal dictum that a woman must marry and find her identity through her husband and children, or else face life with no identity at all, as an "unwanted spinster."

But besides being an institutional oppressor of all women, the bridal magazine was oppressive on a daily basis to me and the other women working there. Paying lip service to the fact that it was, after all, a "women's magazine," the company hired mostly women on the editorial staff (as opposed to the other magazines published by the same company, where, for the most part, the only visible women were secretaries and clerks). In fact, of the seventeen or so members of the editorial staff, all were women, except for one man—that one man was the editor-in-chief, and I was his secretary. While responsibility for the editorial content of The Magazine was nominally in the hands of the various (female) editors, in fact, every editorial decision was either reviewed or instigated by the editor-in-chief, who ruled absolutely by inspiring the staff with fear of the nearly violent temper tantrums he was given to when crossed. He was a temperamental man, unsure at the outset of his own masculinity, and he vented his hostility toward women by taking it out first on the (female) staff, and finally on the readers of "his" magazine, universally referred to as "our little readers" or "those dumb girls" . . .

At The Magazine, I had finally achieved the highest job rung available to girls of limited education or, for that matter, to most girls, no matter what their education. I was a private secretary. As a child, watching the television show "Private Secretary" with Ann Sothern, I had often daydreamed about the glamorous and sexy life a New York secretary leads . . .

Well, I knew that I was letting myself in for such basically uncreative tasks as typing letters, filing, and opening mail. After all, I was a realistic girl, I needed bread, and I was prepared to sell my skills and labor to survive— I had done it before and I didn't expect this job to be much different from the others. I must confess, however, that I was not prepared for what I soon discovered was the bulk of a private secretary's work: balancing my boss's checkbook; making his coffee in an electric coffeepot and then washing the pot and cups; dusting his office; Xeroxing his income-tax records; even at one point washing baseboards. It seemed incredible to me at first that a human being, very much like myself in appearance and basic needs, seemed incapable of the simplest tasks: sharpening his own pencils or answering his own phone. I finally realized, however, that it was probably not that the tasks themselves were so physically debilitating to my boss; the degrading division of labor was just the quickest way of enforcing the sexual hierarchy in employment, just a way of saying, "You're shit and I'm King." . . .

I endured daily humiliation at The Magazine for nearly a year; then finally, with the support and encouragement of my sisters in women's liberation, and inspired by a particularly offensive office situation which all the women had been complaining about for some time, I sent around a signed memo to the female employees on my floor, which read:

As we all know, the door to the sixth floor ladies' room is locked. At the moment, it is so well locked that we can hardly get into it. The lock is in fact broken and requires complicated manipulation to open it. Besides this, the keys which we were all individually given are easily and continually being lost—or stolen by otherwise honest women made desperate by a sudden emergency. For pregnant women (of whom there are several now employed on the sixth floor) the specter of the Ladies' Room Lock holds real terror. In other words, the situation is intolerable.

The reason for our difficulties, we are told, is that the sixth floor is only partially leased by the company. Apparently, the lavatory door is kept locked in order to keep the employees of other firms from using our toilets. I should think that their bathrooms must be in pretty ghastly condition if it is felt that those employees are so desperate to use ours. Surely no one thinks that our lavatory is so clean and beautiful that we really need fear its defacement by outside agitators. Why should we not share our bathrooms with those less fortunate than we?

Furthermore, I have recently uncovered an astonishing piece of news—the men's room door is not locked. This is blatant discrimination against women—although it is only a more obvious manifestation of the discrimination against women which pervades this whole society and which is easily seen in the hiring practices of this company. (How many male secretaries have you met up with lately? And even at the bridal magazine, where mostly women are employed, and the content is geared especially toward women, the publisher and editor-in-chief are men.)

Women! Let us unite for the attainment for our just demands! The toilets belong to the people! No more locks on any lavatory door! No more discrimination against women, in bathroom locks, or hiring practices, or any other area!

Retribution was swift and final; I was fired within a half-hour. My boss ran up to me in a rage, and shouted: "You're just a secretary— you can't do this!" His first concern, apparently, was the challenge I had made to his authority. His second concern was that people might find out about it, specifically the president of the company, and he might be made a laughingstock or worse. Implicit in this concern of his was the fact that he was held responsible for all my actions; as his secretary, I was merely an extension of him, a reflection of his glory or failure. The assumption was that the only reason I had been able to take an independent action was that he had failed to keep me in line properly.

Getting fired was a liberating experience. The Unemployment Board agreed with me that my dismissal was unfair, and they're supporting me until I find another job. But moments of vindication like this are brief, and I know that when my Unemployment Insurance runs out and I have to go back to work, things will be just as bad.

I can no longer fool myself with the fantasy that working conditions might improve at my next job. Each of my past jobs has been, by society's standards, "better" than the last, and each has been dehumanizing in its own way. I can't find my liberation through a "personal solution"; personal solutions do not exist in an inhuman society. I need a movement to help me find political solutions to these problems, which are societal problems, not personal problems . . .

Maybe some readers of this article will think that I was unusual among clerical workers because I knew that I was being exploited and rebelled against it. Maybe some of you think that most clerical workers accept and even like their lot and don't care about changing it. But it's not true. Everywhere I worked the women at the bottom knew that they were underpaid and overworked, denied job security and the possibility of advancement, exploited by male supremacy and a class system. And everywhere we rebelled in a thousand small ways —taking extra time in the ladies' room, misfiling important letters, "forgetting" to correct typos.

What we must do now is resist collectively instead of in isolation. We have feared that by speaking out against our oppression we might lose our lousy jobs and thus our livelihood, which does happen if we speak out alone. We have feared that maybe our present conditions are just the way things are and can't be changed. But these and other fears can be overcome through collective actions and solidarity. We can pool our financial resources to reduce the danger of summary firings; we can share our child-rearing responsibilities to free each other's time for action. We can support each other emotionally and become sisters in oppression and, finally, in victory.

21   The "Dirty Workers"

Lee Rainwater

Schoolteachers, social workers, and policemen in a number of major cities have recently gone on strike, or resigned en masse, or taken mass sick leaves. These events bring to mind the works of Everett C. Hughes, the man who established the investigation of work, occupations, and professions as a major area of social research. In "Good People and Dirty Work," Everett Hughes analyzed some of the societal and social-psychological factors in Germany that fostered the mass murder of concentration-camp victims. He was particularly concerned with the link between the cadre that actually carried out the dirty work and the Germans in general, who were "ignorant" of and silent about what went on in the concentration camps. As in much social-science research, Hughes was able to use an extreme, almost unique social event to advance our understanding of much more common processes. The German murderers raised much more general questions about how societies go about handling situations in which repressive action is considered necessary but few citizens are willing to do what they want done.

The Germans' anti-Semitism made them feel that "something must be done about the Jews," which in turn led them to covertly delegate to the S.S. the task of doing that something. It then became important to the Germans to fuzz over the gory details, to conceal from themselves, as well as from others, exactly what was being done. Hughes suggested that this is a typical way societies deal with out-groups:

The greater their social distance from us the more we leave in the hands of others a sort

of mandate by default to deal with them on our behalf. . . . Perhaps we give them an unconscious mandate to go beyond anything we ourselves would care to do, or even to acknowledge. I venture to suggest that the higher and more expert functionaries who act in our behalf represent something of a distillation of what we may consider our public wishes, while some of the others show a sort of concentrate of those impulses of which we are, or wish to be, less aware.

This shameful work that nevertheless must be done is, then (morally), "dirty work."

It is easy to see the same processes operating in the deeply felt American ambivalence toward the police. But the process operates much more broadly. In our world, there is a large out-group—a separate nation of ghetto Negroes whom most white Americans feel must be controlled and confined. Yet those same white Americans are deeply ashamed and uncertain about *how* Negroes are controlled and confined, and they prefer to conceal from themselves much of the detail of how the doers of this dirty work actually go about their assigned tasks.

As the urban ghettos have grown, so has the cohort of functionaries who receive the covert assignment to "keep the colored out of our way." In the process many institutions officially designed to further well-being and opportunity have become perverted into institutions of custody and constraint. Social-welfare workers find that their profession, designed to help, has been perverted into one designed to spy and to punish. More dramatically, the schools have become custodial institutions in which less and less learning takes place. To conceal their failure, year in and year out the schools promote students who have learned less than they should. The proliferation of policemen in schools, of special schools for "incorrigible" children, and the like, testify to the prisonlike functions that undergird the educational rhetoric and increasingly call into question the national ideology that "education" cures all ills.

Americans are, in general, indifferent to the welfare of their public functionaries— witness the notoriously poor prestige and salaries of these functionaries. This indifference has been so great that those recruited for many public-service jobs tend to be people who are not the main breadwinners of their families, or who regard public-service work as temporary, or who are motivated more by a desire for security than by the usual American expectation of affluence. And, in the same way, society's indifference has served to blunt the drive of public-service workers for equitable compensation and for a reasonable recognition of their right to collective bargaining.

As the ghettos in this country grow, a new dimension is added, a dimension of silence and ignorance about exactly what these functionaries are expected to do, and how in fact they do carry out society's covert order to control and cool out those who must be excluded from ordinary society. If the teachers, social workers, and cops were ever to spell out in detail what their duties are in order to justify their wage demands, they would threaten the delicate balance preserved by silence about their assigned dirty work—no one wants to learn that they are striking for "combat pay."

But the dirty workers *are* striking—for increased pay, of course, but also for other demands that are more directly related to the dangers of dirty work, and to the disrespect society insists on giving to those who do its tacit bidding. The New York teachers, for example, openly and directly challenged the implicit understanding that it is more important for them to be custodians than for them to be teachers. It is gradually dawning on all of these public servants that both their official public tasks (to educate, to protect the citizens, to look after the welfare of the dependent) and their covert tasks (to control

Negroes and make them as invisible as possible) are impossible to achieve.

The dirty workers are increasingly caught between the silent middle class, which wants them to do the dirty work and keep quiet about it, and the objects of that dirty work, who refuse to continue to take it lying down. Individual revolts confront the teachers with the problems of the "blackboard jungle," the police with the problem of "disrespect for law and order," and the welfare workers with the problem of their charges' feigned stupidity and real deception. These civilian colonial armies find their right to respect from their charges challenged at every turn, and often they must carry out their daily duties with fear for their physical safety.

Equally ominous for the dirty workers is the organized Negro challenge to their legitimacy. Not only must they cope with individual resistance to their ministrations, but also, more and more, with militant and insistent local civil-rights groups that expose their failures and tax them with their abrogation of their professional responsibilities to teach, to protect, to help.

It is encouraging that those expected to do the dirty work are rebelling. But it is really too much to expect that they will admit their own individual culpability, at least as long as the rest of us won't. Even so, the more the teachers, the police, and the welfare workers insist on the impossibility of their tasks, the more that society at large, and its political leaders, will have to confront the fact that our tacit understandings about the dirty work that is to be done are no longer adequate.

Of course there are dangers, too. The police are our internal hawks, and they might win—and there are also hawks among schoolteachers (they want unruly children kicked out of school) and welfare workers (who want to escalate the attack on welfare chiselers). As dangerous in the long run, perhaps, are the doves—the teachers and the social workers who want to save the ghetto through education and casework (or that form of neighborhood casework called "community action"). Should either the ghetto hawks or doves carry the day, their victory could become the basis for a new tacit understanding about dirty work, one that would save the country from paying the price it is apparently most reluctant to pay— the price of providing economic resources and open, decent housing to Negroes, so there is no longer a ghetto that requires dirty workers.

VI

Freedom
and Political Action

Picture a college course on American politics. The course had progressed about as far as this book has, and the students had read some of the articles in the previous parts of this book. Then the instructor asked the students to come to the next class meeting prepared to describe what freedom really looked like to them. "Bring something you can carry easily that symbolizes freedom to you. Or come with a short story to tell that illustrates an experience of freedom." What those students had to say about what freedom meant to them is worth repeating.

One person brought her car keys. She said she felt free when she could get in the car and drive away, maybe all the way to Mexico.

Another person brought a balloon. "You'd be free if you could just float up and up, no longer held down by everything that ties you to the earth and all its problems."

Another person told a story about running, running away, running as fast as she could run, until she fell down in a countryside field in the middle of the tall grass, and fell asleep looking up at the sky.

Another person brought a fishing reel. He felt free when he was off on a fishing trip, wading up clear mountain streams in search of fresh-water trout.

Another person brought his back pack. Like the car keys, it symbolized being "on the road," able to go anywhere, being on your own.

Another person brought his skis. He was an expert skier, and felt the experience of flying down an empty mountainside with only his own strength and skill in control was the closest he had ever come to freedom.

Another person brought her guitar. For a while she had played in night-clubs, singing to earn a living, but it had been depressing and frustrating. Now she was just playing for herself. Alone in her room, lost in her music and the intricacies of fingering her guitar, she felt free.

Several other people had similar feelings about freedom. We were going around the circle, giving everyone a chance to talk. Then a tall, quiet young man said, "I can't show you what symbolizes freedom to me, because I burned it. I burned my draft card. Not that freedom is being without a draft card. Freedom to me is the act of burning my draft card."

THE NATURE OF FREEDOM

Speaking generally, and abstractly, being free or having freedom involves being who one really wants to be and become, able to do what one really wants to do. Freedom is always expressed in action, in living. But an abstract understanding of freedom in general is not very helpful. It gives no sense of how a specific person should actually live, no sense of the way a specific person's concrete notion of freedom influences how she actually lives. And the main reason why freedom is worth taking seriously in the first place is only because people's concrete notions of what freedom is lead them to live in certain particular ways. Like believing in the pot of gold at the end of the rainbow, people who really believe that freedom (with its promise of fulfillment and dignity) is to be found by making more money are usually found in hot pursuit of that pot of gold, trying very hard to make more money. A person who believes that freedom is the ability to escape from the confines and entanglements of the world tends to arrange his life so that it can be escaped from.

To speak of an "escape from freedom" or of a "fear of freedom" is mystifying. I might try to escape from what *you* call freedom! Or I might be afraid of freedom if I don't really believe that I am capable of doing what someone (or even my own conscience) tells me to do. But to say that a person might fear, or try to escape from, living in a way that she knows is possible to live and that she knows will bring fulfillment and dignity—that's just confusing. Rather than talk about an escape from freedom, say rather that for some people freedom involves, in fact, escape or submission. Rather than talk about the fear of freedom, say rather that for some people freedom involves struggle with a fear that cannot be defeated.

Of course, a person's understanding of what is freedom is not necessarily fixed, the same all through life. It can and sometimes does change. When large numbers of people all come to live on the basis of a newly discovered and shared understanding of freedom, you have a political movement.

Now the drift of my argument may be getting clearer. The previous parts have described and explained the ways that we Americans live as a nation. The one thing that's left is to answer the question, "Why don't we live differently?" The answer is that, aside from all the constraints due to the quality of our public life, the structure of power, our traditions, and the ideological and workaday limits on our lives—aside, in other words, from what we (feel we) "have to" do—*the understanding that we Americans have of freedom only works to reinforce, not challenge or undermine or alter, our present national way of life.* Very briefly, here's how this happens.

The usual ways we Americans understand freedom, as John Wikse puts it, have to do with "getting away (with something)." The preceding students' statements illustrate that we are concerned with "making it," doing something successfully, and escaping or getting away. An American feels free in the absence of restrictions or when she is powerful enough to overcome restrictions on what she wants to do. These notions of what freedom is reinforce the status quo because (except under certain extraordinary conditions) as we understand them concretely they can be—indeed, they must be —achieved *within* the status quo; they do not lead people to take actions that might significantly change the way we are as a nation and thereby change the things we can do as a nation. As Robert E. Lane concluded in his investigations into "why the American common man believes what he does," when you ask white working-class American men what the perfect society or utopia would look like, they describe exactly the same society we live in, minus health problems, anxiety, loneliness, and overdrawn bank accounts. Of course in our society such hopes are indeed hard to achieve, but they are made "utopian" only by the institutional patterns (the industrial work life, the class system, private property, and other elements of our constitution) that Americans incorrectly think of as rooted in the natural and inevitable scheme of things. Exactly in the same way, our understanding of freedom reinforces the status quo because "getting away" with something or from something can't challenge the status quo when the "something" that is gotten or avoided is a part of the status quo.

More specifically, "making it" means, of course, becoming a "success" in society's conventional ways. "Getting away with something" means, similarly, succeeding at achieving some conventional social goal; but "getting away with" sounds a bit shady, unethical, or criminal. This is of no consequence: crime whose aim is only to get what society defines as desirable never threatens the basic order of society. It should be obvious that anyone whose notion of freedom, like these, consists of achieving wholly conventional goals will not threaten the society if she should become free. However, it might look as though this notion of freedom does tend to produce a challenge to the status quo in another way, since not everyone can be a complete and total "success." All the people who feel blocked from "freedom" (success) should get together and demand a change. But this misses an important feature of "success" as a goal: you can never be sure when you're there. And that means, conversely, you can never feel completely sure (unless you're starving) that you've been gypped, shut out, denied your *legitimate* share of the American dream. As long as you're better off than your parents (and it's a central feature of the status quo to make sure that we are all better off in material ways than our parents), then it's very hard to know whether your grievances are justified criticisms of the society, truly relevant to the lack of freedom in the society, or merely your own personal sour grapes and reluctance to admit that you weren't quite as good as the other guy. For example, for women until recently, conventionally "making it" meant getting married. Now how could a person who was a spinster persuade anyone that she had grievances that were really about the quality or degree of freedom in the society, and not merely about her "failure"?

Educated Americans often try to distinguish between "negative" and "positive" freedom. Negative freedom is "freedom from"—the absence of restrictions and of obligations. Positive freedom is "freedom to"—the ability to do what one wants. But in fact these are just two different ways of saying exactly the same thing. They both describe the condition where a person's wants and desires equal her power and abilities to satisfy those wants and desires. Moreover, this notion of freedom (wants = abilities) is not at all a reliable standard for measuring the amount of freedom a person has. You remain completely free simply by learning to not want to do anyting that you are (or might be) restricted from doing; you remain completely free simply by learning to want to do everything you are (or might be) obliged to do or punished for trying to avoid. In other words, to become free (that is, to make this equation balance), you can simply *decrease* your wants without increasing your abilities! Every commuter who learns to not want to do anything other than get in the car and drive to work every morning is freer, by these (our usual) ways of thinking about freedom, than if he wanted to do something else. Even more to the point, a totally conditioned, robotlike human being is, by these ways of thinking about freedom, no less free than a member of a community of equals who govern themselves entirely! Thinking about freedom in this way, and wanting to feel free, isn't it "natural" that Americans learn to feel free by conforming to expectations and patterns that are part of the status quo? Because that is, in fact, what we do. *Given our usual understanding of freedom, the American who is most concerned with being personally free is least likely to change anything basic in the society.*

Insofar as freedom-as-escape is just another way of talking about "negative freedom," then, by the previous paragraph, escape is also not the sort of freedom that would lead people to make changes in their society. But escape is often understood in a more absolute sense in our country—for instance Ishmael in Moby Dick, or Tom Sawyer, or the "beats" and 'hippies" of recent years who "drop out" of society. In this sense escape means a near-total withdrawal from mainstream society and all its conventions. But here again, this sort of freedom can't change those conventions. Avoidance and nonconfrontation by themselves can change nothing in the dominant society.

It *is* true, on the other hand, that escape may permit one to develop new ways of living, new communities with different constitutions. Americans have always been trying out "intentional" or utopian communities, from New Harmony and Oneida to today's so-called communes. However, none of these as yet has had any influence on the larger society. And the reason is not hard to see. To say that freedom-by-dropping-out would produce major social changes if only enough people do it, as some say today, is to beg the question. If a significant number of people did drop out, they would be immediately confronted with the society that they are trying to avoid and are therefore unprepared for. If it is "obvious" that the black 10 per cent of the population is not going to be permitted to drop out of white society and form a separate black nation, just how is a significant number of any other people going to pull it off? (Although, with unemployment as high as it is, it might be an aid to the economy if 5 per cent of the people would drop out!)

This understanding of freedom as getting ahead or getting away stems directly from our traditional individualism. And, like that principle itself, both these notions suggest that one must "travel light" in order to be free. Working closely with other people, which is necessary if fundamental social changes are to be achieved, is from the viewpoint of individualistic notions of freedom the heart of unfreedom, and to be avoided at all costs! This is only one more way that our understanding of freedom prevents us from living out any serious challenge to the status quo.

On the other hand, what about the notion of freedom as the absence of restrictions, as a goal to lead people to challenge the national status quo? With all the restrictions that we live under, surely a movement dedicated to removing them should pick up massive popular support. But the trouble is that this notion of freedom is purely negative. There is no direction, nothing that needs to be done (and that would be a justification for wanting the restrictions removed). If you see an individual who talks about not being free only in the sense of suffering restrictions, you can be fairly confident that when the restrictions are taken away he won't know what he wants to do. And if you see a political movement that talks only about restrictions on their (otherwise undefined) freedom, you can expect that the movement is "united" only in their sense of being restricted, and that its members are unable to work together for positive changes. At the University of California at Berkeley in 1964, for example, the Free Speech Movement was supported by every student political group from communists to the supporters of Barry Goldwater, and by most religious groups as well. But few could agree with any others on anything except that restrictions on speech were bad, and so the FSM's victory turned out to be a hollow one.

This lack of substance, of agreement on the positive goals, in our usual understanding of freedom is intimately connected with some themes in previous parts of this book. In order for this connection to be clear, it should be enough to point out that this conception of freedom as the absence of restraint is basically a *legalistic* notion. We often hear about "our liberties" being guaranteed by the law, and our "civil liberties" are of course in the Bill of Rights of the Constitution. But our notion that freedom is the absence of restraint is legalistic in a more profound sense than that it happens to be incorporated into laws. This notion of freedom *had* to be incorporated into the legal system, in order for it to have any significance at all. To say that I have freedom of speech, for example, in the sense that even though I am not right now speaking freely, and before I even know what I want to say, my "right of free speech" exists, is to say that my freedom exists in and because of laws. And while a system of laws guaranteeing certain civil liberties, freedom in a negative sense, seems to be a necessary condition for any nonlegal substantial freedom to exist, that legalistic notion of freedom by itself does stand in the way of purposeful collective action—as Schaar suggested in his article in Part II.

But if our usual understanding of freedom in negative, conformist, and legalistic ways only reinforces the very constitutional system that makes our need for another kind of freedom so urgent, this is not to say that there is no way to change the system, nor that there is no way both to live freely and to be working to change the system. In fact, my argument is the opposite. There are ways to live freely and at the same time to be working toward constitutional change. But these ways involve a rather unfamiliar notion of freedom.

Two things in particular make it hard for an American to feel comfortable with the student who said, "Freedom to me is the act of burning my draft card," even aside from the fact that the act was illegal, "unpatriotic," and disobedient. First, he is saying that freedom exists *during a struggle,* and not simply after one has achieved the power to do what one wants. We may be familiar with a feeling that freedom and struggle are connected. But we want to say, I think, that the struggle is *for* freedom, not that the struggle *is* freedom. And secondly, the student is saying that freedom involves *being part of a collectivity* and not, as we usually feel, being independent. Hannah Arendt describes these two aspects of freedom in *On Revolution* by saying that freedom is necessarily a quality of *public action,* a view that she admits opposes the more usual view in the United States that freedom is a quality of private behavior. In other words, traditionally we Americans have regarded freedom as the range of nonpolitical activities that a government or a society permits its members. But it also makes sense to say that a person is free only insofar as she is participating, interacting with her peers, in directing the common affairs of her community.

   This idea is a long way from the notion that freedom is the condition of "getting away (with, or from, something)." It differs, partly, in the way being a part of a cast performing a play differs from playing the stock market. Actions themselves matter, not just the results of action, because you are in public. You can't "get away" with or from much of anything. But you don't have to rely entirely upon the material results of your actions in order to make your actions become meaningful. And this idea of freedom is different from our traditional thinking in the way a struggle for liberation is different from the condition of being personally liberated. A struggle for liberation is participation in determining the community's future; the condition of being liberated is at best only a precondition of such participation (and usually involves only being able to engage in a wider range of nonpublic activities than before liberation).

   The idea that freedom represents a quality of public action satisfies the need for a notion of freedom that is valid personally and that directs one's energies toward the struggle to change this society and its constitution. The self-discovering and self-creating nature of public action, and the fact that public action is inherently significant in itself, all mean that free public action may satisfy the demand (which we Americans will always make) that any valid conception of freedom must contribute to individual fulfillment and dignity. And, on the other hand, to attempt to engage in public action in an unfree society that has nearly eliminated any place for the public is obviously to commit oneself to the struggle for a different America.

   My intention, as I said earlier, is not to argue that one *must* accept the notion that freedom can only be achieved through public or political action. Mainly I just want to get people to take seriously the possibility that this might be so. But there is one further, perhaps significant, point. As I tried to explain toward the end of Part I, given the world we live in, it is probably true that some of the goals Americans pursue today (self-respect, release from anxiety, a sense of competence, meaningful connection with others) cannot be achieved as long as we hold to our habitual belief that freedom is a quality of private behavior. Achieving success, or escaping, or removing some restrictions, will not bring us all the way to those goals, because those goals cannot be fully achieved within our body politic, inside the boundaries of life in the United States. But, on the other hand, it has been the experience of many people that those goals are achieved in the process of struggling to change the society we live in—in the process, that is, of living freely in the public sense.

COURSES OF POLITICAL ACTION

What *sorts* of actions make sense? What should one do? The world of people who are committed to working for fundamental social change is always full of arguments about strategies and tactics. Should one join the "counterculture" and work to form a "commune" or "intentional community"? Should one become a "militant activist," as the newspapers call people who help to organize demonstrations or lead strikes? Is it naive to work for the election of a particular candidate in an election, hoping that he or she will make a difference once in office? What about working at the level of local government, perhaps for community control of police or a more decentralized school system? Or is the only serious type of action to become a "revolutionary," and if so what should a revolutionary do? But is there nothing to the old idea of "boring from within," becoming successful and influential and competent enough "within the system" (as a lawyer or teacher, perhaps) to be of crucial help in engineering basic social changes?

There are lots of possibilities, once one starts taking seriously the notion that living freely will involve living in a public or political way. But choosing among these possibilities often seems to be a hopelessly confusing job. Not only is there the personal question of what sorts of public life or political actions are right for *me?* There is the even more forbidding task of figuring out what sorts of public life or political actions will be right for the *situation.* This task has two aspects: to assess the possibilities in the situation, and to calculate which courses of action will achieve the most desirable possibilities. What kinds of basic, constitutional change are possible in the United States in the coming years, and what kinds of lives and courses of action are most likely to push along those possible changes?

The selections that follow describe different kinds of public life, or courses of political action, that people are trying in the United States today in order to produce basic political changes. In addition to those selections, the various political magazines always have articles on "strategy" and "tactics," and more and more books are available that describe or advocate particular strategies. One fundamental point about action, though, is important enough to be mentioned before going on to consider the political possibilities of our day.

Any particular political action must be seen as *both* an end in itself (or, if you prefer, as a part of a process in which means and ends are not separable) *and* as a means or method of producing certain desirable effects. An action must not be seen only as a means of producing desired effects, as words like "strategy" and "tactics" tend to make us see. Of course, results are what matters. But there is never a result without a process leading up to that result, and the nature of that process (i.e., the nature of the actions leading to the result) determines just what the result really is. As Douglas Lummis put it once, it is true that you can't make an omelet without breaking some eggs. But anyone who thinks that you make a pregnant woman give birth by making her bleed isn't a midwife. He's a butcher.

This may sound as though I am *opposing* violence, but all I mean is that "the same" outcome achieved through violence and through some other process is not going to be the same outcome at all. My point is not at all to oppose all violence on grounds of moral principle. Just as no one approves of any and all acts of violence in principle, almost no one disapproves of all acts of violence in principle. I merely insist on asking what violence does accomplish in practice. (The same goes, it should be apparent, for any tactic.) Think of where racial relations in the south and in the rest of the country stood in, say, 1950. It is undeniable that far more change in racial relations has occurred in the south than the rest of the country. Why this has happened is a complicated question, but certainly it isn't irrelevant that the black freedom movement began in the south in the 1950's on a mass basis with bus boycotts, sit-ins, and grass-roots voter-registration campaigns, and the racist opposition began with bombings and other violence.

But what are the possibilities? In the introductions to the parts of this book I have tried to show both that our various social, economic, and political problems are interrelated ("racism" can't be separated from "structural poverty" and neither can be separated from "alienation," for example), and that these problems are in important part the symptoms of the kind of constitution that governs us, of the kind of society we live in and are taught to believe in. It has been implicit in all of this that I do not believe that our problems are going to be solved easily, certainly not without some major changes in our basic institutions and practices. This is a pretty grim thought. Isn't there *some* way, short of fundamental changes, that we as a nation can deal successfully with the issues that plague us? The answer, in my judgment, is *no*. Short of a major change in the constitution and its ruling system, real success with these issues is impossible. The reason for this is fairly simple.

First, given the way our society works now, obviously we have to deal with our problems through governmental action. But open up any of the standard textbooks on United States government and politics, and turn to the chapter where the author raises the question of how to be an effective, successful political actor. What you will read is that the only way to be effective is to enter the government or to enter or form a pressure group. That is, there are only three ways to be an effective agent of change, within the confines of the present ruling system: to be a bureaucrat, to be a politician, or to be a lobbyist. But, given the nature of our structure of power and interests (described in Part III), even an effective bureaucrat, congressman, or lobbyist must work within rather narrow limits. His effectiveness is necessarily confined to making marginal adjustments on the existing system and its policies. As the good standard textbooks show, any bureaucrat, congressman, or lobbyist who demands a serious change in basic national policies will simply fail. (It should go without saying that the same is true of nongovernmental positions, like corporation executive.) In order to be "effective," such actors must limit themselves to asking for greater rationalization of the economy or society, a slightly larger slice of the GNP for some specific group, or extension of basic citizen rights to some group which has been denied them. And these requests must not interfere with the really serious business of the government: managing the economy and guaranteeing economic (corporate) growth, and guaranteeing the national security (to use the common euphemism).

In other words, as even the professors who support and defend the present system will tell you, all that is possible within the confines of this system is either pressure-group victory (more "welfare," a bigger slice of the economic pie, further equalization of the law), or else "incremental problem-solving" (giving "first aid" to the symptom-problems of our basic institutions). Moreover, they will tell you, the size of your pressure-group victory depends strictly on your group's power—which means, of course, that precisely the groups that are worst off and most discriminated against will have the smallest victory in the pressure-politics sweepstakes.

Of course even a minor victory for some oppressed group is important for that group. But *even* when no United States citizen has an annual income of less than, say, $5,000, and when all discriminated-against groups are treated just the same way as a white, male, Protestant janitor—and these goals are not going to be achieved for a long time, but they *might* be achieved within this system—even when that "utopia" is achieved, we will *still* be faced with the problems of war, unequal distribution of wealth, misuse of natural resources, the social and human costs of our class system, powerlessness, meaninglessness, and all the "psychological problems" concomitant with the lack of real self-government. (Parts I through V should have shown how this is true.) In other words, our present structure of power and interests can if pushed provide minimum economic subsistence and formal legal equality. That's what it's all about. But, although these things are not to be sneezed at, they are obviously not nearly enough. And in order to go further, to begin to be effective with the more profound sicknesses of this society, it will be necessary to make fundamental changes in the society. In order to demilitarize our foreign policy, in order to allocate our economic resources on the basis of genuine social need rather than corporate profit and pressure-group influence, in order to decentralize the national bureaucracies and give people some control over their lives, in order to end the various forms of exploitation and domination described in Part V, in order to encourage saner human relationships and significant community ties—in order to achieve these sorts of goals, there must be a major change in the ruling system, because *as it presently exists* the structure of power and interests cannot do such things.

These last three paragraphs can be summed up as saying that, given everything described in Parts I–V, the ruling system by itself as it is will not be able to solve the real problems that plague this nation, and a few individuals working within that system will be unable to make what we do as a nation become very different from what it is now (because, after all, they won't be able to make what we are as a nation *be* very different from what it is now). Perhaps this seems obvious; perhaps it still seems debatable. At any rate, my position and the reasons for my conclusions should at least be clear. But this does not say everything there is to say about political action and social change. Several key questions have not been touched on at all.

1. What possibility is there that the sorts of incremental, marginal changes that are possible and likely to occur within the present system of power, interests, and policy will add up and snowball into significant changes?

2. What trends appear within the basic pattern of power, interests, and policy, and within the society as a whole? That is, where are we heading if we do *not* consciously and collectively take control of our future?

3. What chances are there that basic changes will occur in the way we are and the things we do as a nation? What might these changes be *to?* In other words:

(*a*) How would a change in the basic pattern of power and interests appear if it occurred through elections (like the New Deal, perhaps), and how likely is such an electoral revolution to occur?

(*b*) How would basic constitutional change appear if it began with an illegal seizure of the tools of violence (army, police) and of what powers of government remained after the violent transfer of control, and how likely is such a revolution to occur?

(*c*) How would a movement for basic constitutional change appear if it began without getting into (established positions of) power, what sorts of changes would be possible to achieve in this way, and how likely is such a movement for structural reform to occur?

I have already indicated, if only implicitly, my judgment about questions 1 and 2, so I will state my answers here without defending them or explaining them at length. There is very little chance that the sorts of changes that are likely to occur within the present structure of power and interests will eventually add up to significant desirable change. We may keep ourselves out of a nuclear war, but we will certainly continue our reactionary foreign policy of preventing sociopolitical changes in other countries that would harm powerful interests in this country, and so we will continue to fight foreign wars. Domestically, as I said above, qualitative changes in our national policy—other than extending legal equality to more people, putting a floor under poverty, and in other ways applying "first aid" to the consequences of our national priorities—just don't seem likely. Likewise, the trends that seem likely to occur, if we do not take conscious collective control over our national policy, are more of the same. More centralization of power, more domination by private interests masquerading as "public spirit," more manipulation by technically advanced bureaucracies, more of the kind of "justice" and "community" and "leadership" that leaves us like frantic or disillusioned children precociously "wise" in the ways of the world and unprepared to change them, and more of the indoctrination that supports the boundaries on lives that are already terribly limited.

The hope for an electoral revolution is the old hope that significant change can be "democratic." But as our own New Deal in the 1930's shows, since relatively few of the positions in the basic structure of power and interests are filled by elections, and since many of those electoral positions are well insulated from the winds of social change, it is terribly difficult to achieve a new "ruling class" all at once. Lacking the ability to unite the government and get it moving in a new direction, then, the "electoral revolutionaries" have to compromise with the people in the government who do not want serious change (and who are, of course, supported by nongovernmental as well as noncentral governmental elements of the structure of power). Moreover, in order to be elected, these "revolutionaries" will have to move through the established party system—an experience not calculated to bring out the revolutionary in anyone!

In other words, for an electoral revolution to occur, three things are necessary. The revolutionary party must gain unified control over the whole government. The revolutionary-dominated government must be able to move the whole country. And the revolutionary party must indeed be composed of capable and experienced people who are dedicated to fundamental sociopolitical change. Without all three of these conditions, no lasting constitutional changes can come out of the electoral system. And all three of them are *very* unlikely, in this country. No third party has arisen successfully since before the Civil War, and the established parties are thoroughly integrated into and supporters of the present structure of power, interests, and policy. Moreover, the constitutional-legal system is specifically designed to prevent coherent positive action by the national government ("separation of powers," "checks and balances," "federalism") unless that action is supported by powerful socioeconomic interests throughout the society—and that support would hardly be likely for a government aiming at making changes in the basic structure of power, interests, and policy.

This is not to say that revolution can't be democratic, but only to say that the revolution would have to occur *before* the election rather than afterward. The "electoral revolution" would have to *reflect* changes that were *already* occurring, or else it would fail. And this leads to the other two questions about the nature and likelihood of basic constitutional change.

In order to assess the possibility of a violent revolution in this country, it makes sense to look at the actual situations that existed just prior to successful or nearly successful revolutions in the past. By pinpointing the conditions in each case that seem to have been necesssry for past revolutions to happen as they did, we can arrive at some notion of what would have to happen here in this country in order for a revolution to occur. In 1970 Barrington Moore, Jr., published such an analysis in the *New York Review of Books,* which is part of the basis of the next few paragraphs.

In every revolution three interrelated developments occurred within the dominant classes prior to the seizure of power by the revolutionaries. First, there is the "desertion of the intellectuals," a popular but misleading phrase because it is not merely desertion and it involves many more people than the intellectuals. Rather, what happens is that some people formulate a serious challenge to the prevailing habits of thought that underlie the existing constitution, particularly a challenge to conventional notions of what should be considered as inevitable suffering and what is in fact remediable suffering, as well as new suggestions about the causes of and the remedies for suffering that is not necessary. In other words, prior to a revolution, people's thinking changes in ways that enable them to see a revolution as making sense for their country. Secondly, there is some sort of conflict within the dominant centers of power. Historically, the conflict between a landed aristocracy and an urban industrial-capitalist class was critical in moving many nations toward the point of revolution against a monarchy or a feudal regime. This conflict is not a mere clash of interests in the sense that the aerospace industry and the major financial institutions and banks have conflicting interests in the Vietnam War. The sort of conflict needed, if a nation is to move toward significant constitutional change, must be more like the conflict between northern industry and southern plantation before our Civil War. It must be a conflict between two basic views of how the nation will "have to" develop (and who should and should not bear the costs of that development). For example, a conflict between "expansionists" and "nationalists"—between, that is, people who believe that the nation can only get more and more involved in the international economy and the internal affairs of other nations, and people who believe deeply that it is only by focusing our whole attention on ourselves as a nation that we will survive —such a conflict between major bureaucratic centers of power would be significant enough to make basic constitutional change possible.

These first two preconditions of revolution can just as well be the basis of nonviolent but significant social change. What tips the scale toward revolution is the third factor: loss of unified control over the army and the police. (This is almost the same as saying that violent revolution breaks out, but it tells you where to look to see if revolution is just about to break out.) But loss of unified control over these instruments of force and violence only matters if certain revolutionary developments occur within the dominated classes of the population. To comprehend these developments, it is necessary to divide all revolutions into three categories; those that had a popular base in the cities, those that rested primarily on a rural base, and those that lacked any popular base prior to the outbreak of the revolution. Considering the present condition of the United States, it appears that no popular revolution is at all likely within the current generation. A popular revolution based on rural areas requires "liberated areas" (such as we had in our Revolutionary War, and the Viet Cong have in Vietnam) which would be militarily impossible to establish in the United States today. A popular revolution based on urban masses apparently requires a sudden increase in hardship coming on top of a longer period of serious deprivation, but the vast majority of our "urban masses" (the very term seems out of place!) are neither deprived enough nor disillusioned enough with the government now to support a revolutionary movement.

This still leaves open the third possibility: a major breakdown of the ruling structure without prior mass support, providing an opening for a seizure of power by a disciplined and highly organized revolutionary party. Whether or not such a possibility exists (and I am inclined to think that it is not as unlikely as the possibility of a popular revolution—given the increasing rage and desperation of some people in this country), this sort of revolution would not be desirable if it succeeded, and would not succeed if it were desirable. In the absence of popular support, it would have to resort to dictatorial methods and probably terror to achieve success. If, out of principle, it refused to use those methods, then lacking widespread popular support it could only fail. So the cost of an unpopular revolution succeeding would be too high; the result could only be tyranny.

Therefore I conclude that no desirable revolution is at all likely to occur in the United States in the near future. No matter how urgent the situation, fundamental changes are not going to start happening right now. But the lesson I draw from this is not that we should all go to sleep, or work to make the present structure of power responsive to our private interests. Rather, I conclude merely that the movement for a new America should not place its hopes on a quick revolution any more than on a quick electoral victory.

This leaves a final possibility. What would a movement for major constitutional change look like if it did not begin through a violent revolution? Would it have any chance of success? Most of the following selections are attempts to describe what such a movement might be like. Essentially all these selections suggest answers to both "what for?" and "how to?" What goals should be achieved, and how can they be achieved?

Perhaps this is the point to say something rather obvious, but that often gets forgotten in discussions of this sort. We don't have to throw out the entire world and try to create a wholly new one in order to come up with positive answers to radical questions. There are things in this country that can be worked on, and people that can be worked with. There is a rich store of inspiration and examples in the lesser-known pages of our history. The whole point of talking about change rather than mere destruction is to keep in mind the fact that we must begin with the skills and tools and materials we have or can get. And there *are* all sorts of concrete things to do. You can join or form a rural or urban commune. You can do educational work, either in a conventional or "free" school or by taking some job or moving into some community and talking with people there. You can work to restructure whatever institution you are a part of. You can get into local politics, working the way many people across the country have begun, to decentralize and democratize the city council and the police. You can get into a political collective, a group of men and women that tries to work together to find and live out various forms of collective action. You can work on the military, either by joining and doing political education inside or by living near a base and establishing some center like a coffeehouse where soldiers can come and talk. You can try to restructure and reorient the basic institutions in the society—the media, universities, labor unions, large businesses, churches, professional associations, courts, and so on—either from within or from the edges. (There are already some such groups among teachers, scholars, lawyers, doctors, scientists, and engineers. For more of this sort of information, look at Mitchell Goodman's *The Movement Toward a New America,* or P. Long's *The New Left* or find a copy of *Vocations for Social Change,* a bimonthly newsletter-type of magazine published by the political collective of the same name in Canyon, California.)

The more difficult questions involve not simply "what to do?" but the likelihood of genuine success. Of course, there never is any definite proof that some line of action will succeed, and it is always possible to convince yourself that any suggestion won't work. So I raise the question of how to succeed not to prove one argument or another, but because it must be raised and dealt with carefully before a person can make up her mind where and how she wants to move, publicly. The sorts of questions that I think need careful consideration include the following, and each of the selections in this part can be read as a different set of answers to these six questions:

1. *Arena:* Should one focus on some relatively small community or on the nation as a whole? Good arguments can be given for concentrating on a local town or city, or in a particular occupation or particular group: the issues are immediate, people can relate more personally, the power of giant corporations and the federal government is not immediately involved, and solutions can be arrived at more democratically. But good arguments can be given for avoiding localistic issues and concentrating on the nation as a whole: small communities easily become privatistic and exclusive, allies in other places and occupations can be found, and the national government has in recent years been more progressive.

2. *Danger:* How likely is a course of action to lead to suppression and/or punishment? Would that retaliation be more likely to help or hurt the cause, on balance? Some people argue that nothing should be tried that is likely to be suppressed or that seriously threatens the members of the movement personally. Others argue that certain kinds of retaliation can be helpful, exposing the injustice and irrationality of the present system or angering people who secretly sympathize with the movement. The government's suppression of the Black Panther Party has been so severe that it seems to me that the Panthers' cause has on balance suffered. But the suppression of the demonstrations in Chicago, 1968, and the behavior of the government and the judge in the political trial that followed may have brought many previously unsympathetic people to view the entire struggle differently.

3. *Allies:* Which groups and classes in the society will be most fruitful to work with? This question requires a subtle balancing of present feelings and long-run interests. Various arguments are made that prison convicts, dropped-out youth, angry blacks, Puerto Ricans and chicanos are the people to work with, because such people "have shown they understand that the system is wrong and must be destroyed." But counterarguments are advanced attempting to show that such groups have no serious argument with the basic constitutional system, except that it has excluded them or treated them badly. (I do *not* mean to imply that these three groups have the *same* potentiality, but that the same argument has been used for all three.) On the other hand, arguments that "the working class" or specific groups of blue-collar or white-collar workers or unions or even "the middle class" have basic long-run conflicts with the present system of policy run up against the undeniable fact that these groups show little indication that they understand their dissatisfactions as due to the basic structure of power and interests. The same sorts of questions should also be asked of other groups that are not usually considered in such discussions: lawyers, doctors, school teachers, engineers and technicians, the elderly, people in "nonmodern" occupations or "left-behind" towns, the unemployed, the career military, and so on.

4. *Time and process:* Should a movement focus on relatively short-run objectives or on relatively long-run objectives? For example, does it make more sense to concentrate on changing the seniority system in Congress and decentralizing control over a city's police force, or does it make more sense to concentrate on those changes that in themselves will be immediately valuable, such as a national transfer of power or the creation of different kinds of local communities? Another way of phrasing this issue is: should one expect that a particular (not intrinsically valuable) objective will lead to a further (desirable) development, or should one concentrate from the start on only those objectives that are desirable in themselves? These questions cannot be answered absolutely, since the chains of means-ends-means- . . . go on indefinitely, but they do need serious consideration if only to avoid empty victories for the short-runners, and never-consummated planning ("carrion-bird politics," as Carl Oglesby calls it) for the long-runners. What does a self-regenerating process of change look like and how can it get started?

5. *Mode:* What kinds of actions are appropriate? How should "educational" or "organizing" activities be combined with "direct-action" activities? Most important, should confrontations be more like Gandhi's *satyagraha* (perseverance in truth, militant nonviolence, or, as Clifford Geertz calls it, "mass taunting," "collective needling") or a more unyielding struggle to the death, with nonnegotiable demands and unconditional surrender? What is really at stake here, I think, is revealed by asking, "What are you sure you will really have won if you have to destroy your opponent emotionally or physically in order to win it?" The Gandhian position is "sim-

ple": you never know absolutely and finally whether your goals are just, and so you must achieve those goals without sheerly forcing your opponent to give them to you. Not using sheer force ensures that your opponent won't surrender unless he recognizes the justice of your goal. The opposing position has been expressed perhaps most forcibly by Frantz Fanon: you may not know what you really want until after you have destroyed the colonial oppressor, but precisely because of that—because your oppressor has made it impossible for you to be fully human—it is necessary to destroy him in order to discover yourself. Someplace not on the dimension that these essentially moral positions define is the "pragmatic" position, that you always get more in the long run if you (appear to) give more in the short run. None of these three is more "absolutist" or "fanatical" than the others, I should emphasize. They are just fanatical about different things.*

6. *Organization:* What sorts of relationships should there be between the members of a movement for basic social change? A centralized organization may or may not be more efficient, both during and after the struggle to seize power, and it has all the disadvantages that Stalin's use of Lenin's centralized bolshevik party revealed. Resting on the belief that the top leaders ought to be followed, centralized organization turns that belief into an order, so that "the top leaders must be followed." But to decentralize, so that everyone in the movement has control over his or her own activities, seems to threaten to make coordinated, large-scale actions impossible. In the abstract, good arguments can be made on each side, and after all, the kind of organization that is chosen must also depend on the answers to the other preceding questions. But to consider all the issues that are raised by the question of organization is far beyond my purpose here, which is simply to insist that the question itself—like the other five—requires careful thought.

ONCE AGAIN ON THE NATURE OF POLITICS

I want to end these notes by reemphasizing a major theme of this book, a theme that might shed some additional light on questions about action, but also on the connection between action and the previous parts of the book. This theme is the nature and significance of politics (and by now it should

*For Gandhi's views, see Joan Bondurant, *The Conquest of Violence,* rev. ed. (Berkeley: Univ. of California Press, 1965; available in paper). For Fanon, see his *The Wretched of the Earth* (New York: Grove Press, 1966). Albert Camus' *The Rebel* (Vintage, paper) is still an excellent discussion of the Gandhian viewpoint in Western language.

Some readers may feel that I have not given fair due to the pragmatic position, which is sometimes called by its supporters the "ethics of responsibility." But as I see it, this sort of pragmatism rests upon the unrealistic assumption that all actions or states of the world can be *compared* and then ranked *objectively* according to "more or less preferred." If this assumption were accurate, then of course there would be no ethical problems at all! If, on the other hand, the ranking is merely subjective or personal, then the pragmatic position turns out to be a mere "do your own thing, but do it rationally," hardly an answer to the *ethical* dilemma that Gandhi and Fanon embrace.

go without further explanation that politics does not mean simply the use of our governmental institutions and conventional political practices).

Each part of this book has talked about politics in different terms. In Part I, politics was the intersection between personal troubles and social issues. In Part II, politics almost disappeared into psychology and history; it had to do with our traditional shared values and ways of thinking, and with the major changes and choices we as a nation have been through during the past hundred years. In Part III, politics was a matter of power and interest, of who gets the most of what there is to get. In Part IV, politics had to do with the quality of our public life, with the kind of justice, community, and leadership we experience and expect to live with. In Part V, politics became a matter of daily life, of social structure and ideology. And in Part VI, obviously, politics is concerned with freedom, action, and fundamental social change.

That politics can be seen in all these different ways should not be confusing. They don't contradict each other. Rather, each one sheds a different light on the nature of our national way of life, which is itself political in all of these different senses.

In other words, rather than saying that the different sorts of things described in the different parts of the books are connected, as I have said before, it is equally true and perhaps even more helpful to understand that *all* of those things *are political,* in the various meanings that the word politics has. To say, therefore, that the basic problems of our country are political is to say that politics (as well as those problems) involves our constitutional institutions and principles, our national traditions, our structure of power, interests, and policy, our kind of justice, community and leadership, our workaday ideology and social practices, and our ways of living and acting freely. To see politics in this way is to grasp the essential interrelatedness of the different sides of our national (personal and collective) life, and to sense the manifold possibilities that a better politics has for us.

"The end of politics in America," then, has two meanings. On one hand, the book has been about the dead end that we have reached, as a body politic. Given the way we are as a nation, the things we do as a nation are not going to improve much. Politics in the sense of an open-ended process of intelligent collective action is over in our country. But on the other hand, the end (goal, purpose) of politics in America is precisely to remake ourselves as a nation, so that what we are can be different in order that what we do, as a nation, can be different. (Conventional) politics is dead; long live (the potentialities of) politics!

Hanna Pitkin has written that the heart of politics is the question, "What shall we do?" It is fundamental, because in the process of discussing and then acting out the answer to the question, we find out just who, indeed, "we" are, and just what it is that we are doing, when we do "it." Unfortunately, for us, because of the kinds of politics we have become accustomed to living with, even to understand what she means is a major effort! On the

other hand, all the more, her formulation shows the potentialities of changing our politics. We've tried just about everything else; at one time or another our national salvation has seemed to lie in religion, business, the
frontier, moral causes, foreign wars, scientific progress, and a thousand
other less lasting fads and fetishes—but always within the confines of our
politics. Wouldn't it make sense, now, to try paying attention to the thing
that has always been the defining, delimiting characteristic of an American
—our politics? Then we might find out (decide for ourselves) just who "we"
are, and just what it is in fact that we are doing. "What shall we do?"

The Ends and Means
of New Politics, American Style

22   The "Port Huron Statement"

Students for a Democratic Society

A first task of any social movement is to convince people that the search for orienting theories and the creation of human values is complex but worthwhile. We are aware that to avoid platitudes we must analyze the concrete conditions of social order. But to direct such an analysis we must use the guideposts of basic principles. Our own social values involve conceptions of human beings, human relationships, and social systems.

We regard *men* as infinitely precious and possessed of unfulfilled capacities for reason, freedom, and love. In affirming these principles we are aware of countering perhaps the dominant conceptions of man in the twentieth century: that he is a thing to be manipulated, and that he is inherently incapable of directing his own affairs. We oppose the depersonalization that reduces human beings to the status of things—if anything, the brutalities of the twentieth century teach that means and ends are intimately related, that vague appeals to "posterity" cannot justify the mutilations of the present. We oppose, too, the doctrine of human incompetence because it rests essentially on the modern fact that men have been "competently" manipulated into incompetence—we see little reason why men cannot meet with increasing skill the complexities and respon-

sibilities of their situation, if society is organized not for minority, but for majority, participation in decision-making.

Men have unrealized potential for self-cultivation, self-direction, self-understanding, and creativity. It is this potential that we regard as crucial and to which we appeal, not to the human potentiality for violence, unreason, and submission to authority. The goal of man and society should be human independence: a concern not with image or popularity but with finding a meaning in life that is personally authentic; a quality of mind not compulsively driven by a sense of powerlessness, nor one which unthinkingly adopts status values, nor one which represses all threats to its habits, but one which has full, spontaneous access to present and past experiences, one which easily unites the fragmented parts of personal history, one which openly faces problems which are troubling and unresolved; one with an intuitive awareness of possibilities, an active sense of curiosity, an ability and willingness to learn.

This kind of independence does not mean egotistic individualism—the object is not to have one's way so much as it is to have a way that is one's own. Nor do we deify man—we merely have faith in his potential.

Human relationships should involve fraternity and honesty. Human interdependence is contemporary fact; human brotherhood

Reprinted by permission.

must be willed, however, as a condition of future survival and as the most appropriate form of social relations. Personal links between man and man are needed, especially to go beyond the partial and fragmentary bonds of function that bind men only as worker to worker, employer to employee, teacher to student, American to Russian.

Loneliness, estrangement, isolation describe the vast distance between man and man today. These dominant tendencies cannot be overcome by better personnel management, nor by improved gadgets, but only when a love of man overcomes the idolatrous worship of things by man. As the individualism we affirm is not egoism, the selflessness we affirm is not self-elimination. On the contrary, we believe in generosity of a kind that imprints one's unique individual qualities in the relation to other men, and to all human activity. Further, to dislike isolation is not to favor the abolition of privacy; the latter differs from isolation in that it occurs or is abolished according to individual will.

We would replace power rooted in possession, privilege, or circumstance by power and uniqueness rooted in love, reflectiveness, reason, and creativity. As a *social system* we seek the establishment of a democracy of individual participation, governed by two central aims: that the individual share in those social decisions determining the quality and direction of his life; that society be organized to encourage independence in men and provide the media for their common participation.

In a participatory democracy, the political life would be based in several root principles:

that decision-making of basic social consequence be carried on by public groupings;

that politics be seen positively, as the art of collectively creating an acceptable pattern of social relations;

that politics has the function of bringing people out of isolation and into community, thus being a necessary, though not sufficient, means of finding meaning in personal life;

that the political order should serve to clarify problems in a way instrumental to their solution; it should provide outlets for the expression of personal grievance and aspiration; opposing views should be organized so as to illuminate choices and facilitate the attainment of goals; channels should be commonly available to relate men to knowledge and to power so that private problems—from bad recreation facilities to personal alienation—are formulated as general issues.

The economic sphere would have as its basis the principles:

that work should involve incentives worthier than money or survival. It should be educative, not stultifying; creative, not mechanical; self-directed, not manipulated, encouraging independence, a respect for others, a sense of dignity, and a willingness to accept social responsibility, since it is this experience that has crucial influence on habits, perceptions, and individual ethics;

that the economic experience is so personally decisive that the individual must share in its full determination;

that the economy itself is of such social importance that its major resources and means of production should be open to democratic participation and subject to democratic social regulation.

Like the political and economic ones, major social institutions—cultural, educational, rehabilitative, and others—should be generally organized with the well-being and dignity of man as the essential measure of success.

In social change or interchange, we find violence to be abhorrent because it requires generally the transformation of the target, be it a human being or a community of people, into a depersonalized object of hate. It is imperative that the means of violence be abolished and the institutions—local, national, international—that encourage nonviolence as a condition of conflict be developed.

These are our central values, in skeletal form. It remains vital to understand their denial or attainment in the context of the modern world.

23   Citizen Politics

Michael Walzer

A great deal of political activity is routine day-in, day-out work, best left to professionals. Other people don't have time for it, though they are often doing work very much like it in organizations whose character is not overtly political. But routine performances are adequate only to routine occasions. In moments of crisis, the professionals often can't cope; or, given new perceptions of injury and injustice, they seem to be coping badly. Then the democratic system offers a standing invitation to the rest of us to enlist in political life, an invitation to commitment and participation. More rarely, the question is not of enlistment but conscription: the routines suddenly collapse, and harsh choices are forced upon large numbers of men and women.

One of the reasons the choices are so harsh is that they involve people in activity and movement who were passive before. These are not incompetent people (not all or most of them, anyway), but they are often innocent of the complications of political life. They are unaware of the personal risks involved, unprepared for enmity and contention, unaccustomed to the sheer endlessness of artful talk and manipulative behavior. Nevertheless, they act. In clubs, campaigns, movements, they articulate their sense of *something wrong* and press for change. This little handbook is for them, because they are inexpert, as I am, and in order that the little we learn will not become a trade secret.

Every man has his own sense of crisis and outrage. So long as this is not shared or widely shared, most of us deal with it, suffer

from it, repress and forget it, in private. The solitary prophet makes his own wilderness of inattention, mockery, and withdrawal by talking to people unwilling to listen. It is (sometimes) worth trying, but most of us learn to keep quiet. Political action is only possible when expressions of outrage and prophecies of disaster meet a lively response, at least within some circle of our own acquaintances. We try them out on our friends. The actual decision to enter the political arena will almost certainly be made by a small group, but it should only be made by a group whose members have what might be called intimations of growth. Where do such intimations come from? Hopefully, from conversations and encounters with other people, hints of commitment, plausible signs of interest. Would-be activists must have some sense of their future constituency; they must know that so many people will support the strike, attend the mass meeting, join the march, before they put themselves forward and call for action.

I want to caution against the intimations of pure theory, the products of a very specialized form of conversation. Political discourse carried on within the narrow circle of academies and sects does not produce—not alone —signs sufficient to justify political action. Later on, I will take up some of the problems of sectarian politics, but one feature of such politics should be mentioned here: the willingness to act, in disregard of present experience, on the basis of one or another theoretical view of the future. Then parties and movements are developed that are grounded on nothing more than the tense expectancy of the faithful, and barring the occurrence of the expected events, and given the likely occurrence of unexpected events, the band of the faithful generally remains small. There are ways of dealing with this difficulty, as the long history of Christianity suggests, but there are many more ways of not dealing with it. Hence the political sects of the Left, each one the product of an initiative for which, whatever the verdict of the future, the present was not ripe.

But sectarian initiatives are at least preceded by extended speculations about consequences and outcomes. Much more dangerous is the recklessness suggested by the maxim of a Jacobin leader in 1793: "On s'engage et puis, on voit." I commit myself, and then ... I see what happens. That is, whether or not I have support, whether or not my commitment is retrievable, whether or not other people are affected, and, if so, how they are affected, I act in the hope of unpredictable goods and even, perhaps, without any hope at all. What this most often means is that my action derives from personal rage and frustration so intense, so unbearable that doing something now seems far more urgent than producing effects later on. I have, in fact, had such feelings, and I have seen other people possessed by them. But political motivation is something quite different. We become political men when we act for public and not private reasons, or at least for public in addition to private reasons, and when we imagine our effects in terms of other people as well as ourselves. Political action is action with or for others, and while we may think our personal feelings very important (as we all do), they are, in fact, less important than the inevitably impersonal feelings for other people that are involved in acting with this group, for this group, against that group of men and women whom we cannot really know.

Large numbers of men and women ready to act together without knowing one another, and in disregard of the professional and his routines—these are the makings of the political moment. The makers of the moment are some smaller number of men and women who recognize the readiness and give it public expression. The readiness itself

has two sources. Common injury, class interest, ethnic solidarity produce a kind of citizen politics most likely to evolve into professionalism, most likely to leave behind permanent defensive alliances and associations. Only the beginning moments of the labor movement (and then of each new union), for instance, provide clear examples of amateur activism—though every strike turns up new activists free of professional sophistication yet politically competent in surprising ways. On the other hand, the struggle for women's suffrage remained throughout a citizens' movement and never produced a professionally run feminist union, in part because no ongoing organization of women was (or was thought to be) necessary once suffrage was won.

Moral outrage, anger, and sorrow for injustices done within our own society, or by our government overseas, produce a kind of citizen politics most likely to remain the province of citizens, largely because its incidence and endurance are so unpredictable. Professional politicians seek out, sometimes, the support of such citizens, but they are not likely to join them. In any case, the politicians are rarely there at the beginning. The first attempts to cope with the crisis, to end the injustice, begin without them, and despite them, when a group of citizens holds a meeting, argues about strategies, and plans a new organization.

BEGINNINGS

The first task is to find the support one believes is there, to reach out somehow to unknown but sympathetic people. In order to do that, the little group of activists must appear to be more than it yet is. Beginnings are rarely straightforward; they trade on unpredictable futures. It is necessary at once that there be a name, a speculation on the movement to follow, but worth thinking about, since names are not easy to change. After the name, an address, a letterhead, a list of sponsors, a statement and a program, a press release. All this may seem embarrassing and pretentious to the men and women who put it together; they can still meet, and probably will, in each other's living rooms. But there is no other way. They must make themselves visible, and it is not enough simply to stand up.

Political movements are begun by throwing together a facade, behind which activists rush about trying to raise a building. Often enough, they fail; the facade collapses before there is any shelter behind it. But if they have chosen their moment wisely, the first little group will find people to help it along. Other groups will spring up on the same model and will want to affiliate with the first, not necessarily because it is larger or more powerful, but simply because it is first. The initiative belongs to its members, as do, for a time at least, the crucial decisions.

Sometimes the original group is already a political association—a sect or party—and its members are political professionals, though most likely of a marginal sort. Then the facade they put up is especially important. They must look like ordinary citizens if they are to attract significant support. This sort of disguise should probably be encouraged; in many cases it is the functional equivalent of good intentions. And, assuming a worthwhile cause and an attractive facade, even knowledgeable activists may do well to join, for the sake of the others, so to speak; and, if necessary, to make trouble later on.

With regard to many issues, national committees of one sort or another already exist, founded, sometimes, long ago, and sustained with more loyalty than wisdom. Nevertheless, it is often sensible to try to begin under the banner of an established organization and to work with or (in time) take over its national office. Otherwise, energy will be wasted differentiating oneself from the existing group and fighting with its staff. There is often real help to be had, and the status of a local branch is nothing to be ashamed of. But if the existing group has come to be identified with defeat, or with some idiosyncratic and isolated leader, or with sectarian styles of political action, then not only a fresh start but also the appearance of a fresh start is vitally necessary. Citizen activists gain a great deal, in such cases, if their movement looks shiny and new.

STRATEGIC CHOICES

Quiet men and women often exaggerate the importance of their own outrage, their long delayed decision to *do something*. If they are moved, how can the rest of the world stand still? But it is always best to plan one's moves on the supposition that most of the world will stand still, that established institutions and social practices will survive the shock. All that has changed is that some group of people has decided to use the pronoun "we," and to act together. Nor is it the case in a democratic society that this decision challenges the political system. Quiet citizens are the resources of a democracy, saved up, we are told, for those moments when professionalism fails. They may feel unconventional; they may behave unconventionally; but their intermittent forays into the political arena are by now one of the conventions of democratic politics. That doesn't mean that what they do isn't important, nor that it isn't sometimes dangerous. Using democratic rights puts them at risk: now there are men and women—now there are enemies—threatened by that use. For this reason above all, it is important for activists to know what they can and cannot do, and never to indulge themselves (or frighten their enemies) with fantasies of social and political changes they cannot actually bring about.

Revolution is such a fantasy, less common than is often thought, but worth dealing with early on. Citizen activists may aim at this or that fundamental change, but they cannot hope to make a revolution. It is not very often that anyone actually *makes* a revolution. Revolutions happen, and all sorts of people find themselves, unexpectedly, participants in the happening. Ordinary citizens will be among them (often yearning not to be), but at such moments it is the professionals, newly recruited professionals perhaps, who take charge. Power of the ultimate sort is at stake, and no one contends for such power in a part-time way, or carries on simultaneously a nonpolitical career, or retires casually from the struggle once some point of special interest has been won. But these are the characteristics of citizen activists; simply listing them helps explain why amateur politics is most often parasitic on the routines of a more or less stable democratic system. The crises and outrages that set off the political activity of ordinary citizens are serious enough, but they occur within a system that is not yet in a state of total crisis and that protects even the irregular responses of its members. Most men and women join the movement counting on that protection. It isn't absolute, as they will learn, but it is a great deal more than revolutionaries have any right to expect.

Giving the system a "last chance" is another fantasy. This suggests that revolution is the next step if citizen activism in general, or this particular citizens' campaign, fails to carry the cause to victory. But activists have no business imagining that they will win right away; they are a minority, probably a small minority, of the country. They must risk failure, and they ought to be aware that the most likely consequence of failure is not revolution at all, but the fragmentation of their movement and the retreat of many citizens from politics. Small bands of sectarian militants may then experiment with disruption and violence, fantastically imitating Jacobins and Bolsheviks. But this is rarely a serious business. One day, hopefully, there will be a new mobilization of activists, a reorganized movement, and another citizen's campaign—that is, another "last chance" for the system. *There is nothing else to do but try again.*

The real choice faced by the men and women who plan these successive attempts is between two kinds of politics, both of which have conventional names, though they can each be pursued in a variety of irregular ways. The two kinds are pressure politics and electoral politics, and I am inclined to think that there are no other kinds. To choose pressure politics means to try to in-fluence those people who already hold power, who sit in official seats, who may even be responsible for the outrages against which the movement is aimed. To choose electoral politics is to try to dislodge those people and plant others in their seats, not necessarily or even probably the leaders of the movement, more likely whatever alternative set of professional politicians the system provides. Of course, the two choices overlap in important ways; they are often pursued simultaneously, with stress being put on the first only until some group of professionals adopts the cause. But it is worth emphasizing the two simply because they exhaust the range: changing the policies men make and changing the men who make policies. Changing the political system within which policy is made is rarely a real option for citizen activists.

It is never easy to know when to shift from pressure to electoral politics, whether at any given moment (and the moments are recurrent) to enter or to avoid the campaign of this or that candidate or party. On the one hand, electioneering is the sort of politics citizen activists are most familiar with, know best, probably do best. On the other hand, they often feel that their break with the routines of the system precludes it. They have come to distrust the promises of professional politicians. They are in search precisely of a politics that does not require them to support candidates who are only barely better than their opponents and who have, most likely, weak and vacillating positions on what the activists believe is the crucial issue. Sentiment of this sort is entirely justified. It is, after all, what makes the movement possible in the first place.

But assuming that pressure politics (petitions, mass meetings, marches, and so on) doesn't lead to a change in government policy, electoral politics is a necessary next step. The movement can't avoid it, even if supporting conventional candidates and parties involves some compromise of its principles. It is only a question of when, and to that there is no specific answer. The general answer is: not until the movement is strong enough to force fairly clear positions upon the professionals and to exercise some control over them once they have won.

This general rule sometimes suggests to activists that they must run their own candidates or that they must join in a new political party. A single-issue educational campaign, even with victory inconceivable, may be a useful activity; whether it is or isn't in any particular case is a tactical decision. A new party is something quite different. It involves the movement in a coalition with many other groups and so defines its position on many other issues; it requires a commitment to an elaborate program and to broad social change. That is a commitment many of the activists would probably like to make, but it is not what first brought them together, and it is not what holds them together with other activists in the movement. Nor is it at all clear that a new party and a struggle for social change on a wide front is the best (the easiest or the quickest) way to carry their own cause to victory. There are, in fact, two very different strategies entangled here, which will have to be separated out in the course of movement debate and action. Two questions are crucial: Should the citizen's movement be committed to single-issue or to multi-issue politics? Should the movement be organized as a single constituency or a coalition? . . .

COALITIONS

When political activists are successful, even minimally successful, they not only add members to their own organizations; they also bring other organizations into action. The people they find are not facsimiles of themselves: they have, or many of them have, different interests and loyalties, different notions about appropriate channels. If they are to become active, they will probably do so only within their own groups. Some of these are established groups, their leaders suspicious of the movement, sensitive about their own prestige; some are as new as the movement itself, their members equally hopeful, but with some scheme or plan all their own. Some of them have only a periph-

eral interest in the cause; some are ready to take it on, full time, at least for a while. In any case, the movement must now consider the relative advantages of the many different kinds of cooperation, alliance, and coalition.

With all the good will in the world, cooperation is not easy, and in practice one must make do with considerably less good will than that. The crucial problem is that the different organizations compete with one another. They find themselves fighting for a limited supply of members, money, media coverage, and so on. To some extent, the single-issue movement can reduce the intensity of these fights and save itself a lot of trouble if it sticks to its own issue, promising, in effect, to go away once the cause has been won. Then it is less of a threat to ongoing groups, such as labor unions and political parties, whose leaders can now hope, if they cooperate, to inherit some of the people mobilized by the movement. But there is bound to be conflict, perhaps especially among groups with more or less similar or overlapping goals. They will disagree about strategies, aim at different constituencies (but compete in practice for the same core of activists), accuse one another of stupidity, fearfulness, and even betrayal.

For all this, alliances and coalitions are possible and necessary. The familiar maxim about strange bedfellows is, in fact, an injunction: it is the aim of political action, of day-to-day argument and maneuver, to get people into the same bed who never imagined they could take a peaceful walk together. But there are political (and moral) guidelines to be followed in establishing these peculiar intimacies, and citizen activists don't always succeed in plotting the appropriate course between puritanical fastidiousness and eager promiscuity. It is mostly a question of time and place, but also, as in moral life generally, of character. Some groups put themselves beyond the pale; sometimes it is necessary to say that with this or that organization, whose official policy requires, say, a defense of Nazi or Stalinist terror, no alliance of any sort is possible. This announcement is itself a political act, which lets people know something they have a right to know about the character of the movement. But when the questions at issue are of lesser moment, citizen activists ought never to make public display of their virtue. With ordinary corruption and opportunism, as with disagreeable opinions, they can deal —and they had better deal with them. The only question is on what terms. . . .

TACTICS

There are only a limited number of things to do, so it is important, first, to do them well and, second, to do them enough. Movement debates about tactics, however, rarely focus on these two imperatives. They are often disguised arguments about leaders, issues, strategies, organizational structures. And it does make sense, at least sometimes, to avoid the larger questions until they are forcibly raised by the pressures of day-to-day activity and the need for (what look like) tactical decisions. But activists should always be aware of exactly what is being decided. If canvassing is organized by ward and precinct, a future electoral campaign is being set up (and if not, not); if every local group is authorized to bring its own signs to the demonstration, a federal and, possible, multi-issue movement is being established, and so on.

But tactics have also an interest and value of their own. Leaders and movements survive, after all, largely on tactical successes. Day after day, they must find things to do, from which activists will carry away a sense of meaning and effect and which other people also will notice and remember. What sorts of things? . . .

WINNING AND LOSING

It is best to win. It is also best to appear to be winning, and since the movement is involved in an ongoing series of activities, it is usually possible to plan for a series of successes. These will mostly be small triumphs, and triumphs, perhaps, only by the movement's own measure: a successful rally, a march larger than the last march, more names on a petition than anyone expected (expectations should be low), this or that conventional politician turning around, agreeing to speak, looking for support. Such victories make the growth of the movement apparent, and movements grow, in fact, by appearing to grow. Hence the importance of the demonstration and the sequence of demonstrations which must be aimed, above all, at communicating a sense of expansion, of numerical increase and greater social range.

There is always pressure among the activists, however, to escalate rather than expand; that is, to heighten the militancy of successive demonstrations, revealing to the country the increasing zealousness of (a part of) the movement. But escalation of this sort almost always decreases the numerical strength and narrows the social range of political action, often in disastrously sudden ways. It may even be better, though psychologically much more difficult, to move in the other direction: to lower the level of militancy over time in order to maximize growth. In any case, one appears to be winning, and one actually wins, only by reaching and involving more and more people.

It is possible to survive minor defeats, but it isn't always desirable to survive a whole series of minor defeats. If sectarian isolation is the only recourse, it is probably best to dissolve altogether and, assuming the continued significance of the cause, let some new group of people come together, differently organized, differently led, to carry on the struggle. The history of a political cause often takes this form: a number of organizations and movements, rising and falling, peaking at different points, some of them collapsing and vanishing. Only after a long time does one or another achieve enough strength to win. A history of this sort is possible because citizen activists have other things to do (other causes to work for). The movement isn't the whole of their lives, nor should it be. Activists should remember this too: they have worked hard; they can (sometimes) withdraw from the field with honor. Their part-time activity is not indispensable to the cause; the cause is not indispensable to their own lives. . . .

A CALL TO POLITICAL ACTION

[P]olitical life is different in different geographic and social locations, in different parts of the country, in different parts of the city. It also changes, obviously, from one historical moment to another. Politics is sometimes interesting, urgent, dangerous; more often, in any decent society, it is none of those things. The judgments we make of these different moments are bound to be ambiguous, and not only because some people flourish amidst urgency and danger, while others feel the full impact of the old Chinese curse: May you live in interesting times! A quiet and routine politics often conceals injustice and oppression, while "interesting times" are moments not only of risk but also of opportunity—for mobilization, revolt, social change. And citizen politics is one of the most important ways in which opportunity can be seized.

We are cursed and blessed with "interesting times." The struggle for racial equality and the struggle against the Vietnam War have mobilized large numbers of previously passive citizens, but they have also sharply divided the country, strained its political institutions, generated sporadic and increasingly serious violence. Doubtless the causes for all this lie deeper than the immediate issues suggest, though it is difficult to overestimate the extent to which the Vietnam War especially is a national disaster (and a disaster perpetrated, it should be remembered, by professionals and experts). But that is not the whole story of our troubles. The political moments of peace and equality have coincided with a more profound crisis.

In the United States today, a society whose government and economy have been progressively removed from the effective control of its citizens, or whose citizens feel themselves to be powerless and disorganized, suddenly faces a series of revolts. These are spurred by real injustices, but are not necessarily dependent on injustice for their energy and force. Very often the revolts don't have an obvious terminating point or a clear political character. Reflecting as much the general crisis as the concrete necessities of any particular cause, citizen politics has

taken on the most inchoate forms, failing to achieve either national leadership or collective discipline, generating a kind of random militancy. The causes for which activists are recruited are not always the reasons, or the most important reasons, for their activities.

Nothing has a more disorienting effect upon political action than the sense of powerlessness—except, perhaps, powerlessness itself. It produces what might best be called political promiscuity, a feeling that anything goes, a desperate search for immediate if superficial effects because real effects are by definition beyond reach. And since the most desirable immediate effects are those of extremity and outrage, it produces at the same time a steady escalation toward revolutionary struggle (or, at least, revolutionary rhetoric)—as if powerlessness, which can't be overcome by increments and stages, might be transformed in one unexpected stroke. This whole style of citizen activism appeals most of all, I think, to new activists, whose escape from one or another passive role is most recent and whose sense of political possibility is barely developed. It does not serve the cause, whatever the cause is: instead, it invites the defeat and repression for which it is also a subtle kind of psychic preparation. What can the powerless hope for except defeat?

Citizen politics is not easy in the United States today; it would be foolish to pretend that it is, or to hold before the eyes of new activists the formal model of a democratic system. In almost every area of social life they are certain to encounter entrenched and efficient bureaucracies which evade, resist, wear down, or simply absorb the force of their protest. The decline of political parties and of legislative authority has clearly reduced the accessibility of the political system and made the work of newly activated citizens much harder than it once was. Nevertheless, there is abundant evidence to suggest that access is still possible and that bureaucracies can be pushed this way or that (even when they can't be seized and transformed).

A citizens' movement, carefully organized, intelligently led, can win important victories, on both the local and national levels, short of Total Victory. Both the civil rights and Black Power movements of the 1960's, and the peace movement too, had significant effects on American politics. They reached new constituencies, forced professional politicians to pay attention, built up local power bases, won changes in executive policies and bureaucratic procedures. These (small) victories ought to have been more heartening than they were, and might have been followed up in more successful ways, had there existed a larger number of activists scornful of apocalyptic talk and ready for the risks and sacrifices of an ongoing politics.

What would that look like? Why is that so hard? It requires self-control and organizational discipline, for one thing, and then the acting out of the kind of politics I have tried to describe, where every step is measured and pleasure is rarely immediate or ecstatic. It requires activists to live with and make compromises with men and women whose opinions they abhor, for no other reason than that these men and women are (temporarily perhaps) more powerful, or more numerous, or simply because they are *there*. An ongoing politics is not one whose participants can possibly hope to deliver "all power to the people" tomorrow or next month. For they represent only some of the people and must hope to win what they can win; a little more power for this or that newly organized group. And that is only possible if they work at it long and hard enough. . . .

Right now it is important to work at it long and hard. The causes for the sake of which so many of us enlisted are serious enough, but the dangers of defeat once the battle has been joined, as it has been joined in the United States today, are more serious still. It has been joined, in part, by young militants without a community base or a coherent strategy; by sectarian ideologues even more out of touch but with an all-too-coherent strategy; by isolated terrorists insanely committed to the efficacy of The Act, responsible to no one. Without the long-term activism of adult citizens, the central political movements of our time belong to them. And there is nothing more certain than that the revolution of their heated fantasies will end in a brutal and squalid repression, a bitter defeat not only for them.

The militants, sectarians, and terrorists regard themselves as the vanguard of the people; perhaps so, but they are a lost vanguard, and it is not even remotely likely that the people, whoever they are, will follow. The real question is whether citizen activists can find another way. Surely there are many thousands of Americans who will join them if they can, forging a political movement that is committed but also sane and steady in the pursuit of its goals and that makes itself an instrument as well as a symbol of democratic possibility. Nor is there any reason to think that these Americans are less fervent than those who have marched away with the lost vanguard. They are, perhaps, more modest— as befits participants in a citizens' movement. Any many of them probably look forward to a time when political action is not so urgent as it is today. They are not the sort of people who will ever win glory. *But no one else can carry us forward to a society less oppressive, less unjust, more routinely democratic than the one we have now.*

24   Sisterhood Is Powerful

Robin Morgan

Every time drastic change has shaken the established social order, some drive for women's rights has surfaced—only to be put down, or told to "wait until after," after the revolution or whatever else concerned the men. The women's suffrage movement in the United States grew out of the drive to abolish slavery. The current women's movement was begun largely, although not completely, by women who had been active in the civil-rights movement, in the anti-war movement, in student movements, and in the Left generally. There's something contagious about demanding freedom, especially where women, who comprise the oldest oppressed group on the face of the planet, are concerned. Thinking we were involved in the struggle to build a new society, it was a slowly dawning and depressing realization that we were doing the same work and playing the same roles *in* the Movement as out of it: typing the speeches that men delivered, making coffee but not policy, being accessories to the men whose politics would supposedly replace the Old Order. But whose New Order? Not ours, certainly. . . .

Suffice it to say that women, who had been struggling on a one-to-one basis with their men, began to see that some sort of solidarity was necessary, or insanity would result. (Perhaps the most vicious weapon used against women is the psychological line that tells us, "If you're not satisfied with your life, if you can't *adjust* to the feminine role, then something is wrong with *you;* you're frigid, neurotic, castrating, hung-up, a Lesbian, a bitch." This is one tactic they've never been able to use successfully on black

Reprinted from the "Introduction" to *Sisterhood Is Powerful,* edited by Robin Morgan. By permission from Random House, Inc. Copyright © 1970 by Robin Morgan.

people, because that oppression has always been so blatant—but what happens to women ranges from the most subtle to the most brutal, and they've tried to convince us that we want it that way. The argument is "convincingly" reinforced by very real threats, economic, emotional, and social.)

In 1964, Ruby Doris Smith Robinson, a young black woman who was a founder of SNCC (then the Student Non-violent Coordinating Committee) wrote a paper on the position of women in that organization. It was laughed at and dismissed. In 1965, Casey Hayden and Mary King, two white women who had been active in SNCC and other civil-rights organizations for years, wrote an article on women in the Movement for the now-defunct journal *Studies on the Left.* Women began to form caucuses within the Movement organizations where they worked; men's reactions ranged from fury to derision. In 1966, women who demanded that a plank on women's liberation be inserted in the SDS (Students for a Democratic Society) resolution that year were pelted with tomatoes and thrown out of the convention. But the caucuses went on forming, and gradually became small groups all on their own, as women more and more came to see the necessity of an independent women's movement, creating its own theory, politics, tactics, and directing itself toward goals in its own self-interest (which was also the self-interest of more than half the world's population).

Synchronistically, the National Organization for Women (NOW) was formed, in 1966. One of its founders was Betty Friedan, author of *The Feminine Mystique.* A civil-rights organization pledged to "bring women into full participation in the mainstream of American society . . . exercising all the privileges and

responsibilities thereof in truly equal partner-
ship with men." NOW's membership was
mostly comprised of middle- and upper-middle class women (*and men;* it is almost the
only group in the women's movement that
allows male members), professional, middle-
aged, white women. The organization, which
now has members in every state of the union,
as well as about fifty chapters in twenty-four
states, has been called (by some, affection-
ately; by others, pejoratively) "the NAACP of
the women's movement" because it fights
within the System, lobbying legislators,
concentrating on job discrimination, etc.
NOW helped win the airline stewardesses'
fight against mandatory retirement when a
woman married or reached the age of thirty-
five; the group was also almost solely
responsible for the Equal Employment
Opportunities Commission ruling that segregated male-female help-wanted ads in newspapers were discriminatory and illegal. They
have worked hard to change abortion laws
and to call attention to educational discrimination against women.

NOW is essentially an organization that
wants reforms about the second-class citizenship of women—and this is where it
differs drastically from the rest of the Wom-
en's Liberation Movement. Its composite
membership (and remember the men) determines, of course, its politics, which are not
radical. An ecumenical view (which I hold on
alternate Tuesdays and Fridays) would see
that such an organization is extremely valid
and important; it reaches a certain constituency that is never going to be reached by,
say, a group called WITCH, or the Coat Hang-
ers, and it does valuable work, as well. On
certain Mondays and Thursdays, however, I
fear for the women's movement falling into
precisely the same trap as did our foremoth-
ers, the suffragists: creating a bourgeois
feminist movement that never quite dared
enough, never questioned enough, never really reached out beyond its own class and
race. For example, with a few courageous
exceptions, most of the suffragists refused to
examine the family as a structure oppressive
to women. Because of this type of failure,

they wound up having to settle for the vote.
We now see what that got us. The only hope
of a new feminist movement is some kind of
only now barely emerging politics of *revolutionary feminism.* ... That politics comes
from what has been called "rap sessions,"
"bitch sessions," or "consciousness-raising"
which the small groups of radical women began to form around 1966–67. The technique
attracted a lot of ridicule from men; it seems
that when the Chinese used such a technique, "Speak Pains to Recall Pains," it was
right-on revolutionary, but when women
used it, it was "group therapy" or a "hen
party." ... Some groups in the Women's Liberation Movement used consciousness-raising techniques only for a few months before
moving into direct actions; others remained
primarily talk groups and/or study groups;
still others developed along both lines, probably the most healthy combination of "theory
correcting practice, practice correcting theory." ...

In November of 1967, thousands of
women participated in the Jeanette Rankin
Brigade March on Washington to protest the
Vietnam War. There, a group of radical
women, alienated by the dignified Establishment aura of the march, split off to discuss
the possibilities of building an autonomous
women's movement. Over the next year,
brought into clearer focus by women's liberation meetings at various "liberated" colleges (such as Columbia, that spring and
summer), such a movement began to
emerge.

At present, there are women's groups (or
cells), some with names, some without, some
in confederations, some named after the
night on which they meet, in every major city
in the United States, and in many cities of
secondary and tertiary size. Large cities like
New York, Chicago, or Los Angeles tend to
have between fifty to two hundred groups
alone (New York has over two hundred small
groups at last count—and growing rapidly).
Every university in which there has been
even a modicum of student activity, radical
or otherwise, has a women's liberation group
already functioning on campus or in forma-

tion. High-school women are organizing, and OWL (Older Women's Liberation) has come into existence to meet the needs of those women we tend to dismiss as our mothers until we realize that they're also our sisters. There are women's liberation groups in Canada, England, France, Mexico, Japan, Sweden, Germany, Holland, Finland, Tanzania, Australia, and other countries I'll no doubt hear about the minute it's too late to include them in this Introduction.

Alternative institutions are springing up: women's liberation child-care centers and cooperative nurseries; all-women's communes; halfway houses for women separating, divorcing, or recently widowed; abortion counseling and referral services; women's liberation books, magazines, newspapers, and theater groups that can create our own new media, and bail funds to free our political prisoners—among them, prostitutes.

Until recently, the movement seemed to be composed mostly of young white women from middle-class backgrounds (more about this later). But this is beginning to change, partly because the general consciousness about the oppression of women is spreading through all groups and classes, and partly because the women's movement has set itself the task of analyzing divisions (race, class, age, hetero- and homosexuality) that keeps us apart from each other, and is working very concretely to break down those divisions.

Black women, who are obviously doubly oppressed, have, for the most part, chosen to fight beside their black brothers, fighting racism as a priority oppression. But male chauvinism is rampant in the Black Liberation Movement, as well, and there are now women's caucuses forming within black organizations. The SNCC Black Women's Liberation Committee was probably the first; groups of women in the Black Panther Party are getting together, too.*   Women's liberation cells

*Two recent developments of major importance are: the new Black Women's Alliance, and the "Machismo is Fascism" statement by Puerto Rican women in the Young Lords Party.

have, separately and together, been working toward what would be a perfectly organic alliance with welfare-rights organizations, which are made up of women, most of whom are black and brown. We share a common root as *women,* much more natural to both groups than the very *machismo* style of male-dominated organizations, black, brown, *and* white. . . .

The Women's Liberation Movement is the only radical movement I know of today which is dealing with the issue of class—*on a concrete as well as a theoretical basis.* A number of people have written about the "caste and class" analysis: that women could be class enemies but remain caste sisters. Women function as a caste because we class-climb or class-descend *via* our men, and because, in our inter-class and intra-class functions, we still take our definitions *from* men—and those definitions are always that of appendages. Thus the ruling-class woman has no real power herself—she is merely the exquisitely decorated property of a man rich enough to have one slave who does absolutely nothing. Other people do things for her, and they are, of course, poor black and brown and white women. Nevertheless, it is still the "job" of the upper-class woman to "supervise" these tasks: the menu-planning, endless shopping, genteel hostess routine—which is just a diamond-studded variation of the usual female role.

Caste and class analysis notwithstanding, women from working-class backgrounds have been alienated by what has seemed to be a middle-class women's movement. Only recently, people have begun to discover that the women's movement *is* diverse in class origins. One reason for the previous image was that working-class women are of course compelled to strain after middle-class values (what mothers call "marrying well," and sociologists call "upward mobility"), and to *act* middle-class. We all began to discover that a large percentage of the movement comes from working-class backgrounds. Concurrently, as different small groups began to do consciousness-raising on the issues of class and race, whole new areas of political insight opened up in terms of the different forms of oppression experienced by ourselves and our sisters. . . .

It is now the spring of 1970. During the past few months, wildcat strikes by women workers at General Electric, Bendix, and the New York Bell Telephone Company surprised both management and labor; the women felt they had been sold out by the union, which was more concerned about its male members. The first serious woman jockey was pelted by rocks before a major race. Housewives in Stockton, California, went on strike for wages and for a clear definition of their "job"—in writing. Women's caucuses have been formed or are forming in the American Political Science Association, the Anthropological Association, the Modern Language Association, the History Association, and the American Association for the Advancement of Science, among other established professional gatherings. Welfare mothers have been disrupting welfare centers all over the country to protest the bureaucracy that robs them of human dignity. Roman Catholic women are in revolt over the Pill, and Catholic nuns demand greater autonomy from the male clerical hierarchy. Instead of delivering her expected grateful goodbye speech on television, the outgoing Miss USA exposes the commercial way in which she has been used, and denounces her exploiters. Women are marching, picketing, and mounting a variety of actions against abortion laws in every state. Boycotts have been started against billionaire corporations like Procter & Gamble or Lever Brothers, which manipulate women as consumers but are blatantly discriminatory in their own hiring and salary practices. Each television network, and all the major magazines, have had stories on the Women's Liberation Movement—almost all of them written by women because of the movement policy of speaking only to female reporters. Women's Liberation Centers are being set up by local groups all around the country, to try to deal with the women who are pouring into the movement every day. Nurses are organizing. Women in the Armed Forces are organizing. Women have attacked, dis-

rupted, seized, or completely taken over certain media institutions: *Rat* and *High School Free Press,* two major underground radical newspapers, have been taken over completely by women. *Newsweek* women employees brought suit against the magazine for discrimination in salaries, promotions, and assignments. The "mill-in" at the *Ladies' Home Journal* gained, if not a liberated *Journal,* a concession to have at least a liberated supplement in a future issue of the magazine. And in the first "occupation and barricade" action done by women, the executive offices of Grove Press were seized and held for six hours until police were called in. (The sisters were charged with felonies.) The women at Grove were demanding that the millions of dollars earned from pornographic books that degrade women go to set up child-care centers for community and working mothers, a bail fund to free prostitutes, and training programs to prepare women for decent and well-paying jobs. Other demands were that the huge profits made from books written by black and Latin American revolutionaries go to the black and Spanish-speaking communities, to be distributed by the women of those communities.

Meanwhile, a blue-ribbon Presidential panel on the status of women (a panel headed by, of course, two men!) turned in a report warning that women were getting angry, and that unless the government began to act quickly against sexist discriminatory practices, a new "feminist movement that preaches revolution" could become a danger to the established order. Later that month, Nixon solved the whole problem. He created the first two women generals (of the Army) and invaded Cambodia, slaughtering students at Kent State, Augusta, and Jackson on the way. As usual, the women generals had nothing to say about it; they weren't asked. Col. Jeanne Holmes (the highest ranking woman in the Air Force) recently wrote that there was a revolution brewing among women in the military; she implied that any organization that so discriminates within itself (against women) could hardly be other than oppressive in its general policies.

We know that it is not enough to look

around in awe at the rising tide of anger over the lack of "women's rights." We know that we want something more, much more, than the same gray, meaningless, alienating jobs that men are forced to sacrifice their lives to —on the contrary, the technology is such that, if we weren't concerned with sending back color pictures from the moon and were concerned with putting machines to work creatively, no one would have to do those jobs, and no one would have to starve without them. We know that the vote proved useless for our needs (perhaps for those of men, too). We know that the so-called sexual revolution was only another new form of oppression for women. The invention of the Pill made millions for the drug companies, made guinea pigs of us, and made us all the more "available" as sexual objects; if a woman didn't want to go to bed with a man *now,* she must be hung-up. It was inconceivable, naturally, that she might not like the man, or the Pill, or for that matter, sex. We know that "hip culture" and "radical life style"—whatever those mean—have been hip and radical for the men, but filled with the same old chores, harassment, and bottling-up of inner rage for the women, as usual.

But what *do* we want? That's what they always ask us, as if they had expected us, like tidy housekeepers, to come up in five short years with the magic remedy cleanser that will wipe clean the unbelievable mess men have created from their position of power during the past five thousand years.

We're beginning to grope toward some analyses that feel right. We know that two evils clearly pre-date corporate capitalism, and have post-dated socialist revolutions: *sexism* and *racism*—so we know that a male-dominated socialist revolution in economic and even cultural terms, were it to occur tomorrow, would be *no* revolution, but only another coup d'état among men. We know that many historians, scientists, and anthropologists (among them, Briffault, Morgan, Mead, Lévi-Strauss, Childe, Montague, Gorer, and Benedict) note a connection between the concept of property-ownership (primitive capitalism) and the oppression of women. Anthropology has taught us that women probably invented agriculture, were the first to domesticate animals, invented the concept of weaving and of pottery, and (according to Gordon Childe) invented language, which filled a need in their communal work (rather than the necessary silence of the hunters). Anthropologists continue to turn up examples which prove that competitive, aggressive, warlike cultures are those in which sexual stereotypes are most polarized, while those social structures allowing for an overlap of roles and functions between men and women (in tasks, childrearing, decision-making, etc.) tend to be collectivist, cooperative, and peaceful. There are numerous theories about early matriarchal societies, and how and when they were overthrown. . . .

One thing does seem clearer as time goes on: the nuclear family unit is oppressive to women (*and* children, *and* men). The woman is forced into a totally dependent position, paying for her keep with an enormous amount of emotional and physical labor which is not even considered work. As Margaret Benston points out, "In sheer quantity, household labor, including child care, constitutes a huge amount of socially necessary production. Nevertheless, in a society based on commodity production, it is not usually considered as 'real work' since it is outside of trade and the marketplace. . . . In a society in which money determines value, women are a group who work outside the money economy." In essence, women are still back in feudal times. We work outside capitalism, as unpaid labor—and it is the structure of the family that makes this possible, since the employer pays only the husband and, in fact, gets the rest of the family's services for free.
. . .

But if the family as it now exists, with its paranoiac possessiveness of wife and of children, its isolation, and its plain unviability (one out of three American marriages ends in divorce), if this family disappears, what will it be replaced with, and who will determine that? It's obvious that when men think up alternatives (such as divorce or "just living together" or communal living) those alternatives have been known to royally louse women up, so that this time we must create the alternatives that *we* want, those we imagine to be in our self-interest. I, for one, think that some form of extended family structure (something like the old Jewish or Italian families, though not along blood lines, but living companions of choice) might be an answer. The way in which women have so far been used in "alternate culture" communes, however, has made me extremely wary. Instead of cooking Betty Crocker casseroles in Scarsdale, she's stirring brown rice in Arizona or on the Lower East Side, and instead of being the "property" of one man, she's now the "property" of all the men in the collective. It's a thoroughly terrifying subject to explore: what *are* our alternatives? . . .

. . . The only thing I know for certain is that *this* time we women must seize control over our own lives and try, in the process, to salvage the planet from the ecological disaster and nuclear threat created by male-oriented power nations. It is not a small job, and it does seem as if women's work is never done. . . .

Meanwhile, a worldwide revolution is already taking place: Third World peoples, black and brown peoples, are rising up and demanding an end to their neo-colonial status under the economic empire of the United States. The blood of Vietnam, Laos, and Cambodia is mixing with the blood of Jackson, Watts, and Detroit. *How,* we are asked, *can you talk about the comparatively insignificant oppression of women, when set beside the issues of racism and imperialism?*

This is a male-supremacist question. Not only because of its arrogance, but because of its ignorance. First, it dares to weigh and compute human suffering, and it places oppressed groups in competition with each other (an old, and very capitalistic, trick: divide and conquer). Second, the question fails to even minimally grasp the profoundly radical analysis beginning to emerge from revolutionary feminism: that capitalism, imperialism, and racism are *symptoms* of male supremacy—sexism.

Racism as a major contradiction, for example, is surely based on the first "alienizing" act: the basic primary contradiction that occurred with the enslavement of half the hu-

man species by the other half. I think it is no coincidence that all the myths of creation, in all religions, have to do with a "fall from grace" simultaneously with the emergence of set sexual roles.

It also seems obvious that half of all oppressed peoples, black, brown, and otherwise, are *women,* and that I, as a not-starving white American woman living in the very belly of the beast, must fight for those sisters to *survive* before we can even talk together as oppressed women. (Example: in Biafra, most of the millions who died of starvation were women and children. But men were well-fed, since the army needed them kept in good fighting health. That is the essence of male thinking at its most arrogant, *machismo,* militaristic, and *patri*otic. That is sexism.)

More and more, I begin to think of a worldwide Women's Revolution as the only hope for life on the planet. It follows, then, that where women's liberation is, *there* is, for me, the genuine radical movement; I can no more countenance the co-optive lip-service of the male-dominated Left which still stinks of male supremacy than I can countenance the class bias and racism of that male "Movement." I haven't the faintest notion what possible revolutionary role white heterosexual men could fulfill, since they are the very embodiment of reactionary-vested-interest-power. But then, I have great difficulty examining what men in general could possibly do about all this. In addition to doing the shitwork that women have been doing for generations, possibly not exist? No, I really don't mean that. Yes, I really do. Never mind, that's another whole book.

What I began to say earlier, though, was that the differences between "politico" and "feminist" women (as with other divisions of class, race, age, occupation, etc.) are possibly smokescreens, defenses from seeing a frightening truth, resistances to a consciousness that no matter what we are, say, do, or believe, there is no getting away from the shared, primary oppression of being female in a patriarchal world.

You, sister, reading this: I have no earthly way of knowing if you are already involved in women's liberation, and if so, how deeply; perhaps you have never yet been to one women's meeting, but only read and heard things about the movement in magazines and on TV; perhaps you find you have picked up the book out of anger, or defiance, or on a dare, or from genuine curiosity, or cynical amusement—or even as part of your job or your school course. I hope this book means something to you, makes some real change in your heart and head—and I take a terrific risk in saying such a corny thing, because I don't mean it as any sort of "hope you liked the book" statement. No, I mean it desperately, because if we who have put this together have failed you somehow, then we have failed ourselves seriously—because *you* are women's liberation. This is not a movement one "joins." There are no rigid structures or membership cards. The Women's Liberation Movement exists where three or four friends or neighbors decide to meet regularly over coffee and talk about their personal lives. It also exists in the cells of women's jails, on the welfare lines, in the supermarket, the factory, the convent, the farm, the maternity ward, the streetcorner, the old ladies' home, the kitchen, the steno pool, the bed. It exists in your mind, and in the political and personal insights that you can contribute to change and shape and help its growth. It is frightening. It is very exhilarating. It is creating history, or rather, *herstory.*

And anyway, you cannot escape it.

25   Seizing the Time

Bobby Seale

Brother Huey P. Newton put the Black Panther Party into motion. Brother Huey is the Minister of Defense and leader of the Black Panther Party. He is presently a political prisoner, but he is still the philosophical theoretician, the practitioner, the head director, and top official spokesman for the Black Panther Party. It is impossible to talk about the Black Panther Party without first talking about Huey P. Newton, because brother Huey put it all into motion. We sometimes talk about "the genius of Huey P. Newton."

I met Huey P. Newton in the early sixties, during the Cuban blockade when there were numerous street rallies going on around Mer-
ritt Junior College in West Oakland. One particular day there was a lot of discussion about black people and the blockade against Cuba. People were out in front of the college, in the streets, grouped up in bunches of 200,250, what have you. Huey was holding down a crowd of about 250 people and I was one of the participants. After he held the conversation down to what in those days they called "shooting everybody down"—that means rapping off information and throwing facts—people would ask Huey a question or refer to something he said. They tried to shoot Huey down by citing some passage in a book concerning the subject matter being discussed, and before they knew it, Huey whipped out a copy of *Black Bourgeoisie* by E. Franklin Frazier and showed him what page, what paragraph, and corrected the person.

I guess I had the idea that I was supposed to ask questions in college, so I walked over to Huey and asked the brother, weren't all these civil rights laws the NAACP was trying to get for us doing us some good? And he shot me down too, just like he shot a whole lot of other people down. He said, it's all a waste of money, black people don't have anything in this country that is for them. He went on to say that the laws already on the books weren't even serving them in the first place, and what's the use of making more laws when what was needed was to enforce the present laws? So all the money that the people were giving to Martin Luther King and the rest who were supposed to put these laws on the books for black people, was a waste of the black people's money. I was ready to accept that when he started citing many more facts to back up his point of view.

Huey always brings out basic, practical things; that's the way he talks to you, that's the way he explains things to you. He gets to a point where you can't get around, so you have to face things.

That's the kind of atmosphere I met Huey in. And all the conflicts of this meeting, all this blowing that was going on in the streets that day during the Cuban crisis, all of that was involved with his association with the Afro-American Association. A lot of arguments came down. A lot of people were discussing with three or four cats in the Afro-American Association, which was developing the first black nationalist philosophy on the West Coast.

They got me caught up. They made me feel that I had to help out, be a part and do something, to help out some way. One or two days later I went around looking for Huey at the school, and I went to the library. I found Huey in the library, and I asked him where the meetings were. He gave me an address and told me that there were book discussions. And then he told me the name of the book they were discussing at the time, which was *Black Bourgeoisie.*

Huey was a large influence on the whole campus. I got to know where Huey was on campus. I wasn't a running partner of Huey's then, but I was catching him on the streets. We would all wig out behind brother Huey, and I guess everybody respected Huey's mind and also Huey's guts. He had something about him, that he didn't drive over people, but he would never let anyone drive over him. Especially in a violent and rowdy fashion because—I didn't know it at the time but I learned later—Huey had a kind of hidden reputation on the block with the brothers.

There were cats all over East and West Oakland who had reputations for being bad, and they were known throughout the community for being bad. Huey didn't have this kind of reputation. The bad cats terrorized the community—and Huey terrorized the bad cats. You heard a lot of stories about Huey. Like one night at a party, Huey accidentally stepped on some brother's shoes, and Huey stepped back and he said, "Excuse me, brother." The brother—he was bad, one of those bad dudes—he said, "Motherfucker, 'scuse me, don't reshine my shoes." Huey knew his brothers very well. When the dude slid back to the side and dropped his arm slightly to the right, hanging behind his right thigh, Huey saw this. He knew this was the time to fire. Next thing you knew, Huey fired on him and decked him, and all the other bad dudes at the party who were this decked dude's friends or partners wanted to know who this cat thinks he is. And so they jumped up and said that Huey needs his ass kicked, and Huey told them, "I'll fight all of you one at a time or all of you at the same time and you won't wait outside for me, I'll be waiting outside for you." And then he walked outside and waited and dared them to come outside.

And this is something I think Huey understood too, that he would shock them because he was as bad as the noted dudes in the area. He shocked them because he had nerve enough to fight all of them. They would come outside and think they could get around him, or start sneaking around him to try and deck him, and the next thing you knew, Huey would come out with a fourteen- or fifteen-inch machete and he'd be righteously trying to whip heads and cut up some ass, and he would have niggers running everywhere.

There's another thing about Huey. I remember one time, there were some black nationalists, cultural nationalists, on the campus who used to project all this cultural nationalism.* They were so engrossed in this cultural nationalism, they just *hated* white people simply for the color of their skin. This is where Huey and I got this thing about cultural nationalists. Huey had opened the door for a sister to go through. You know how a man opens the door for a woman? There happened to be a white girl, coming right behind the sister, and so the white girl walked in. So one of the cultural nationalists ran up to him and said, "How come you opened the door for that white girl?" And Huey turned around and looked at him. He said, "Look man, I'm a human being and I'm not a fool. I opened the door for the sister. There happened to be a white girl behind her. The white girl's not attacking me. She's not brutalizing me. So there's nothing wrong with me keeping the door open for her to pass through, too." And the cultural nationalists just went out of their minds, exaggerating the shit. That's just one point to show Huey's humanism toward all other human beings; this is the way he is. . . .

One day I went over to his house and asked him if he has read Fanon. I'd read *Wretched of the Earth* six times. I knew Fanon was right and I knew he was running it down—but how do you put ideas like this over? Huey was

laying up in bed, thinking, plotting on the man. I knew what he was doing. He used to tell me how he was plotting to make himself some money on the man. He was always involved with day-to-day survival like the average brother on the block.

He said no, he hadn't read Fanon. So I brought Fanon over one day. That brother got to reading Fanon, and man, let me tell you, when Huey got ahold of Fanon, and read Fanon (I had been always running down about how we need this organization, that organization, but never anything concrete), Huey'd be thinking. Hard. We would sit down with *Wretched of the Earth* and talk, go over another section or chapter of Fanon, and Huey would explain it in depth. It was the first time I ever had anybody who could show a clear-cut perception of what was said in one sentence, a paragraph, or chapter, and not have to read it again. He knew it already. He'd get on the streets. We'd be walking down the street and get in some discussion with somebody, and throughout the process of this discussion and argument, Huey would be citing facts, citing that material, and giving perception to it. At that time he was giving the same basic concepts as he's giving now, but now he's in a wider and broader area, because he's had a lot of experience in leadership in the Black Panther Party. His development now is at the head of the revolutionary struggle. But he always had this vast ability to do things along with a proper perspective, and he could run it down and get things going.

Huey was one for implementing things, and I guess this is where the Black Panther Party really started. . . .

THE PANTHER PROGRAM

One day Huey said, "It's about time we get the organization off the ground, and do it now."

This was in the latter part of September 1966. From around the first of October to the fifteenth of October, in the poverty center in

---

*Cultural nationalists and Black Panthers are in conflict in many areas. Basically, cultural nationalism sees the white man as the oppressor and makes no distinction between racist whites and non-racist whites, as the Panthers do. The cultural naturalists say that a black man cannot be an enemy of the black people, while the Panthers believe that black capitalists are exploiters and oppressors. Although the Black Panther Party believes in black nationalism and black culture, it does not believe that either will lead to black liberation or the overthrow of the capitalist system, and are therefore ineffective.—Ed.

North Oakland, Huey and I began to write out a ten-point platform and program of the Black Panther Party. Huey himself articulated it word for word. All I made were suggestions.

Huey said, "We need a program. We have to have a program for the people. A program that relates to the people. A program that the people can understand. A program that the people can read and see, and which expresses their desires and needs at the same time. It's got to relate to the philosophical meaning of where in the world we are going, but the philosophical meaning will also have to relate to something specific."

That was very important with Huey. So, Huey divided it up into "What We Want" and "What We Believe." "What We Want" are the practical, specific things that we need and that should exist. At the same time, we expressed philosophically, but concretely, what we believe. So we read the program one to one. Point One of "What We Want" and Point One of "What We Believe." Point Two of "What We Want" and Point Two of "What We Believe." This is the way the people should look at it. It puts together concisely all the physical needs and all the philosophical principles in some basic instructive thing that they can understand, instead of a bunch of esoteric bullshit. . . .

When we got all through writing the program, Huey said, "We've got to have some kind of structure. What do you want to be," he asked me, "Chairman or Minister of Defense?"

"Doesn't make any difference to me," I said. "What do you want to be, Chairman or Minister of Defense?"

"I'll be the Minister of Defense," Huey said, "and you'll be the Chairman."

"That's fine with me," I told him, and that's just the way that shit came about, how Huey became the Minister of Defense and I became the Chairman of the Black Panther Party. Just like that.

With the ten-point platform and program and the two of us, the Party was officially launched on October 15, 1966, in a poverty program office in the black community in Oakland, California. . . .

Here is the ten-point platform and program as it appears each week in our paper:

BLACK PANTHER PARTY PLATFORM AND PROGRAM WHAT WE WANT WHAT WE BELIEVE

1. *We want freedom. We want power to determine the destiny of our Black Community.*

We believe that black people will not be free until we are able to determine our destiny.

2. *We want full employment for our people.*

We believe that the federal government is responsible and obligated to give every man employment or a guaranteed income. We believe that if the white American businessmen will not give full employment, then the means of production should be taken from the businessmen and placed in the community so that the people of the community can organize and employ all of its people and give a high standard of living.

3. *We want an end to the robbery by the white man of our Black Community.*

We believe that this racist government has robbed us and now we are demanding the overdue debt of forty acres and two mules. Forty acres and two mules was promised 100 years ago as restitution for slave labor and mass murder of black people. We will accept the payment in currency which will be distributed to our many communities. The Germans are now aiding the Jews in Israel for the genocide of the Jewish people. The Germans murdered six million Jews. The American racist has taken part in the slaughter of over fifty million black people; therefore, we feel that this is a modest demand that we make.

4. *We want decent housing, fit for shelter of human beings.*

We believe that if the white landlords will not give decent housing to our black community, then the housing and the land should be made into cooperatives so that our community, with government aid, can build and make decent housing for its people.

5. *We want education for our people that exposes the true nature of this decadent American society. We want education that teaches us our true history and our role in the present-day society.*

We believe in an educational system that will give to our people a knowledge of self. If a man does not have knowledge of himself and his position in society and the world, then he has little chance to relate to anything else.

6. *We want all black men to be exempt from military service.*

We believe that black people should not be forced to fight in the military service to defend a racist government that does not protect us. We will not fight and kill other people of color in the world who, like black people, are being victimized by the white racist government of America. We will protect ourselves from the force and violence of the racist people and the racist military, by whatever means necessary.

7. *We want an immediate end to POLICE BRUTALITY and MURDER of black people.*

We believe we can end police brutality in our black community by organizing black self-defense groups that are dedicated to defending our black community from racist police oppression and brutality. The Second Amendment to the Constitution of the United States gives a right to bear arms. We therefore believe that all people should arm themselves for self-defense.

8. *We want freedom for all black men held in federal, state, county, and city prisons and jails.*

We believe that all black people should be released from the many jails and prisons because they have not received a fair and impartial trial.

9. *We want all black people when brought to trial to be tried in court by a jury of their peer group or people*

from their black communities, as defined by the Constitution of the United States.

We believe that the courts should follow the United States Constitution so that black people will receive fair trials. The Fourteenth Amendment of the U. S. Constitution gives a man a right to be tried by his peer group. A peer is a person from a similar economic, social, religious, geographical, environmental, historical, and racial background. To do this the court will be forced to select a jury from the black community from which the black defendant came. We have been and are being tried by all-white juries that have no understanding of the "average reasoning man" of the black community.

10; *We want land, bread, housing, education, clothing, justice, and peace. And as our major political objective, a United Nations-supervised plebiscite to be held throughout the black colony in which only black colonial subjects will be allowed to participate, for the purpose of determining the will of black people as to their national destiny.*

When, in the course of human events, it becomes necessary for one people to dissolve the political bands which have connected them with another, and to assume, among the powers of the earth, the separate and equal station to which the laws of nature and nature's God entitle them, a decent respect to the opinions of mankind requires that they should declare the causes which impel them to the separation.

We hold these truths to be self-evident, that all men are created equal; that they are endowed by their Creator with certain inalienable rights; that among these are life, liberty, and the pursuit of happiness. That, to secure these rights, governments are instituted among men, deriving their just powers from the consent of the governed; that, whenever any form of government becomes destructive of these ends, it is the right of the people to alter or to abolish it, and to institute a new government, laying its foundation on such principles, and organizing its powers in such form, as to them shall seem most likely to effect their safety and happiness. Prudence, indeed, will dictate that governments long established should not be changed for light and transient causes; and, accordingly, all experience hath shown, that mankind are more disposed to suffer, while evils are sufferable, than to right themselves by abolishing the forms to which they are accustomed. But, when a long train of abuses and unsurpations, pursuing invariably the same object, evinces a design to reduce them under absolute despotism, it is their right, it is their duty, to throw off such government, and to provide new guards for their future security. . . .

* * *

Late in November 1966, we went to a Third World brother we knew, a Japanese radical cat. He had guns for a motherfucker: .357 Magnums, 22's, 9mm's, what have you. We told him that we wanted these guns to begin to institutionalize and let black people know that we have to defend ourselves as Malcolm X said we must. We didn't have any money to buy guns. We told him that if he was a real revolutionary he'd better go on and give them up to us because we needed them now to begin educating the people to wage a revolutionary struggle. So he gave us an M-1 and a 9mm.

There was a law service section up in the poverty program office, and Huey studied those law books, backwards, forwards, sideways, and cattycorners; everything on gun laws. And I was right there with him, trying to study them too, run them down, and understand them. Huey knew that he could carry a rifle or a shotgun. His probation officer had run this down to him—he could carry a rifle or a shotgun, but he couldn't carry a pistol. So I carried the pistol, and Huey P. Newton carried the M-1. . . .

So we floated around the streets, and we patroled pigs. We followed pigs. They wouldn't even know we'd be following them. That's the way that shit went down in the very beginning. That went on for a month,

back there in December 1966. Sometimes we'd just be high, going to a party. We might not have guns. Other times, we'd have guns. Still other times we weren't even going to a party. We'd just be going to a meeting. We'd have our shit with us, and while we were going to the meeting we'd patrol those pigs, trying to catch them wrong. We'd see a pig, we'd get keyed off the meeting. We'd just forget about the meeting, and patrol that pig, just drive around behind him, a long time. After that, we'd go to the meeting. That's how interrelated that shit was. We went to a lot of meetings.

About this time Huey said, "Let's get these brothers together and let's get us an office." That was very important to Huey, because the establishment of an office meant that something was functional. The people in the black community could relate to it. Around the corner from my house, about a block and a half away, there was a vacant store. Huey and Bobby Hutton went and got it for us. Bobby Hutton said, "I'm a member of the Black Panther Party." And Huey says, "You're the first member, a righteous member." He righteously came in then as a righteous member. From there, we got our little pay checks from the poverty program—Bobby Hutton, Huey, and I. We put all our money together and paid the first rent on the first office. We rented that first office for $150 a month on Fifty-sixth and Grove in Oakland.

We got off in that office and we painted a sign in the window—Black Panther Party for Self-Defense. This is what it was named at the time and a lot of people came by in those first days that we opened that office. We opened it January 1, 1967. We announced that we were going to have a first meeting of the Black Panther Party on Saturday, one week later. We opened up the office with the new name on the window and brothers came into the office and sat down and heard what we had to say. We passed out the ten-point platform and program of the Black Panther Party. . . .

Huey was on a level where he was ready to organize the black brothers for a righteous revolutionary struggle with guns and force. It came to a point where, every day, we walked in and out of the Black Panther office, around to my house or around to Bobby Hutton's house, or somebody's house, with guns on our sides, and got in a car, or two or three cars, or four or five cars as it built up, and patroled the pigs on Friday and Saturday nights. Sometimes when we went to a meeting during the week we patroled the pigs. We had a camera or two, a law book, and were working on getting some tape recorders in patroling the pig cops. . . .

BADGE 206

One night Huey, Little Bobby, and I were patroling this pig in North Oakland. We had been patroling him for a couple of hours. We'd be about a block away from him wherever he'd go. Sometimes we'd stop and lose the pig, but ten, twenty minutes later he'd make it around again, he'd be back where he was, and we'd patrol him some more. Little Bobby had an M-1, I had a .45, and brother Huey had a shotgun and a law book on the back seat. Brother Huey was driving my old '54 Chevy. I guess we patroled for quite a while, then on Fifty-eighth Street we saw the pig stop up at the corner. We stopped at the corner, and he backed up and parked right in front of the stop sign at the corner of Fifty-eighth and Grove. I remember us saying we were tired of patroling this pig, "let's go in." It was about 8:30 or 9:30 when we drove down the street and stopped next to the pig. We were stopped at the stop sign. I looked over at the pig. Naturally we were carrying guns in Oakland in those days. The shotgun barrel was sticking up. I was holding on to the shotgun while Huey drove. I was on the righthand side of the front seat and the shotgun was to my left, next to my left leg. It was standing straight up resting on its butt. I looked over at the pig, the pig looked back and looked over to me and to Little Bobby, who had his M-1 in the back seat between his legs, the barrel of it showing through the window, too.

Huey had completed his stop and he started off again and started turning right, right in front of the pig's car. As we were turning right, the pig flashed his lights on and he flashed his high beams on. Huey kept moving. He didn't stop and didn't speed up. See, those pigs don't shake Huey at all. I guess we drove no more than twenty feet when we could see the red light flashing. He was starting his engine up and pulling out of the spot where he was parked, making a right turn right behind us. Huey kept moving. He got ready to make a left turn right there at the next little corner. He made his left turn and said, "I'm not going to stop till he puts his damn siren on because a flashing red light really don't mean nothin', anything could be a flashing red light." Well, the pig cut his siren on as he was turning the corner following us and when he cut his siren on, Huey stopped. We'd been stopped by pigs a number of times, pigs who'd seen us with guns and didn't know what to do. We were down with it because Huey had put us together and knew how to handle the situation.

This pig surprised us because he stopped his car as soon as we stopped. He stopped his car about twenty-five feet in back of our car. Some pigs stop right up behind you, but he was twenty-five feet from us. He got out of his car and as soon as he did, and came walking from his door, we could hear this pig hollering, "What the goddam hell you niggers doing with them goddam guns? Who in the goddam hell you niggers think you are? Get out of that goddam car. Get out of that goddam car with them goddam guns."

I said, "Huey, this motherfucker's trying to get killed, man. Listen to him."

As he walked up to the car, he said, "Get out of that car."

Huey said, "You ain't putting nobody under arrest. Who the hell you think you are?"

The pig snatched the door open. When he snatched it open, he said, "I said get out of that goddam car and bring them goddam guns out of there."

Huey said, "Man, what the hell?" By this time the pig came all the way up, his head inside the door, and he's reaching across Huey real fast. This all happened so fast. He was grabbing hold of the barrel of the shotgun, and I tightened up on it and pulled it away from him. At the same time I was pulling the shotgun away from him, Huey grabbed this pig by the collar, pushed his head back up against the roof of the car, then shifted around and got his foot and kicked him in the belly, shoving him all the way out of the car. The pig fell backwards about ten feet from the car but as he was going out, no sooner had Huey finished putting his foot in this pig's belly, kicking and pushing him out of the car—and the pig was being propelled and off balance, away from the car—then Huey was grabbing hold of the barrel of the shotgun. No sooner did brother Huey's feet hit the ground, but he was jacking a round off into the chamber, "Clack upp," and taking three quick steps.

The pig looked up and looked around, and Huey P. Newton was standing there saying, "Now who in the hell do you think you are, you big rednecked bastard, you rotten fascist swine, you bigoted racist? You come into my car, trying to brutalize me and take my property away from me. Go for your gun and you're a dead pig." The pig folded his hands up. By this time I'd gotten out of the car on the other side, put the .45 in my hand, and pulled the hammer back. As soon as Huey finished saying what he had to say, Little Bobby jumped out on the back of our car and jacked a round off in the M-1. The pig heard these clicks and looked back at Huey, and the pig folded his hands up. In other words, he was taking his hands away from his gun. Huey had said, "Go for your gun and you're a dead pig. Don't you know by the Fourteenth Amendment of the U.S. Constitution that you can't remove a person's property from them without due process of law." Huey was mad, loud, and articulate.

The pig began to walk and he kind of did a half-moon, walking around and away from Huey, trying to walk back to his car. Huey just stepped back holding his gun on him and the pig came walking back to his car hollering, "They got guns. They got guns. They got

guns." He got on his radio, "Niggers down here got guns. Get me some help down here. Niggers got guns, they got guns." This pig was scared.

Black people began to come out of their houses, wanting to know what was going on. Huey said, "Come on out, black people. Come on out and get to know about these racist dog swine who been controlling our community and occupying our community like a foreign troop. Come on out and we're going to show you about swine pigs." People got to coming out. It must have been around 9:30 because we were in the back of Merritt College and people in night school were coming out, and I guess seventy or eighty had gathered up there before the other pigs got there. They had about fifteen cars come down there—fifteen cars and pigs everywhere. So me and Huey and Little Bobby were there with our guns. The people were there. I think Little Bobby placed his gun right back on the back seat again. He was sitting in the seat and he shut the door and got back out. Huey and I had been warning Little Bobby about keeping in his possession the written permission he had, and to carry with him the written permission thing from his father to carry and keep the gun because he was still under eighteen at the time, and I think he didn't have it. He realized that he'd better lay the gun down.

Huey was talking to most of the people and running it down to the people about how racism was rotten. How these pigs were brutal and murderous racists. And every time Huey said something I'd say it right behind him, I'd say the same thing, I'd say, "That's right." And he would say, "Racist dog pigs occupy our community, come down here to brutalize and kill and murder us. I'm tired of it," and I'd say, "That's right, racist dogs, pigs occupying our community like a foreign troop that occupies territory. Black people are tired of it." Every time Huey said something, I'd say something. The pigs must have thought that we was crazy niggers. A pig walks up and says, "Let me see that weapon!"

Huey says, "Let you see my weapon? You haven't placed me under arrest."

"Well, you just let me see the weapon, I have a right to see the weapon."

Huey says, "Ain't you ever heard of the Fourteenth Amendment of the Consitution of the United States? Don't you know you don't remove nobody's property without due process of law?" Huey got loud at those last words. "What's the matter with you? You're supposed to be people enforcing the law, and here you are, ready to violate my constitutional rights. You can't see my gun. You can't have my gun. The only way you're gonna get it from me is to try to take it."

Then another pig walks up to me, "Come over here by the car."

"I ain't going no goddam place. Who the hell you think you are? You ain't placed me under arrest."

"But I have a right to take you over to the car."

"You don't have no right to move me from one spot to another."

Huey P. Newton, the Minister of Defense, teaches us and runs it down to us that whenever a cop moves a person from one spot to another, then he's technically under arrest, and if the cop states that you're not under arrest, or doesn't say you're under arrest when you ask, then he has no right to ask you to move from one spot to another.

"You just got through telling me I wasn't under arrest, so I'm not moving nowhere, I'm staying right here."

"Well, you let me see that gun."

"I said you can't see my gun," and I ran down the Fourteenth Amendment of the Constitution just like Huey had run it down. The pigs were frustrated, mad, and didn't know what to do.

"Well, I got a right to look at the serial number."

"I already know what the serial number is," I said.

"I got to make sure it has a serial number." So I held my gun in my hand and he looked at it with his flashlight. "Hold it up, let me see."

"No, I ain't holding up nothing. You got a flashlight so you look at it from that distance right there, because you don't get near this gun." So I read the serial number, and I said, "There's the serial."

The pig took the serial number down and after that a police lieutenant came down, and he kept saying, "Well, if we charge him, we'll probably lose the case, just for them having guns, we'll probably lose the case because they turn around the Second Amendment of the Constitution about them having a right to carry guns as long as they ain't concealed."

Then one big fat pig says, "Well, we gotta find something. We gotta find something to do to them." He was looking down, he started looking the car over and he said that the license plate was being held on by a coat hanger. It was secure all right, but it was just put together with a coat hanger. "Let's give them a ticket for this here, this here license plate is not adequately secure." He asked Huey for some identification and Huey handed him his license. They said his license looked kind of old so they gave him a ticket for not having a good new license. Huey later went to court, pleaded not guilty on both counts, and beat both tickets.

The pigs jumped up and left the scene and the black people were asking what was happening. While Huey was calling the pigs all kinds of names and stuff, a lot of the brothers said, "Right on time, Huey. Tell it. Right. Run it down, Huey." Huey talked to the people some more and a lot of them said they were going to come down and join the Black Panther Party. And we did get some of the older brothers and sisters and some younger brothers and sisters out there to join. Even a number of white people had a chance to watch that.

Badge 206 was the cop. The cop who almost got his head blown away that night. I kept telling him he was acting a fool. Badge 206. Badge 206. We never forgot his badge. I remembered his badge, Huey remembered his badge. We put his number on the front page of our newspaper. . . .

THE DEATH OF DENZIL DOWELL

The Black Panther Party was called to Richmond by the Dowell Family. They had heard of the Black Panther Party over in Oakland. Mark Comfort came down to the office at Fifty-sixth and Grove, and told us that the Dowell family would like us to come over because Denzil Dowell had been killed in Richmond by a Contra Costa County deputy sheriff.

We went out there that day and saw the Dowell family. They began to explain all the details about how certain people had said they heard ten shots, and the papers and the local media there were saying that only two or three shots were fired. And how the coroner's office had originally told them he was shot nine or ten times, but the police department said he was only shot once or twice. How the pigs had lied about Denzil Dowell, the brother, telling about how he was trying to burglarize some place.

His brothers, Carl Dowell and George Dowell, explained how the pigs knew Denzil by name, because they had arrested him a number of times. The pigs had made threats that they were going to get Denzil. It was just a cold-blooded killing of a black man. Some pigs were trigger-happy and wanted to shoot somebody, shoot a "nigger."

They explained all this to us. Then the family took us over to the site where they killed brother Denzil Dowell, and showed us just where the bullets hit certain walls and the direction they came from, and how the pigs lied and said that he ran and jumped a fence. The blood was twenty yards away from the fence. They must have dragged his body over to the other side, and then over another fence. The blood was in two different places.

We were investigating, and a lot of black people in the black community there came out. They had noticed us Panthers, with our guns and everything. I guess there were ten or twelve of us who went out there together and went through the whole process of investigation, of looking over what had happened, and listening to the information that people were giving that contradicted all the crap that the pigs and the newspapers had run down. And the people were looking.

We were standing on the corner there in North Richmond. There were about 150 people around, some in cars, some standing across the street. Some of the younger brothers, fifteen, sixteen, some twenty years old, were asking us about the guns, and we were explaining to them about the Black Panther Party. All of a sudden some sister hollers out, "Uh, oh . . . here come the *cops.*"

When the sister hollered, Huey jacked a round off into the chamber of his eighteen-inch shotgun with a loud click and clack. When he did that, I unhitched the strap that held the hammer down on my .45, and it clacked too. People started moving back. Some of them went across the street. Some got in their cars and drove up the street. Then the pigs came down and Huey stepped to the curb. I followed Huey and stepped to the curb, a few feet down from him. The pigs were surprised all of a sudden. They looked and noticed who was ready and standing tall for them. The pigs kept driving, drove right on off—in fact, they speeded on up and drove on away. Then the people moved on back, and some of them jumped around across the street, figuring there was going to be a shoot-out, but we just stood tall, ready to defend ourselves. We were educating the people that we would die here for them. This was the position we always took with brother Huey P. Newton.

We told the people there that we were going to have a rally that coming Saturday, on the corner of Third and Chesley, right down the street. We said we'd run down and educate them about the fact that we'd have to start using guns to defend ourselves, because the racist pig cops were coming to our community and murdering our brothers and sisters. Brother Denzil Dowell was killed, and we'd found information out about two, three other brothers who'd been shot up back in December, in North Richmond there. The brothers had been shot in the armpits, which clearly showed they had their arms over their heads. Two brothers were killed in December and around April 1 Denzil Dowell was gunned down by those pigs. Huey told them we were going to have a rally concerning this, to tell the people it was necessary for us to arm ourselves for self-defense.

We went forth to have this rally, and we got about twenty brothers together with their pieces and their uniforms. We had the rally right there on the corner of Third and Chesley. We got guns and a force to defend ourselves. "Ain't no pigs going to come down here and stop our street rally. We're going to exercise our constitutional rights to free speech. And we're going to have a rally right here on the corner." Most of North Richmond doesn't have sidewalks at all. But for that section on the corner there, in front of this liquor store, there's an eight-to-ten-foot sidewalk between the curb and the store. We got right out there on the corner, and all the brothers out there in this community saw us with the guns. We lined up all along the streets.

Imagine an intersection now. On one corner we put four, five brothers, and they were spread out about twenty, thirty feet from each other, coming around the corner. Across the street, we put a brother on the corner, then two brothers down from him, thirty or forty feet apart. Then on the corner where Huey and I were speaking, right there in front of the liquor store, we lined that corner up going east and west. Then we lined the other corner up as you go north and south. So the whole intersection was lined up with Panthers all up and down the corners, going north, east, west, and south on both sides of the streets. And we had our guns, shotguns, pistols, and everything.

The people began to line up and brother Huey told me to go ahead and start blowing. So I started blowing to the brothers there, running down to them about the ten-point platform and program, what kind of organization we had now, about the fact that brother Denzil Dowell had been killed by some racist dog Gestapo pigs. And the fact that we must begin to unify and organize with guns and force. That the Black Panther Party had come to North Richmond, and the Black Panther Party is there to serve the people, it's going to be a black people's party. I guess about two or three hundred people gathered around. In fact, people in cars just stopped, and the whole section on the one side of the street was just a line of cars. And on the other side, coming right up to the intersection, there was another line of cars. Some cars were still moving by, going on the

other side of the street, driving up the wrong side of the street.

I was blowing there, and then all of a sudden they start sending some sheriffs in. The people had noticed that we were there, we were there with our guns, we were back again. The pigs started driving down the streets, the sheriff's pigs. Huey whispered, he said, "Run it down about the pigs, Bobby. About how we're going to hold this street rally, and how we're going to exercise our right of free speech. No pig's going to stop it." And he said, "Tell them about the reason why no pig's going to stop it. It's because we've got guns and force here to protect ourselves, to protect the people."

So I ran it down to the brothers, and pointed to the pigs, and the pigs got nervous. I noticed one of the pigs stopped across the street and sat there, and started listening. Four of the brothers came across the street and surrounded the pig car, standing about nine, ten feet away from it. One brother had a .357 Magnum, Warren Tucker had a .38 pistol hanging on him, and Reginald Forte had a 9mm pistol. One brother didn't even have a gun and he got up there too. Then the pig got nervous. He started trying to light a cigarette, but the cigarette just fell out of his hand, with all these people looking at him. The black people had guns and force, ready to deal with the pigs, and the pig couldn't take it any more, he couldn't light his cigarette he was so nervous, he just up and drove away. The people yelled and raved at the fact.

Huey P. Newton had placed the notion in their minds that we organize. I think the people respected the fact that Huey had all of the brothers organized, because he had them all stationed up and down the streets, covering the intersection, guarding the lives of the black people, while we went forth to organize the people. They respected this organization that Huey put down. Huey put down a form, a discipline, that the gun was for our protection, and not for bull jive. So the pig had to split.

Another pig was sitting there. This other pig came up in a car and some of the people's cars moved along. But one man said,

"Well, I ain't moving my car. I'm going to sit here and listen." And this cop got caught in between the cars and he couldn't move and he had to sit there and listen to everything. He couldn't do nothing. And that brother didn't move his car. He had a Cadillac too, and he and his woman were sitting in the Cadillac, sitting right at the head of the intersection. So this pig's car was right in between, and he couldn't move, he just had to sit there and listen, and look at 300, that's right, he had to look at 300 mad niggers—mad at the pigs for killing Denzil Dowell. And twenty Panthers out there armed with guns, disciplined, standing thirty or forty feet apart, on every corner of the intersection. So it was tied down.

The people dug it and they said, "Right on." And Huey went on and blew to the brothers and sisters and told them how we're going to get organized and how we're going to start using guns and force in an organized and disciplined manner. In a very revolutionary manner we're going to go forth, and we're going to defend ourselves against any racist attacks. And we're going to patrol these pigs, we're going to patrol our own communities, even the old people are going to have to patrol from their homes and houses. And everybody has to have a shotgun in his home, everybody. Then George Dowell blew about how his brother, Denzil, had been murdered by the pigs. We said we were going to have another meeting over on Second Street, and Huey said we're going to block the whole street off, and ain't no pigs going to be allowed up the street ... *at all.*

At the second Richmond rally, three or four hundred people came up. They drove their cars all inside the street, and brothers got on top of cars and top of roofs all up and down the street, from one corner to the next, and it was a pretty long block. The whole street was cluttered with cars. We were at one particular address, where I think some relative of George Dowell lived. This was right around the corner from George Dowell's mother's home. All the people came around and we had applications there for people to join the Party. I guess just about everybody out there joined the Party that day, from little young fourteen-year-olds and twelve-year-olds.

We blocked the whole street off. Brother Huey blew, I blew, brother Eldridge Cleaver came over and he blew to the people, and the people dug it, and the people filled out the applications.

One incident happened there. I noticed that one of the brothers moved some four, five guns to one of the corners. We were in the center of the block. Some more of the extra brothers had been moved down to one of the corners. The corner on the north end. The brother explained to me (I was blowing at the time) that one of the pigs had come up at the corner down there, so the brothers blocked the street off. One of the pigs was sitting there. So a couple of other brothers went over to a vacant lot and stood with their M-1's and 30-. 06's, looking at the pig's car. They couldn't have been thirty yards from the pigs. Stood staring right at the pigs' car, and the pigs looked around and one of them saw another brother walk up near his car, and stand there almost like at parade rest, but with his hand just a few inches from his .357 Magnum. And the pig looked at him when he got up there, then he looked at his partner, and he said, "That's a .357 Magnum he's got!" And when he said that, the pig turned his engine on and he got out of there and didn't come back.

Then a helicopter came around. We blocked off the whole street and held a people's rally, with power, gun power. Gun power's the only thing that backed it up. So all they could do was send a helicopter over, flap, flap, flapping all day long to try and bother us. This time it wasn't only the Black Panthers who came, but other people came there, with their rifles, with their guns, and with their pieces. I noticed some older brothers come out and they were shaking hands with a lot of us, and they had their pieces under their shirts. They just carried them concealed. And some sisters. One sister came out and jumped out of her car with an M-1. We saw the black community people getting uptight and ready. And the helicopter kept flapping over and Huey pointed up at the helicopter as it was going over and said,

"Always remember that *the spirit of the people is greater than the man's technology.*" And the people said, "Right on." I remember we got way over 300 applications.

The community people got together and George Dowell's sisters and brothers and friends got together and began to have a regular session. And everyone would come to the meeting with the people of North Richmond. The brothers had their guns on. They were tired, sick and tired, and they loved brother Huey. They thought brother Huey was out of sight. He was a beautiful leader, and Huey began to instruct them on many things, on many ways they can go about dealing with the real problems. One of the sisters brought up the problem at one of the nightly sessions that one of those schoolteachers beat up and slapped down a couple of black kids in school. She wanted the Panthers, the Black Panther Party, to go to the school, and she was going to get a lot of mothers and parents to go to the junior high school where her kids went. We all got together and scheduled it for that Monday.

On Monday we took three carloads of Panthers down to the school. All of them were armed down to the gills. We got out of the cars with our guns and stood on the sidewalk. Right at the sidewalk there's a fence to the school yard. All the little black kids ran over to the fence, and all the little white kids ran away from the fence, and went and hid somewhere inside the school. Then the mothers came driving up. They went inside the school building to patrol the halls of the school. They patroled the halls during lunch period, and went and told the principal that they didn't want any more brutality upon their kids in the schools. "We're concerned citizens, and we'll whip your ass and anyone else's that we hear of slapping our children around."

After about twenty minutes, while the mothers were patroling the halls, the pigs drove up. This little, young, rookie, jive pig, trying to look mean and thinking he was bad or something, walked up to the car; the brothers were sitting there in the car, looking back at him, because Huey had trained his brothers, don't be moving in a rash manner. And they got shotguns, four motherfuckers, M-1's. He looks in the car and sees all these pieces and he moves back in a hurry. He got all nervous. "Wha' . . . wha' . . . what the guns for? What the guns for?" And I think Huey said, "We're the Black Panther Party, why?" "Uh, uh, da, da, doo, do you have any license? Do you have any driver's license?" And Huey gave him his license.

"Well, you're Huey P. Newton."

"Minister of Defense Huey P. Newton, of the Black Panther Party." And the pig was just shaking. He didn't know what to do, so he gave Huey his license back and went and got on his radio and called up another pig. They kind of hung off, away from us, looking and not knowing what to do. Shook, because there's too many niggers and too many guns down there for them.

They called up another car and the principal of the school came out, and tried to talk to the pigs. Their cars were parked a little way out in front of the sidewalk that leads into the door of the school, about thirty, forty yards or so behind ours. All they could do was sit there and wonder. And that's all they did, was sit there and wonder. We went there with the mothers and they patroled the halls for the lunch period, and then we left. . . .

26   A Strategy for Labor: Nonreformist Reform

André Gorz

Is it possible *from within*—that is to say, without having previously destroyed capitalism—to impose anticapitalist solutions which will not immediately be incorporated into and subordinated to the system? This is the old question of "reform or revolution." This was (or is) a paramount question when the movement had (or has) the choice between a struggle for reforms and armed insurrection. Such is no longer the case in Western Europe; here there is no longer an alternative. The question here revolves around the possibility of "revolutionary reforms," that is to say, of reforms which advance toward a radical transformation of society. Is this possible?

Straight off we must rule out the nominalist objection. All struggle for reform is not necessarily reformist. The not always very clear dividing line between reformist reforms and nonreformist reforms can be defined as follows:

A reformist reform is one which subordinates its objectives to the criteria of rationality and practicability of a given system and policy. Reformism rejects those objectives and demands—however deep the need for them—which are incompatible with the preservation of the system.

On the other hand, a not necessarily reformist reform is one which is conceived not in terms of what is possible within the framework of a given system and administration, but in view of what should be made possible in terms of human needs and demands.

In other words, a struggle for nonreformist reforms—for anticapitalist reforms—is one

which does not base its validity and its right to exist on capitalist needs, criteria, and rationales.[1] A nonreformist reform is determined not in terms of what can be, but what should be. And finally, it bases the possibility of attaining its objective on the implementation of fundamental political and economic changes. These changes can be sudden, just as they can be gradual. But in any case they assume a modification of the relations of power; they assume that the workers will take over powers to assert a force (that is to say, a noninstitutionalized force) strong enough to establish, maintain, and expand those tendencies within the system which serve to weaken capitalism and to shake its joints. They assume structural reforms.[2]

[1] Is it reformist, for example, to demand the construction of 500,000 new housing units a year, or a real democratization of secondary and higher education? It is impossible to know beforehand. One would have to decide first whether the proposed housing program would mean the expropriation of those who own the required land, and whether the construction would be a socialized public service, thus destroying an important center of the accumulation of private capital; or if, on the contrary, this would mean subsidizing private enterprise with taxpayers' money to guarantee its profits.

One must also know whether the intention is to build workers' housing anywhere that land and materials can be cheaply bought, or if it is to construct lodgings as well as new industry according to optimum human and social criteria.

Depending on the case, the proposal of 500,000 housing units will be either neocapitalist or anticapitalist.

[2] Each time I use the term structural reform, it should be understood that this does not mean a reform which rationalizes the existing system while leaving intact the existing distribution of

Nevertheless, is it not inevitable that powers gained by the workers within the capitalist framework be reabsorbed by the system and subordinated to its functioning? This question is essential for the Marxist movement, and the only possible answer (which is the answer of the great majority of Italian Marxists, whether Communists or, such as Lelio Basso and Vittorio Foa, left-wing Socialists) is the following: the risk of subordination exists, but subordination *is not inevitable.* The risk must be run, for there is no other way. Seizure of power by insurrection is out of the question, and the waiting game leads the workers' movement to disintegration. The only possible line for the movement is to seize, from the present on, those powers which will prepare it to assume the leadership of society and which will permit it in the meantime to control and to plan the development of the society, and to establish certain limiting mechanisms which will restrict or dislocate the power of capital.

It is not, therefore, the opportuneness of "counter-powers" which is in question, but their nature and their relationship to the power of the capitalist State. The alternative is not between the conquest, exercise, and constant enlargement of powers by the workers, on the one hand, and the necessarily abstract will to seize power, on the other. The choice is between subordinate powers and autonomous powers.

By subordinate powers must be understood the association or participation of powers; this does not mean to delegate to the (capitalist) State the task of improving the system.

Structural reform is by definition a reform implemented or controlled by those who demand it. Be it in agriculture, the university, property relations, the region, the administration, the economy, etc., a structural reform *always* requires the creation of new centers of democratic power.

Whether it be at the level of companies, schools, municipalities, regions, or of the national plan, etc., structural reform always requires a *decentralization* of the decision-making power, *a restriction on the powers of State or Capital,* an *extension of popular power,* that is to say, a victory of democracy over the dictatorship of profit. No nationalization is *in itself* a structural reform.

workers in an economic policy which urges them to share the responsibility on the level of results and execution, while at the same time it forbids them to become involved in the decisions and the criteria according to which this policy has been decreed. For example, the union is invited to "participate" in a policy predetermined by others on the company level and to "share" in carrying out this policy. The union is permitted to "challenge" the implementation, or even the effects of capitalist administration. But it is hoped at the same time that it will in fact not be able to challenge the *effects,* since it has been made an accomplice to the premises from which they follow. And as an additional precaution, management provides for an "arbitrator" to make sure that the challenge to the effects does not place these premises in question.

By *autonomous* power, on the other hand, must be understood the power of the workers to challenge, in opposing the effects and the methods of implementation, the very premises of the management's policy; to challenge them even in anticipation, because they control all the particulars on the basis of which the management's policy is elaborated. ... Such autonomous power is a first step toward the subordination of the exigencies of production to human exigencies, with the conquest of the power of autonomous control as an ultimate goal.

The exercise of this kind of autonomous power cannot be restricted to purely negative opposition. But it is also clear that this power will never be granted, nor even conceded, by the employers without a struggle. This power must be won by force. And even when it is won (as in the case of the Italian metal workers, after nine months of struggle, May 1962 to February 1963), this power can be exercised only at the price of constant mobilization. Moreover, it will inevitably tend to extend beyond the framework of the large enterprise, because the policy of a monopoly or of an oligopoly is in such close reciprocal relation with the economic policies of the State, the life of the city, the community, and the region.

Far, then, from leading toward the integration and subordination of the labor movement to the State, the autonomous power of the workers—in the large enterprises, but also in the cities, the towns, public services, regional bodies, cooperatives, etc.—prepares the way for a dialectical progression of the struggle to a higher and higher level. Autonomous power is at once the generator and the indispensable relay station for the elaboration and pursuit of the integral objectives of a policy aimed at replacing capitalism.

Moreover, this autonomous power is an indispensable element in the training and education of the masses, making it possible for them to see socialism not as something in the transcendental beyond, in an indefinite future, but as the visible goal of a praxis already at work; not a goal which the masses are supposed to wish for abstractly, but one to aim for by means of partial objectives in which it is foreshadowed.

What is involved here is indeed a strategy of *progressive* conquest of power by the workers, a strategy which does not, however, exclude the possibility of or even the necessity for a revolutionary seizure of power at a later stage.

Is such a strategy a step backward, because it abandons the idea of seizing power right away, of installing socialism with one blow? That would be the case if a revolutionary seizure of power were possible, or if the preparation for this seizure maintained the masses in a state of mobilization. But such is not the case. It is impossible—above all for Marxists—to pretend to explain the masses' present state of demobilization by the absence of revolutionary fervor on the part of their leaders. In truth, the state of demobilization today is due to the fact that neither the possibility nor the form nor the content of the workers' potential political power has been defined.

As long as the condition of the workers was immediately and absolutely unbearable, the conquest of power was an immediate end in itself. At present, however, the conquest of power is not a goal which will gain support unless it is made clear toward what ends—unrealizable under capitalism—the workers' power will be *the means*. Why socialism? How will it be achieved?

The answer to these questions is today a necessary first step. Mobilization for the conquest of power and of socialism—abstract terms which no longer in themselves serve to mobilize the masses—must pass through the "mediation" of intermediate, mobilizing objectives. The struggle for partial objectives which arise from deep needs and bring into question the capitalist structure, the struggle for partial autonomous powers and their exercise should present socialism to the masses as a living reality already at work, a reality which attacks capitalism from within and which struggles for its own free development. Instead of dichotomizing the future and the present—future power and present impotence, like Good and Evil—what must be done is to bring the future into the present, to make power tangible *now* by means of actions which demonstrate to the workers their positive strength, their ability to measure themselves against the power of capital and to impose their will on it.

27   Holding onto Ourselves

Paul Potter

I want to make an assertion now, and I want to ask you to think about it as carefully as you can from your own experience to see whether or not you feel it is right. That is, I want you to ask the question, is this right for me and does it seem right for the people I know. The assertion is that the thing that most Americans want more than any other thing is love. I know that this is not what a radical is supposed to say; I know that I am supposed to say that Americans are crazed about possessions and power and status or material security, but it is my conviction that all of those things are secondary wants, that they are the things that eventually people accept because they can't get love.

Or ask the question this way. What is it the people you know really want out of life, what is it they're after, what exactly is it that people always seem to be chasing? And when I think about this question, the first thing that occurs to me is that some of the people I know *are* chasing or once chased images of power and glory and prestige and were really fascinated and excited and strongly attracted to these images. But each year more of the people I know begin to act like they think those images have tarnished; and each year the age at which people realize those images are tarnished gets younger. And even the people I know who are striving in the good old American way to get ahead really don't seem to put so much stake in it and maybe even are a little bit embarrassed to admit that they have ambition to achieve. It's as if right under the surface of official American admiration for money and prestige people want something else. And I think that

something is love, a desire to be whole and free. Or to say it another way, what I think the people I know want is love—even though they are supposed to want a Barracuda or a promotion and even though they themselves sometimes think they do.

As a matter of fact, the craving for love is so close to the surface as to be part of American folklore. The Baptist minister in the small farm town in Illinois where I grew up had a favorite sermon which he gave several times a year about the rich and prestigious man who died miserable. He managed to draw a moral something like "rich people should go to church," but the point of the story was clear nonetheless; the point is there is a widespread popular suspicion that "making it" will not solve "the problem." And even though the country is explicitly set up to allay this suspicion by rewarding people well for their competitive accomplishments, the suspicion hangs on and gets stronger. And each year, more and more Americans, in whatever way they express it, are beginning to catch on to the fact that this country isn't all it's cracked up to be, and whether you sweat your ass off in a factory or press your white collar in a computer, you know it. The problem, the thing that can't be satisfied, is love —or that, at least, is what I think my friends would call it.

But whether they call it love or something else, I don't believe Americans think they can get it. There is another piece of American folklore about the resignation that signals maturity, the final, fatalistic peace that comes when a man realizes he will not accomplish his dreams. To be mature in this country is to know you won't find what you want but to still play out your life. Growing up, after a point, is thought of as giving up, even though it is never portrayed that way.

Giving up is always made to look like maturity. That is what you might call a bit of American realism.

So we have these two things; first that people want love; and second, that they don't think they can get it—even though not getting it in the end turns out to be dignified. Taken together these two ideas constitute a fairly thorough condemnation of America, even though that is not what people talk about when they are condemning America.

. . .

But you will want to know what exactly it is I mean by love, because the way I have been talking so far suggests that what I mean by love is not necessarily what most people mean by love when they talk about it, but is something more abstract. And although I think the best way to understand what I mean to say is to try to understand it intuitively out of your own experience, I will try to be more clear. Because I will agree that the way I talk about love here is not the way we normally talk about love even though I think the two ideas are closely connected. On the few occasions when we do talk about love we usually talk about love for a specific person—some one person who we love or who loves us. Or more likely, we talk about love when the experience of trying to find love is so wrenching and twisting that we are forced to overcome our shyness about love and confide our pain in a close friend. That is the way we talk about love—quietly and intimately and specifically. Our talk about love is focused on the specific hope that the right woman (women) will come along, that everything will be easy and natural, that all the hidden constraint and unhappiness that marks our relationships with all people will at last be left behind with at least one person. (Just one person, to love and hold and cherish.)

But if you think about what that one specific woman is supposed to do for you, the way she is supposed to make you feel—you will realize that even our specific aspirations for love are for things that are quite abstract. What we fantasize we would feel—or what we have felt during those relatively brief moments when love has been alive for us, is something as abstract as wholeness or openness or peace. But even though these things are quite abstract, they are real, and their reality goes beyond something we want with just one person. Their reality describes what we want from life. So that when I say what we want most from life is love, I mean that what we want is to be whole and free. What we want is to find peace through overcoming the conflict between ourselves and others, to find a way to be open with at least one other person even though that desire symbolizes our desire to be open with all of our world.

OTHER WORDS THAN LOVE

There are other words besides love we can honor. There is self-respect (self-love); there is beauty (the recognition of that which can be loved and cherished in other things and people and in ourselves); there is control over our lives (for what, for what); there is community (of what); there is passion and compassion (the capacity in each of us to what). These and other words are what we use to describe what we want and what this society perverts. And they are important words. But all of them have come to sound a little euphemistic to me. They are words we use because we are embarrassed to say we want love—need love, feel broken inside day to day because we are denied love. And so long as they prevent us from saying that, they are bad euphemisms. Because without their roots in our own immediate human ache, they are too distant. Community becomes something enjoyable, a pleasanter way to live, rather than an absolute human necessity. Beauty becomes something that could be spliced together in a good Hollywood film studio. Compassion sours and becomes the distant emotion called pity. Passion becomes an excuse for mutilating the world.

LOVE AND WHOLENESS

I have said that love is our desire to be whole, to overcome the conflict between ourselves and others, but I have obviously to make my meaning clearer. And I want to do so in a way that shows that what I mean by love is what in fact most people feel when they feel a capacity to love, and not just some philosophical abstraction that is unrelated to experience. Note that I say *feel*, not *think*, because what we think about love is only confusedly related to what we feel. What we think is mixed up with what we have been *taught* to think which like other things we've been taught is a way of discrediting and repressing the meaning of our experience. To understand what we *feel* we must ask ourselves carefully the question, what is it we have felt when we were in love, and think hard, really hard, about what it was like, what we really carried inside us when we were loving and being loved, what really happened. And if you can answer that question and at the same time have some intuitive sense of trust in your answer, then you can say that you are talking about what it feels like to be in love.

When I try to do this, what I come up with is that one of the things I have felt most strongly when I was in love is an acute, self-conscious sense of myself, a heightened awareness of all my being, a knowledge that was in touch with parts of me that previously I had only vaguely sensed existed, but a self-consciousness that arose not from some fear of what other people might see when they looked at me, but a self-consciousness from deep within. That is, what I think I have felt is a sense of my *whole* self. And what is more, I have felt glad with what I felt. Not because it was beautiful (although it is when I am in love that I feel more beauty than I feel at any other time) but because I feel the ragged edges of my own existence without feeling that I must turn away from any of them for fear of being hurt. I am aware not only of all that is beautiful in me, but all that is ugly, and I am able to look at the ugliness with a matter of factness, a detachment, a recognition that the ugliness is really a part of an external shell I would gladly discard were it only safe. And to the extent I am aware of other people, and invariably I am more acutely aware of other people, I am less

afraid to let them see me and less offended if they don't. And what is more, less afraid to look myself—at them as well as me.

And what I feel of the person I love comes first from my sense that she is the source of this new feeling inside me. My sense of her comes from the feeling that here is a person I can trust knowledge of myself to who will not use that knowledge to hurt me (like everyone else has, does). My sense of her is that I have trusted another person to keep part of myself inside of her, which is the deepest trust anyone can put in anyone. But even my statement of it is a little bit nervous, because the suggestion that you let somebody "keep" part of you is framed in the language of an old fear—that they might actually keep part of you, take it away, destroy it, you. The happier expression of that same feeling, which none of us are ever quite able to love enough to let happen, is that you and another person are in some way one, that you share something of each other in such rapport, that you never fear that it will be taken away. And if you do not fear losing yourself in another person, if your heightened sense of yourself is so complete and so strong that you know that that person's identity does not threaten your own and never will, then what you feel is that you and another person share of one another in such a way that you *are* each other, share an essential identity which is the same.

But we are too nervous about love to ever really allow ourselves to become that way. Our sense of ourselves is so permanently incomplete, our earliest love of parents so systematically abased, our sense of self so regularly taken away from us by other people, that the very notion that we should be one with another person is slightly repugnant to most people. We can only think of it as a loss (albeit a loss of our poor, defensive, embattled sense of self).

When I am in love, I usually feel (even though I fail to demonstrate) the capacity to love more than one person. And that is particularly true if it is a "good" love relationship, i.e., not one in which I am lost in her or she in me. The tension (conflict, fear) that has been reduced between her and me becomes almost a symbol of how tension could be reduced between me and others. And that capacity is latent and infectious. Other people respond to me differently, are aware of my awareness.

All of these images and many more are images of wholeness and unity. Love is the attempt to be whole. It is the desire to overcome the tension between ourselves and others as the only conceivable route to wholeness. It is the expression of our frustrated oneness with the universe.

But even here, I have talked about love as if it were a personal capacity, and that is because it is almost impossible to talk about my experience of love in any other way. I find myself saying things like, "We do not let ourselves," or, "too nervous to ever really allow," when what I should say is, "We have been too terribly injured, made too neurotically nervous to be able to love." But the deepest part of the social ideology about love is its personalness and privateness, and try as I may that social ideology keeps reinserting itself in my interpretation of experience. It is almost impossible for me to imagine love as a social experience, as a society. So I keep seeing my failures as personal failures. And the social ideology that makes me see things this way is extremely critical for the maintenance of this society. Because so long as people think of their inability to love as a personal failure, they will continue to believe with part of themselves that love is really an illusion, a romantic, adolescent idea, pretty to look at in the movies, pleasantly painful to remember from your own adolescence, but in the last analysis, something to be turned aside cynically, like fantasy and unreality. Like so many other things, the experience of love is turned against itself. We are made to feel that the experience of love is so absurd in this society that it really can't be an experience at all but must obviously be a fantasy. . . .

LOVE IS IMPOSSIBLE

The fact that this society has constructed us so that we can never ever let go of enough of our defensiveness to ever really love someone honestly and deeply, the fact that love is impossible, makes love seem closer to me. The knowledge that I am not permitted to love relieves me of an enormous sense of failure and guilt, which in turn has made it much easier to forgive myself for all the terrible things I have done to other people, which in turn relieves me of the responsibility of denying my guilt and blaming my atrocities on another person, which means that I don't have to be so hostile to other people and myself, which means I can relax a little bit about me and other people, which means I can actually open up a little bit, which means I get closer to love.

Knowing that love is impossible gets me out from under the thumb of two tyrannies. The first, I call the tyranny of liberation—which stated most sharply is the belief that love is possible. In our society, the belief that love is possible is called "youthful idealism." It is an optimism about love that has grown not out of what we have observed in our parents' "love relationship," but out of a feeling for what we have been denied. Particularly when you are young, you know that love is real, because of a constant craving ache we have for it. And since we have grown up in a society that has told us that what is real is possible and what is impossible is unreal, we naturally assume that since love is real it is possible. The connection of our knowledge that love is real to the society's contention that what is real is possible creates an image of liberation. We now believe that we can attain love and the personal liberation that promises. But we can't and don't; we are far too crippled.

But when we fail to accomplish the possible, when we can't find love, we either blame ourselves for our failure, or we conclude that since love now seems impossible, it must be unreal, an adolescent fantasy. Either way, our belief that love is possible leads to despair and cynicism about love. And either way works out perfectly for the status quo. Because our failure and disillusionment and despair remains focused on ourselves. Our belief that love is possible, our image of liberation, tyrannically forces us to carry the weight of our failure, prevents us from ever identifying the source of our humiliation.

The tyranny of liberation is believing that the reality of our needs can overcome what this society has done to us. That is not only wrong, it is arrogant. It is one of our most impotent conceits. Regardless of what we say about the power of the military and the corporations, we seem to be incapable of believing that the society that crushed our parents could crush us in the same way. We assume we will do better than them. (We deny that they could ever have been like us.) What we cannot comprehend is that our parents too might have had images of liberation once. We fail to see this because our parents make it almost impossible to see. Because when their own tyrannical images of liberation crushed them, they lost track of the reality that had been tangled up in those images, they buried their own vivid sense of need when they discovered it was impossible. And better yet, for the purposes of the society, they conspired to deny that there had ever been real need there at all, learned to call it fantasy, learned to insulate themselves from the pain of their loss by pretending that the crumbs of self-respect and the pale reflections of love that the society had allowed them were really quite enough. And although we "see through" the pretense and recognize that much of our parents' lives are sham, we fail, in collaboration with our parents, to ever see the pain that made the pretense necessary. We believe so deeply in our own images of liberation that we walk right into the same trap that our parents did. We pursue love and fail. We balance ourselves for our failure.

But to realize that love is impossible is to begin to work out of that trap. Love *is* real. But love is not possible. To understand that love is impossible but real is to formulate a revolutionary proposition about the society that made love impossible. It is a way to make our vivid knowledge of the reality of love into an anchor that can be used to fight this society. It is a way to begin to make images of liberation that will liberate us, not conquer or tyrannize us.

The second tyranny, which is really the cor-

ollary of the tyranny of liberation, is the tyranny of failure. Despite the fact we start out "believing" love is possible, we know that it is not, consciously or intuitively. Our whole lives have been records of failure to find love. Probably the very earliest memory anyone can have in this society is of his failure to keep the love of his parents—of "realizing" one night when you were an infant that your mother had just denied you her love because you'd wakened her once too often. And from right then on, our lives are records of love getting twisted and denied and used like a whip and just plain lost, so that we know from before we ever start a conscious quest for love that we have failed to find it. And it is natural enough that we would want to guard ourselves against the pain of trying and failing once again. So even as our sense that love is possible, our image of liberation, is propelling us into yet another attempt at love, our knowledge that we have failed to find love is making us be cautious and hold something back (or its corollary, throw everything away). We haul our protection against failure along like a watchdog, always ready to tell us if we've gone a step too far with another person, always fending off overtures from other people that are a wee bit too threatening, always guarding a path of retreat we can use for quick escape. My knowledge of failure and my fear that it will be repeated premeditates and predetermines that my attempt at love will fail. In order to protect myself from more pain, I must so thoroughly hedge my commitment in one way or another that any "serious" relationship is doomed to starve to death regardless of how much time I put into it.* It starves for lack of commitment. It starves because part of me has already planned failure so as to ease the pain. It starves because I am afraid to try to make it work.

*The other way of hedging commitment is to so thoroughly hold yourself back as to have it appear that you have thrown yourself away, submerged your identity in another person's. In the name of loving someone else, we give up on the responsibility to portray our experience as vividly as we can; we make the relationship basically dishonest by hiding.

But of course the tyranny of liberation, the belief that love is possible, the pretense that characterizes all our love relationships, demands that we deny the reality of our failure, demands we deny that the watchdog is there, demands that we pretend that we are really trying to make a love relationship work.

But the knowledge that love is impossible liberates us from the need to deny failure. It makes failure seem matter of fact—which it is. Because if love is impossible, it is a matter of fact that we have and will continue to fail to find it. And to the extent we are able to acknowledge and experience the inevitability of failure, we can let go of the pretense that it isn't there, and to the extent we can do that, we are enabled to have more honest relationships with people we wish to love, and to the extent we can do that, we get closer to love.

The knowledge that love is impossible makes love seem closer to me.

LOVE AND POLITICS

There is undeniably a big rift between our notion of politics and our notion of love. Our feeling for the word politics is so radically different than our feeling for the word love that there is little chance we would ever think to connect them—and this is true whether we call our politics "new" or "old." People who say out loud that what they want out of life is love, usually call themselves antipolitical. People who call themselves "political" and particularly people who call themselves "revolutionary political" usually say love is a bourgeois need which must be subjugated to revolutionary necessity.

But if the impossibility of love flows directly from the nature of the society we live in, then people who say they are concerned about love must be interested in politics. There is no way out of it. So it is important to try to understand the origins of the intuitive feeling we have that love and politics exist in two radically different spheres.

And if you think about it, it seems obvious that our whole big notion about politics is that politics has to do with controlling the very alien universe we live in; we believe that politics is a fight over who's going to manage the factories and although we "know" this is important, try as we can, we cannot make management of the factories feel like an issue that is very important to us. We can understand it on paper and debate it in a bull session, but we can't feel it very well; control of the factories and other such issues still seem alien. Politics is alien. It is not directly about us. It has not connected our needs to the factory—and I don't believe it can. Our need is not to control factories; it is to make factories unthinkable, to destroy the society in which men spend their lives working and living in various kinds of factories. (Try thinking about a suburb as a middle-class factory, churning out batch after batch of delicate, middle-class mechanisms.) Politics is alien because even its most revolutionary adherents have not been able to draw clear, straight, sharp lines between our need and political goals.

And it is odd that this is so, because the first lesson the New Left was supposed to have learned from its first and best teacher, C. Wright Mills, was how to "make the connection between personal troubles and public issues." That was supposed to have been the most basic, rudimentary instruction we got about political education. Our task as radicals was to show people how to make the connection between their own grief and misery and the social structure that produced it. So, for example, we were supposed to have learned that this society makes a man hate himself when he can't find decent work, when the truth of the matter is that for millions there are no jobs and that decent jobs exist for almost no one. But we consistently and stubbornly refuse to apply the same insight to ourselves, to recognize that our own failure to find love is not a personal shortcoming but a condition of life in America.

In the first place, we have always acted as if we thought Mills' dictum was to be applied to somebody else, not ourselves. We try to connect somebody else's oppression to that great big old alien framework called politics. But it is only when we try to connect our own need to find love to politics and public issues that we realize how revolutionary Mills' dictum was. To make a solid, binding connection between anyone's deeply felt oppression and politics means everything has got to change. First we must thoroughly explore and rework our whole idea of what love is so that we recognize its social implications. And that is not an understanding that can be sloganized or simplified into an "organizing line."

Second, we simply have to shatter all those old political ideas so that political goals are the most vivid, meaningful goals of our lives. Our whole big sense that politics is about the control of an alien world has to go. Politics has to be thought of as the destruction of the alien world and the construction of a whole new kind of power. Only then can the connection be made. . . .

What I have talked about so far . . . can be fairly concisely summarized. Because basically, I have been trying to illustrate, with a variety of metaphors, one simple thing—that even though human nature, which I call a capacity to love, has been defiled, our experience still gives us an intuitive recognition that we have been oppressed.

But recognizing we are oppressed is only the beginning. That knowledge, in and of itself, doesn't point out a direction to move. The way most of us experience oppression is as an amorphous, omnipresent sense that is so diffuse that we cannot locate its source or articulate any of our feelings about it. On the few occasions when we do strike out against it, we strike out blindly and impotently, blow up or "lose control," and of course feel childish and ashamed of ourselves afterwards, whether or not we are forced to admit that by way of apologizing to the people we "offended." Alternatively, we build great, rationalistic constructs to describe Oppression, which may sound quite articulate, but do not connect to us.

What we need is more than knowledge that we feel oppressed. What we need is a way to sharply define that oppression and disentangle ourselves from it. Properly understood, the process of defining oppression

is not a process of abstraction; we are not simply looking for a set of diagrams or generalizations we can make about the society. Our first task is to concretize, not abstract. Our first task is to bring back, validate, make more vivid, our own authentic experience. We need to get in touch with our own pain and joy and try to remember what caused them. That is a funny kind of abstraction; it is abstraction that takes place only when we have recalled all the details we were told to forget, only when we have gotten further into the particulars of our own experience than we have ever been before.

Stated another way, what this society makes us feel is a deep inauthenticity about ourselves. Even our outbursts of rage seem wrong—inappropriate and immature. What we are looking for is authentic identity, a description of ourselves that we trust intuitively. And the only way to grasp that new identity is to sort ourselves out from them, to reverse the process that has led us to internalize our own oppression. I call this process of sorting out separatism—quite literally to separate yourself from your allegiance to the system that oppresses you. And it is that process I want to talk about . . . . In addition, I want to talk about the fact that large groups of people share the experience of oppression in such similar ways (share the same basic political metaphors) that they can separate themselves (search for authentic experience and identity) collectively. I call such real or potential collectives, classes; I call the shared metaphors of experience they have, class experience. . . .

Making concrete the thing I call an antithesis (separatism) can be done in a variety of ways. I want to start with what I think is most visibly what the middle class "stands for" and what we stand for. That is important to me because I can remember a time, not so long ago, when I felt that it was important to affirm certain aspects of my middle-class heritage, to acknowledge that many of the values of the middle class were my own. Now when I reflect on those values, I am amazed at how superficial my understanding of them was, or more likely, how hard I was trying to be generous and inclusive in my definition of who "we" were.

Let me begin where it is simplest. *The middle-class image of the good society is at its root competitive.* It is an image of men struggling against men, whether in athletics or international trade or the new grey-flannel, ad-business man—the nicest house, the finest car, the best taste, the most beautiful children—the erudition of the professor as he puts down an upstart student, the quick jibe, the biting sarcasm, the finesse of the modernist political candidate as he parries newsmen's questions with wit and factualism under the glare of hot lights and the pressure of high stakes. Even where the society admires collaborative efforts, "teamwork," it is always an adjunct to competition, as again with athletics or business, or the space-race teamwork of NASA, the Huntley/Brinkley team beating out the old-style CBS news coverage, the teamwork of the tactical police crushing a street demonstration before it could become a riot.

The middle class feeds on the society of constant grading and evaluation, the never-ending social intelligence game that gets formal glorification in schools, chicken-judging contests (I was champion Champaign County chicken judger when I was twelve), the office, the art festival/contest, popular music ("And now, Number One"), classical music ("And now, see whether you recognize this all-time favorite"), but more insidiously, and perhaps more important, if you're young, at a dance or in a swimming suit or driving a car or making small talk, or even when you finally make the team, in still getting judged, graded, classified, ranked on a hundred competitive scales, by a thousand competitive eyes.

Our image is at root collaborative. It is an image of a society where men's estimate of themselves or each other is not developed out of a contest where one man wins and another loses—where one is one up and the other is down. . . .

The middle class stands for expertise. It makes sense, since that is what the middle class is all about. It is composed of the people with the technical and social skills that are required to run the progress machine, and it is sufficiently self-impressed and specialized to have created a cult of itself, a cult of the expert. Let me illustrate with a TV ad by a New England bank, which is trying to sell people on the idea of a "personal investment counselor." The ad shows the man sitting in the middle of a circle of empty, folding chairs, in a rather bleak, darkly lit room. As the announcer reads off the categories of the man's personal counselors, the room fills up (and brightens up) with a doctor, lawyer, clergyman, insurance man, everything you need, except of course, a personal investment counselor, who soon enters the room brightening everything to its peak and relieving our anxiety. All the counselors would look identical to anyone reared outside of Western civilization, but our well-trained eyes can instantly pick up the deliberate distinctions added to the TV stereotype—the somewhat more somber look of the minister, the older, reassuring, mature feeling about the doctor, the harder, pin-stripier edge to the lawyer, the affable, nondescript quality of the insurance man. Everything is perfect, except the man in the middle should be a quadruple amputee. It is clear that is what we are meant to feel he would be without these trusty servants.

This society has not only created a dependence on experts, but has rationalized our insecurity about the control they have over our lives into a cult of the expert. You may not have the faintest idea what the physician is doing to you, so to compensate for the anxiety that creates, you choose to believe in him—and if not him, then medical science. There are intuitively well-known hierarchies of experts (with the physician very near the top), but they all represent, more or less, the amputation of important life functions from our control and understanding. It is worth noting that working-class experts fall near the bottom of the hierarchy, e.g., the mechanic, who is so intimately involved in our egos since he works on our cars, is almost universally distrusted. There is no more reason to distrust him than a doctor; in fact, generally, I suspect that mechanics have a relatively more thorough knowledge of their field than doctors do of theirs and are just as honest. But the mechanic is distrusted, largely, I suspect, because he lacks the pedigree—quite literally the breeding, manner, and qualities of middle-class social skill that would put us at ease. The need for pedigree, then, becomes an essential part of education, at least as important as the technical knowledge that the expert masters. And that need is increasing. The more specialized and fragmented the society becomes, the more need there is to keep it glued together with extensive and careful pedigrees. The top engineering schools, for example, now cram more and more liberal arts down the throats of their students; it is not just vogue; it is a critical effort to hold the society together.

The kind of glue I'm talking about is the kind whose reality we've all been trained to disbelieve; it is *ideological;* it is a faith in the essential soundness and coherence of an incomprehensible system that is ratified by the fact that the system emerges triumphant everywhere we look. It is not a faith that can be simply subscribed to by proclamation. One must be initiated into it over a long period of time. One of the reasons the middle class was so horrified by Lyndon Johnson was because of his Texas vulgarity. He was a professional politician of the old style. What was wanted was a man of middle-class sensibilities, a man with the style and manner of an expert who could reassure the middle class that "our kind of guy" was at the controls. Kennedy, who was our kind of guy, was forgiven the Bay of Pigs and the Cuban Missile Crisis—acts so brash that had Lyndon Johnson committed them, they would have aroused a stream of unending horror and vituperation.

What the middle class wants is not so much a set of political acts, but a style of political craftsmanship that assures it that a bearer of the faith, an expert, progress-oriented leader is at the controls of our technically complicated civilization.

We stand for the destruction of the elevation of the expert and the cult that surrounds

him. Perhaps the simplest assertion the New Left has made is that people have the capacity to make *all* the judgments about the critical things that affect their lives. If a man is so estranged from his body that he has nothing to do but place it limply in the hands of a doctor, then he is philosophically, physically, and emotionally in bad health, regardless of what the doctor does for him. If a man's ego is deeply involved in a machine and he is completely incapacitated and dependent when the machine breaks down—his need is not for a trustworthy expert to fix the car but for a new relationship with the machine or no machine at all. If civilization is too complicated for ordinary men to direct, then it is civilization that is at fault and not the people. If we must have Shakespearean experts in order to "understand and appreciate" Shakespeare, it just may be that we can get along without Shakespeare. Expertise is the bond of faith, the ideological glue that covers up our mutilation. We would be whole.

The middle class stands for security through possessions. The accumulation of property and wealth is the most significant measure of that possessiveness. But the most dynamic characteristic of possession and security is the acquisition of status. The possession of status, power, and stature, the quest to be somebody big, someone that people know about, someone who is feared more than he fears, someone who moves in exclusive circles, who has prestige—that is the real drive of middle-class possessiveness. What people are looking to possess is a *position* above other people—in a sense, the possession of people as subservient.

A man possesses a woman. She is subservient; she gives him status. If she resists being chattel, she detracts from his status. He must compensate; he must be a more powerful lawyer, a more wealthy, successful business man. If he does not, if he fails to possess in both these spheres, then he is henpecked, a poor hulk of a man, a person without respect. One man's security is dependent on the diminution of another.

We are not involved in your quest for possessions, human or material. You have given us no model of what integrity in human relationships is like but we know that is what we want. So long as one man's security is another's insecurity, we will be content to share our insecurity. Your property is boring; there is too much of it; it is tasteless and heavy; it sits there, for the most part unwanted and unused. It dominates your lives; you must constantly protect it, refurbish it, insure it, paint it, mow it, shingle it, display it, and attend to it emotionally when it chips, splits, or cracks. When your children go away from you, your devotion to it becomes pathetic. . . .

We are not middle class. But if we are not middle class, what are we? What is the new name and the new identity we will take for ourselves? What is the name of the system that oppresses us? Is the name that important, is it really? And if you think about it, the answer is yes, it obviously is.

But it is just as obvious that we have not yet reached the point where we can give ourselves a name. It is not possible now. And it may not be possible for a long time. We have got to let go of a lot more than we have so far before we can think clearly enough to come up with a new name. And in part I think it is the frustration of people trying to find that new identity that makes them flip-flop so drastically and rally to their sense, when they can't find it, that they are traitors to what they believe in, and consequently to see the revolutionary impulse as coming from some other group.

But if I was forced to give the system a name now, I would not call it capitalism. I would perhaps say that it was hate and we are love. That it is unattended fear, and we are the courage to attend it. That it is isolation and we are community. I would not call it capitalism because the abolition of private ownership and production for profit is not enough. It does not promise, as Marx thought it would, to create a free and communalistic society. That is a problem that is beyond capital, i.e., that is beyond the question of whether the equipment that manufactures the material wealth of a civilization is "privately controlled" or "socially controlled." I

would not call it capitalism because we suffer as much from the logic of a technologically constructed civilization as we do from capitalism itself. What we experience is depersonalization through bureaucracy, standardization of human beings to meet bureaucratic and technological demands, the destruction of the family and the primary community, the impossibility of love—and all those things are rooted in a deeper essence than is described by the term capitalism.

We are not middle class. We are love; we are courage; we are community. They are hate, fear, and isolation. That is the beginning of a better understanding. . . .

We are on the threshold of something new. That is a growing conviction in me and it is confirmed not by the logic of what I write but by the fact that as I talk to people around the country I find more and more who in different ways express recognition of the same threshold. It is not that any *one* has the definition. No *one* can have it. It is that many find their thoughts being turned (forced) in the same direction.

More and more people begin to talk about the lack of authentic identity (authentic definition). But their talk is not the parlor room talk of people who experience pointless frustration. It is not the never-to-be answered, "Who am I" that Freud's disciples have taught us to intone endlessly as a token of our own abasement. It is rather people saying first to themselves and then to others, "What is this thing that engulfs me, that propels me, that soaks up all my energy until I want desperately for it to let me go—but that keeps pushing me on? What has swallowed me and my friends? What is this pit we have fallen into? Who are WE?" And the question brings back an echo. Strikes a resonance in other people.

Who are WE? It is a question that has an energy of its own. Part of the energy and insistence of the question makes me uneasy. I fear that one day I will whisper it and someone will shout back an answer and force me to deal with it. And I am not sure that I am ready for an answer, even though I sense that the answer is already in me and everybody around me but waits and waits and waits because we have not yet been forced to find the courage to listen to our own sentence, to grasp our own destiny. But the question will not now wait for us to answer it. It will make us answer to it.

People are beginning to see beyond the edges of their own amorphousness. Amorphousness is the feeling people have who struggle without definition. The movement is full of activity but all of it is without adequate definition. For a while the war provided definition—purpose, a reason to struggle, a simple, unambiguous definition of what it was all about. Before that civil rights had provided definition. And most recently, the demand of blacks for recognition in the university has given definition. But all these definitions break down because they are external and people again experience the amorphousness of no definition. In part, this explains the popularity of current sectarian styles and parties. They play at rigid clarity and they recruit people who must have it even if it means swallowing themselves.

To experience the amorphousness of the movement is to try to do something without knowing why. Or . . . to start doing something thinking you know why, only to find that the explanation can't hold the weight of reality—yours or theirs.

When I say people have begun to see beyond the edges of their own amorphousness, I mean that we have begun to understand that there is a force pushing the fog that surrounds us. We may not know what that force is, but we do understand it as the reason we keep attempting to *do* things. And the reason is not so much a logic as it is a perception that we have slipped into a stream, have been pulled gently into a current that is moving us even if we don't fully grasp it. We have gained a certain humility with that insight. We have learned that the world is bigger than our own logic. And as we have understood that we have begun to stop thrashing so wildly against the current, even have begun to feel that we are part of the current.

We can begin to see that the thing we call a movement is not defined by a set of projects, insurrections, and events. It is not a shopping list of activities that people around the country have thought up to do. All of those things are part of another thing, are encompassed by it, pushed ahead by it, dragged under by it, but always, insistently, moved by it. We are part of a social force.

One way of thinking about the activities we undertake is that they are attempts at definition. But none is adequate—largely because they define the universe with too narrow a logic. Nonetheless, while they last, they are important. They give people things to do and a partial rationalization for why they are being done. They keep us from going back or going crazy by keeping us busy, keeping our hands occupied. It makes sense that now at a time when all projects seem to break down either in the direction of amorphousness or rigid sectarianism that many people begin to grasp that the movement in some very fundamental way is no longer describable as or even dependent on a set of activity. Rather it has become a social force, a cleavage in America, and tens of thousands of young people are discovering that they are on one side of that cleavage, swept up in the force that created it, without an adequate definition of that force (and themselves) and with less and less chance each day that goes by of getting back to the other side of the cleavage. But the new consciousness erases the old mystification of projects without filling up the time. How can you continue to work on what you were working on once you recognize its essential make-work character? The result of amorphousness, of empty time, is that people are being forced out of projects and well-defined niches and up against themselves and each other without a sense of direction, with only an ache for definition and a sense of motion and turbulence.

More and more people who are on the edge of the movement, who are potential recruits to it, who participate in some of its activities, are aware of the inadequacy of its definition for them, find that despite their attraction to it, there is nothing in it that speaks to their need. Eventually they find themselves in an equally amorphous, though perhaps more honest thing called the youth culture. Both the drop-out culture and the movement must be understood in the end as part of the same social force. But they do not define it.

In the current situation, the pressure for definition is enormous. Each day more and more people are dislocated, consciously or unconsciously, broken loose from their old feelings that they could get by in America, jarred or eased or jolted or floated into a new self-recognition that where things used to look okay and possible, now something starts feeling terribly wrong.

Each day there are new engineering students who find they can't concentrate on calculus. Each day more young women wonder how they could ever be housewives, more housewives remember something they once felt very strongly. Each day more kids look up at their teachers with total incomprehension; and each day a few more kids understand for the first time what this school business is really all about.

And as new people are dislocated, others find it even more inconceivable that they could ever be part of this country's design for them, begin to feel that there is no turning back, begin to realize that they know too much now to ever be able to successfully forget what they have learned, realize that they are committed by their knowledge to live in a new land. And this sense we have of being part of a social force also gives us the sense that there is a road to this new land and that we are on it or are at least looking for it. And there are all sorts of hawkers along the way shouting, "This way to the new land. This way to the new land." And either we've tried their wares before and know that they are no good, or we begin to notice that as the hawkers scream they keep running alongside of us, trying to make us understand, trying to reach us, trying to keep up so they can keep shouting at us—being pulled along by the force that is pushing us in spite of themselves.

And as this social force grows in volume and intensity, it begins to come right smack up against itself on the one hand and the reality of the society's reaction to it on the other. Young people are beginning to realize that they are no longer the children of a "privileged" class, but are instead the hated, feared minority that the mainstream society describes and increasingly treats as vermin. And in the crossfire of these pressures from the society and each other's inability to sustain definition, there is more and more need to create a revolutionary, separatist, self-definition of ourselves. There is less and less chance to escape dealing with the question of who we are. It is when the last of the old self-definitions has been dashed into amorphousness and the only place left to look for self-definition is to one another that we will realize who we are, remember the thing we forgot so long ago, be able to announce in our own name that we are part of the revolution in America.